# Power over Themselves:
# The Literary Controversy about Female Education in England, 1660–1820

Veena P. Kasbekar

**Professor of English Emerita**

Power over Themselves:
The Literary Controversy about Female Education in England, 1660-1820
by Veena P. Kasbekar
Copyright © 1980, 2022 Veena P. Kasbekar
Published by SkillBites LLC
All rights reserved.



ISBN 13: 978-1-952281-51-8 paperback
ISBN 13: 978-1-952281-52-5 eBook

1797 Portrait by John Opie
National Portrait Gallery of London

# Author's Note

The controversy in Britain about women's education, as seen in its literature, was the subject of my dissertation at the University of Cincinnati. Because it discusses 325 primary sources from 1660–1820,* including 36 French works, along with 134 secondary sources, I hope it will prove of additional use to current scholars of Women's/Gender Studies, English, and Education. I have retained the original MLA documentation style, especially footnotes, finding them more immediately relevant to the context than endnotes. Retirement and the pandemic gave me time to revisit my research and again revel in the literature which finally enabled higher education for women. After graduating from Bombay University (now Mumbai University), I did my Master's, appropriately, at the first women's higher-ed institution in the U.S., Mt. Holyoke College in Massachusetts. To make my research accessible, I have kept the price reasonably low but intend to donate all proceeds to the women's shelter in Columbus.

Veena P. Kasbekar, PhD
Professor of English Emerita
Ohio University Chillicothe

---

* Every primary source in the bibliography was discovered and read as a *book*. No digital research today can replace the almost sacred thrill (to me) of actually handling and reading eighteenth-century texts in a climate-controlled Archives/Rare Books Room, although it certainly makes all my primary texts readily accessible to all. Harvard and other universities were very generous in mailing their books to supplement my library's holdings.

# Acknowledgements

Many thanks to Dr. Leslie Chard, my dissertation advisor at The University of Cincinnati, and to Judy Weintraub, CEO SkillBites LLC, for her unstinting guidance through the publication process.

# Dedication

This work is dedicated to the memory of my parents, Dr. P. G. and Vimal P. Kasbekar.

# Table of Contents

Introduction .................................................................... 1

Chapter 1: The Conservative Tradition, 1659–1787 ....................7

Chapter 2: The Progressive Tradition, 1673–1787 ..................... 57

Chapter 3: The Radical Tradition, 1788–1799 ........................ 101

Chapter 4: The Reactionary Tradition, 1788–1799 ................. 159

Chapter 5: Merging Traditions, 1800–1820 ............................ 199

Primary Sources .............................................................241

Secondary Sources ........................................................ 259

Index ............................................................................ 265

# Introduction

This work deals with the controversy about female education in England from 1660 to 1820, that is, from the restoration to the throne of Charles II to the end of the reign of George III, as well as from Mary Astell (1666–1731) to Jane Austen (1775–1817). It is an intellectual record of certain aspects of the eighteenth century, largely neglected until the feminist critical revival in the twentieth century: it contains a history of women's literature and a history of prescribed, as well as proscribed, women's thinking, education, and professionalism, as well as of their dreams, aspirations, and visions.

Of course, feminist aspirations were not in the ascendance from the Restoration to the end of the eighteenth century. Rather, Alexander Pope's conservative dictum that "Whatever is, is right" (*Essay on Man*, 1734) ruled politics, religion, society, and the family. All Britons were believed to be in their God-ordained place, from the sovereign at the top of the hierarchy to the lower-class laborer or indigent at the bottom, as well as all the gradations in between. Moreover, this hierarchy was necessarily patriarchal: upper-class Anglican men constituted the superior class and man himself the superior sex. As politically inferior beings, women were often lumped into a class by themselves and relegated to the social and familial duties expected of all their sex. However, as procreative beings who enabled the ruling class to propagate itself and as instructors morally responsible for the upbringing of their children, upper-class women alone were granted certain privileges, notably the right to a certain amount of education.

In the eighteenth century, the term "education" developed two specific connotations. In its more philosophical sense, it came to mean all the processes throughout a lifetime that went into forming individual female character. In its narrower sense, it stood for the instruction given women in the formative years, generally ending before the period of marriage. Since the general purpose of education was to teach social usefulness rather than to convey pure knowledge, it aimed at efficiently training women about their duties according to gender and class. Importantly, because the age believed in class distinctions, only the upper classes were deemed worthy of a liberal education, men far more so than women. Most of the literature on female education written at this time, both fictional and non-fictional, was therefore geared towards the gentlewoman, rather than the middle- or working-class woman. This work therefore concentrates largely on the instruction of upper-class women, although it includes educational theories about the other two classes.

Since my intention was to write an intellectual rather than a social history of women, my research deals more with prescriptive theories about education than with specific institutions. (As doctoral source material, I used, sometimes resurrected, literature both by and about women of this period.) It must be here understood that the term "literature" generally meant not just the belles-lettres but all fictional and non-fictional forms that satisfied the two main criteria of instruction and amusement. Thus, it included works in the arts and sciences that were not written explicitly for specialists but had a general didactic purpose. The literature considered in the following chapters is chosen specifically for its relation to female education, whether directly, as in the non-fictional works, or indirectly, as through the fictional genres. Hence, making allowances for its fictional world, the didactic novel has been regarded as equally prescriptive as the philosophical treatise and the educational tract.

During this period, such literature was used both to uphold the sociopolitical system as well as to attempt to change it for the betterment of women. The resulting controversy over the education of women, especially gentlewomen, reached its peak in the 1790s, a time when the question of the rights of man in France brought to a head the corresponding question of the rights of woman in Britain. French theory had all along influenced English thinking; the added political impulse gave this decade a particular significance. As the period that saw the highest point of the controversy, the 1790s became the focus of my research. In this decade, as before, the controversy consisted of conflicting theories about the learning capacities, educational possibilities, and professional capabilities of gentlewomen. These theories, in their extreme form, have been labelled the "radical" and the "reactionary"; each developed respectively and directly from the progressive and conservative philosophies of women's education that had evolved over the previous hundred years. To understand the later theories more thoroughly, it was necessary to examine the entire century prior to the 1790s, especially since two influential events in the history of women's literature and education took place in the last quarter of the seventeenth century: Aphra Behn (1640-89) became the first professional woman writer in England and Mary Astell the first feminist woman to advocate college education for her sex.

Eighteenth-century attitudes towards women and their education necessarily changed according to each of the four main philosophies. The chief point separating the two sides—conservatives and reactionaries, progressives and radicals—was their attitude towards women as human beings. Conservatives and reactionaries believed that "whatever is" was eternally right; hence, they attempted to maintain the existing social and sexual hierarchies by regarding women as purely societal and familial beings and by relegating corresponding duties to them. The progressives and radicals likewise believed women to be social beings with societal and familial duties, but, importantly, they also saw them as individuals. The chief contribution of the progressives to female education was the theory that a gentlewoman could best carry out her duties by intelligently understanding them instead of performing them mechanically, inexpertly, or not at all. To this, the radicals added the theory of self-sufficiency for gentlewomen, not only in terms of their minds, bodies, morals, and intellects, but also their professional outlets when necessary. The progressives and radicals thus demanded more choices for gentlewomen, to enable them to take control of their own lives, while the conservatives and reactionaries believed in dictating terms to them, to maintain the patriarchal structure of society. In a sense, the split can also be regarded as the conflict in eighteenth-century Britain between the neoclassical insistence on the importance of the social being and the emerging pre-Romantic belief in the preeminence of the individual.

The four systems of thought were not, however, exclusive of one another. In the course of the eighteenth century, the non-feminist theories were imperceptibly influenced by the opposing ones, as much by the force of argument as by changing economic conditions in the status of women. Also, individual writers themselves sometimes switched allegiance between groups, not only from one work to another and one theory to another, but also from their lives to their works. Thus, the classification of writers cannot always be rigid; the four terms are generally only loosely descriptive of most of the writers considered. Moreover, just as the traditions fall into classifications, so also do certain authors present themselves as key figures in each tradition. The important progressive names were Mary Astell (1666–1731) and John Locke (1632–1704); the important radical leader was Mary Wollstonecraft (1759–97). The major conservatives were Hannah More (1745–1833) and Anna Laetitia Barbauld (1743–1825), and also perhaps Jean-Jacques Rousseau (1712–78); More and Barbauld lived on to represent the reactionaries as well. Especially in the 1790s and after, conservative criticism was directed not only against the opposing tradition but at the opposing party's spokespersons too, even while sometimes incorporating their ideas. Thus, in spite of a certain polarity, the four major theories were essentially interrelated. In the following chapters, I have focused on the contribution of all four theories to the improvement of female education; in the case of the non-feminists, this necessarily included a discussion of both regressive and progressive tendencies in the works considered.

The improvement that took place in female education by the end of the eighteenth century as a result of this controversy was more ideological than actual. However, in the first two decades of the nineteenth century, changes became apparent in the gradual converging of the two theoretical trends. These trends are again labelled "progressive" and "conservative" since external pressure had killed overt radicalism by the beginning of the new century. Fortunately, by this time, progressive theory itself had sufficiently infiltrated into conservative thinking; visions of what could be and prescriptions of what should be now began to set the stage for actual changes to take place in the Victorian age. The greatest achievement of this particular period was the novels of Jane Austen; the combination of female talent and rational thinking, so apparent in them, offered conclusive proof of the competency of female mental ability and professional capability under conditions of proper nurturance. Austen's last two publications appeared in 1817; George III ended his long reign in 1820. In many respects, 1820 therefore seemed a fitting date to conclude this discussion on the controversy that reached such battle proportions in the 1790s.

Since this work deals with the history of ideas, in the following five chapters I have chosen a topical as well as chronological synthesis of the four-hundred-and-fifty or so primary and secondary works consulted to provide a more composite picture of the literary controversy. Each of the following chapters analyzes the controversy in four main respects: in terms of the political and intellectual background; the works used and the theories and places of education proposed; the four main systems of instruction prescribed, here labeled of the head (intellect), the heart (morals), the person (class-related fashionable traits), the physique (health); and the professional possibilities suggested.

Through this synthesis, I have attempted a critical history of prescriptive women's education in the eighteenth century. My purpose in undertaking this project was primarily feminist; I wished to add to the body of information presented on the status of women in former times. Moreover, although not agreeing with Austen's Catherine Morland that history is written "only for the torment of little boys and girls," I have sympathetically responded to her lament that it has consisted mostly of "the quarrels of Popes and Kings with wars or pestilences in every page; the men all so good for nothing, and hardly any women at all, it is very tiresome."[1] The following pages therefore consist of the history of the literary controversy about women's education;[2] more importantly, they contain the written history of women's growing concern about their own lives and their realization that education would give them power, if not over men, at least over their children—and themselves.

---

[1] *Northanger Abbey* (1818; rpt. New York: Dutton, 1907), p. 85.

[2] In the first two chapters especially, I have had to be selective rather than comprehensive in the choice of works.

# CHAPTER 1

# The Conservative Tradition, 1659–1787

As it was in the beginning
Is now and ever shall be
World without end. Amen.
　　　　Magnificat

Whatever is, is right.
　　　　Alexander Pope, *An Essay on Man* (1733-34)

## I.  Political and Intellectual Background

The church, state, militia, and judiciary in eighteenth-century England were in the hands of a small elite that was male, Anglican, and upper-class, and whose rights were unequivocally upheld by a conservative body of thought. To retain its power, this group deemed it necessary to control the larger groups under it, namely women, religious Dissenters,[1] and the middle and lower classes. Like their male counterparts, English gentlewomen, with whom this work is primarily concerned, were generally Anglican and necessarily upper-class. Yet,

---

[1]  All the information on Dissenters in this chapter is from Anthony Lincoln's *Some Political and Social Ideas of English Dissent* (Cambridge: University Press, 1938) and will not be further documented.

unlike the men, their sex prevented them from assuming power in politics (except, ironically, as Queens), in religion, defense, and lawmaking, and especially over themselves. In spite of their higher social status, in a way gentlewomen found themselves educationally among the most oppressed of the four groups. For, unlike the Dissenters, they could not unite to found their own educational institutions; unlike the middle class, they were financially powerless; unlike the poor, they could not respectably work for self-support. Thus, through the dual barriers of sex and social class, conservative theory attempted to keep women in their place by limiting their educational and professional possibilities.

The sphere of gentlewomen was seen as the home and the sphere of gentlemen, the world at large, their only common ground perhaps being their *noblesse oblige* towards the poor.[2] Educational theorists like the French Archbishop François Fénelon (1651–1715) supported this sexual bifurcation of duties by telling women that their private work was as important as men's public efforts in keeping society at large running smoothly. It was therefore regarded as the vocation of either sex to carry out its separate duties adequately; it was the purpose of their differing education to train them for their different roles in life. As befitting the supposedly inferior sex, women's education was to be geared to making them serviceable daughters, wives, and mothers of the men who held immediate power over them as fathers and husbands. The position in which a woman had the least control over her destiny and almost no legal rights was that of a married woman; little wonder, then, that it was towards this very state or profession that conservative educational theory attempted to propel her.

Many prominent upper-class women, from royalty down through the nobility to the gentility, accepted the idea of their sexual inferiority and the necessity of their sexual duties in order to win social respect for themselves. However, this social respect gave these women leeway to satisfy their personal interests when need be; the coexistence of the two seems an indication of the social change gradually going on in the eighteenth century. The Queens of England from the Restoration to the first two decades of the nineteenth century were a case in point. Although they occupied the highest position allowed a woman in England, they did not, in general, violate their gender-

---

[2] All the information in this chapter on the education of gentlemen is from George Brauer's *The Education of a Gentleman: Theories of Gentlemanly Education in England, 1660–1775* (New York: Bookman Associates, 1959) and will not be further documented.

related duties, especially to their husbands. Thus, the Stuart Queens, Mary (reigning 1689–94) and Anne (1702–14), were much respected for their conjugal subservience even though they both eschewed their filial duty to their Catholic father, James II (1685–88), to accept the English throne for themselves. Unlike her sister Mary, Anne did not insist on sharing the throne with her husband, but like Charlotte Sophia of Mecklenburg-Strelitz, wife of the Hanoverian George III (1766–1820), she appeared to be a model wife. To their credit, it must be pointed out that George of Denmark (Anne's consort) and George III also proved themselves devoted and faithful spouses, unlike English kings from Charles II (1660–85) to George IV (1820–30). In *Who's Who in History*, Geoffrey Treasure describes the reigns of Anne and George III, at the beginning and end of the eighteenth century respectively, as fortunate periods of great royal "domestic respectability" in England.[3]

In their roles as mothers, however, the Queens were not generally happy, for a variety of reasons. Of the Stuart Queens, Catherine of Braganza, wife of Charles II, was barren; Anna Hyde, first wife of James II, produced two unfilial daughters; Mary had two miscarriages and was thereafter childless; Anne had thirteen miscarriages and five children who died young. Of the Hanoverian Queens, Sophia Dorothea gave George I (1714–27) two children, an heir and a daughter, before he divorced her on the suspicion of adultery (her son believed her innocent) and incarcerated her for life in a German castle. Caroline of Anspach, wife of George II (1727–60), bore a rebellious son Frederick (who, to his father's satisfaction, died before him); further, she suffered an umbilical rupture, which she carefully concealed from her husband for fear of losing his affection. Charlotte, wife of George III, had fifteen pregnancies; of her surviving children, she was unhappy in her eccentric or extravagant sons, although her daughters proved more tractable.[4]

---

[3] *England, 1714–1786*, vol 4 (Oxford: Blackwell, 1969), p. 287. The historical data in these paragraphs are from *Who's Who in History*, general ed. C. R. N. Routh, III–V (1965, 1969, 1974). Information on French royalty in the ensuing pages is from *The New Encyclopaedia [sic] Britannica* (Chicago: Hemingway Benton, 1974), VI–VII.

[4] These daughters were stifled with parental affection and a repressively monitored moral education. George III was reluctant to allow them to marry and cloistered them as long as he could in virginal seclusion.

The domestic respectability of the family life of George III, the proverbial dullness of his court[5] as opposed to the gay Restoration court of Charles II, and the length of his reign, coming as it did after seven shorter reigns in the previous hundred years, probably did much to stabilize civil and social conditions in England. Conditions in France seemed in sharp contrast during the hundred-year period under discussion. France underwent two long, expensive reigns under Louis XIV (1638–1715) and Louis XV (1715–74) and a far shorter one under Louis XVI (1774–93), the unfortunate contemporary of George III.[6] According to accepted French morals and traditions, the French Kings kept a series of mistresses and presided over dissolute courts; their adherence to Roman Catholicism, however, gave more marital security to their Queens. Nevertheless, French Salique law proved itself more stringent than English law in barring women from ever succeeding to the French throne. Thus, political conditions and religious affiliations in England and France were very different in the hundred years or so discussed in this chapter. In spite of such political dissimilarities, the patriarchal constitutions in both countries generally led their respective theorists to agree about the purpose and extent of the education of gentlewomen. In fact, the influence of French theorists was of significant importance in the controversy over the issue that raged in England throughout the eighteenth century.

Unlike in France, the influence of English conservative gentlewomen-writers on the education and literary status of their peers does not seem to have begun until around the mid-eighteenth century.[7] In the 1760s, ’70s, and ’80s, especially, highly educated gentlewomen like the Dissenter Anna Laetitia Aikin (1743–1825, Barbauld from 1774) and the group known as the Bluestockings[8] slowly effected changes in the social acceptance of conservative literary women.

---

[5] Recorded, among others, by the novelist Fanny Burney, who worked as Second Keeper of the Robes to Queen Charlotte from 1786–91.

[6] The frivolity, political intrigues, and personal beauty of his Queen Marie Antoinette were in direct contrast to the plainness and love of home and duty of Charlotte in England.

[7] Actually, from the Restoration to around 1750, female English theorists were largely progressive in their attitude towards women's education.

[8] Bluestocking salons were originally attended not only by women but also by well-known male figures like Samuel Johnson, Joshua Reynolds, and Edmund Burke. The term Bluestocking did not develop pejorative connotations until the late eighteenth century. Among the best-known London hostesses of Bluestocking soirées were Elizabeth Montagu, Elizabeth Vesey, Frances Boscawen, Hester Thrale, and Mary Delaney. Their assemblies were also successfully imitated in the provinces; Anna

The Bluestockings particularly under consideration are Elizabeth Montagu (1720-1800), Elizabeth Carter (1717-1806), Hester Chapone (1727-1801), Hannah More (1745-1833), and Fanny Burney (1752-1840). Their positive influence, however, was owing to their progressive lifestyles rather than to their genteel educational precepts, for the generality of upper-class women, for these writers (aside from Chapone) exhibited a duality between their lives and published opinions. Like the Queens of England just discussed, they courted social approval by paying assiduous attention to the external principles of female decorum and propriety and by emphasizing the importance of female duties. This approval stood them in good stead when they successfully attempted entry into activities hitherto seen as purely male.

In education as well as lifestyle, these women were exceptions to the norm of womanly behavior. In her article, "Mistresses of Orthodoxy," Miriam Leranbaum records that contrary to prescribed female education, these women were given what was called a classical or "masculine" education by interested fathers or father-surrogates.[9] Except for Burney, a slow starter, they were all eager scholars and voracious readers from a very early age. In fact, as young girls, they received and gave themselves the stimulating education suggested for gentlewomen by progressive forebears like Mary Astell.

As adults, their observance of gender-related duties was only slightly less aberrant than their unorthodox education had been. The moralizing More and respectably intellectual Carter remained single: the former, after being stood up three times at the altar by the same man; the latter, by choosing to devote her life to study instead of to marriage. With the double standards typical of the Bluestockings, Carter is noted to have said, "Marriage is a very right scheme for everybody but myself."[10] The others were all married. In her forties and against initial paternal approval, Burney rushed into marriage with a penniless but upper-class French emigré; Barbauld married a good

---

Seward, the "Swan of Lichfield," headed the group in Johnson and David Garrick's hometown; Lady Millar led the one at Batheaston; Amelia Alderson [later Opie] was a popular member among the Norwich intellectuals.

[9] *Proceedings of the American Philosophical Society*, 121, No. 4 (August 12, 1977), p. 284.

[10] Quoted in Joyce Horner's *The English Women Novelists and their Connection with the Feminist Movement* (1688-1797), *Smith College Studies in Modern Languages*, 11, Nos. 1–3 (Northampton, MA: The Collegiate Press,1929–30), p. 52. Carter, however, resented William Hayley's mistaken enthusiasm in dedicating to her his *Philosophical, Historical, and Moral Essay on Old Maids* (3 vols, 1785).

but emotionally unstable clergyman who in later life attempted to kill her; Chapone became a widow after only ten months of marriage; Montagu, perhaps prudently, married a wealthy man twenty-nine years her senior and efficiently managed his money and coal fields after his death. Among all these women, only Burney had a child that lived into adulthood: Montagu's son died in infancy, while Chapone and Barbauld exemplified the inexplicable infertility of many writing women of the eighteenth and nineteenth centuries.

The deviance of some of the Bluestockings is also apparent in their personal efforts in behalf of society and literary women. The hostesses endeavored to wield a beneficial socio-intellectual influence on the habits of society ladies by promoting intelligent conversation in their soirées, in concerted opposition to cards and scandal, supposedly the two popular pastimes of their genteel contemporaries. Moreover, in an age that stigmatized the literary lady, Montagu and Carter actively encouraged the talents, but not necessarily the professionalism, of aspiring female contemporaries (Leranbaum, p. 291).

Through their published works, the Bluestockings also opened up or popularized new literary fields for women, such as polemical criticism (Montagu's refutation of Voltaire in her *Essay on the Writings and Genius of Shakespear* [*sic*], 1769); translation (Carter's translation of Epictetus from the Greek, 1758); and biography (Hester Piozzi's *Anecdotes of the Late Samuel Johnson*, 1786, which anticipated James Boswell's more famous work by five years). The voluminous (posthumously published) letters of the Bluestockings Montagu, Chapone, Carter, Vesey, and Catherine Talbot (1721–70) to each other also give a lively picture of the emerging New Woman and of the social life of the times. They discuss politics and classical and European literature, exchange news about famous contemporaries, and express their deep affection for one another (defying a common eighteenth-century concept that women could not be friends). The social and literary approval given the works of these intelligent women must surely have played its part in increasing the respectability of writing as a profession for women in the second half of the century. But professionalism did not come easily to gentlewomen themselves. Wealthy socialites like Montagu penned their works as genteel, intellectual amateurs, much in the style of their nobly born seventeenth-century forebears who chose to pen elegant letters, poems, and scholarly works. On the other hand, and unlike them, remuneration rather than genius or elegant exercise encouraged unprovided gentlewomen to turn to professional (generally fictional) writing, once Aphra Behn (1640–89) pioneered the field in the third quarter of the seventeenth century. Unexpected circumstances forced gentle-women like her and Mary de la Rivière Manley (1663–1724) to realize that when it came to survival, financial independence was more important than fear of social stigma. In the course of the eighteenth century, more and more impoverished upper-class women turned to writing for profit, although they sometimes attempted to salvage their gentility by publishing anonymously.

In spite of or perhaps because of a growing number of women writers, literary professionalism in women was often not taken seriously. Women's work was trivialized as the consequence of what was often called an "itch to scribble"; early in the century, Pope sarcastically dismissed literature by women as a result of a fit of the "Spleen" (*Rape of the Lock*, 1712). Moreover, women's work was, by nature, supposed to be mediocre; eminent writers from Elizabeth Montagu to Anne Louise Germaine de Staël (1766–1817) lamented the social pressure put on a female writer of genius. In a letter to her friend Lord Lyttelton, dated October 21, 1760, the former complained about the existing double-standards in the reception of writers:

> Extraordinary talents may make a woman admired, but they will never make her happy. Talents put a man above the world in a condition to be feared or worshipped; a woman that possesses them must always be courting the world, and asking pardon, as it were, for uncommon excellence.[11]

The fear of social censure made many conservative writing women add a conventionally apologetic, humble, self-deprecating preface to their works. They were careful to point out that they published only at the urgent entreaty of friends or to prevent pirated editions. The difference between the self-confidently assured tone of a man's preface and the pleading tones of a conservative woman's preface is made apparent by comparing representative samples from the works of Edward Moore (1712–57) and Hannah More. Although dedicating his poetic *Fables for the Female Sex* (1744) to the Princess of Wales, Moore arrogantly asserted in his preface: "I wrote to please myself, and I publish to please others."[12] On the other hand, a female player in More's school-play, *The Search After Happiness* (1773), apologizes in the prologue for the temerity of the cast: "With trembling diffidence, with modest fear / Before

---

[11] *Letters* (1813; rpt. New York: AMS Press, 1974), IV, 311.

[12] Rpt. in *The Young Lady's Pocket Library* (London: n.p., 1790), p. 169.

this gentle audience we appear."[13] Paradoxically, it was only by denying their artistic worth that many women writers felt they could be accepted as literary artists.

Yet it seems that social censure at large did not necessarily include the withholding of private male approval. From around the mid-century on, two literary giants, Samuel Richardson and Samuel Johnson, encouraged moral and talented women writers in their work, much as Carter and Montagu did. In France too, the *philosophes* Montesquieu (1689–1755), Voltaire (1694–1778), Diderot (1713–84), Condillac (1714–80), and Helvétius (1715–71) attended the salons of literary and intellectual women of their time and paid their respects to female talent. The French philosophers have often been called progressive by twentieth-century critics, but, more than Richardson and Johnson, they often displayed a duality between their private and printed word.[14] For instance (except perhaps for d'Holbach), they recognized that women's grievances stemmed from a faulty education and not from natural inferiority, yet they generally accepted as normal the unnatural socio-political differences existing between the sexes.

All in all, whether or not writing gentlewomen gained public respect or financial self-sufficiency, "the numbers of novels, children's books, essays, poems, plays, translations, travels, and controversies published by women between 1750 and 1790 testify to a massive public debut of educated and self-educated female opinion."[15] In the second half of the century especially, literary gentlewomen were no longer driven crazy as the unfortunate Margaret Cavendish, Duchess of Newcastle, was in the seventeenth century. Women were making their voices heard in important matters relating to themselves, especially on their own education; whether they wrote as conservatives or progressives is perhaps not so important as the fact that they dared to publish their views at all.

It is unfortunate, of course, that when it came to publication for profit, conservative educational theory often triumphed over private feminism in

---

[13] *The Search after Happiness*, 6th ed. (Bristol: sold by Bonner et al., 1775), p. ix.

[14] The *philosophes* also discussed aspects of women's lives on which English conservatives were totally silent for reasons of decorum or religious difference, as, for instance, female life processes like menstruation and pregnancy, the social acceptability of female conjugal infidelity, the importance of Catholic sacraments to women, and the significance of convents for both the education of young women and the incarceration of older surplus females.

[15] Ellen Messer-Davidow, a fellow grad at UC, provided this insight.

the works of women writers like the Bluestockings. Most male writers, on the other hand, especially theorists and clergymen, were more consistently conservative than the women writers and therefore popular with most educators throughout the century. Thus, the works of the Marquess of Halifax (1633–95) and Archbishop Fénelon, written in the late seventeenth century, were prescribed for women as often as the chronologically later works of Jean-Jacques Rousseau (1712–78) and Drs. James Fordyce (1720–98) and John Gregory (1724–73), written in the 1760s and '70s. Significantly, however, progressive attitudes occasionally surfaced even in these works, while other writers switched allegiance not only in their lives and works but also in different works themselves. So it is with regard to the predominant nature of their prescriptive texts, both fictional and non-fictional, rather than to their occasional forays into feminism, that the writers in this chapter have been labelled conservative.

## II. Works, Theories, Places of Education

If one can form a judgement from the large amount of literature written for and increasingly by her, the literacy of the eighteenth-century gentlewoman seems to have greatly increased from the beginning to the end of the century. It is important to remember the distinction between literacy and education; according to one eighteenth-century connotation, the latter term often included the development of a person's whole being, throughout a lifetime, and was not limited to mere language skills or to formal or gender-related instruction in youth. However, if language skills in general improved among gentlewomen, how is one to interpret Jonathan Swift's famous accusation that upper-class women often could not even sign their own names? The answer seems to be that, as with the poor later in the century, the abilities to read and write did not always coexist in gentlewomen earlier in the century. Hence, it would be perfectly logical to assume that a percentage of women were able to read, even if they could not pen their own signatures. It is likewise necessary to remember that the low level of literacy of the boorish, fox-hunting squire and the superficial knowledge of the Augustan town-fop were equally proverbial in literature.

Since the education of the youth of either sex was not a national concern in this period, a large body of theoreticians of both sexes wrote a voluminous amount of literature on female instruction. In careful detail and using various fictional and non-fictional forms, they discussed such related issues as the learning capacity of gentlewomen; the nature and purpose of their education according to gender, class, and marital status; the best place of instruction for them; and the curricula of what I see as the four main types of instruction available to them. All these factors were necessarily related to the economic status of women and therefore manipulated, at least in theory, to limit the extent of female professionalism and independence. The conservatives did not belong to a school as such, yet certain generalizations can be made from their works regarding their composite opinion on various aspects of female education.

Since an increasing number of gentlewomen were beginning to read, prescriptive literature written specifically for them became an important means of spreading ideas on education. Both non-fictional and fictional works aimed to instruct, either directly or indirectly. The non-fictional literary forms most frequently used were courtesy books, letters, treatises, and essays. The best-known courtesy or conduct books of this period were all by men. They were, in chronological order: Fénelon's *Traité sur l'éducation des filles* (1687; *The Education of Girls*) and *Les Aventures de Télémaque* (1699; *The Adventures of Telemachus, the Son of Ulysses*),[16] the Marquis of Halifax's *The Lady's New Year's Gift: Or Advice to a Daughter* (1688), William Kenrick's *The Whole Duty of Woman* (published anonymously in 1753 as "By a Lady"), James Fordyce's *Sermons to Young Women* (1765) and *The Character and Conduct of the Female Sex* (1775), John Gregory's *A Father's Legacy to His Daughters* (1774), and Henry Home, Lord Kames's *Loose Hints upon Education, Chiefly Concerning the Culture of the Heart* (1781).

Theorists also used the epistolary form as a more informal and entertaining means of instruction. Among the educational letters used in this chapter are Jonathan Swift's *A Letter to a Very Young Lady on her Marriage* (1727); Lady Sarah Pennington's *An Unfortunate Mother's Advice to her Absent Daughters* (1761); Hester Chapone's *Letters on the Improvement of the Mind* (1772), *Letters on Filial Obedience* (rpt. 1807), *Letter to a New-Married Lady* (rpt. 1821); and, incidentally, Philip Dormer Stanhope, the Earl of Chesterfield's *Letters to his Son: On the Fine Art of Becoming a Man of the World and a Gentleman* (1774) and *The Art of Pleasing; or Instructions for Youth* (3rd ed. 1783). The French *philosophes* included discussions on female capacity and education in

---

[16] In cases where a French work is used in translation, the original title is followed by the English title in parentheses.

their treatises and essays, as, for instance, in Montesquieu's *De l'esprit des lois* (1748; *The Spirit of the Laws*), Condillac's *Essai sur l'origine des connaissances humaines* (1746; *An Essay on the Origin of Human Knowledge*), Diderot's "Sur les femmes" (1772), and so on.

The belles-lettres forms dealing with women's education included poems, plays, fictional letters, and the newly introduced genre of the novel. The poems used in this chapter are those by Alexander Pope, Hannah More, and Edward Moore. In drama, at both the beginning and end of this period, satiric comedies on intellectual women were a popular medium for both the stage and the "closet"; the best-known ones were perhaps Molière's *Les Femmes savantes* (1762; *The Learned Ladies*), *Les Précieuses ridicules* (1659; *The Affected Ladies*), and Richard Brinsley Sheridan's *The Rivals* (1775). Montesquieu's *Lettres persanes* (1721; *Persian Letters*) and Mary Walker's *Letters of the Duchess de Crui and Others, on Subjects Moral and Entertaining, wherein the Character of the Female Sex, with their Rank, Importance, and Consequence, Is Stated, and their Relative Duties in Life Are Enforced* (1776) combined fiction and treatise, using different letter writers to present different points of view.

Of all the fictional genres, the most commonly used form of instruction was the novel, traditionally believed to have been introduced in 1740 with the publication of Richardson's epistolary *Pamela*. Until the controversial decade of the 1790s, when the *tendenz* novel or "novel of purpose" became popular, works of sentiment and sensibility remained the most fashionable types. Jean-Jacques Rousseau's *Julie, ou la nouvelle Héloise* (1764; *Eloisa: or, a Series of Original Letters*), Frances Sheridan's *Memoirs of Miss Sidney Biddulph* (1761–67),[17] Oliver Goldsmith's *The Vicar of Wakefield* (1766), Henry Mackenzie's *The Man of Feeling* (1771), and Johann Wolfgang von Goethe's *Die Leiden des Jungen Werther* (1774; *The Sufferings of Young Werther*) were among the most widely read of these sentimental novels. They served an implicit educational purpose by demonstrating how the heroine's or hero's education directly influenced her or his reaction to the vicissitudes of life and love.

Other novelists were concerned explicitly with the question of female education. Burney wrote courtesy-book novels like *Evelina;*[sic] *or the History of a Young Lady's Entrance into the World* (1778) and *Cecilia, or Memoirs of an Heiress* (1782), which met with approval even from the Royal family. Others like Thomas Day in *The History of Sandford and Merton* (1783–89)

---

[17] She was the mother of the playwright Richard Brinsley Sheridan and a well-known writer in her time.

and Rousseau in *Émile, ou de l'éducation* (1762; *Emilius, or, an Essay on Education*) wrote educational treatises in the thin guise of fiction. *Émile* remained one of the most controversial books on female and male education in the eighteenth century. More than any other form, the serious novel, at least in theory, must have answered to the eighteenth-century literary criteria of instruction and entertainment.

The four major novelists of this period, Samuel Richardson,[18] Henry Fielding, Tobias Smollett, and Lawrence Sterne (among whom only the first was a feminist), were all male, yet novel-writing seems to have been regarded as a particularly female phenomenon in the eighteenth century,[19] the first novel by a gentlewoman perhaps being Sarah Fielding's *David Simple* (1744). Women appear to have preferred this form to any other, for several reasons. Their education was supposed to be primarily moral; Richardson's influential emphasis on (prudential) morality in his fiction gave them an excuse to use their own instruction both to benefit themselves financially and to amuse and edify their female readers. Bridget MacCarthy points out that as women gained in self-confidence (in spite of the humility of their prefaces) and began to master their tools, they grew more comfortable writing as women, and realized that "with their increasing hold over the reading public they need no longer subscribe to a masculine attitude in fiction."[20] Moreover, as women writing about women to mostly women, they could work from a female perspective where the "other" was the father, husband, and son, instead of themselves as just submissive, retiring daughter, wife, and mother.[21] Aside from instruction, novel reading and writing also served as a pleasant escape for women, encouraging them both to read and exercise their literary talents.

Circulating libraries grew up all over England to satisfy the rage for novels. Conservative theorists naturally saw reason for alarm at the preference of women, flightier females in particular, for novels rather than (dry) edifying

---

[18] Novelists like Richardson, Mackenzie, and Goldsmith sometimes combined their own poetic and fictional talents through the medium of versifying heroines or heroes, creating a novel form that was popularized in the 1790s by practitioners like Charlotte Smith and Ann Ward Radcliffe.

[19] It is probable that, like Jane Austen's hero Henry Tilney in *Northanger Abbey* (1818), men read (and wrote) novels with equal pleasure.

[20] In *Women Writers: Their Contribution to the English Novel 1621-1744* (New York: Salloch, 1948), p. 86.

[21] Hazel Mews, *Frail Vessels: Women's Role in Women's Novels from Fanny Burney to George Eliot* (London: Athlone Press, 1969), p. 24.

works. Hence, throughout this period, comic writers attempted to laugh women out of this so-called dangerous folly. The "novel-reading miss" whose head was turned by her fantastical diet of novels and romances became a frequent subject of satire in comedies and often even in novels themselves, famous examples being Molière's two *précieuses ridicules*, Sheridan's Lydia Languish (*The Rivals*, with its caricatured Mrs. Malaprop), Charlotte Lennox's Arabella (*The Female Quixote*, 1752), and Smollett's Lydia Melford (*Humphry Clinker*, 1771).[22] More seriously, stern critics from Fénelon to Fordyce, Chapone, and More attacked the novel and romance as giving a perniciously false impression of life. But novelists like Rousseau (in *La Nouvelle Héloise*) and Burney (in *Evelina*) defended their craft; the former by recommending greater realism in novels, the latter by pleading for the encouragement of moral novels since it was not possible to "extirpate" the genre itself.[23]

Through the various forms of literature discussed above, the conservatives sought to disseminate their views on female education. Although they did not subscribe to a uniform system of thought, they held certain common beliefs about the relationship of female capacity to women's education, notably, that woman was a creature inferior to and dependent on man for survival; that marriage was a gentlewoman's ultimate vocation; and that her education was to be chiefly man-oriented, therefore, domestic and practical. Such an education was believed just, not limiting, for God himself had irrevocably cursed woman to a subordinate position, through the sin of her foremother Eve (after whom knowledge was to be denied to all women). Thereafter, it was agreed, Nature seconded and Custom enforced the sexual hierarchy and the consequent differences in roles, capacities, and duties of women and men. Education was always to follow a person's sexual "grain"; hence, the woman who chose to overstep gender-related boundaries became sacrilegious, unsexed, and socially deviant. In the gentlewoman's code especially, the last was as great a crime as the first two, for "singularity" of behavior was not the mark of good-breeding. The essence of good-breeding, according to Chesterfield, was *l'art de plaire* or the art of pleasing, but while the gentleman was to please society in general, the gentlewoman was to please man in particular. Rousseau

---

[22] Novels dealt with fiction close to contemporary life, romances with stories of distant times and people, especially from the ancient classics. Clara Reeve deals with the distinction between the two in her *Progress of Romance* (1785).

[23] Preface to *Evelina* (1778; rpt. London: Oxford UP, 1968), p. 8.

went so far as to declare that a woman was born only to please and to serve the "superior" sex. In the section on Sophie, the everywoman in *Émile*, he gave a detailed account of female education based on the theory of sexual inferiority. Nature, he said, framed women to be "passive and feeble" for man's delight:

> The education of the fair sex should be intirely [*sic*] relative to ours. To oblige us, to do us service, to gain our love and esteem, to rear us when young, to attend us when grown up, to advise, to console us, to soothe our pains, and to soften life with every kind of blandishment; these are the duties of the sex at all times, and what they ought to learn from their infancy.[24]

(It must be pointed out that this imperious demand for woman to serve and to mother both father and son came from a man who deposited each of his offspring, as it was born, at the foundling hospital.)

Considerations of class were as important as those of gender in the formulation of conservative theories on female education. As a sex, all women were regarded as inferior to man but as a class, gentlewomen were seen as superior to others of their sex and therefore deserving of a better education. Gender and class were, then as now, related issues. Both were used to keep women in their place and thereby to preserve the social status quo, for changes such as economic betterment (especially for the poor), social mobility (especially for the middle class), and female emancipation (this, impartially, for all classes) could only lead to political upheaval and subsequent loss of power for the male elite.

The conservatives used religion as a powerful ally in their attempt to suppress women as a sex as well as the poor as a class. They promised both groups the joys of the afterlife for unquestioning forbearance and patient suffering in this, because patience and acceptance would adequately stifle hankerings after change and betterment. Above all, women and the poor were enjoined to wear their chains cheerfully in order to preserve the happiness of the sexes and of the ruling and serving classes. The novels of the time were especially insistent on the class issue and were full of cautionary lessons to lower- and middle-class girls against upsetting the social stasis. Their particular targets were lower-class girls who dressed and thought above their class, like Molly Seagrim, the gamekeeper's daughter in *Tom Jones* (1749); orphaned village girls

---

[24] *Emilius* (London: Nourse and Vaillant, 1763), II, 177, 189.

like Fanny Hill in John Cleland's prurient novel, *The Memoirs of a Woman of Pleasure* (1748–49); and servant girls like Defoe's eponymous Moll Flanders (1722), who were educated above their class by kindly, unthinking mistresses. Such women were depicted as more likely to be victims of seduction and the consequent horrors of prostitution and thieving than to marry their masters, Cinderella-fashion, like Richardson's prudent Pamela.

Aspiring middle-class girls were also warned that they would become likely candidates for seduction by upper-class rakes.[25] Another argument used to keep them in their places was that they could never transcend the ill-breeding and commercial-mindedness of their class and therefore made fools of themselves when they attempted to ape gentility. Lennox's vituperative portrayal in *Henrietta* (1758) of the arrogant, mean-minded, middle-class heiress, Miss Cordwain, and Burney's humorous depiction in *Evelina* of the vulgar Branghtons and Mr. Smith are only two of the many fictional examples warning middle-class women against social climbing.

In fact, however, the error of the aspiring middle-class woman did not lie in her misunderstanding of the term *respectability* as meaning only economic non-productivity (commonly called idleness). Her error was that in an age when members of her class sometimes equaled or exceeded the nobility in its wealth, she failed to understand fully that her strength, if of wealthy parentage, lay entirely in her dowry money and to demand social advantages for it.

Gentlewomen, especially, were untutored in money matters; for the most part, conservative theory was built around keeping them from a knowledge of the social and professional connection between themselves and money, except in relation to household accounts. According to Rousseau, a woman's education was only to pertain to that which was practical and useful—to society and not herself. So, since nature and class defined a gentlewoman's role in society, it was believed practical not only to educate her to carry out her duties well but also to weed out options systematically, both in her mind and in society.

The conservatives advocated practicality even with regard to the place of female education, the alternatives for gentlewomen being the home or boarding schools. Throughout this period, educators like Fénelon, Rousseau, and Thomas Day were unanimous in recommending home education, in the belief that a love of domestic life could be fostered in young girls only by habituating them to it from an early age. Following John Locke (1632–1704), Rousseau

---

[25] Seduction, drunkenness, and gaming were the social vices of gentleman-rakes.

and others saw this home education as taking place under the mother's tutelage, for a mother best understood her daughter's capabilities and needs. This system had the dual purpose of ensuring that both the daughter and mother stayed at home and was prescribed as much for the upper- as the middle class.

The other educational option was the boarding school. Such schools appear to have sprung up all over the country, from fashionable resorts to market towns. However, boarding-school education was roundly decried throughout the century, not only by conservatives, but also by most of their progressive counterparts and by the radicals and the reactionaries of the 1790s. The objections of the conservatives were both gender- and class-related. They argued that instead of being under the mother's careful supervision at home, young ladies were subjected to either unscrupulous, lower-class adventurers or indigent and harassed gentlewomen, both types proving incompetent in the business of edifying young minds. Further, instead of a quiet, repressive, domestic education, schoolgirls were supposed to receive an outgoing "fashionable" education, which consisted only of frippery and frumpery; a superficial knowledge of ornamental accomplishments such as dancing, singing, and music;[26] a smattering of ill-spoken French and Italian; a frivolous outlook on life; and a love of escapist novels and romances. Such an education, it was argued, could only give growing girls a giddy instead of a sober turn of mind. In Smollett's *Humphry Clinker*, the crusty hypochondriac, Matthew Bramble, complains to his friend, Dr. Lewis, that the faults of his highly inflammable niece Lydia all stemmed from her institutional instruction. In his opinion, next to a nunnery, a boarding school was the worst kind of seminary ever contrived for young women.

Perhaps an even greater crime than poor academic training, in the eyes of this class-conscious century, was that the common education given in boarding schools forced upper-class girls to mix indiscriminately with their social inferiors. (This objection was also made regarding a young gentleman's education in a public school [it is generally known that Britain's private schools for upper-crust boys are called public schools].) Yet the alternative of home education could not be enforced for all young ladies since, as was often bitterly pointed out, fashionable mothers chose to spend their time in a continual round of dissipation instead of in tending their daughters' minds and morals. What the theorists therefore did was strive to keep middle-class girls,

---

[26] "Fashionable" education is discussed in Section III as "education of the person."

especially farmers' and tradesmen's daughters, away from boarding schools, preaching to them that it was to their own benefit and happiness not to mingle with their superiors. Through letters and articles in his periodical, *The Mirror* (1779–80), Henry Mackenzie vividly dramatized the self-conscious unhappiness of thinking, middle-class girls like Harriet B— (I. No. 51) and Mary Muslin (II, No. 96) who return from their boarding schools with too much false sensibility ever to be satisfied in their gauche parents' homes again. In Day's *Sandford and Merton*, Harry's sensible father, farmer Sandford, takes preventive measures against such familial discord by refusing Mr. Merton's gift of £100, declaring that its acceptance would turn his daughters' heads; they would demand a boarding-school education and thereupon cease to be useful women.

Unlike the middle class and the gentility, lower-class girls were specifically recommended some institutional education, presumably because their mothers were too illiterate to instruct them on their own. The schools suggested were naturally not boarding schools but Charity and, later, Industry and Sunday schools. As early as 1696, the Society for Promoting Christian Knowledge had founded Charity schools in England; in the 1780s, reformers like Robert Raikes and Sarah Trimmer started Sunday and Industry schools for the poor. The purpose of all three types of schools was not always to increase literacy among the poor (although much seems to have been done in this respect); often the intention was to teach them submission to their social superiors, on religious grounds.

If class barriers controlled the educational limits of the various classes, it was specifically the sex barrier that denied higher education to upper-class women. The universities of Oxford and Cambridge were meant only for Anglican men, generally of the upper class.[27] There were no colleges for women, in spite of Mary Astell's earnest plea for such a seminary, made towards the end of the seventeenth century (1694).[28]

Around 1774, Astell's dream had a chance to come alive but was aborted at the instance of Anna Laetitia Aikin, herself classically educated and well known as a poet and essayist. Under her married name of Barbauld, Aikin was soon to become famous as an exemplary school teacher of young boys,

---

[27] Like women, male Dissenters too were denied entry into English universities, but they had the option to attend Scottish universities or the Dutch university at Leyden.

[28] See Chapter 2, Section II, under "Places of Education."

as well as a writer of popular lessons and prose hymns for children.[29] The story of this projected college deserves attention. Barbauld's biographer, Grace Atkinson Ellis, records that the rich Bluestocking Elizabeth Montagu and others proposed that the talented, brilliantly educated Anna Aikin assume charge and instruction of an "academy or college for young ladies," beginning at age fifteen. The scholars were to receive a "more extended and elevated system of education for women" than hitherto given in most schools and be taught in a "regular, systematic manner the various branches of science."[30]

Either totally misunderstanding or deliberately de-emphasizing the importance of the institution proposed, Aikin refused. She envisioned the college, meant as an academy for higher instruction, as a mere boarding school and therefore felt age fifteen to be far too late to begin schooling. That, she believed, was the age to be under the mother's tutelage and to learn the social graces. Moreover, she misinterpreted the nature of the curriculum, which proposed a truly learned knowledge of the sciences, to mean superficial learning like that of Molière's *précieuses* and *femmes savantes*. With blatant double-standards, she argued that regardless of her own superior education, the only knowledge women in general needed could be picked up in conversation with a father, brother, or male friend, and from such books as they suggested. She further confused the proposed intellectual curriculum with genteel accomplishments, good-breeding, "air," and conversation, in all of which she felt herself deficient, ignoring the possibility that she had been picked as a role model of an intelligent yet dutiful woman rather than as a mere fashionable governess.

The conservative gentlewomen who had so daringly proposed the college were overcome by the force of her arguments and weakly abandoned the project. The modern-day feminist shares Johnson's sense of frustration, recorded in Dr. Charles Burney's *Recollections of Dr. Johnson* (also in Boswell's *Life*), at Anna Aikin's wasted powers (and her incidentally regressive contribution to the history of women's education in England):

Miss Aikin was an instance of early cultivation, but in what did it terminate? In marrying a little Presbyterian parson, who keeps an infant boarding-school, so

---

[29] The boys' school she and her husband ran at Palgrave became known as one of the best of its kind in the country.

[30] *Memoir, Letters, and a Selection from the Poems and Prose Writings of Anna Laetitia Barbauld* (Boston: Osgood, 1874), I, 56. Ellis quotes the full letter containing Barbauld's reply, pp. 56–61.

that all her employment now is 'To suckle fools, and chronicle small beer.' She tells the children, 'This is a cat, and this is a dog, with four legs and a tail, see there! You are much better than a cat or a dog, for you can speak.' If I had bestowed such an education on a daughter, and had discovered that she thought of marrying such a fellow, I would have sent her to the Congress. (Quoted in Ellis, I, 73)

Barbauld's double-standards were only symptomatic of the standards of conservative educational thought of her day. Moreover, such conservatism denied gentlewomen not only higher formal studies, but also education by experience, through the sort of continental tour that was supposed to add the final touches to a gentleman's education. The ideal of domesticity naturally excluded extensive travel; when it came to the female mind and intellect, theorists preferred physical confinement at home to mental enlargement abroad. They therefore complained that after their "formal" education, young ladies were paraded by mothers around London and the bathing spas instead of kept in retirement at home. As Margaret Phillips and W. S. Tomkinson express it in *English Women in Life and Letters*, "Miss" put away her books at sixteen for the "more serious business of life—routs, masquerades, balls, and husband-hunting. Bath commenced her education proper, Ranelagh and Vauxhall finished it."[31]

In spite of the cautionary advice of theorists, then, the final stage in a well-bred gentlewoman's education was an introduction to "the world," that is to fashionable English society, perhaps as a compensation for the lack of college education and of a continental tour. But the actual purpose of this "coming out," as it was called, was not so much pleasure per se as the desperate business of charming a well-off man into marriage and thereby securing a legal competency in life. The projected training in domesticity and the deliberate exclusion from exposure until the final display of the merchandise were carefully worked out steps in the education of a gentlewoman. Their purpose was to reinsure her return to domesticity in what was seen as the most (and often only) serious business of a woman's life: matrimony and motherhood.

---

[31] *English Women* (Oxford: Oxford University Press, 1927), p. 196.

## III. Education of the Person, the Physique, the Heart, and the Head

If, in its philosophical sense, education was sometimes regarded in the eighteenth century as the business of a lifetime, in its more practical aspects, a gentlewoman's formal education was assumed finished by the time she was married. Thereafter, it was up to her or her husband to cultivate her knowledge further. She received her formal instruction through four main disciplines, if they may be so called: of the person, the physique, the heart, and the head. The first comprised what was called a fashionable education, that of the heart was seen as a shrewd moral education, that of the head was an intellectual education. The degree of physical education changed according to the degree of health believed necessary for a gentlewoman to carry out her prescribed functions. In a sense, fashionable education was a training in the external arts of charming and securing a husband; moral education included a training in the more calculated arts of keeping his affection and therefore his financial support as long as he lived. Conservatives regarded moral education as the most important of the four types, yet intellectual education must have proved equally so, for it must have given the gentlewoman a mental retreat within herself when emotional and affectional support from family members failed.

In the eighteenth century, it became the fashion among moral theorists, both feminist and non-feminist, to attack the excesses of the first type of education, namely, of the person, especially when it was the only sort of instruction a gentlewoman received. In Susanna Keir's novel, *Interesting Memoirs* (1785), the lively, intelligent Charlotte Villiers gives a description of just such an education and its effects. She teasingly recites to the vapid heroine Louisa a mock-catechism on "the whole duty of woman":

Question. For what end did you come into the world? Answer. To get a husband. —Q. What is the way to get a husband? A. To dress, dance, chat, play, and go to all manner of public places, except church for fear of being called a fanatic. —Q. What is the duty of a husband? A. To please his wife. —Q. What is the duty of a wife? A. To please herself.[32]

---

[32] *Interesting Memoirs*, 2nd ed. (London: Strahan, Cadell, 1785), II, 38.

"To please herself." Charlotte speaks facetiously, but the conservatives were alarmed that the system of fashionable education, especially that given at boarding schools, would spread from noblemen's to farmers' daughters and present a very real threat to the social and sexual hierarchy. This could not be allowed; male educators like Rousseau and clergymen like Fordyce high-handedly insisted that since woman was formed to please man, she should be educated only to appear attractive to him and not to live a fashionable life herself.

As for the moral conservatives, in spite of their antipathy to an entirely fashionable education, most of them acknowledged that the standards of gentility demanded some attention to the education of the person. So they gave gentlewomen detailed if somewhat varied advice on each aspect of the curriculum, which included an attention to beauty, an attention to dress, and a knowledge of the ornamental accomplishments, namely, dancing, drawing, music, and needlework. They were not unanimous in their stand on the importance of physical beauty, the first requisite in the art of attracting a man and securing him in marriage. In his heroines, Sophia, Fanny, and Amelia (as well as in his heroes), Fielding equated external allure with internal goodness. So far so good, but this platonic equation also implied the unjust corollary that ugliness was connected to spinsterhood and to such defects as "masculine" learning (as in Mrs. Western) and jealous mean-mindedness (as in Amelia's sister).

Contrary to the platonic duality, moralists like Chapone denied the importance of physical beauty and preached instead that mental beauty was both superior and less ephemeral.[33] More practically, Swift and others pointed out that mental beauty helped keep the husband's affection alive after his passion for his wife's body had decreased. This principle was not unsound, considering that the wife would thereby be ensuring her own maintenance.

Next in importance to beauty, in the list of female attractions, was adornment of the person through dress. Rousseau, his disciple Kames, and others believed that women had a natural inclination to this vanity. From the beginning to the end of this period, none of the English and French conservatives neglected to give their advice on this all-important article in their works on female education. Fénelon, Swift, Moore, Pennington, Fordyce, Gregory,

---

[33] A living example of the plain-faced yet dutiful and moral wife and mother was Queen Charlotte herself.

Kames, and others recommended qualities in dress that they desired to see in gentlewomen in general, such as simplicity, neatness, and an avoidance of "singularity." Rousseau and Gregory deliberately confounded simplicity with simulation and suggested a studied artful artlessness in dress, so as to attract the viewer by setting his imagination on fire. This advice was faithfully followed in fiction not only by the ethereally good heroines, always so humbly unaware of their charms, but also by the more sexually down-to-earth female characters, such as Fielding's parodic Shamela Andrews and Cleland's prostitute Fanny Hill.

The use of the same arts by whores and heroines in fiction to get and keep their men implies a certain degree of desperation in the economic situation of women in the eighteenth century. Or it implies a significant unsoundness in the conservative line of thought which attempted to train a young lady in the arts of a mistress, in order to seduce her husband into spending time with her in the evenings, instead of seeking social pleasure at male clubs or sexual pleasure with other women. Earlier in the century, a Frenchwoman, the marchioness Anne Thérèse de Lambert, advised her daughter to hold men's attention not only by a series of agreeable accomplishments but also to "strike their fancy with a variety of graces and merits to keep up their inclinations, and make the same object afford them all the pleasures of inconstancy."[34]

It was to secure a husband and entertain him and his family rather than for professional independence or personal pleasure that certain conservatives encouraged young ladies to go through a rigorous training in the accomplishments, which, as stated before, generally included dancing, drawing, music, and needlework. The first of these accomplishments was prescribed for gentlemen too, as an aid to graceful posture. But there were added motives in recommending dancing to gentlewomen. Balls and routs, public and private, were regarded as propitious places for young ladies and gentlemen to meet, and, as many a fond mother seemed to hope, to fall in love and marry. Burney's Evelina (educated in retirement rather than polished by association with "high life") meets the handsome, good, proper Lord Orville at just such a ball but is comically tongue-tied and awkward, instead of enticing, having previously danced only with schoolgirls.

---

[34] *Avis d'une mere à son fils et à sa fille*, 1728; rpt. in *The Young Lady's Pocket Library as Advice of a Mother to her Daughter* (London: n.p., 1790), p. 130.

There were other reasons put forward for learning dancing. Pennington and Chapone (in *Improvement of the Mind*) regarded it as a healthful exercise, at once useful and ornamental. Believing that everything natural according to sex and age was good, Rousseau recommended it as suitable to the period of youth. Gregory allowed his daughters the accomplishment but shrewdly cautioned them against showing even innocent spiritedness in this enjoyment, as it could be misconstrued for laxity of private morals and conduct.

Along with the generally prescribed accomplishment of dancing, writers discussed the more specialized arts of drawing and music. Music included singing and the playing of instruments, especially the harpsichord. Pennington and Chapone seconded Fénelon's principle that only young ladies with talents and genius be indulged in these accomplishments, with careful supervision. For those without inclination, the long hours of practice these arts required were considered a waste of time and labor, for although a woman was never to pass her time idly, idleness being the devil's workshop, she was never to be uselessly employed either.

The conservatives were, on the whole, unanimous in their approval of needlework as a suitably feminine employment. Rousseau and Kames both asserted that girls instinctively preferred needlework to reading and writing since it aided their natural vanity and taught them to adorn first their dolls and then themselves. Fordyce allowed gentlewomen fancy-work as an elegant amusement; Chapone advocated plain needlework to middle-class women as saving the expense of a seamstress.

While almost all writers favored the above domestic accomplishments, no such unanimity was felt about the recreation of card-playing. Only members of the nobility from Lord Halifax to Lady Pennington allowed it as a necessary social evil. On the other hand, the Bluestockings staunchly opposed card-playing as quite unnecessary. In her poem, *The Bas Bleu: or Conversation Addressed to Mrs. Vesey*, More applauded the Bluestocking hostesses Vesey, Montagu, and Boscawen for saving the day for conversation rather than cards:

Long was society e'er-run [*sic*],
By Whist, that desolating Hun.
Long did Quadrille despotic sit. That
Vandal of colloquial Wit.[35]

---

35 *The Bas Bleu* (London: Cadell, 1786), pp.69–70.

Likewise, in Johnson's periodical, the *Rambler* (1750–52), Chapone sturdily attacked the vicious addiction to gambling in upper-class women.[36] Gaming was seen as triply dangerous—it ruined not only finances and morals but also physical health.

Like card-playing, the question of female physical health and education was a controversial one. Patriarchal-minded thinkers like Fordyce and Gregory urged gentlewomen to dissimulate and conceal their good health, if any, because men favorably connected the idea of female weakness and debility of form with softness and delicacy of constitution. Women were believed by nature to be the weaker sex, and men were apparently never so happy as when the female form bore out this opinion. But Lady Filmer, the sole feminist letter-writer in Walker's *Letters of the Duchess de Crui and Others*, rightly pointed out that if women in general seemed "hypocondriac [*sic*] and vapourish," the fault lay not in the laws of nature but in the tyranny of men, who "condemned women to a retired, idle way of life."[37] Likewise, conservatives from Chapone to Day showed themselves sufficiently influenced by the progressive liberalism of Locke to advocate that gentlewomen combat ill-health by attending to the development of both mind and body through the adequate exercise of both.

Surprisingly, in *Émile*, the arch-misogynist Rousseau also supported the development of female health. Gregory, Kames, and Day suggested genteel exercises like walking and riding; Rousseau went further and insisted on a vigorous system of physical education and exercise for women, to begin in early childhood. He also condemned the custom of using tight bodices, stays, and mechanical props to contort the female form into unnatural shapes, a horror to which young ladies seem often to have been subjected, especially in boarding schools. Rousseau's recommendation of exercise and free body growth for gentlewomen seems wonderfully woman-oriented until one understands the rationale behind his argument: physical education would make gentlewomen as robust as the ancient Spartan women and serve the same purpose—it would give their men strong, vigorous, male offspring. Rousseau's approval of female robustness was as male-oriented as Fordyce's and Gregory's

---

[36] Ethel Rolt Wheeler, *Famous Bluestockings* (London: Methuen, 1910), pp. 146–48. Of course, men gambled too, often to the ruin of their families, though virtuous wives were not supposed to complain. Thus, Fielding's Amelia patiently starves herself while her dissolute husband wastes their meager resources on a mistress and gaming.

[37] *Letters* (London: Robson, Walter, and Robinson, 1776), I, 97.

preference for female fragility; all three men subscribed to the conservative belief that a woman's main reason for existence was to be a satisfactory wife and mother to men.

The emphasis that moral education, or education of the heart, placed on women's duties as daughters, wives, and mothers made it the most popular among the four "disciplines" for conservative thinkers. In addition to duties, this type of education also aimed at safeguarding the gender- and class-related virtues of gentlewomen and eliminating their gender- and class-related vices. It is interesting to note at this point that an early training in moral habits was emphasized as much in the education of a gentleman as a gentlewoman.[38] However, the important point of difference was that while the sexual duties of a gentlewoman to men were constantly reiterated in literature on female education, the duties of a man to his wife and daughters seemed to have been not very important. In fact, they are given no mention at all in George Brauer's careful research on the education of the eighteenth-century gentleman. Since he *does* discuss the father's duty to educate his son (a point also made by Rousseau in *Émile*), one must interpret his silence on the question of female relatives as one of personal prejudice, either his own or that of the theorists on male education. Conservative thought, after all, insisted that a man's life was largely public, a woman's almost exclusively private, and that their education should emphasize this difference.

The training to a sense of her duties was therefore to begin early in the life of a young lady. In his *Traité sur l'education des filles* (1687), Fénelon expounded a theory that Locke was to make famous three years later in his widely read *Essay Concerning Human Understanding*, namely, that the brain has nothing stamped on it at birth (*tabula rasa*). The archbishop turned this theory to chauvinistic purpose by insisting that the first impressions on the female mind should therefore be those of submission and restraint. Rousseau and disciples like Kames and Fordyce agreed with earlier writers like Montesquieu (*Lettres persanes*, 1721) on the necessity of early habituating women to accept their inferiority and subjection to "so imperfect a being as man" (*Emilius*, I, 199).

The primary duty of the young unmarried lady in eighteenth-century England was to her parents; the main emphasis of writers on filial obedience

---

[38] Except by Rousseau, who said of male children: "The only habit we should suffer a child to contract is that of contracting none" (*Emilius*, I, 50).

was in the choice of a marital partner. However, attitudes to this question seemed to differ before and after 1753, when Lord Hardwicke's Marriage Act was passed to prevent clandestine marriages (and thereby to protect property rights), by giving parents and guardians full rights over the marital status of minors."[39] This act became a turning point. Before this date, the importance of filial duty in the choice of a spouse had not figured large in literature. (Queen Mary and Queen Anne's acquiescence in the exile of their father James II could not have encouraged theorists to expatiate on filial piety during their reigns either.) Even a sexist writer like Moore upheld the rights of women to choose their own husbands, in "Fable IV: The Wolf, the Sheep, and the Lamb" (1744).

After the mid-century, however, theory and fiction were flooded with pro and con rhetoric on the preeminence of filial duty. Surprisingly enough, the ultra-conservative theorists Fordyce, Pennington, and Kames agreed with the erstwhile feminist Chapone that women must be free of parental authority in the choice of a mate, although they owed filial duty in other respects. In her youthful days, Hester Mulso (Chapone) had actually condemned her literary mentor Richardson for his over-emphasis on Clarissa's duty to her undeserving father (*Letters on Filial Obedience*).

Post-1753 fiction writers, on the other hand, swamped the market with "tear-jerker" novels of sensibility which milked the issue of blind filial obedience. Not many heroines had parents in the course of the novel; those that did often fell dutiful prey to the unjust coercion of either their own parents, as with Sidney (*Sidney Biddulph*), Julie (*La Nouvelle Héloise*), Elwina (in More's famous play, *Percy*, 1777), and Elfrida (anonymous, *Elfrida, or Paternal Ambition*, 1786), or of their lover's, as with Burney's Cecilia and Keir's Louisa. In its general outline of unconsciously masochistic child and consciously sadistic parent, Sidney's case is representative of the plot-dynamics of all the others, although the endings differed. Sidney clearly acts on principles of duty and love to her mother; the mother's behavior, however, is shown to be selfish and unjustified. She hastily condemns and dismisses Sidney's fiancé, Faulkland, ostensibly because he is believed to have wronged another woman, but pathologically because her own first lover had jilted her and she seeks to pass her pain on to Sidney. When Sidney is on her deathbed, after a life of incredible suffering as a daughter, wife, and mother, her brother George sums up the

---

[39] *DNB* (rpt. 1949–50), XXI, 1264.

cause of all her misfortunes: "She sacrificed the happiness of her whole life to a too rigid duty."[40]

Theorists believed that like filial duty, conjugal duty required an equal if not greater amount of sacrifice on the gentlewoman's part. Yet they also proposed means to ease her life. Halifax was not quite sanguine that his beloved daughter would be lucky enough to find a good man, men being what they were, so he taught her the duties of patient submission to a husband who could possibly be beneath her in moral caliber. Conservative education also aimed to modify female behavior by training the gentlewoman not only to be contented with her lot but also to impart her contentment to her husband. Aside from charming him with her accomplishments, she could teach him to prefer his home to the world outside by making it a cheerful place where she continually fed his ego and solaced him from his worldly problems, while taking care to suppress her own domestic frustrations and emotional needs. This was an unequal but not unsound policy if she wished to retain her husband's love or support, considering that the patriarchal nature of society decreed that "to make a good husband is but one part of a man's duty, but it is the chief duty of a woman to make a good wife."[41]

The second important gender-related duty of a married woman was to be a good mother, even though as her husband's property herself she had no legal rights to her own children. It was typical of the dichotomy between the rights of men and the duties of women that the father owned the right to his children while the mother owed them the duty of looking after their well-being. Fielding's *Amelia* and Frances Sheridan's *Sidney Biddulph* were among the few novels that dealt realistically with the heroine, not as persecuted, all-perfect virgin, but in terms of her trials as a wife and mother.[42] In general, however, in spite of the emphasis of the theorists on the importance of the mother to her daughters, fictional heroines were seldom depicted as having a mother. To compensate they were sometimes given mother-surrogates, whom they invariably and sentimentally called "My more than mother!"

---

[40] *Sidney Biddulph* (rpt. London: Harrison, 1786), IV, 396.

[41] Kames, *Loose Hints upon Education* (Edinburgh; Bell, 1781), p. 228.

[42] Frances Sheridan's great-granddaughter, Caroline Norton (1808–77), struggled tirelessly to limit the legal control of husbands over wives (Sheila Rowbotham, *Hidden from History*, London: Pluto Press, 1973, p. 49).

The frequent absence of mothers in fiction is a source of interest to feminist critics. Perhaps the absence of the mother's watchful protection in eighteenth-century fiction embodied a conservative lesson to women: they could not survive independently and respectably in the public world and were therefore to retreat, at the end of their "journey," to the insularity of their own proper and dependent sphere, the home. For this dutiful compliance, the heroine was generally rewarded with an unexpected legacy, a gathering of old friends, and, significantly, complete control (termed "protection") by male relatives in the form of a lover-husband of high birth and a returned, long-lost father or uncle. Appropriately, at the end of the novel, the heroine vowed eternal duty to her newly made or found male kinsmen.

Besides the above gender-related duties, conservative theory also enjoined on gentlewomen certain general virtues. These virtues were based on religious precepts, which were therefore emphasized as of prime importance in female education. In advocating religion, however, individual writers were motivated by differing reasons. For instance, Gregory and Day believed that religion armed women against the inevitable evils of life; Chapone felt it gave them habitual sweetness and politeness. Fordyce regarded it as useful for both the next life and this: it taught women that they had souls responsible to God (*Sermons*, II) and it rendered them more virtuous and lovely in the eyes of man (*Character of the Female Sex*). With typical double-standards, Gregory and others excused the male sex, supposedly busy with worldly issues, from making religion the basis of their lives.[43] It took a woman novelist to demand equality of religious standards for both sexes; Keir had the hero's father insist on a religious education for his son as the "only sure basis of morality" (*Interesting Memoirs*, I, 43).

The virtues required of gentlewomen were derived not only from religion and morality but also from ideals of civility and good-breeding. Together, they formed an impressive list that grew out of all proportion as the century progressed. In the hundred years or so spanned by the conservative tradition under discussion, some of the more frequently prescribed virtues were

---

[43] Unless, of course, they were clergymen, which meant, in essence, that men were to preach religion, women to practice it. However, unlike Gregory and his ilk, certain theorists on male education emphasized the importance of religious and moral instruction in the education of a gentleman too.

obedience, submission,[44] compliance, humility, meekness, patience, dependence, modesty, reserve, prudence, decency, decorum, politeness, elegance, simplicity, delicacy,[45] sensibility, reputation, sincerity, love, chastity, cheerfulness of temper, and continual employment (in terms of time not money). All the conservative men agreed that these were essentially feminine qualities, given women by Nature and Providence, therefore justly cultivated by education. Fordyce arrogantly summed up his contribution to this list by saying, "These the men are taught by nature, by education, and by custom, to consider as your duty and their right."[46]

Perhaps the virtue most cherished in gentlewomen by patriarchal conservatives was chastity, largely seen as a female moral.[47] Conjugal fidelity was believed more important in the woman than the man, not merely because—to go back to the basic relationship between women, money, and a male-dominated society—she and her children were the man's property, but because she ought not to pass on his landed or monetary possessions to her bastards.[48] (Pamela correctly pointed out that men themselves, by their own marital infidelity, made other men's bastards.) The connection with property, however, made the ideal of chastity a technical rather than a moral virtue. In the case of unmarried women, it was confounded with technical virginity (Richardson's superlatively coy *Pamela* perhaps remains the classic eighteenth-century example of this equation).[49]

Closely allied to chastity was the female virtue of "reputation." Theorists of the third quarter of the century, like Kenrick, Pennington, Rousseau, Chapone, and Gregory, all agreed that it was not enough for a woman to be virtuous in body or even in conscience; she had to protect her reputation in the eyes of the world too. Fortunately for women, public reputation could be

---

[44] Gentlemen, on the other hand, were to be educated from childhood in habits of independence and freedom.

[45] The heroines' scrupulous sense of delicacy was a prime means of eking out the plot through several volumes, where a commonsensical response would have brought about immediate *éclaircissement.*

[46] *Sermons*, 8th ed. (London: Cadell, Dodsley, 1775), II, 225.

[47] The four major male novelists all capitalized on the revolutionary idea of the sexually chaste male, in the characters of Sir Charles Grandison, Joseph Andrews, Humphry Clinker, and Uncle Toby. Only Richardson, however, viewed his titled hero's chastity seriously rather than as high comedy.

[48] Bastardy or illegitimacy is a particularly patriarchal concept, dismissing the legitimacy of both mother and child.

[49] See Chapter II for a fuller discussion of the notion of chastity in *Pamela* and *Clarissa*.

maintained even if the private conscience were not quite clear. According to the fictional examples of the time, prudence could prove a good substitute for Christian conduct, moral behavior, or true goodness, while deceit, circumspection and an all-encompassing behavioral vigilance were as necessary as virtue itself to every woman. Thus, Pamela and Elwina (in More's *Percy*) prudently preserve their sexual (although not mental) chastity and are applauded by the world and themselves for their "virtue." Clarissa, on the other hand, loses the reputation so dear to her; by an initial act of hubris, she imprudently exchanges her family's protection, however nominal, for that of the rake Lovelace. In "Fable XV: The Female Seducer," Moore summed up the relation between a woman's reputation and her happiness in life: "Unhappy sex: who only claim / A being in the breath of fame" (p. 228). He was not sympathizing with women in this poem so much as asserting that men decreed the fragile nature of female reputation and that women's lives were justly worth naught once their reputation was lost, whether or not through their own agency.

Novels like *Clarissa* and *Sidney Biddulph* and letters like Pennington's *Unfortunate Mother's Advice* dealt with the question of a virtuous woman's loss of reputation or happiness in life through the specific agency of man or God. The only virtue that keeps Sidney alive is her patient resignation in the face of the "inevitable evils that are sometimes allotted, even to the best" (I, 7). Frances Sheridan and Pennington both advised women that since they were powerless in their male-dominated society, unrebellious acceptance alone could help them maintain their mental tranquility. But More echoed Halifax in showing women how to invert the power structure by pretending to yield to traditional roles. Thus, in her school-play, *The Search after Happiness*, she made the virtuous mentor Urania teach intentional dissimulation to her students: "By yielding she obtains the noblest away / And reigns securely when she seems t'obey" (p. 38). It is ironic that conservatives from Halifax to Gregory and More preached to women the vices of cunning and deceit (often believed natural to the sex) to enhance their female virtues.

Mary Delaney (1700–88), the long-lived and much-respected eighteenth-century Bluestocking, who knew writers from Swift's generation through Richardson's to Johnson's, showed herself both more optimistic than Frances Sheridan and Pennington and more just than Halifax, More, and Gregory in her appraisal of virtue. She believed that happiness could be safeguarded not only by the assistance of Providence but also by a truly good and virtuous education for both sexes.[50] The conservatives discussed in this chapter agreed with her to the extent that they added to their superhuman demands of femininity certain "masculine" virtues as well, such as good sense, courage, fortitude,[51] resolution, steadiness, and spirit, but only when the situation so demanded.

The one so-called female virtue that conservatives equally allowed men, at least in the sentimental novels of the time, was sensibility. Sensibility could be defined as the nervously active capacity of a person to respond with intense emotionalism to every source of frustration, sorrow, and to every charitable act. With the happy exception of Arabella, Lennox's romantic but delightfully thick-skinned Female Quixote, virtuous novel heroines (as well as heroes like St. Preux in *la Nouvelle Héloise* and Harley in *The Man of Feeling*) were all subject to this tremblingly alive attribute. The eighteenth-century "novel-reading miss" supposedly gauged her own sensibility by her corresponding emotional response to the heroine's distresses; the present-day reader is irritated rather than moved by the heroine or hero's self-paralyzing emotionalism. Rational-minded critics in the eighteenth century also realized the dangers of cultivating this quality to an extreme limit; in her poem on "Sensibility" (1782), addressed to the Bluestocking Boscawen, More accepted its presence only if combined with religion. Adelaide, the nun in Keir's *Interesting Memoirs*, allied it to fortitude, at least in theory, warning the weepy heroine Louisa that too much sensibility was incompatible with human happiness. Over-indulged, the conservatives often cautioned, sensibility could prove a painful vice rather than a sustaining virtue to women, whose lives were seen as full of trials anyway.

Not all conservatives believed in the power of a virtuous education to teach women to act morally and prudently or of early habits and continual self-monitoring to control a woman's propensity to vice. Misogynists like Pope considered the sex to be innately immoral and undependable and therefore totally incapable of improvement by either nature or education. To Pope, "Nothing [is] so true as what you once let fall, / Most women have no

---

[50] Letter to Richardson dated August 16, 1751, in *The Correspondence of Samuel Richardson*, ed. A. L. Barbauld (London: Phillips, 1804), IV, 46.

[51] Thomas Day carried this principle to sadistic limits in real life. He shot blank cartridges into the petticoats of his adopted ward, Sabrina, or dropped hot sealing wax on her arms then chastised her for screaming with fear instead of bearing the pain with fortitude.

characters at all."[52] This instability of character was supposed to lead to specifically female vices. In *The History of Fanny Burney*, Joyce Hemlow lists the courtesy-book sins that women were supposed to be prone to and therefore to avoid: vanity (which the men called woman's prime foible), coquetry, affectation, singularity, artifice, levity, imprudence, and passion.[53]

Moralistic theorists roundly decried passion, especially sexual passion, in gentlewomen; nevertheless, some of the fiction writers explored female sexuality in great detail, particularly as prevalent among the lower classes, the dissolute aristocracy, and romantic heroines of sensibility. The writers here fall into two camps, according to whether they used their material for prurient and comic or liberal-minded and serious purposes. In the 1740s, '50s, and '60s, Fielding in *An Apology for the Life of Mrs. Shamela Andrews* (1741), Cleland in *Memoirs of a Woman of Pleasure* (1748–49) and *Genuine Memoirs of the Celebrated Miss Maria Brown, Exhibiting the Life of a Courtezan [sic] in the most Fashionable Scenes of Dissipation* (1766), and Diderot in *La Réligieuse* (*Memoirs of a Nun*)[54] wrote in the tradition of male pornographic literature, exploiting so-called sexual and social taboos in women such as masturbation, lesbianism, incest, bigamy,[55] and extra-marital sex. They found prostitution, sexual abuse, sexual exploitation, and forced incarceration in a nunnery fit subject for comedy and made Maria, Fanny, and Shamela glory in their sex lives, in parodic contrast to those of sexless beings like Burney's Evelina.

Illicit commerce between the sexes has generally been accepted in patriarchal societies; illicit love (illicit only because opposed by parents and therefore not always legalized by marriage) has not. In the 1760s and '70s, Sheridan in *Sidney Biddulph*, Rousseau in *La Nouvelle Héloise*, Goethe in *Werther*, Mackenzie in *Julia de Roubigné* (1782), and More in *Percy* describe the intense passion of their heroines, not just as women in love but women as sexual beings.[56] As fictional women of the eighteenth century, however, these heroines dutifully

---

[52] *Moral Essays: Epistle II*, "To a Lady," *Selected Poetry and Prose* (1735; rpt., New York: Holt, Rinehart, and Winston, 1972), p. 245.

[53] *The History of Fanny Burney* (Oxford: Clarendon Press, 1918), p. 22.

[54] Written in 1760 (with d'Holbach, Grimm, and others) as a joke; published posthumously in 1796. Tr. Francis Birrell (New York: Brentano's, 1928), pp. vii, 227.

[55] Even the moral, eponymous heroine Elfrida finds herself unwittingly a bigamist.

[56] In real life, Hester Thrale was ostracized by her three-year house-guest, Fanny Burney, and her peers, the Bluestocking ladies, for violating decorum in declaring her passionate love for Piozzi, her second husband (Hemlow, p. 177).

sacrifice love to filial obedience and marry their parents' choice, generally an older, unromantic man. But they continue to believe in the sanctity of love and glory in their eternal (but sexually chaste) passion for their sentimentally faithful and equally chaste lovers. Although giving their bodies to others, these heroines believe themselves allied in soul to their lovers; Werther too exults in his "sin" of loving and being loved by the married Lotte and commits suicide, hoping to meet her in heaven. Clara, Julie's confidante, gives her the radical encouragement, soon to be popular in the nineties in both England and France, that true love and the enjoyment of its fruits, even without the sanction of marriage, was not criminal. Like Mary Wollstonecraft and William Godwin in the 1790s, Rousseau's hero St. Preux urges Julie that marriage is the "mere formal ceremony of a public declaration,"[57] for their tie is made sacred by their love. Unlike the works of the three English writers, Rousseau's and Goethe's novels remained subjects of angry, moralistic attack throughout the remainder of the century for daring to celebrate the vice of illicit passion.

Besides the more clearly defined vices such as those already discussed, writers also gave women contradictory messages on what to avoid in behavior. Towards the end of the seventeenth century, Fénelon enjoined silence on women; by mid-eighteenth century, Rousseau allowed loquacity as natural to them. Squire B— allowed Pamela wit; Fénelon, Gregory, and others condemned it as a dangerous quality in women. Wit aside, laughter also seems to have been suspect. In view of all the restrictions theorists imposed on women and the long list of virtues they recommended, it is not surprising that virtuous heroines in fiction of the time almost never laughed. They were good women, possessing to a superlative degree, "far above their sex," all the courtesy-book virtues. Their authors, generally more than half in love with them, applauded them with such epithets as "divine" and "angelic," the tradition beginning with the long-suffering Clarissa. But these women did not laugh. In fact, Burney's Evelina seems to have been almost the only heroine in the English novel from its inception in 1740 to 1813 (the year when Austen gave the world her marvelous creation, Elizabeth Bennet, in *Pride and Prejudice*) to possess this refreshing ability consistently. Sheridan's Sidney and Burney's Cecilia begin with laughter but end with the heroine's more general behavior pattern of faintings and tears. The only comic relief in sentimental novels came from the heroines' epistolary best-friends, who almost all, beginning with Anna Howe

---

[57] *Eloisa*, 3rd ed. (London: Becket and de Hondt, 1764), I, 107.

in *Clarissa*, possess the heartening qualities of vivaciousness, independence, wit, assertiveness, and a feminist pride in their own sex. Although the heroine's friend generally appears more attractive and wholesome to the modern reader than the heroine herself, there is no doubt that the novelists intended their tearful, dependent, non-assertive, virtuous heroines to be perfect models of the lauded system of moral instruction here called education of the heart.

Conservative opinion was far more divided regarding the final system of instruction, namely, the education of the head or intellect, than it was on that of the heart. While moral education was universally encouraged by theorists and fiction writers, intellectual education was often decried by the more old-fashioned members of society.[58] Such ultra-conservatives considered it essential to suppress learning in women (as in the poor) in order to maintain social stability and sexual inequality. Learning would enable women to think for themselves; such thinking would prove dangerous, for it might reveal to women the injustice of their condition. The best way, therefore, to keep women from revolt was to thoroughly convince them of their own intellectual inferiority to men and to assure them that it was in their interests to further curb their already small mental capacity. Thus, practiced in the arts of the very deceit they both advised for and attributed to women, Halifax told his daughter he imposed severe restraint on her out of a regard for her happiness; Fordyce prefaced his *Sermons* with the self-serving lie that he wrote out of an unfeigned regard for the female sex. Gregory admitted, more honestly, that he wished by repression to make his daughters more respectable and amiable in the eyes of men.

Others among the male denigrators of female learning were not quite as polite. With insulting arrogance, Swift wrote to the "very young lady" on her marriage that he had very little respect for the female sex or intellect, for, "after all the pains you may be at, you can never arrive in point of learning to the perfection of a schoolboy."[59] Pennington slavishly repeated this comparison in her work. She did not acknowledge Swift as the source; his high-handed

---

[58] "Old-fashioned" refers here specifically to the seventeenth century and the Middle Ages in England. In the sixteenth century, Renaissance gentlewomen were often encouraged to undertake learning. It is perhaps important to note that for the eighteenth-century gentleman too, moral education was valued over intellectual instruction while learning was still somewhat distrusted as an aid to virtue.

[59] Rpt. in *The Female Repertory* (Edinburgh; M'William, 1808), II, 211.

opinion had become widely known by the time she published her advice to her daughters.

Around the mid-century, Chesterfield, who regarded women either as man's sexual playthings or fashionable monitors, tried to condition his young, illegitimate son, Philip Stanhope, to distrust and despise female capabilities. In 1748, he wrote to him: "Women are only children of a larger growth; they have an entertaining tattle and sometimes wit, but for solid reasoning, good sense, I never knew one in my life that had it."[60] In "Sur les femmes" (July 1772), Diderot used the same metaphor as Chesterfield, although with some attempt at fairness. He pointed out that it was not merely the cruelty of nature, by which he meant the painful processes of menstruation and child-birth, but also the cruelty of civil laws that rendered women "des enfants imbeciles."[61] However, the entry under "femme," in the *Encyclopédie* which he co-edited with d'Alembert, attributed women's "inferior" mental capacity to a frequently believed physiological basis: women's organs were more delicate than men's and therefore less capable of intellectual stimulation.[62]

The above theoretical attempts to systematically repress learning and in-dependence in women could not, perhaps, have gone very far without the cooperation of certain influential female voices themselves, like those of More and Burney, among others. It is ironic that in her poem, "The Slave Trade" (1787), More pleaded on behalf of African slaves what she denied her own sex: liberty of thought and mind and freedom to act on one's own feelings and affections. It was unfortunate for the female sex that such famous social and literary figures, either without conscience or consciousness, advocated that other women fit themselves into a man-ordained niche rather than follow their own unconventional examples.

When even respected literary women solemnly denied in their works the worth of female ability, it was no great wonder that male fiction writers from sentimental novelists like Rousseau and Goethe (in *Werther*) to first-rate comic playwrights like Molière and Richard Brinsley Sheridan did likewise.

---

[60] Letter XLIX, dated London, September 5, 1748, in *Letters to His Son* (1774; rpt. New York: Tudor, n.d.), p. 107. The blindness of his prejudice is made obvious when one remembers that he was a con-temporary of the great Anglo-Saxon scholar, Elizabeth Elstob (1683–1756), and the classical scholar, Elizabeth Carter. Theorists on the education of gentlemen also did not approve of Chesterfield's *Letters* as a suitable text because of the immorality they advocated.

[61] In *Oeuvres complètes* (n.p.: Le Club Franchise du Livre, 1971), X, 44.

[62] *Encyclopédie* (1751–76, rpt. Genève, Pellet, 1777), XIII, 957.

The learned lady became a source of ridicule rather than esteem in their fiction. An important fact to note, however, is that nowhere in the conservative literature of these hundred years, except perhaps in the case of Mrs. Atkinson in *Amelia*, was the woman of true learning depicted. Rather, it was the romantically inclined, novel-, poetry-, and play-reading young lady like Sheridan's Lydia Languish or the supposedly rational, pseudo-intellectual gentlewoman, like Molière's Armande, who was attacked for abusing her learning and neglecting her duties. The learned woman was also satirized as a vain, self-deluded, semi-literate older woman, like Sheridan's immortally comic character, Mrs. Malaprop. "Ah," she is made pretentiously to lament to Absolute; "few gentlemen now-a-days know how to value the ineffectual [intellectual] qualities in a woman!"[63]

Aside from ridicule, writers attempted to frighten female readers away from an interest in learning by insinuating that its cause was generally an ugly face and its consequence a single life, naturally an economic terror to women brought up with the idea of dependence on a husband. Warnings of the loveless fate of ugly, single, often affected women were rampant in male literature of the time. Among the more famous examples were Mrs. Western,[64] whose six feet of height and masculine person "prevented the other sex from regarding her, notwithstanding her petticoats, in the light of a woman"[65]; Harley's small-minded spinster aunt in *The Man of Feeling* (1771); the man-shunning Sophronia in Goldsmith's periodical, *The Citizen of the World* (Letter XXVIII, 1762); the crabby, husband-hunting Tabitha Bramble in *Humphry Clinker* (1771); and the progenitor of them all, Bélise in *Les Femmes savantes* (1672). Thus, a large volume of literature, both theoretical and fictional, was written on woman's supposedly natural idiocy, on her abuse of learning, and on the effects of this abuse.

The total picture, nevertheless, was not entirely bleak. A few conservatives, like Chapone in *Improvement of the Mind*, took the progressive side on this issue. Following Astell, they declared that it was the lack of mental cultivation, not innate incapacity, that kept woman in an inferior position to man. Learning would teach a woman to carry out her familial duties more effectively; ignorance, on the other hand, could lead a woman unknowingly

---

[63] *The Rivals* (rpt. London: Oxford UP, 1968), p. 77.

[64] "Mrs." was a courtesy-title given to a single woman of genius.

[65] *Tom Jones* (1749; rpt. Baltimore: Penguin, 1971), p. 255.

to betray her all-important duties to man, as the restrictive Arnolphus finds out in Molière's *L'École des femmes* (1663; *A School for Women*).

Perhaps the best fictional plea for knowledge and compatibility in the wife was made in Sterne's marvelously comic masterpiece, *Tristram Shandy* (1760–67). It was a "source of misery" and a "consuming vexation" to the intellectualizing Mr. Shandy that his wife never asked him the meaning of things she did not understand:

> That she is not a woman of science, my father would say [quoted Tristram]— is her misfortune—but she might ask a question. —My mother never did.... [Instead] she contented herself with doing all that her godfathers and god-mothers promised for her—but no more; and so would go on using a hard word twenty years together—and replying to it too, if it was a verb, in all its moods and tenses, without giving herself any trouble to enquire after it.[66]

Her unquestioning, dutiful complacency, so earnestly enjoined by educators of women from St. Paul to Lord Halifax "broke the neck, at the first setting out [said Tristram], of more good dialogues between them, than could have done the most petulant contradiction" (p. 613) of such "henpecking" *femmes savantes*, one supposes, as Molière's Philaminte. In her intellectual response, then, the ideally trained, properly educated, and companionable wife would have to be somewhere between Mrs. Shandy and Philaminte.

Besides intelligent companionship, another accepted way for gentlewomen to sidestep the whole issue of improper female learning and thereby to avoid both the intolerance of men and the jealousy of other women was to merge their intellectual education entirely into the role of woman as maternal educator.[67] The ideal education for girls until marriage, as already seen, was under the mother's tutelage. Young boys in petticoats, like the comically ill-fated infant Tristram, were also to be directly under the mother's intellectual

---

[66] *Tristram Shandy* (rpt. New York: Bobbs-Merrill, 1940), pp. 472, 613.

[67] At the daughter's marriage, the mother-preceptor was supposed to hand over to the husband-tutor, an idea popularized by Rousseau's *Émile*. The husband or chaste lover as tutor was an important part of the plot of Burney's novels. Cecilia frankly declares that she would rather be pupil than tutor to her husband, although the more fashionably educated Lady Honoria Pemberton reminds her that most women married to get rid of their tutors.

tuition.[68] Using almost identical terms, in their respective second *Dialogue of the Dead* between "Mercury and a Modern Fine Lady" (1760) and an essay "On Enthusiasm and Indifference in Religion" (In *Miscellanies in Prose and Verse*, II, 1775), the childless society-ladies Montagu and Chapone berated the woman of *ton* who neglected her domestic concerns and left the education of her daughters to chambermaids[69] and dancing- and music-masters. This evasion was interpreted as the mother's neglecting herself for eternity, for St. Paul had condescendingly admitted that women could be "saved" by instructing their children.

Apart from the call of duty, gentlewomen were allowed intellectual education for only two other reasons. First, as women of the leisured class, they could receive a certain amount of instruction, but as elegant amusement rather than as serious study. Knowledge for its own sake was not encouraged in the education of the gentility of either sex; hence, Voltaire,[70] Chapone, and others regarded it merely as an accomplishment, more or less like the ornamental ones discussed under education of the person. So, instead of scholarship, Gregory termed intellectual instruction "amusement"; Fordyce, "elegant and polished knowledge" (*Sermons*); and Pennington, mental improvement and conversational aid.

The second concession to learning made by theorists from Halifax to Fordyce was in favor of gentlewomen of "extraordinary" talents or genius. A good example of the positive effects of such cultivation was the scholar, Elizabeth Carter. Throughout the second half of the eighteenth century, and even after her death in 1806, she was regarded as a role-model because she combined her erudition (and private feminism) with the accepted feminine traits of piety, good-heartedness, and modesty. She not only knew the classical languages of Greek, Latin, and Hebrew, but also modern languages like French, Italian, Spanish, Portuguese, German, and Arabic. She loved the sciences, especially astronomy, and took part in religious controversy with her friend Dr. Seeker, Archbishop of Canterbury, to whom she pointed out examples

---

[68] The mother was supposed to educate her sons until the tutor or public school took over. Fond mothers were accused of meddling with the tutor's instruction and thereby rendering it useless.

[69] The conservatives, like most of the progressives, radicals, and reactionaries, agreed that servants were to be treated fairly but not familiarly and kept away from children as far as possible, for fear of adversely influencing them.

[70] In the pseudo-feminist dedication to the marquise du Chastelet, prefixed to his play, *Alzire* (acted in 1736).

of deliberately sexist translations in King James's Bible by which churchmen sought to keep woman in her place (Wheeler, p. 282). She also singly educated her youngest half-brother for the university, thereby astonishing the Cambridge faculty. But in spite of enjoying the special privileges of genius, Carter did not escape the duties of her sex: she once wrote to her beloved friend, the learned Catherine Talbot, that she had no time to write the life of Epictetus because she had a dozen shirts to make.[71] Nor did she escape the personal criticism applied to literary women; Johnson praised her for being able to bake a pudding as well as translate from the ancient Greek. A woman was always to be first a dutiful woman; only then, if time, accident, and men permitted, could she attempt to develop herself as a human being.

In spite of the controversy among themselves as to whether or not and under what conditions a gentlewoman should be intellectually educated, the conservatives collectively came up with a surprisingly solid curriculum for her. The subjects prescribed seemed owing to a variety of influences. As with the Dissenters, the reading, writing, and orthography of the English language, as opposed to those of the classical languages, were encouraged for gentlewomen. (Grammar was a controversial subject; many glibly believed it was sufficient for women to pick it up in conversation with men instead of from books.) As in the education of gentleman, the modern languages of French and Italian were allowed by some theorists as fashionable accomplishments; the less liberal believed languages unnecessary for women. The inclusion of the four rules of arithmetic was due to the gentlewoman's role as supervisor of household accounts, while history, geography, and chronology, subjects regularly prescribed in the eighteenth century, were first made fashionable by Queen Mary.[72]

The curriculum also included scriptural studies (for reading rather than discussion) and an appreciation of God's creation through a study of astronomy (a controversial subject) and of natural and moral philosophy. The reading lists for these orthodox subjects were mind-boggling in intent and dry in material, as seen by those drawn up in Clara Reeve's *Progress of Romance*, Pennington's *Advice*, and, especially, in the progressive Stephanie de Genlis's *Adèle et Théodore* (1782). Actually, most of the theoretical and fictional

---

[71] Letter dated March 5, 1755, in *Memoirs of the Life of Mrs. Elizabeth Carter*, ed. Montagu Pennington (1807; rpt. London: Cawthorn, 1825), I, 186.

[72] Dorothy Gardiner, *English Girlhood at School* (London: Humphrey Milford, 1929), p. 429.

works discussed in this chapter were "regulars" represented in any young lady's library, except for the pornographic novels and perhaps lesser-known moral ones like *Elfrida*.

In addition to the generally accepted subjects listed above, individual theorists allowed women certain unorthodox subjects. For instance, Day had Sukey Simmons learn geometry (mathematics was often strictly prohibited to women) and Kames allowed botany (which prudish critics decried as involving a study of the sexual nature of plants). Walker permitted poetry, often considered as inflammatory as novels, romances, and plays to the already over-exercised female imagination; Molière's *femmes savantes* demanded ethics, physics, and politics. French educators like Fénelon also wisely insisted on a legal education regarding property and estate for young ladies, although the archbishop carefully reminded his female readers that they were incapable of understanding the further complexities of law. The lack of legal and financial education seems to have been severely felt in the English system too. In Letter No. 81 of Mackenzie's *Mirror* (II), "Olivia" laments that she is left with a fortune but no instruction in how to manage it and is consequently harassed by tenants and by property problems.

Whatever personal concessions individual theorists might make regarding certain subjects, there were four areas which almost all the major educators agreed should not be allowed women—classical learning, the "abstruser" sciences, politics, and religious controversy. These were generally seen as either beyond female comprehension or intellectually dangerous to it. Yet Fénelon permitted Latin; Gregory and Rousseau permitted "any art or science" on the grounds of accident, individual genius, or the husband's prerogative of educating his wife in whatever subjects he pleased.

Religious controversy was viewed as a more serious matter. Although education of the heart relied heavily on religion, women were to follow its precepts as a matter of dutiful faith rather than through rational belief. Fénelon, Montesquieu, Rousseau, and Gregory warned young ladies against interpreting the scriptures for themselves or falling into the subtleties of philosophy and divinity.[73] It took a woman, Hester Chapone, to require of her niece (in

---

[73] Philosophical and religious controversy was especially encouraged in Dissenting schools for men. Unlike the boorish Hanoverian George II, Queen Caroline, wife of George III, was also greatly fond of debate on these subjects.

*Improvement of the Mind*) that she examine for herself evidence of the Christian religion in order to become rationally convinced of its divine authority.

Knowledge of the workings of the state as of the church (and its scriptures), the two bastions of male power, was tenaciously guarded by gentlemen for their own sex and class. Thus, Chesterfield and others declared that women had no right to "meddle" with politics. In their fiction, such writers showed that only intellectual malcontents or unsexed females such as the *femmes savantes* or Mrs. Western were interested in the politics of the day. In their private letters, however, the outwardly decorous Bluestocking ladies displayed an unfeminine knowledge of not only contemporary politics, but also of classical learning and the best European literature of their time.

Having once placed reading and some learning in the power of women, at least theoretically, conservatives could not really police the forces of enlightenment at work for women in the eighteenth century. In the absence of a national policy on female education, neither could they legally enforce their cautionary principles on female development. All they could do was prescribe, exhort, and warn, in an attempt to channel women into a cheerful acceptance of their second-class status and education.

As just seen in this section, they did this by formulating their own version of the four main systems of female instruction, according to their own estimate of female capacity and of women's gender-related expectations and duties. In their emphasis on matrimony and motherhood and their basic Anglican, upper-class stance, they did not expend much energy on connecting a gentlewoman's education with professional possibilities. The relation between gentlewomen and money was to take place through the intermediary of man, not through women's own labors. For the conservatives, it was enough if ladies minded their own persons and hearts and heads and walked in the prescribed path of familial and social duty.

## IV. Professionalism

Although guilty of it themselves, eighteenth-century conservatives disapproved of professional occupation by upper-class women; it involved a loss of caste and was unwomanly as well. Commercialism supposedly soiled the hands of gentlewomen and -men. Here, as everywhere, men were financially better off than women; they were provided for by fathers or by the patriarchal socio-political constitution of England, while women were not. Landed fathers provided for eldest sons, passing on their estates and family name to them by the system of primogeniture; the state supported younger sons of the nobility and gentility by making available to them honorable positions of power and command in the government, church, militia, and judiciary. Gentlewomen, on the other hand, were excluded from such means of self-support on account of their sex.

Thus, gender and conservative thinking dictated to upper-class (indeed all) women the three "professional" states open to them: the married, the single, and the "fallen." Although the education of the heart, geared largely to the first state, was the system most prescribed by conservatives, it was the education of the person and of the intellect that provided some means of independence to indigent ladies. Necessity made such women defy society and carve out employment for themselves; some could put their ornamental or intellectual accomplishments to profitable use by selling their needlework or through the newly emerging professions of teaching or writing. Unprotected or utterly desperate women had the unfortunate "profession" of prostitution. Other options there were none, at least in the books of the conservatives.

In spite of the scant attention paid by such theorists to the question of female professional independence, both fictional and non-fictional works of the time testify to the existence of unprovided gentlewomen, brought up originally in expensive habits of idleness. With minds and intellects scarcely trained to console or support themselves in case of adversity, these women sometimes found themselves jolted into poverty by the death of their fathers or insolvency of their husbands. In Mackenzie's *Mirror*, an unfortunate young lady deprecates the imprudence of "educating a girl in luxury and elegance, and then leaving her to all the hardships of poverty and neglect."[74] Of the three main alternatives left a single woman, none seems to have been particularly palatable although she could contract a loveless marriage, merely for security. Chapone followed the progressive Sarah Fielding (in *David Simple*) in describing such a marriage as "legalized prostitution," a brutally telling phrase later popularized by the radical Mary Wollstonecraft. Otherwise, such a woman could choose three conditions lessening her social standing—low-income independent work, financial retrenchment, or humble dependence on a brother or relative. (Austen's *Sense and Sensibility* and *Mansfield Park* exemplified the last option even decades later.) Unprovided gentlewomen,

---

[74] No. 65, *The Mirror* (1779–80; rpt. 2 vols in 1; London: Parsons, 1794), II, 47.

especially when single, became economically expendable to the brother's family unit and to the social structure at large. Conservative fiction blatantly supported this patriarchal system, making single women seem grotesque deviants from the norm of accepted female behavior.

The possession of a competence necessarily changed the social status of a single gentlewoman. Implicitly assuming a degree of financial security, Fordyce, Chapone, and Kames theorized that single women too could lead useful, contented lives and be accepted in society. More practically, Gregory promised his daughters the security of a financial legacy, in addition to his literary one, in the hope that they would prefer the independence and ease of singleness to becoming "the slaves of a fool's or tyrant's caprice."[75]

Although celibacy was not generally advocated, almost none of the theorists spoke optimistically of a woman's chances for economic security in the married state. A woman had no legal rights in marriage, not even to inherited or earned money.[76] Yet marriage continued to be recommended as a woman's best source of dependence and of social and financial security. The low economic status of the eighteenth-century woman, even of the socially superior gentlewoman, is made clear by a look at the semantic degeneration of the words "wife" and "spinster" in the seventeenth and eighteenth centuries. Before the seventeenth century, these words signified the economically productive "weaver" and "spinner"; by the eighteenth century, they took on connotations of expensive or expendable appendages, namely "unpaid housekeepers" or "china dolls" and "old maids."

But because marriage remained the main option for gentlewomen, conservative theorists taught women how to make the best of their situation. In her *Matrimonial Creed*, Chapone wisely echoed the advice of the feminist Astell that since a wife must submit to her husband anyway, it was better for her to choose, at the outset, a man she could honestly acknowledge her superior in understanding and judgement. The men, such as Kenrick, Fordyce, Gregory, and Kames gave women the benefit of their own experience in advising them to marry a man for his good sense, good morals, good temper, good family, and

---

[75] *A Father's Legacy* (1774; rpt. London: Strahan, Cadell, 1784), p. 109.

[76] Prudent parents made settlements on their daughters to protect them in case of the husband's insolvency. In general, it was widows and single women rather than married women who had rights to their own money.

adequate fortune, rather than merely for his looks, money, or title.[77] Intimately informed of their own nature as they presumed to be of woman's, these theorists rightly warned her against marrying rakes, sots, philosophers, fools, atheists, servile suitors (who then turned tyrants), and men with a family history of madness. According to the novels of sensibility of the time, except for the all-perfect hero, most men fell into the category of undesirable mates, for any or many of the above reasons, rakishness probably being the most popular one.[78]

It is not necessary to gauge how closely the percentage of male rakes and villains in novels approximated to statistics or met with social ostracism in real life. On the other hand, "fallen" women, that is, women fallen from the state of technical chastity, led a grim existence, for almost all the writers deal with this third possible way of life for all classes of women. The literature of the period talks of servant or middle-class girls, duped or aspiring above their social status, and hapless, unprotected young ladies, especially those without a dowry, who unsuspectingly exchanged their virginity (their only asset) for false promises and betrayal by upper-class men. It seems that thereafter both society, especially women, and often their own parents, who had nurtured them in their follies by a false education, sternly shut the door on them. In *The Vicar of Wakefield* (1766), Oliver Goldsmith's uncompromising solution for the "lovely woman [who] stoops to folly" was death.

His theory was countered, surprisingly enough, by patriarchs like Fordyce and Gregory, who joined occasionally liberal conservatives like Keir, to plead for the humble re-entry of such penitents into society, in order to save them from further degradation. For, with the loss of social acceptance, it seems such women had only three alternatives: to die of starvation, to be kept, or to give in reluctantly to prostitution.[79] As a desperate alternative to married security, prostitution has probably been the only paid profession consistently open to women since the beginning of patriarchal civilization.

The novels of the period, however, show that the one dubious benefit of the difficult lives of astute prostitutes, as opposed to the cushioned servility

---

[77] The necessity of adequate fortune is demonstrated in the embittered married and family lives of Henrietta's (1758) and Elfrida's (1786) moneyless parents, who marry for love. However, both these heroines prove themselves resolute and "singular" enough to secure independence through their own efforts.

[78] In contrast, Pope believed "every woman is at heart a Rake" (*Moral Essays: Epistle II*, p. 251).

[79] According to Phillips and Tomkinson, from 1758 on, the Magdalen Hospital in Prescott Street, London, cared for such "unhappy women" (p. 324).

of the married gentlewoman, was the shrewd knowledge the former acquired of money and of women's relationship to it. Prostitute-heroines, from Defoe's Moll Flanders and Roxana to Cleland's Fanny Hill and Maria Brown (*Genuine Memoirs*, 1766) display an intelligent knowledge of the intimate relation of money to their lives, tutored as they are in the "science" by various madams. For them, money is not merely a means of subsistence; it also becomes a means of buying their own independence from their customers in order to settle down in easy circumstances with the husband of their choice.

At the other end, respectable fictional characters often display the gentility of their upbringing through a total lack of monetary sense and therefore of self-survival. As a single woman, Burney's Cecilia gives away her entire paternal legacy to her so-called friends, the Harrels, and further renounces her uncle's conditional legacy in order to marry a man whose father despises her for her inferior birth. Likewise, delicacy keeps Sidney Biddulph from accepting her former suitor Faulkland's gift of £300, at a point in her life when she is starving, moneyless, ill, orphaned, widowed, and sole supporter of two little daughters. The plots of the general run of novels throve on such female indigence, yet their oft-used dénouement of an unexpected legacy at the end was too facile and unrealistic to suggest any concrete means of support for gentlewomen.

The answer to the undesirability of prostitution and the unreliability of sudden windfalls was self-support through the use of one's fashionable and intellectual education. Since conservative writers showed little interest in paid female professionalism, the following discussion is, of necessity, also based on the actual lives of working gentlewomen. Acting was generally considered immoral; therefore, among the very few respectable positions open to gentlewomen were teaching and writing.[80]

The emphasis on educating gentlewomen to become efficient maternal preceptors seems to have incidentally opened up the field of teaching to them.[81] Yet their teaching ability depended to a large extent on the adequacy of the education they themselves had received; according to the earlier mentioned article on Mary Muslin in *The Mirror*, few school or private governesses were either intellectually or morally competent for their task. On the

---

[80] The term "respectable" is used loosely. Whenever the professions of teaching and writing involved financial recompense, they also involved a drop in social respectability.

[81] Village dame schools were run by generally older, indigent, semi-literate lower-class women.

other hand, in real life, Hannah More's father deliberately trained his five daughters to be independent through teaching. The More sisters remained single and successfully ran a school for young ladies in Bristol for over thirty-two years; it ended in 1789, having gained for itself the reputation of being the "best conducted establishment for the education of young ladies in the United Kingdom."[82] Thereafter, in the 1790s and early 1800s, they ran Sunday schools for the poor in Cheddar. But whether or not competent like the More sisters, the number of governesses and female pupils must certainly have increased in eighteenth-century England (in spite of the majority of male teachers), for both modern critics and eighteenth-century writers testify to the mushrooming of boarding schools all over the country.

In the third quarter of the seventeenth century, Aphra Behn's suddenly reduced circumstances led her to break the barriers of female literary amateurism by opening up the field of fictional writing to women. Unfortunately, the freer morals of pioneer playwrights like Behn and Manley led to the denigration of professional women actors and writers in the first half of the eighteenth century, although the famous tragedienne Sarah Siddons redeemed the profession a couple of decades later. By the third quarter of this century, however, female writers seem to have been more respected, as individuals if not as a class, perhaps because of the example of the Bluestockings, the support of literary titans like Richardson and Johnson, and also the increasingly moral and educational tenor of their own works. Intellectual mothers like Lambert, Pennington, and Walker combined motherhood with literary aspirations by publishing their letters on education to their daughters. For the handful of writers who produced a "best-seller," writing even proved to be a profitable business. Carter received nearly £1,000 for her translation of Epictetus; Burney capitalized on the success of her anonymous and ill-paid first novel *Evelina* by earning £250 for the far inferior *Cecilia*.[83] In general, however, writing and teaching could not have proved as profitable for gentlewomen as the law and other professions were for gentlemen, yet society grudgingly came to recognize them as financial outlets for the impoverished upper-class woman.

---

[82] Jane Williams, *The Literary Women of England* (London: Saunders, Otley, and Co., 1861), p. 337.

[83] I do not agree with Joyce Horner that Burney's writing and publishing without the need for money showed that women novelists no longer needed to feel ashamed of their profession (p. 61). Many women still published anonymously, even though their authorship often came to be known later. Fearing detection and her father's disapproval, Burney herself disguised her handwriting in the manuscript of *Evelina* and had it clandestinely delivered to the publisher.

As for the middle-class woman, conservative theory persistently denied her the somewhat mixed blessing of upper-class professionalism. Instead, it suggested that like her forebears, she stay at home making jams, jellies, and household linen; training her daughters in domesticity; and helping her husband in his shop (like the bustling, scolding, simultaneously nurturing shoemaker's wife in Thomas Dekker's play, *The Shoemaker's Holiday*, 1600). Yet these writers gave the middle-class woman double messages about the relation of her sex and class to her work. On the one hand, they lamented that women of this class were developing an unhealthy disrespect for their own social status and beginning to despise the very commerce that allowed them to be idle and hire help. On the other hand, at least until the time of Austen and probably later, they continued to belittle trade and trade-connections in their works.

The poor seem to have been the only class of which both sexes were expected to work for a living.[84] Conservatives believed that both boys and girls of the laboring classes were to be trained early for financial usefulness. On weekdays, girls were to attend schools of industry. Here, they were to be taught useful domestic arts like cookery, laundry, needlework, and cleaning, which would train them to be moral, hardworking maidservants and frugal, economical wives. Boys who attended Charity schools were meant for hard labor or to be apprenticed to trade schools, in order to prepare them to earn their own living and support their families, instead of leaving them to the care of the parish. In this way, both women and men of the lower classes would become productive members of society instead of financial burdens to it.

At every social level, then, conservative thought sought to regulate women's education and professional possibilities in terms of their relevance to men and to society. Whatever the achievements of individual women, the needs and desires of the collective sex could not be given any importance if the existing hierarchies were to continue unchallenged. Thus, "the educational and fictional literature of the time tried to convince women that dutiful womanhood was a vocation just as deserving of women's efforts and fidelity as church, state, commerce, and the professions were vocations deserving of men's efforts" (Ellen Messer-Davidow, then a fellow doctoral student).

So women were to be conditioned to owe duties to everyone around them but themselves. Were they at least to be allowed someone—a female

---

[84] In *Women Workers and the Industrial Revolution 1750–1850* (New York: Crofts, MCMXXX), Ivy Pinchbeck gives detailed information on labor-class women.

friend, for instance—to whom they could unburden their cares? No, not by male theorists like Swift, Kenrick, Fordyce, and Gregory, perhaps for fear that women talking to women, women discussing their injustices, women bonding together would create insurrections that could upset the social order so dear to the conservative eighteenth-century mind. Consequently, they assured women that friendship between members of their own sex and age could never exist. But not all conservative women were ready to accept this sexist opinion. Even a staunch non-feminist like Anna Aikin (later Barbauld) was disturbed by it. In a letter dated London, February 1771, she wrote to her friend Miss Belsham: "It is not true, what Dr. Fordyce insinuates, that women's friendships are not sincere; I am sure it is not. I remember when I read it, I had a good mind to have burnt the book for that unkind passage" (quoted in Ellis, I, 42).

Yet throughout this period, women continued to be warned to "beware women" and to make friends only with the superior species of men who could be trusted to improve them. A woman without a man as father, brother, husband, or chaste consort therefore became a social deviant. It was not just paternalistic men, however, but women too, like Lennox and Frances Sheridan who, in their fictions, extolled the goodness of their heroines by demeaning the rest of womankind. Keir's *Interesting Memoirs* was the only conservative eighteenth-century novel, to my knowledge, in which all the female characters were shown as supportive of each other, even if their interests clashed as vitally as did those of Louisa Seymour and Lady Granville (over the former's love for the latter's son). Likewise, Louisa and Charlotte Villiers (the Granvilles' choice for their son) were made to show their sense of sisterhood, not only by their affection instead of rivalry for each other, but also by their joint efforts to reclaim penitent Sally, a seduced maid-servant. As a novelist, Keir showed indifferent talent; as a woman, she demonstrated that friendship between women need not be condemned, for it did not necessarily upset the social order.

Some of the novelists, although not the theorists, agreed that women could be friends in companiable pairs, if not as a sex.[85] The epistolary form introduced by Richardson set a rigid pattern for the exchange of detailed letters between "bosom" female friends, one of whom was the tearful heroine, full of sensibility and beset by obstacles, and the other her lively, commonsensical friend. This model began with Clarissa Harlowe and Anna Howe and worked

---

[85] Although female friendship between boarding-school girls was objected to by theorists, male friendships in public schools were often encouraged, as leading to influential connections in later life.

its way through imitations like Julie and Clara (*La Nouvelle Héloise*), Julia and Maria (*Julia de Roubigné*), Lydia Melford and Letty Willis (*Humphry Clinker*), and Louisa and Adelaide (*Interesting Memoirs*), to name only a few.

In real life too, there were examples of educated or literary women living in amicable pairs, among them, Frances Sheridan and Pennington's daughter; Montagu and Gregory's daughter (later Mrs. Alison); and Montagu's sister, Sarah Scott (separated from her husband) and Halifax's sister, Lady Barbara Montagu. Did Miss Pennington, Miss Gregory, Scott, and Lady Montagu choose to remain single for part or all of their lives to avoid following the overwhelmingly repressive precepts of their more famous relatives? How much did Chesterfield's cynicism about women owe to the fact that he was the son of Halifax's systematically repressed daughter?

The answer, Locke (in *An Essay Concerning Human Understanding*) and Condillac (in *Essai sur l'origine des connaissances humaines*) would have told us, lay in individual circumstances, not in accidental heredity, for within the same families it was possible to have conservative as well as progressive thinkers. (Also, according to circumstances, the same individual could sometimes subscribe to both ways of thinking.) So, obviously, on the larger societal scale, too, there were women who supported the existing socio-economic system and women who did not. The conflict, then, seems to have been one between patriarchal versus humanitarian viewpoints rather than between the sexes themselves on the question of women's rights to a self-fulfilling education and all the benefits it entailed. The fear of the humanitarian progressives was that the conservatives, left unchallenged, would become so complacent that they would react with regressive rigidity towards any new measure concerning the betterment of women, without first considering its validity.

Dickens has aptly expressed this fear in *A Tale of Two Cities*, a story set around the stormy decade of the 1790s:

The precept, that "Whatever is, is right"; [is] an aphorism that would be as final as it is lazy, did it not include the troublesome consequence, that nothing that ever was, was wrong.[86]

---

[86] *Tale of Two Cities* (1859; rpt. New York: Collier Books, 1974), p. 70.

# CHAPTER 2

# The Progressive Tradition, 1673–1787

I would calmly ask, is it reasonable, that a candidate for immortality, for the joys of heaven, an intelligent being, who is to spend an eternity in contemplating the works of deity, would at present be so degraded, as to be allowed no other ideas than those which are suggested by the mechanism of a pudding, or the sewing of the seams of garment?

[American] Judith Sargent Murray, "On the Equality of the Sexes," 1790

Let not your Ladiships [*sic*] be offended, that I do not (as some have wittily done) plead for Female Preeminence. To ask too much is the way to be denied all.

Bathsua Makin, *An Essay to Revive the Antient [sic] Education of Gentlewomen*, 1673

## I. Intellectual Background

The year 1673 was an important one in the intellectual history of upper-class Englishwomen. It saw the publication of two feminist tracts in England and France: Bathsua Makin's *An Essay to Revive the Antient Education of Gentlewomen* and François Poulain de la Barre's *De l'Égalite des deux sexes.*[1] These works were by no means completely original in their ideas, yet for the purposes of this chapter they will be regarded as the parents of the progressive tradition, representing as they did the two main arguments that differentiated it from the conservative one. Poulain de la Barre affirmed that gentlewomen were equal not inferior in rational capacities to men of their own social class; Makin argued that as rational human beings they deserved an education commensurate with their innate as well as class-related capacities. Both writers attacked the conservative restriction of female education to largely gender-related duties. Following their example, all later progressives voiced their passionate belief in rational education as the key to better conditions for gentlewomen.

These beliefs seem to have paralleled and were perhaps even influenced by the radical and ultimately subversive nature of contemporary Dissenting thought. For just as the radical Protestants dispensed with the importance of priests in their relationship with God, so also did the pioneering feminists of the Restoration and eighteenth century dispense with the importance of man in the relation of woman to her environment. Instead, they saw the gentlewoman as an individual in her own right, rather than merely as the social and familial being the conservatives assumed her to be. Three generations of feminists carried this ideological progressivism into the last decade of the eighteenth century, when it was combined with the ideologies of the French Revolution and culminated in Mary Wollstonecraft's definitive work, *A Vindication of Rights of Woman* (1792). These generations are best represented by Mary Astell (1666–1731) and Judith Drake (fl. 1696)[2] in the 1690s, Lady Mary Wortley Montagu[3] (1689–1762) and Samuel Richardson (1689–1761) in the mid-eighteenth century, and the comtesse de Genlis (1747–1830) and Mary Wollstonecraft (1759–97) in the 1780s (and nineties).

---

[1] Translated by "A. L." as *Woman as Good as the Man, or the Equality of both Sexes* (1677). Information on both Poulain de la Barre and Makin is from Myra Reynolds, *The Learned Lady in England 1650–1760* (Boston: Houghton Mifflin, 1920).

[2] I follow Myra Reynolds (as also the National Union Catalogue [NUC] and the publisher Curl [1741]) in ascribing the anonymously published tract, *An Essay in Defence* [*sic*] *of the Female Sex* (1696) to Drake rather than Astell, on the basis of "internal and external evidence." Reynolds calls its author "the most brilliant woman writer of her period" (p. 306). A fourth edition of the polemic was published as late as 1791, at the beginning of the decade when the question of the rights of women came to a head in England.

[3] Henceforth referred to as Wortley Montagu to differentiate her from her relative, the Bluestocking Elizabeth Montagu.

Although Wollstonecraft is sometimes regarded as the mother of English feminism, the title seems more legitimately to belong to Mary Astell, according to the accounts of both her first biographer, George Ballard (*Memoirs of Several Ladies of Great Britain*, 1752), and her twentieth-century biographer, Florence Smith (*Mary Astell*, 1916). Like most of the upper-class women writers of the late seventeenth century, and unlike the later Bluestockings, Astell expressed her feminism openly and fearlessly, even calling herself a "Lover of her Sex" in her pioneer tract, *A Serious Proposal to the Ladies, for the Advancement of their True and Greatest Interest* (Part I, 1694; Part II, 1697). Like the later Bluestockings, she was a member of a warm circle of intellectual and literary gentlewomen. Among her better-known friends were Elizabeth Elstob, the Anglo-Saxon scholar; Lady Elizabeth Hastings, who contributed to the support of Astell's Charity school in Chelsea; and the younger, more vivacious Lady Mary Wortley Montagu, whose posthumous works disseminated Astell's ideas on education well into the eighteenth century.

Of Astell's intellectual cohort, Judith Drake, little was known as late as the early 1980s although online information is available now on her friends and personal life. Her single work, *An Essay in Defence of the Female Sex* (1696), on the other hand, shows her to be a militant feminist with a largely secular outlook on life and a lively sense of humor. Also, she seems to have been fortunate in a brother who appreciated her writing ability (as his laudatory poem indicates), at a time when such talent was not always commended in women. Unfortunately, in attributing her work only to "A Lady," she represented the anonymity successfully (and regrettably) sought by or conferred on many writing women of this period.

If some writers preferred or could afford secrecy, there were others who eagerly sought encouragement where they could find it. Straitened means, no doubt, added to their openness about their professionalism. For instance, unlike Astell's coterie, which consisted largely of provident gentlewomen, the female coterie that collected in the mid-eighteenth century around the printer and novelist Samuel Richardson often included indigent, self-supporting writers, such as the feminists Sarah Scott (sister of the wealthy socialite and Bluestocking Elizabeth Montagu) and Sarah Fielding (sister of the novelist Henry Fielding and cousin of the affluent literary amateur Wortley Montagu). Like Scott and Fielding, Wollstonecraft, who began her literary career in the penultimate decade of the eighteenth century, was also a professional writer, working under the pressures of an unhappy home life but buoyed by a resilient instinct to survive. In common with her more solvent predecessors, Astell and Wortley Montagu, and indeed, with most of the female intellectual elite of her time, Wollstonecraft owed her own education to extensive private reading and to friendly tutoring from male mentors. Wollstonecraft turned her education to profitable use by working as governess and companion, by teaching, and by writing, although her bold conduct in the 1790s alienated many instructors from her sound precepts.

A far more respected educator in her time, among both the progressives and the conservatives, was the countess of Genlis, a French aristocrat and tutor to the children of the house of Orléans, cadet house of the Bourbon royal family. Whatever their public reception, however, all feminists from the time of Astell to that of Wollstonecraft shared a steadfast private belief in female ability and in the positive effects of an intellectually sound education. Although their immediate achievements were limited, their importance lies in their creation of a gradually receptive intellectual climate which ultimately resulted in the educational and professional changes for women that took place in the nineteenth century. As Myra Reynolds puts it:

> What was actually accomplished in the century before 1760 was a lavish sowing of seed, a steady infiltration of new ideas, a breaking up of old certainties as to women's place in domestic and civic life, and an accumulation of examples proving women capable of the most varied intellectual aptitudes and energies. (p. 456)

This "lavish sowing of seed" was mostly done by encouraging literacy among gentlewomen. Although literacy was not confused with a sound education, feminist writers recognized its importance in raising consciousness among gentlewomen. Increasingly, books came to be written for women, often by women. Thus in 1695, Astell published (albeit anonymously) her polemical *Letters Concerning the Love of God*, with the specific hope that women might be encouraged to read books if written by a member of their own sex. In 1711, "Mr. Spectator" claimed credit for the general intellectual improvement in his female readers; he considered himself responsible for making them better scholars, conversationalists, and letter-writers (in both meaning and orthography) than town-fops in general and the gentlemen at Will's coffeehouse in particular.[4]

_______________________

[4] Joseph Addison, No. 92, Friday, June 15, 1711, *Spectator*, 2 (rpt. London: Tonson, 1733), 49.

As the century progressed, magazines written specifically for women came into being. Cynthia White, in *Women's Magazines 1693–1968*, and Alison Adburgham, in *Women in Print: Writing Women and Women's Magazines from the Restoration to the Accession of Victoria*, point out that in the second half of the eighteenth century, thought-provoking, intelligent magazines for women were published, which concentrated on the female intellect and education instead of on the adornment of the body. These included Charlotte Lennox's monthly periodical, the *Lady's Museum* (1760–61), and a magazine with a very long run, the *Lady's Magazine* (started 1770), which White describes as the first professional effort to create a magazine acceptable to intellectual women of the leisured classes.[5]

In keeping with the thinking of her time, Wortley Montagu approved of periodical-reading as an aid to moral virtue, especially among the idle elite of both sexes, who, she felt, could not be bothered with more serious material. For them, some reading was better than none at all.[6] For those who enjoyed reading, periodicals seem to have been the first step to the reading of larger works, either novels and romances or moral works and histories. By 1778, Samuel Johnson, himself a periodical writer, was able to declare: "All our ladies read now, which is a great extension."[7]

Through the written word, the progressives launched the initial step of their campaign—to arouse in women a pride in the achievements of their ancestors, and therefore in themselves. They first turned to history, one of the many subjects prescribed for gentlewomen by the conservatives. Writers like Wortley Montagu applauded the administrative capacities of Queens like Elizabeth I, instead of abhorring the traits as masculine and therefore undesirable in women. Polemicists from Judith Drake, at the beginning of this period, to the anonymous author of *Female Restoration, by a Moral and Physical Vindication of Female Talents;[sic] in Opposition to All Dogmatical Assertions Relative to Disparity in the Sexes* (1780), towards its end, became aware that time and the malice of men had deliberately destroyed, misrepresented, or

---

[5] *Women's Magazines 1693–1968* (London: Michael Joseph, 1969), p. 31.

[6] Letter to Lady Bute, from Louvere, June 23, 1754, *Mary Wortley Montagu* (New York: Athenaeum Press, n.d.), p. 233.

[7] Wednesday, April 29, 1778, in James Boswell, *Life of Samuel Johnson* (1791; rpt. Oxford: Clarendon Press, 1934), III, 333.

suppressed knowledge of the heroic deeds of women, to conceal the "weakness and illegality" of male power.[8]

In 1779, William Alexander published his *History of Women, from the Earliest Antiquity to the Present Time, Giving Some Account of Almost Every Interesting Particular Concerning that Sex, among All Nations, Ancient and Modern.* Among other things, he celebrated women's contributions to society and to the progress of civilization itself, especially the invention of spinning and sewing and in the field of medical knowledge. His history was the earliest such extensively researched work of its kind, written with the specifically feminist intent of encouraging women to "look into the history of their own sex," instead of wasting their idle hours on novels and romances.[9] Catherine Macaulay Graham went a step further; in writing a comprehensive *History of England from the Accession of James I to that of the Brunswick [Hanoverian] Line* (1763–83), she became one of the first female historians in England.

Closely connected with history, and also a popular subject for gentlewomen, was the field of biography. In 1752, George Ballard published the first biography of literary women from the fourteenth to the mid-eighteenth century, in his *Memoirs of Several Ladies of Great Britain who have been Celebrated for their Writings or Skill in the Learned Languages, Arts, and Sciences.* (As already seen, among his biographies was one of Astell, one of the rare direct references to her in the mid-eighteenth century.)

The pride of the progressives in female achievement appeared not only in fields traditionally ascribed to men, such as learning, history-writing, and political government, but also in fields traditionally connected with women, and hitherto degraded as such. Writers from Judith Drake in the late seventeenth century to William Alexander and Mary Wollstonecraft in the 1780s all pointed out that male partiality for their own pursuits and studies made them undervalue women's pursuits and studies, which were equally useful and important, although directed to different ends. Drake understood the cause and nature of this sexism to lie in the natural inferiority of men in such fields: "This Presumption arises from an Erroneous Conceit, that all those things in which they are little concerned or consulted, are Triffles [*sic*] below their care or notice which indeed they are not by Nature so well able to manage" (p. 84). These trifles included important duties that affected both sexes, like

---

[8] Drake, *Defence of the Female Sex* (London: Roper and Wilkinson, Clavel, 1696), p. 23.

[9] Advertisement, *History of Women*, 3rd ed. (rpt. London: Dilly, Christopher, 1782), I, n.pag.

childbearing, the education of children, and the management of servants and household affairs, without which, continued Drake, men's houses would be in chaos. The anonymous author of *Female Restoration* extended her appreciation of women's work to even the ornamental accomplishments, such as Dresden work, which, she felt, required as much time and intelligence as learning, literature, and the metaphysical sciences.

The female achievement with which women writers were most involved was, of course, their own craft. The progressives applauded both one another's writing and their own. Unlike certain conservatives, Drake praised Aphra Behn for pioneering the field of literary professionalism and recommended her as a role model for other writers; Astell pointed to the French letter-writer Anne Dacier, the romance writer Madeleine de Scudéry (often decried by the conservatives), and the English poet Katherine Philips ("the matchless Orinda") as writers worthy of emulation. In her preface to her friend Wortley Montagu's *Letters from the Levant,* the first travel book of its kind by a gentlewoman, Astell proudly exhorted her fellow writers: "Let us freely own the superiority of this sublime genius as I do, in the sincerity of my soul; pleased that a woman triumphs and proud to follow in her train."[10] This preface was written in 1724; in spite of Astell's urging, however, Wortley Montagu "modestly" refused to have the work published in her own lifetime. Yet in her old age, Wortley Montagu herself urged Britons to emulate the pride of the Italians in their female writers. Similarly, in *Tales of the Castle;*[sic] *or Stories of Instruction and Delight,* de Genlis's maternal instructor, Mme de Clemire, informs her children of the accomplishments of famous European women artists—writers, musicians, composers, painters, and actresses—to make them aware of female talent and ability.[11]

Aside from the appreciation of their peers and forerunners, progressive writers from Drake and Astell to Wollstonecraft and *Female Restoration* also demonstrated a new toughness in their prefaces while assessing their own literary merit. Instead of the cringing (if conventional) humility of their more conservative peers, we see only a slight concession made to modesty.

---

[10] *Letters from the Levant* (1763; rpt. 1838; rpt. New York: Arno Press and the New York Times, 1971), p. iv.

[11] *Les Veillées du château* (1784), translated into English by Thomas Holcroft. Holcroft followed the eighteenth-century English custom of free translation and arbitrary interpolation.

Wollstonecraft was the boldest of them all: "I shall not swell these sheets by writing apologies for my attempt."[12]

But the stalwart feminism of such writers could not stem the scurrilous public resentment sometimes expressed about women and their literary achievements. Astell, Wortley Montagu, and Wollstonecraft, among others, were subjected to humorous or bitter satire, aimed at their private lives rather than their literary accomplishments. Thus, Astell's celibacy and Wollstonecraft's (later) sexual freedom were considered as much matters for ridicule as Wortley Montagu's initial social popularity and later marital separation and slovenliness of dress. As the eighteenth century progressed, literary criticism came increasingly to demand a rigid sexual and moral purity from female writers. Even pseudo-feminists like John Duncombe, who claimed his *Feminead: A Poem* (1754) to be the first poetical appreciation of women poets, and William Woty, in his *Female Advocate: A Poem* (1770), were guilty of applying personal criticism to the writers they considered. At the same time that he encouraged women to write poetry, therefore, Duncombe warned them against what he called the "disgraceful" examples of Aphra Behn, Mary de la Rivière Manley, Susannah Centlivre, Laetitia Pilkington, and V—. He praised only poets who combined genius with duty, and cited the works of Sappho, "Orinda," Anne Finch (Countess of Winchelsea), Catherine Cockburn, Elizabeth Rowe, Eliza Carter, and others as shining examples of female artistry.

Besides the unfairness of such personal criticism, the progressives identified two other deterrents to the development of female talent. The biographer Ballard and writing women themselves from Drake to de Genlis complained that true merit in a woman's work often led society to attribute the work to a man (as Rousseau did in *Émile*). In fact, Drake ascribed her reasons for anonymity specifically to this social malignity. On this question, as elsewhere, her tone was cheerfully buoyant instead of whiningly martyred. With mock-maternalism, she wrote of her "First Born":

Our Sex are by Nature tender of their Offspring, and may be allow'd to have more fondness for those of the Brain, then [*sic*] any other; because they are so few and meet with so many Enemies at their first Appearance in the World.

(Dedication to the *Defence*, n.pag.)

---

[12] Preface, *Thoughts on the Education of Daughters* (1787; rpt. New York: Garland, 1974), p. iii.

More bitterly, de Genlis put forward another reason for the frequent absence of female artistic talent. She pointed out that women's talents for music, composing, painting, acting, or writing were deliberately suppressed into closet-art instead of nurtured for achieving public fame. With brilliant insight into the reasons for the failure of female talents, de Genlis anticipated Virginia Woolf's explanation for the literary non-existence of Shakespeare's mythical sister, Judith (in *A Room of One's Own*, 1929). In de Genlis's *Tales of the Castle*, the maternal instructor, Mme de Clemire, tells her son Cesar that a man of letters or any other professional ability, seeing talent in his daughter, will deliberately "rob his scholar of that confidence which inspires fortitude, and that ambition which surmounts difficulties. . . . Had she the genius of a Corneille or Racine," she would not be allowed to succeed, for she is constantly told to write nothing but novels, pastorals, or sonnets, that is, genres then regarded as less significant forms of literature.[13] In many respects, then, the progressives felt that familial, social, and literary criticism all conspired to inhibit women's achievements in both life and literature.

Yet even in the face of all these odds, women began and continued to read and write throughout the course of the eighteenth century. In spite of basic differences in ideologies and aims, writers of both progressive and conservative tendencies came to realize that the condition of gentlewomen depended on the type of education they received. If in their personal lives the progressive women were closer to their precepts than such conservative counterparts as the Bluestockings, nevertheless, in their achievements, adherents of both sides proved to their age that their sex could, indeed, be intelligent, talented, and, if well-educated, professionally successful.

## II. Works, Theories, Places of Education

The main difference between the progressives and the conservatives was, necessarily, the resistance of the latter to change. Throughout this period, the tendency of the progressives was to reject rather than passively accept the stasis implied in Pope's widely believed conservative maxim that "Whatever is, is right." Thus, *Female Restoration* argued that it was wrong to continue

---

[13] *Tales of the Castle* (1785; rpt. London: Scatcherd and Letterman, Longman, Hurst, et al., 1819), II, 158.

in (harmful) old ways, merely because that was how things had always been. What the theorist Vicesimus Knox said of the prohibition against women's learning Latin can be applied to the authority of custom in general. He advocated the challenging of custom by practical change, quoting Erasmus's learned matron to validate his point:

> Why do you tell me of the generality of people, the very worst pattern of conduct? Why do you talk to me of custom, the teacher of all that is bad? Let us accustom ourselves to that which we know is best: so that will become usual that was unusual, and that will become agreeable that was disagreeable, and that fashionable which appeared unfashionable.[14]

Earlier, in the 1690s, Astell and Drake had asserted that women could bring about change only by accepting responsibility for it: they could not help their conditioning as children, but they themselves were to blame if as adults they continued to neglect their betterment through education.

One suggested way adult women could educate themselves was by reading the literature written for them. Like the conservatives, the progressives used various non-fictional and fictional forms to reach their public. The non-fictional forms included polemics, letters, histories, and biographies, some of which have already been mentioned in Section I. Serious polemics sometimes appeared in the form of tracts and pamphlets, loosely called "essays" or "thoughts," as in the case of Locke's *Essay Concerning Human Understanding* (1690) and Wollstonecraft's *Thoughts on the Education of Daughters* (1787). The marchioness Anne Thérèse de Lambert's *Advice from a Mother to her Daughter* was a personal pamphlet along the lines of a courtesy book;[15] Wortley Montagu's formal letters on her experiences in Turkey (1716-18, during her husband's ambassadorship) and her later informal ones from France and Italy (1739–61) gave lively social histories of the times and sound advice on female education.

The fictional forms consisted of articles in periodicals, of poems, and of novels; the last included the works of major progressives like Sarah Scott, Samuel Richardson, and Robert Bage. Children's books were becoming popular with both writers and readers. For instance, Sarah Fielding, in *The Governess; or*

---

[14] *Liberal Education: or, a Practical Treatise in the Methods of Acquiring Useful and Polite Learning*, 6th ed. (1781; rpt. London: Dilly, 1784), p. 265.

[15] This pamphlet is sometimes progressive and sometimes conservative, so has been discussed in both Chs. 1 and 2.

*Little Female Academy* (1749), and de Genlis, in *Les Veillées du château* (1784), wrote realistic stories of lifelike children in their school or home environments, a trend that was beginning to replace earlier moralistic or horrifying tales. In their efforts to educate their sex to a sense of their own worth, feminists thus reached out to female children and adults through the various literary genres.

The progressives were well aware of the difficulties to be encountered in attempting changes in society's set patterns of thinking. In her preface, the author of *Female Restoration* pinpointed what she saw as the two main adversaries: "the vulgar and almost all the learned." She believed that the vulgar based their opinions on custom which could be "easily refuted" by showing that women's state of dependence was due to their conditioned ignorance and not to any natural incapacity; the learned would come around on their own when they saw the truth and reason of women's claims.[16] The reforms demanded by the progressives, however, were not simple ones. They radically challenged the more accepted conservative modes of thought in insisting that woman was equal to man and, like him, a rational, capable being, worthy of thinking and acting for herself, and therefore deserving of a good education.[17]

The progressives put forward many reasons to substantiate the above theory. First, their appreciation of female achievement and its contribution to human progress made them postulate that female ability should be assessed from the best rather than the worst examples. Thus, intelligent, assertive women, whether like Elizabeth I in real life or like Judith Lamounde in fiction (Robert Bage, *James Wallace*, 1787), were to be seen as representative of their sex and not as freakish anomalies.

Furthermore, progressives like Poulain de la Barre, Astell, Defoe, Wortley Montagu, "Sophia" (of the *Sophia Pamphlets*, 1739–40),[18] Woty, Alexander,

---

[16] *Female Restoration* (London: MacGowan's, 1780), pp. iii-iv.

[17] *Female Restoration* argued, with inexorably clear logic, that if it were true that women were unequal to men, because, as the misogynous Aristotle and his followers had said, they were imperfect men, then "with as much reason as these philosophers, women could say that men are but imperfect women" (p. 66).

[18] Two of these pamphlets were written by "Sophia," one by an anonymous opponent. They were *Woman not Inferior to Man; Or A Short and Modest Vindication of the Natural Rights of the Fair Sex to a Perfect Equality with the Men, by Sophia, a Person of Quality* (1739); *Man Superior to Woman, Containing a Plain Confutation of the Fallacious Arguments of Sophia in her late Treatise entitled Woman not Inferior to Man* (1739); *Woman's Superior Excellence over Man or a Reply to the Author of a Late Treatise, entitled Man Superior to Woman in Which the Excessive Weakness of that Gentleman's Answer to Woman not Inferior to Man is Exposed* (1740). The *Sophia Pamphlets* were collectively published in 1757 as *Beauty's Triumph* (Reynolds, p. 313).

Knox, and *Female Restoration* argued that it was blasphemy even to doubt the existence of natural capacity in women, for it was given by God to them, equally with the other sex. Astell believed it showed contempt for God to suppose that women were made only to admire and serve men and to lead an animal life. *Female Restoration* asserted that the scriptures did not mention a word of sexual inequality on biological grounds; moreover, she continued brilliantly, the argument of the rib could be applied only to Eve, for no other women were indebted to their husbands for their creation. This refutation of Biblical authority remained an important feminist argument from the progressive Drake in the 1690s to the radical Mary Hays in the 1790s.

It is amusing to see how the progressives, like the conservatives, energetically enlisted Nature too on their side in the controversy about female capacity, both intellectual and physical. The progressives insisted that intellectual imbecility was not natural in women; it was the result of a poor or faulty education. Astell, Drake, Ballard, Alexander, and Knox pointed out that women's inferiority was due to a lack of opportunity and was therefore circumstantial and acquired, rather than innate and natural. Both sexes started out equal, for the mind at birth, according to Locke, was a mere *tabula rasa*. In fact, young girls showed themselves sharper in wit and intelligence than boys, argued Defoe (*Essay upon Projects*, 1697) and *Female Restoration*. But, the progressives lamented, custom and prejudice soon warped and stifled this early disposition and rendered women unequal to men. Of all the progressive works, however, only Drake's *Defence* and the anonymous *Female Restoration* asserted that women were superior to men even as adults and in spite of the greater opportunities given men by hierarchical social prejudices.[19] With less humor and greater bitterness than in the above two works, Wortley Montagu condemned the force and prevalence of male prejudice:

> The same characters are formed by the same lessons, which inclines me to think (if I dare say it) that nature has not placed us in an inferior rank to men, no more than females of other animals, where we see no distinction of capacity; though I am persuaded, that if there was a commonwealth of horses (as Doctor

---

[19] The two most feminist progressives, Drake and the author of *Female Restoration*, have a refreshing, lively style that is, ironically, reminiscent of two of their antagonists, the playwrights Molière and Sheridan. I suspect the ease and sense of fun of all four, so different from the grave didacticism of some of their peers, stemmed from the security of their complete belief in their ideas. Their tones and methods were therefore not defensive and explanatory but rather relaxed and expository.

Swift has supposed), it would be an established maxim among them, that a mare could not be taught to pace.

(Louvere, March 6, 1753, Mary Wortley Montagu, p. 265)

Likewise, on the question of female physical inferiority, the progressives came to the important realization that men appropriated intellectual wisdom to themselves merely on the grounds of superior physical strength. In his *History of the Decline and Fall of the Roman Empire* (1782), Edward Gibbon reinforced this argument by pointing out that in every age and country, the wiser or at least the stronger sex "usurped" state power and "confined" the other sex to the "cares and pleasures of domestic life."[20] Similarly, in his *Système social* (1773), the *philosophe* baron d'Holbach agreed with the general theory that women were better treated in civilized than in "savage" societies, but he lamented that even in refined societies, women's minds were deliberately made to vegetate uselessly.

In fact, from the end of the seventeenth century on, feminists like Drake and Defoe began to compare the degraded socio-political position of women not with that of their "savage" sisters of earlier times but with the Black American slaves of their own period. (Behn's *Oroonoko, or the Royal Slave* was published in 1688.) The metaphor of slavery continued to be a popular one on this issue in the eighteenth century, especially with the radicals of the 1790s. To arouse female consciousness, progressives like Drake, Alexander, and *Female Restoration* gave vivid historical sketches of the systematic repression of women too in all ages and climes. However, and for the same end, they also counterbalanced these descriptions with a parallel account of female successes. *Female Restoration* gave examples of women who had been equal in intellectual talents and abilities to men in government, law, warfare, religion, learning, morality, and patriotism. "How then," the author asks, "does history corroborate the imbecillity [*sic*] of the women?" (p. 32).

Through this process of historical revaluation, Poulain de la Barre, Astell, Ballard, de Genlis, Alexander, and *Female Restoration* became aware that the natural rights of women had been usurped by men solely on the basis of greater physical strength. *Female Restoration* further exposed the weakness of men's claim to preeminence. It argued that strength of body was not a sure

---

[20] *Decline and Fall* (1776–88; rpt. London: Cadell and Davies, Johnson, et al., 1807), I, 241.

criterion of superiority even in men: robust bodies were not always joined to an extensive understanding; otherwise, porters, even beasts, would possess more intelligence than great geniuses.

Most importantly, the progressives came to the major realization that man's greater strength was a result of conditioning rather than of innate physical superiority over the female body. On the question of female physical ability, as elsewhere, the difference between the progressives and the conservatives is apparent in their terminology. For instance, Drake and *Female Restoration* spoke in positive terms of the Amazons, the ancient race of strong warrior women, identifying their strength with a desirable state of female liberty, while conservatives like Henry Fielding scornfully applied the epithet to so-called unfeminine characters like Mrs. Western, the learned single woman in *Tom Jones*.

The revaluation of female strength naturally led to a questioning of all the arguments that stemmed from it. Poulain de la Barre, Drake, Alexander, and *Female Restoration* came to see that it was arbitrary man and not Providence or Nature (as the conservatives alleged) who conferred rights upon his own sex. They also saw that the generality of women mindlessly concurred with the belief in the preeminence of man because Custom (the third member of the conservative trinity) had given the façade of naturalness to what was originally an unjust usurpation. This was not all. Alexander and others pointed out that the prejudices of custom had been further solidified by legal sanction, men naturally making the laws in their own interest rather than in that of the female sex. With gallant arrogance, even a would-be progressive like Samuel Johnson justified such laws: "Nature has given women so much power that the law has very wisely given them little."[21]

Although by the end of the seventeenth century, feminists were beginning to question man-made laws and customs, in one significant aspect, they remained children of their time. Astell,[22] Locke, and Defoe at one end of this period and Knox, de Genlis, and even the earlier Wollstonecraft at the other favored a severe classism in education, by which each level of society was to be educated according to its rank. Believing in the power of influence by acquaintance, they even recommended that children be kept away from

---

[21] Letter to Dr. Taylor, August 18, 1763, *Life*, V, 226.

[22] Smith, Astell's biographer, sees her upper-class bias as her greatest limitation (p. 54). However, it seems unfair to judge Astell by the standards of contemporary liberalism.

servants, who would fill their heads either with ignorant superstition or with vicious ideas. De Genlis and Wollstonecraft defended their classism in relation to servants on the principle that differently educated people ought not to be familiar with one another as equals, for "nobility of birth is only an imaginary advantage, but education establishes a real inequality among men. A rational, enlightened, well-informed person cannot be intimate with one who is rude, ignorant, imprudent, and full of prejudice" (de Genlis, *The Tales of the Castle*, I, 7).

Philanthropical progressives like Catherine Cappe had a solution to such prejudice. In an extract dated 1785, from an account of a spinning school for the poor, she proposed that female children of the laboring classes be given a school education in morals, domestic duties, and reading so that later, as servants, they would be sober, honest, industrious, and obedient, instead of ignorant and vicious. Such an education for the poor would benefit both the upper and the lower classes, she urged, and thereby contribute to the general social good (*An Account of Two Charity Schools for the Education of Girls*, 1800).

The question of institutional education as opposed to a home education was as important to the progressives as the conservatives. It has already been seen in Chapter 1 that the conservatives preferred gentlewomen to be closeted in the privacy of the home. Boarding schools supposedly being what they were, this bias was shared by many of the progressive writers too. Further, Locke's suggestion that the mother educate her children, especially her daughters, was responsible for reinforcing the theory of home education for girls. It must here be pointed out that he rejected the public school system for boys too, in favor of home education under first the mother and later the tutor. Astell, Addison (*Spectator*, I, No. 73), Knox, d'Holbach, and de Genlis also emphasized the education of children as one of the mother's primary duties. In *Adelaide and Theodore;*[sic] *or Letters on Education*, de Genlis went so far as to make the entire d'Almane family, along with an Italian tutor and an English governess, move from Paris to their retired country estate for the children's education.[23]

Defoe, Alexander, Knox, and Wollstonecraft also recommended home education as opposed to the dubious education received at boarding schools. Wollstonecraft regarded the mother's active participation as of prime importance but

---

[23] *Adèle et Théodore, ou lettres sur l'éducation* (1782; translated, 1783).

postulated that if a mother proved negligent in her duty, it was preferable to send the daughters to a boarding school rather than have them stay under the same roof and be exposed to the even more corrupting influence of servants. Besides home education, another of the few subjects on which most of the progressives and conservatives agreed was the ill effects of boarding schools, which supposedly left the students emptyheaded and vain, if not actually immoral.

Even if most boarding schools proved unsatisfactory, the idea of some form of institutional education and/or retreat for women was not entirely rejected. Visionaries like Makin, Astell, Defoe, Scott, and Richardson projected seminaries for gentlewomen as places of either retirement or instruction. Both reasons, especially the former, were valid for Englishwomen at the time. The closing down of nunneries in England in the sixteenth century had suddenly deprived women of religious retirement as an alternative to marriage, and consequently rendered the dependent "old maid" an undesirable social element, without leaving her any place of independent retreat. On the other hand, at least until the revolutionary 1790s, eighteenth-century Frenchwomen continued to enjoy the privilege of convent-retirement under the Roman Catholic religious system. In his introduction to Diderot's *La Réligieuse*, Francis Birrell points out that in eighteenth-century France, convents had become comfortable hotels, where middle-aged women lived calm and respected lives (p. x).

The idea of convents for women seems to have been afloat again around the mid-eighteenth century; a close approximation in England to this sort of haven appears in a novel by Sarah Scott. Herself separated from her husband and living with Lady Barbara Montagu, Scott created *Millenium Hall* (1762); this was the retreat of five middle-aged single ladies, unhappy in love or marriage, who joined their fortunes together to live in friendship and charitable works. Like Richardson in *Sir Charles Grandison* (1753–54), even the conservative Charlotte Lennox, in both *The Female Quixote* (1752) and *Henrietta* (1758), had two of her characters lament the lack of Protestant nunneries as places where Englishwomen could either renounce the world or be renounced by uncaring relatives.

The other function of French nunneries was to educate young ladies. Their educational system seems to have been as injurious in effect and as accomplishment-oriented as the common run of English boarding schools and therefore as heartily despised by serious-minded people. Wortley Montagu said of convents in general: "I would as soon put a girl in the play house for education as send her among them" (*Mary Wortley Montagu*, p. 308).

Not all schools, however, were unworthy as female educational institutions; conscientious governesses like Makin and, in the next century, the More sisters ran efficient schools that afforded a very good education to young gentlewomen. Reynolds describes Makin's school at Tottenham High Cross, to advertise which she published her *Essay* in 1673, as "the first known attempt to organize a scheme of definite and solid study for girls" (p. 280). Astell's project, as outlined in *A Serious Proposal*, went further: like the French convents, her ideal seminary made provisions for the education and habitation of young ladies as well as of surplus gentlewomen (Reynolds, p. 361).

Astell's proposal for a college of higher education for women was perhaps the most important contribution of the progressives to female education. She was by no means the first feminist in the seventeenth century to think of such a scheme, yet because her reputation carried weight in her own time (she lived on until 1731) and because of the century-long influence of her ideas, even after her name itself was almost forgotten for a few decades, she deserves recognition as the first champion of higher education for women. Furthermore, even if aborted from actualization a few times during the eighteenth century, Astell's plan, along with the related ones of Defoe and Richardson, was responsible for generating a lively controversy about college education for women in this period. As such, all three projects will be dealt with here in some detail.

In *An Essay upon Projects* and in *Sir Charles Grandison*, Defoe and Richardson, respectively, outlined plans for seminaries that bore close parallels to Astell's scheme.[24] In keeping with the classism and moral emphasis of their times, all three projected their proposals only for women of good birth and impeccable morals. The boarders were to be allowed to enter and leave the institution willingly and to be free from vows of any kind.[25] Since it was intended for ladies, the college was not, in general, to be a charitable institution.

---

[24] Some of the phrases and ideas in Richardson's plan were plagiarized from the *Serious Proposal* as ideas of the all-perfect Sir Charles himself. It is noteworthy that on reading the novel, Wortley Montagu, who knew Astell intimately until the latter's death, was reminded of her own "favorite scheme" of an English monastery, at age fifteen: "Had I then been mistress of an independent fortune [I] would certainly have executed it, and elected myself lady abbess" (Louvere, October 20, N.S., 1752, *Works* 1803; rpt. London: Longman, Hurst, Rees, et al, 1817, IV, 184).

[25] Astell's biographer, Smith, reminds us that in the seventeenth century, a feminist governess, Mary Ward (1585-1645), had founded an educational institution for women on similar lines, without vows (p. 62).

Defoe instituted a non-refundable fee; Astell proposed the then-princely sum of five hundred pounds if the boarders could afford it. Richardson recommended that individuals pay according to their circumstances and that the ladies engage in genteel work (a very practical idea), the profits of which would help support the institution and give them a small sum for personal expenses. (This system of self-sufficiency was often recommended for Charity schools too.)

The main difference between the three proposals is the religious emphasis on Astell's part as opposed to the secularism of the two men. Although criticism of Part I of the *Serious Proposal* made Astell insist in Part II that her purpose was "Academical [rather] than Monastic,"[26] in the earlier part she actually called her institution a "Monastery," then changed the word, to avoid "superstitious" connotations, to a "Religious Retirement" (Part I, p. 36). She intended her college to serve the double purpose of providing either a retreat from the world or training in how to live more worthily in it. The tasks of her "Religious"[27] would be to spread the glory of God; to love one another; to enjoy innocent pleasures; and to communicate useful knowledge, which they would obtain by study and contemplation. Such a seminary would benefit not only its lodgers but also help "stock the kingdom with pious and prudent Ladies" (I, p. 43). It is worth noting that Richardson, who dared to call his seminary a Protestant nunnery (in spite of its "Popish" overtones), was simultaneously cautious enough to change "ladies," with its inclusion of single women, to "wives" although like Astell he too saw the project as conducive to "national good."[28] These institutions were thus to serve both public and private good. Astell also intended her retreat as a shelter for unprotected heiresses, for "superannuated virgins" who might otherwise rush into undesirable matches, and for portionless daughters of landed gentry. Among his projected boarders, Richardson included widows and the wives of absent, seafaring husbands.

As importantly, Astell, Defoe, and Richardson meant their institutions to serve as good schools for the daughters of persons of quality. In charity, however, Astell agreed to accept daughters of gentlemen fallen into financial decay, hoping that their good education would serve as their dowry. Defoe

---

[26] *A Serious Proposal*, Part II (1697; rpt. London: Wilkin, 1701), p. 286.

[27] Astell used this word as a noun, as in the French "réligieuse" for "nun." Astell obviously intended a lay sisterhood for her seminary.

[28] *Sir Charles Grandison* (rpt. Oxford: Blackwell, 1931), III, 383.

acknowledged his respect for Astell's proposal but insisted his seminary was envisioned on the secular lines of a public school, "wherein such ladies as were willing to study should have all the advantages of learning suitable to their genius."[29] None of the three theorists determined the size of the institution in terms of its students and boarders. However, Astell's plan seemed to have been for a single college; Defoe's was proposed on a nationwide scale, with ten institutions for London, and at least one in every county, in which last he was followed by Richardson.

Their ideas for a female seminary did not die. As late as 1792, in her *Plans of Education*, Clara Reeve expounded a scheme similar to the above three plans. Unfortunately, even though Astell's proposal (if not her name) remained before the public eye throughout the eighteenth century, her idea was too radical and woman-oriented to be accepted by some of her own contemporaries. For instance, Richard Steele satirized her as "Mrs. Comma, the great scholar" in the *Tatler*.[30] Jonathan Swift made a scurrilous attack on the morals of the inmates of "Madonella's" Platonic College[31] and ridiculously exaggerated its supposed curriculum: "Instead of Scissors, Needles, and Samplers; Pens, Compasses, Quadrants, Books, Manuscripts, Greek, Latin, and Hebrew are to take up their whole Time." On holidays, he continued, they will be taught light weaponry and "Amazonian tacticks."[32] More detrimental to Astell's proposal than the *Tatler* satires was Bishop Burnet's fear of a "Popish" revival, which, alas, made him persuade Queen Anne to retract her offer of £10,000 to found the college. Ironically, it was Bishop Burnet who was one of Wortley Montagu's childhood mentors, encouraging her in her classical, that is, "masculine" studies. But in fairness to the Bishop, who in later life lamented the lack of a "monastery without vows" (Smith, p. 22), it must be remembered that as near in time as the years 1685–88, James II had attempted to restore "popery" to England.

The eighteenth century, then, seemed destined not to see the first college for women but rather to create the social and intellectual atmosphere for it through the dissemination of progressive thinking. But Astell's basic assertion

---

[29] In *The Earlier Life and the Chief Earlier Works of Daniel Defoe*, ed. Henry Morley (London: Routledge, 1889), p. 146. The curriculum recommended by the three writers is discussed in Section III.

[30] No. 166, Tuesday, May 2, 1710, *Tatler*, 3 (rpt. London: Nutt, Knapton, Sprint, et al, 1728), 245.

[31] No. 32, Thursday, June 23, 1709, *Tatler*, I, 214–17.

[32] No. 63, Saturday, September 3, 1709, *Tatler*, II, 84.

was remembered all through the century, that women had too long been rendered "cheap and contemptible" because men had deliberately monopolized good education for themselves. As early as the seventeenth century, she and Makin proposed giving the gentlewoman an "ingenious and liberal education" which centered on her own improvement but was not incompatible with the duties of either married or single life. Its purpose was to render her virtuous in the eyes of God and herself, and thereby make her "as perfect and happy as 'tis possible to be in this imperfect state" as also in the hereafter (*Serious Proposal*, I, 19, 12). But Defoe was pessimistic that this happiness for women through reformed education would come about in his lifetime. He realistically asserted that the times were more suited for theoretical acquiescence than for practical change, and that the defects in female education "will be more easily granted than remedied" (*Essay upon Projects*, p. 152).

Astell was not daunted. Her project for gentlewomen having failed, she showed her flexibility by founding a Charity school for the daughters of the poor in Chelsea, funded by her friend Lady Hastings (Smith, p. 32). As already seen in Chapter 1, an increasing number of Charity schools came into being in the eighteenth century for children of the poor. By the 1780s, benevolent gentlewomen like de Genlis's baronne d'Almane and her daughter Adèle in fiction and Catherine Cappe in real life came to concern themselves with the welfare of the poor, especially in terms of their education. Cappe's detailed account of the Grey Coat School in York, which had existed from the beginning of the century, was businesslike and intelligent yet showed active sympathy for the students themselves. Her special concern for forlorn, friendless orphans who needed the patronage of such a school echoed Astell's concern for similarly unprotected heiresses. Also, without the over-emphasis on religion of philanthropists like her contemporary Hannah More, Cappe's aim seemed to be the health, welfare, and economic self-sufficiency of the girls themselves, both while at school and later, when apprenticed out as servants. As Astell hoped her plan would people the nation with worthy gentlewomen, so Cappe and her co-workers hoped the pupils they supervised in the Grey Coat and Spinning Schools would provide York with decent, industrious, orderly, and self-disciplined maids. Both Astell and Cappe equated their concern for young women, whether with or without parental protection, with their concern for public good, this connection perhaps making their plans more acceptable to society.

In spite of all the feminist works written, the theories put forward, and the schools projected for daughters of the upper classes, in actual fact reformers seem to have had more success in their endeavors for only the lowest class. However, in their varied ways, the progressives continued to keep the controversy alive at least on paper and in the minds of the readers—whether with the religious earnestness of an Astell, the witty logic of a Drake, the saddened realism of a Wortley Montagu, or the pedagogical primness of the earlier Wollstonecraft.

## III. Education of the Head, the Physique, the Person, and the Heart

The progressives differed in important respects from the conservatives on the issue of the four major areas of female education—the intellect, the physique, the person, and the heart. They assessed woman on the basis of her mind rather than solely for her external appearance or gender-related usefulness. Their attention was, therefore, focused on the education of the head, working healthily in conjunction with the body, rather than on adorning the person, and although the heart continued to be important, it now included character traits that were androgynous rather than merely "feminine."

The basis of the progressive argument in favor of an intellectual education for the gentlewoman was, as already seen, the belief in her innate rational ability. Makin, Astell, Drake, de Genlis, Alexander, Knox, and Wollstonecraft asserted that this ability ought to be cultivated; women were to be allowed "the means of examining and judging the rational," so they would not be "imposed on with tinsel ware" (*Serious Proposal*, I, 20). In his *Essay Concerning Human Understanding* (1690), Locke had emphasized the need for men to learn to think and know for themselves, since all knowledge was grounded on experience. Women writers from Astell and Lambert to de Genlis (in "Delphine: Or the Fortunate Cure," *Tales*), the author of *Female Restoration*, Wollstonecraft, and Anna Seward (*Letters of Anna Seward: Written between the Years 1784 and 1807* [1811]) applied this theory to their own sex. As Wollstonecraft put it: "Too many of our sex suffer theirs [reason] to lie dormant. . . . I wish them to be taught to think" (*Education of Daughters*, pp. 99). A definite shift in emphasis is, however, discernible from Astell's time to Wollstonecraft's. Religious knowledge only for opulent ladies gave way to secular benefits for all gentle-women, whatever their economic background: "Taste and thought open many sources of pleasure, which do not depend on fortune" (Wollstonecraft, p. 55).

Although all the progressives believed in the ability of women to think for themselves, they differed in the degree of their belief. Strong feminists like Drake and *Female Restoration* were convinced of female preeminence and alleged that men deliberately distorted terminology to make women sound inferior. As Drake expressed it: "I know our Opposers usually miscall our quickness of thought, Fancy and Flash, and Christen their own Heaviness ('Dullness' and 'Stupidity') by the specious names of Judgement and Solidity" (*Defence*, p. 19). With a similar and characteristically eighteenth-century conviction of the importance of words and their proper usage, *Female Restoration* supported Drake's semantic grievance: "No weight should be given to certain [such] common expressions, which draw their etymology from the present unnatural state of the sexes" (p. 53).

More placatingly, Astell and Knox urged that women were equal rather than superior to men in their learning capacity; as such, their "reason may properly receive the highest possible cultivation."[33] In Addison's periodical, the *Guardian*, the "editor," Nestor Ironside, argued from the perspective of the liberal male:

> Learning and knowledge are perfections in us, not as we are men, but as we are reasonable creatures, in which order of beings the female world is upon the same level with the male. We ought to consider in this particular, not what is the sex, but what is the species to which they belong.[34]

But gender continued to be an issue, the different progressives responding to it in different ways. Feminists like Drake and *Female Restoration* wittily inverted the doctrine of female physical inferiority by proposing that if Nature had, indeed, fashioned men for action and labor, then it must have intended women for thought and exercise of the mind. At another level, Nestor Ironside suggested that since women's tongues were naturally in motion, why

---

[33] Knox, No. LXXXVI, *Essays Moral and Literary* (1778–79; rpt. London: Dilly, 1785), II, 21. In *Essays*, II, Knox posed his most feminist ideas in a letter by a learned but virtuous daughter of a clergyman, perhaps to escape direct responsibility for propagating the ideas himself.

[34] Tuesday, September 8, 1713, *Guardian* (rpt. London: Jones, 1829), p. 227.

not set gentlewomen to talking wisely instead of scandalously? Moreover, he continued humorously, since their husbands were generally strangers to learning, it was "a great pity there should be no knowledge in a family" (No. 155, p. 227). "Ironside," Astell, and Duncombe suggested that such learning could prove a social asset to educated gentlewomen; it would render them useful and agreeable in company, intelligent conversation replacing the less desirable alternatives of gaming, idle visiting, and malicious gossip.

In *Sir Charles Grandison*, grandmother Shirley questions why it is necessary for women to affect a "childish ignorance" in mixed company."[35] In private life too, she believes, there is a degree of knowledge very compatible with women's duties, which would make them fit and useful companions to a man of sense; and fit teachers of his children too, Locke would have added. Actually, the progressives argued, far from interfering with her gender-related duties, a cultivated intellect would help a gentlewoman to understand them better and therefore effectively carry them out. As Wortley Montagu pointed out, it was ignorance and not knowledge that was the cause of all the idleness and mischief in women. Mentoria, the governess in Ann Murry's educational work, *Mentoria; or, the Young Ladies Instructor*, exhorts her young female pupils in this regard:

> Let me entreat you to avoid the fetters of ignorance; as the chains which confine the mind are the worst slavery a human creature can experience: yet, unlike most other bonds, they may be broken by the strong efforts of our reason.[36]

Wollstonecraft, in particular, relied on the metaphor of slavery in outlining the dangers of ignorant as opposed to intelligent obedience in the family hierarchy: "She who submits, without conviction, to a parent or husband, will as unreasonably tyrannize over her servants; for slavish fear and tyranny go together" (*Education of Daughters*, p. 63). Even more important than their concern over the adequate performance of duties was the insistence of the

---

[35] (I, 355). Her own intelligent, well-educated granddaughter Harriet is, however, guilty of such deceit when she tells a gentleman that she does not know what is meant by the "learned languages." In the course of the seven volumes of the novel, Harriet turns from a lively feminist to a mirthless conservative; much as Richardson's friend, the sprightly Hester Mulso of the feminist *Letters on Filial Obedience* and the *Matrimonial Creed* was to turn into the moralizing Mrs. Chapone of the *Letters on Improvement* and *Letter to a New-Married Lady*.

[36] *Mentoria* (1778; rpt. London: Dilly, 1796), p. 204.

progressives that a gentlewoman could benefit herself by cultivating her mind. They argued that the pursuit of knowledge would prove a rational occupation to fill her leisure hours and would provide a source of diversion and relaxation from mental cares and passions. All things considered, they concluded, learning would prove an asset instead of a danger to women of the upper classes.

The conservatives who denigrated learning in gentlewomen therefore seemed mistaken in their bias. It has already been seen in Chapter 1 that writers like Molière had attacked the shadow for the substance in consistently deriding the pseudo-intellectual for the truly learned women. The progressives countered with the plea that true learning was not detrimental to female behavior because it was always accompanied by modesty. With a possibly unconscious display of their own learning, Astell and Wortley Montagu drew on the classical support of Socrates and Thucydides to affirm that the most knowing women would honestly admit they knew nothing. More shrewdly than philosophically, the latter also advised her daughter, Lady Mary Bute, to conceal her daughters' learning, if any, with as much assiduity as "crookedness or lameness" for it invariably drew forth the "envy and hatred" of both sexes (*Mary Wortley Montagu*, p. 259).

According to Knox, it was only the abuse of learning (which involved a smattering of knowledge) that led to arrogance, masculine boldness, injudicious ostentation, and critical severity in women. In *Essays Moral and Literary*, he listed all the activities he felt came under the head of superficial and ill-directed learning: the reading of magazines, works by modern skeptics, and sentimental novels; the talking of politics; and the writing of indifferent poetry. Moreover, he continued, both sexes hated the affectation of learning and authorship in women of little merit. But, argued Drake and *Female Restoration*, neither did all gentlemen use their knowledge intelligently. Men also sometimes frustrated the effects of a liberal education by turning into the "Learned and Unlearned Blockhead," that is, the pedant and the carousing, fox-hunting squire, or the atheist and the debauchee (Drake, p. 35). The abuse of learning was, therefore, a human and not a female fault.

So it was generally agreed by the progressives that learning put to proper use could be an actual benefit. Learning was seen as particularly profitable for three special categories of gentlewomen: single, indigent, or opulent. Like her disciple Wortley Montagu, Astell believed that single women profited from knowledge because their minds were not contracted by familial obligations. Wortley Montagu offered a more personal inducement: "I know, by experience, that it is in the power of study not only to make solitude tolerable, but agreeable" (*Mary Wortley Montagu*, p. 263). Learning was considered a practical necessity for indigent women, for it could be put to professional use, even though eighteenth-century society in general frowned on the working gentlewoman.

With regard to women of leisure, Knox reasoned that although wealth did not totally exempt them from domestic cares, it gave them more free time, which could be best spent in studying. To such women, he suggested what he called a "classical" education, meaning a study of the French and English classics and not of the so-called learned languages. The classical languages themselves were often confused with learning per se; Drake felt that lazy women often pleaded ignorance on the grounds of a lack of knowledge of Greek and Latin. Like the Dissenters, she found English a perfectly adequate medium of instruction and subject of study; she even suggested a semantic enlargement of the word "learning" to include not just a knowledge of the ancient languages but also of one's own times.

On the other hand, believing in the inadequacy of translations, Wortley Montagu recommended the knowledge of languages to her granddaughters so they could read works in the original, but she simultaneously cautioned them that even with a knowledge of classical languages, a woman must not make the mistake of calling herself learned, for languages were only "vehicles of learning rather than learning itself" (*Mary Wortley Montagu*, p. 257). She followed Astell in considering true knowledge to consist in "knowing things, not words." With Lockean methodology and the practical intent of arriving at the truth through some degree of self-education, Astell taught her readers the processes of knowing: understanding, reasoning, examining, thinking, and judging.

The progressives differed among themselves on the question of how much exactly a gentlewoman should know. Alexander cautiously recommended that gentlewomen receive a less liberal education than gentlemen because "Nature seems not to have intended them for the more intense and severer studies" (I, 73). On the other hand, fully aware of her own capabilities, Wortley Montagu declared it "the highest injustice to be debarred the entertainment of my closet, and that the same studies which raise the character of a man, should hurt that of a woman" (Letter from Brescia, October 10, 1752, *Works*, IV, 168). Alone among both parties, de Genlis went to a surprising extreme; in *Tales of the Castle* she affirmed that the erudition which enlarged the faculties was worth more than the accomplishments or even qualities of the heart. Astell understood this erudition to be chiefly a knowledge of God; her younger and more secular friend Wortley Montagu interpreted it to mean "every branch of knowledge," with the qualification of Locke and Astell (and the eighteenth century in general) that it be according to one's "genius."

The next question was one of curriculum. Makin, Astell, Drake, Defoe, Richardson, Wortley Montagu, Knox, and Wollstonecraft first suggested the usual courses. These included the basics of English, reading, writing, and spelling; standard female subjects, such as history and geography; aids to housewifery such as arithmetic, accounts, economy; the polite languages, French and Italian; and genteel reading, as of the English classics. Drake displayed a strong nationalist feeling for English literature by recommending its drama, poetry, prose, satire, and essays. Many progressives variously suggested subjects that were strongly opposed by some of the conservatives. These included poetry, often regarded as too inflammatory for women; such masculine subjects as religion, philosophy, politics, logic, grammar, mathematics (perhaps under the influence of the Dissenters); solid sciences like astronomy and chemistry, and the classical languages of Greek and Latin (generally considered only the gentleman's prerogative). Like Fénelon, de Genlis also recommended legal education on property and estate laws so that gentlewomen could manage their own estates if male protection failed.

Astell, Murry, Wollstonecraft, and *Female Restoration* especially insisted on the importance of religious education for gentlewomen, with the significant condition that they understand the fundamentals of Christianity and therefore be Christians by conviction rather than irrational faith. Unlike the male conservatives, Locke recommended a true knowledge of God as the first necessity to the formation of a gentleman too.

The progressives were not, however, united in their approval of some of the more radical subjects. Astell condemned speculative truths, the knowing of many languages, historical details, logic, and rhetoric as leading to self-vanity and not God. Even feminists like de Genlis and Knox declared politics unsuitable for women, in sharp contrast to its enthusiastic advocates, Poulain de la Barre and *Female Restoration*.[37] There was one more field which the

---

[37] *Female Restoration* sometimes reads as if it were the work of an enterprising young feminist who looked into her great-grandmother's library and improved upon the ideas of Drake and Poulain de la Barre.

latter two advocated for women and on which most of the progressives and conservatives were silent: medicine. Recognizing women's ancient connection with the art of healing, the author of *Female Restoration* believed that her sex not only qualified her to practice medicine but also to invent new remedies. For this purpose, she prescribed a study of anatomy; her boldness is made obvious when one remembers that even botany was often condemned in the eighteenth century as involving a study of the sexual nature of plants. She also recommended the study of physics, "polity," jurisprudence, "natural equity," a knowledge of oneself, and of the principles of human conduct; and then, she added with her usual merry humor, her scholar may want to learn the more feminine subjects of history and geography. In short, as Defoe and Wortley Montagu also agreed, gentlewomen could tackle any learning gentlemen could (I, 35).

Just as the more cautious progressives were uneasy with women's encroaching on the so-called masculine subjects, there were also those who differed on the question of novel-reading as an intellectual pastime for women. Wortley Montagu was especially fond of novels. In her youth, she had eagerly swallowed the French romances and even Manley's scandalous *New Atalantis* (1709); in her old age, beginning from September 1749, her daughter, Lady Mary Bute, sent boxes of novels of all kinds, including "trash," to her retreat in Italy. Like Drake, Wortley Montagu encouraged her granddaughters to read plays, romances, and novels as both incidental learning and literary diversion, although with the proviso that their mother point out to them the absurdities in such fiction. Such reading, she insisted, was instrumental in soothing troubled minds and in constructively employing gentlewomen's many idle hours. Mr. Spectator agreed with the latter argument in his appraisal of the widow Leonora's library, which consisted of both romances and useful books—if well directed, Leonora could have been greatly improved, but, in any case, she was better occupied than the frivolous ladies.[38] The anonymous female author of *Elfrida, or Paternal Ambition* (1786) sensibly spoke out "in favor of novel reading that it is like all other modes of amusement, capable of use and abuse" (I, 222).

Astell did not agree. She regarded the reading of plays and romances as a sort of learning worse than the greatest ignorance because it only induced foolish behavior; both she and the Wollstonecraft of the 1780s condemned

---

[38] Addison, No. 37, Thursday, April 12, 1710, *Spectator*, I, 144-47.

the false views of human feelings (especially of the "dangerous" emotion of love) that they gave the impressionable young reader. But in her actual capacity as governess, the latter allowed the daughters of Lady Kingsborough to read novels, realizing that the mother's express interdiction only led to clandestine reading of the love stories, because the girls' affections were starved.[39] Thus, in spite of all the arguments against it, novel-reading too came to have its place in the intellectual curriculum prescribed by the progressives for gentlewomen.

Not too many of the progressives seemed concerned with the education of the daughters of the middle class, except for the staunchly feminist Drake and *Female Restoration*. The former believed it practical for the wives of English tradesmen to learn arithmetic and accounts so they could help their husbands in commerce, as the Dutch women did. The latter lamented that lower-middle-class girls had no leisure to think because they had to spend all their time in learning a trade or calling suitable to their sex and class.

Unlike the gentlewoman, then, the middle-class or labor-class girl was to be educated according to her earning capacity. This connection is especially seen in Catherine Cappe's outline of the curriculum of the Grey Coat Charity School for the years 1786 and 1787. Most of the subjects were those that would make labor-class girls into efficient servants: spinning, knitting, sewing, washing, milking, and general housework. But importantly, according to Cappe's plan, they were also taught to read and write, a benefit that was hotly debated even in the 1780s. In fact, one of the specific duties of Cappe and her benevolent co-workers, who took over the supervision of the Grey Coat School from the unscrupulous presiding master and mistress, was to inspect the pupils in these two fields, at least twice during their term of office. In an account written in 1785, Cappe justified the teaching of reading, at least, to the poor: "At this time of day it will hardly be urged an objection, that they are taught to read."[40] Although reading was regarded by many writers, both progressive and conservative, as a genteel accomplishment only for the rich, liberals like Cappe did not believe it was to be denied to the poor.

---

[39] Eleanor Flexner, *Mary Wollstonecraft; A Biography* (Baltimore: Penguin, 1972), p. 77. Flexner also records that Wollstonecraft was dismissed from service by Lady Kingsborough because the latter was jealous of her daughters' affection for their governess.

[40] *An Account of Two Charity Schools for the Education of Girls* (York: sold by Johnson, Hatchard, Mawman, et al., 1800), p. 97.

The criteria of sex and class affected every aspect of female education, including physical education, especially in the opinions expressed by male progressives. Yet, at face value, some of the men seem marvelously woman-oriented. In the *Tatler*, we see Steele attacking real or affected feebleness or debilitating softness in women (No. 248, Thursday, November 9, 1710) and even the conservative Thomas Day condemning false delicacy in gentlewomen as "vicious indolence and inactivity" (*Sandford and Merton*, p. 375). Locke recommended that except for certain concessions made to the preservation of beauty, girls should be bred up as hardily as boys, with bland food, loose clothing, and cold baths; further, they were to be accustomed to all types of weather and given plenty of fresh air and exercise (in *Some Thoughts Concerning Education*, 1693, and in "Letter to Mrs. Clarke, February, 1685"). Assuming that "savages" of both sexes were equal in mind and body, Alexander concluded that the enervated state of civilized gentlewomen was a "result of art" and not nature; sedentary life; low, abstemious diet; and exclusion from fresh air were the education and conditioning by which women were rendered feebler in mind and body than men.

The emphasis these men put on health and hardiness in the gentlewoman seems pleasantly feminist and liberal for the times until one remembers the patriarchal end they all envisioned. Like the male conservatives Rousseau and Kames, they believed that health in women was important only because healthy mothers made healthy babies, and healthy babies ensured the continuance of the father's all-important family name. Moreover, healthy women were regarded as useful women: according to Locke, they made better housewives ("Letter to Mrs. Clarke").

Among the progressive women, de Genlis ("Delphine" and "Pamela" in *Tales*) and *Female Restoration* agreed with conservatives like Chapone and Walker that their sex needed to exercise vigorously to render their bodies strong and active. The end which they envisioned was, presumably, woman's own physical well-being. Radical as usual, the author of *Female Restoration* boldly proposed that corporeal strength would render women strong enough even to undergo the fatigues of war and business, and, therefore, to lead active professional lives. With characteristic humor, she said of this new degree of strength: "It is sufficient, as I have no intention of conferring upon my Sex the honorable employment of Porters" (Preface, p. xi).

According to the seminal educationist Locke, the ideal of the well-rounded gentleman or gentlewoman was, however, neither the muscular porter nor the sedentary philosopher. In spite of his sexist bias regarding the reasons for female physical education, he radically influenced theories on the upbringing of children for all succeeding ages by reminding his own generation of Juvenal's famous correlation: "*Mens sana in corpore sano.*" If one were to be happy on earth, he insisted, both mind and body had to be cultivated. Believing as it did that the female intellect deserved such cultivation, progressive thought followed Locke on the question of the adequate development of the female body too. There were echoes of Locke's theory in the *Spectator* (Steele, No. 66, Wednesday, May 16, 1711), Sarah Fielding's *The Female Academy*, Duncombe's *Feminead*, and Wollstonecraft's *Thoughts on the Education of Daughters*. With the conventionally moral sternness of her earlier writings, Wollstonecraft further warned women that if the mind were left untutored in early youth, age would confine it to the body and sink it into sensuality. Only by sufficient attention to both her physical and intellectual development, therefore, could a gentlewoman be regarded as truly educating herself.

In spite of emphasis on intellectual development, if we are to believe the large number of critics, progressive and conservative alike, the most widespread system of education centered merely on the person. Like all moral theorists of the eighteenth century, the progressives exposed the abuses of this system. Thus, in the *Spectator* papers, Steele criticized this form of instruction as a systematic training in coquetry instead of good housewifery:

> When a girl is safely brought from her nurse, before she is capable of forming one simple notion of anything in life, she is delivered to the hands of a dancing master; and with a collar round her neck, the pretty wild thing is taught a fantastical gravity of behaviour, and forced to a particular way of holding up her head, heaving her breast, and moving her whole body; and all this under pain of never having a husband, if she steps, looks, or moves awry. This gives the young lady wonderful workings of imagination, what is to pass between her and this husband, that she is every moment told of, and for whom she seems to be educated.[41]

Furthermore, according to Defoe, a girl's youth, thereafter, was spent in learning stitching, sewing, and making baubles: "They are taught to read indeed, and perhaps to write their names or so, and that is the height of a woman's

---

[41] No. 66, Wednesday, May 16, 1711, *Spectator* (rpt. London: Jones, 1840), p. 96.

education" (*Essay upon Projects*, p. 144). Women's intellectual powers were left to nature, or worse, "warped and biased by fantastical instruction, dignified by the name of education" (Alexander, II, 55), while those of gentlemen were developed and expanded by a liberal system of education, either at home or in public schools[42] and at the university.

Almost all the major progressives—Makin, Poulain de la Barre, Astell, Defoe, Drake, Addison, Steele, de Genlis, Wortley Montagu, Alexander, Knox, and *Female Restoration*—realized that gentlewomen's frivolity, intellectual incapacity, even profligacy were due not only to circumstances but also to an overemphasis on this faulty system of education. First among the evils believed to warp the female mind was the undue attention paid to physical beauty. Moralists, therefore, both conservative like Chapone and progressive like Astell, Duncombe, de Genlis, and Knox, argued in favor of the cultivation of mental rather than personal beauty. They affirmed that the former was more attractive to a man of sense and also profited the gentlewoman herself, both in her moments of leisure and in declining age. It is important to remember that the progressives attacked the abuses of this system only; they did not insist on dispensing with it altogether. Thus, the more advanced progressives like Drake, Defoe, Wortley Montagu, and *Female Restoration* were realistic enough to accept the importance of physical beauty, both for itself and for the social advantages it offered. Their appreciation of female attractiveness was a part of their appreciation of all things female; it is not to be confused with the sexual approval of men like Fielding, who also celebrated the charms of their heroines.

As important as the realistic progressive assessment of female beauty was its assessment of female ugliness. In their own ways, various writers dealt with this subject. Knox patronizingly "consoled" plain-looking women that their "want of personal beauty [was] a frequent cause of virtue and happiness" for it led them to cultivate their minds and become more dutiful daughters, wives, and mothers (*Essays*, I, 162). The *Spectator* (in "Laetitia and Daphne, or the Art of Assisting Beauty")[43] and Scott, in *Agreeable Ugliness, or the Triumph of the Graces* (1754), went further—they vindicated the ugly sisters in stories from the Cinderella fairy-tale stereotype which associated wickedness and

---

[42] At least theoretically. In fact, public school and university education seem to have been rife with abuses too.

[43] Taken from the *Female Repertory* (Edinburgh: M'William, 1808), II,188–92.

cruelty with an ill-looking face. In both the essay and the novel, unlike in "Cinderella," the beautiful sister proves empty-headed and morally deficient, while the ugly sister shows that unattractiveness or physical deformity can coexist with a good heart, a good intellect, and virtuous principles, and, importantly, win the hand of the hero/prince. Scott clearly stated her aim in the dedication to her novel: "Ugliness, then, is the thesis of the novel, and the aim is to show that beauty of heart and mind is superior to physical beauty."[44]

After beauty came dress. The difference in thinking between the two schools of thought is dramatically emphasized in their attitude to dress: none of the major conservative English and French writers neglected to give their opinion on it; most of the progressives did. Aside from Locke's stress on loose, free clothing for children of both sexes for the purposes of health and growth, only Alexander, Knox, and Wollstonecraft touched on dress. Wollstonecraft simultaneously attempted to de-emphasize its importance in the adornment of the person and to vindicate the natural female shape by pointing out that "unnatural protuberances" caused distortion rather than a pleasing symmetry. The men veered toward the conservative line of thinking; Knox warned young gentlewomen against the slovenliness of literary ladies (No. CXLII, *Essays*, II), while Alexander, with his consistent mixture of feminism and sexism, followed Rousseau in describing a passion for dress as "natural to the sex" (I, 279).

As with dress, the cultivation of ornamental accomplishments such as music, drawing, dancing, and needlework was not a major issue with the progressives. Their concern with accomplishments was less for the purpose of entertaining a husband than as a source of personal diversion. With her customary piety, Astell allowed only religious music as providing rational entertainment. Wollstonecraft allowed music and painting as "fine arts . . . affording rational and delicate pleasure," but only if the person's inclination led her to them (p. 42). With the progressives' bias for intellectual cultivation, she added writing and the development of style under this head too. With his usual accent on gentility, Locke recommended dancing for children of both sexes to improve posture and to cure sheepishness of behavior. Wortley Montagu recommended needlework, believing it "as scandalous for a woman not to know how to use a needle, as for a man not to know how to use a

---

[44] Quoted in Walter Marion Crittendon, "The Life of Mrs. Sarah Scott—Novelist (1723-1795)," Diss. University of Pennsylvania 1932, p. 84.

sword" (*Mary Wortley Montagu*, p. 261). With similar conservatism, Samuel Johnson sweepingly declared needlework to be "one of the greatest felicities of female life," contributing to a woman's longevity [how?], amusement, and sanity (quoted in Wheeler, p. 323). Richardson, in *Pamela*, was alone among the progressives to allow cards as a genteel pastime for the upper-class woman. However, Pamela advocated cards as a necessary evil only after she herself was promoted from a servant girl to the wife of Squire B—; one remembers that among the conservatives too, only titled writers like Lord Halifax and Lady Pennington had permitted card-playing. Johnson, Alexander, and Wollstonecraft, on the other hand, steadfastly opposed the pastime as leading to the vice of gaming.

In spite of allowing gentlewomen some cultivation of the accomplishments, the progressives were divided in theory on its general usefulness. At one end of the spectrum, Alexander and Wollstonecraft condemned the disproportionate amount of time that was spent in learning what they saw as superficial skills, or, as the former put it, in "teaching the girl what the woman will relinquish" (I, 11). At the other end, de Genlis wholeheartedly encouraged gentlewomen to develop such skills and bitterly lamented that they could not be put to professional use.[45] In his socio-historical *Origin of the Distinction of the Ranks* (1779), John Millar approved of gentlewomen cultivating the elegant arts in opulent countries. He believed that the arts not only heightened a woman's attractions in the eyes of men but also introduced her more into public life and thereby adapted her to an intercourse with high society.

But the general emphasis of the progressives in their attitudes to the four main systems of education was on the welfare of gentlewomen themselves, rather than on their usefulness to men or on the figure they presented to the world. This emphasis on self was especially important in the fourth main system of education, namely of the heart or of the morals and conduct. From the beginning to the end of this period, from Astell's *Serious Proposal* to the anonymous *Female Restoration*, it was contended as an inalienable right that women had souls equal to men's in the sight of God and therefore owed duty to their Maker and to themselves rather than to man, as Rousseau and his

---

[45] The critics Josephine Kamm, in *Hope Deferred: Girls' Education in English History*, and Dorothy Gardiner, in *English Girlhood at School*, both attacked de Genlis for what they called her retrograde influence in encouraging the accomplishments, especially in boarding schools, where her works were often required texts. But the fault must have lain in the abuse of her advice, for she equally advocated a solidly intellectual education for gentlewomen, presumably with far less success.

disciples so arrogantly insisted. Astell recommended self-esteem through "Vertue," conscience, and right action, as the motivating force leading to happiness in heaven and on earth. She also added the corollary of self-responsibility—if women were downtrodden in her day, they themselves were to blame: We hide our faults and lack of ambition to be higher, she said, under the borrowed name of "Vertue"; we *choose* to be content with our servile lot out of "sloth" and "idleness" yet hypocritically call them "humility" and "modesty" (*Serious Proposal,* Part II, pp. 36–37). She pursued her point in *Some Reflections upon Marriage* (1700). In a metaphor almost never used for women at the time, she satirically advised women who loved their submission to glory in avoiding "that audacious attempt of soaring beyond their sphere!" and to continue to "Huswife [*sic*] or Play" (Smith, p. 99).[46] Wollstonecraft too believed in self-responsibility; if woman was weak and went astray, she herself and not the stars were to blame. The progressive emphasis, then, seems more honest than the conservative; it stressed conscientious action and ultimate moral accountability to oneself, rather than prudent circumspection and preservation of reputation in the eyes of the world.

This accountability to oneself was also seen in the patterns of behavior the progressives recommended to gentlewomen in their capacities as daughters, wives, and mothers. Unlike the conservatives, they upheld the rights rather than the duties of gentlewomen in their familial roles; wherever they acknowledged the necessity of duty, they pointed out its mutuality instead of one-sidedness. On the primary question of filial duty, Astell advised parents that kindness in education helped arouse affectionate gratitude in children and reminded them that to bring children into the world was less an obligation than to ensure that they lived happily and wisely in it. Likewise, her disciple Wortley Montagu reminded her own daughter that the maternal and filial affection between them arose from a rigid sense of duty. On the same principle, Wortley Montagu refused to mourn her own father's death in 1726 because he had neglected his duty of loving and educating his children (early rendered motherless): "*Au bout du compte,* I don't know why filial piety should

---

[46] Astell realized the extent of the effort necessary to budge oneself out of a comfortable rut. It was easier, she admitted, to follow the beaten track than to launch into the main ocean to make new discoveries. Her image of braving open seas is powerful and excitingly new, for conservatives in both eighteenth-century fiction and non-fiction preferred the image of woman as a small ship hugging the protective shore against sea gales and rocks.

exceed fatherly fondness. So much by way of consolation" (Letter to her sister, Lady Mar, *Mary Wortley Montagu*, p. 61).[47]

On the question of marriage as well, Wortley Montagu rejected parental authority in the choice of a partner. She herself eloped with Edward Wortley Montagu in 1712, when her father refused the match. In fiction too, one sees a woman of total piety like Clarissa actively rejecting her parents' choice for her, although she also actively suffers for it. In his novel, *The Fair Syrian* (1787), Bage offered a simplistic and rather unrealistic compromise on this question. The lovers in his subplot, namely the French Marquis and Aurelia, meekly obey their parents' ban on their marriage; as a reward, the author kindly kills off both parents after a suitable time-lapse, leaving the dutiful offspring with freedom of choice as well as large legacies.

Since authoritarian fathers and husbands could not be killed off in real life too, the progressives suggested more practical measures to cope with marriage and wifehood. Astell refuted her contemporary Halifax's high-handed advice to wives to bear all meekly, by suggesting a preventive measure for unhappiness in marriage: a better education would teach young women to avoid modern gallants and, consequently, marriage with unworthy men. Unlike the later preference for early marriages expressed in *A Vindication of the Rights of Woman* (1792), Wollstonecraft suggested a more cautious measure in *Thoughts on the Education of Daughters*: Girls should not be made to marry too young for they could not manage a household when scarcely out of childhood themselves and still incapable of thinking.[48] With her characteristic bluntness, she argued that women were born for other purposes than merely "to draw nutrition, propagate, and rot" (p. v). Both Defoe and Knox agreed that neither were gentlewomen meant to be stewards, housekeepers, cooks, laundresses, or slaves in their capacities as wives. But the overall view of marriage was not bleak: Defoe, Knox, Astell, Wortley Montagu, and d'Holbach

---

[47] Another well-known writer, Anna Seward, was not quite so intrepid in her dealings with her authoritarian and jealous father. At his bidding, she gave up her beloved poetry-writing, in her teens, for the more feminine pursuit of needlework. Her twentieth-century biographer, Margaret Ashmun, laments this early restraint, a common phenomenon in eighteenth-century society: "Ancestor worship, that oriental curse of occidental women, constrained her to yield obedience to a prosy, if amiable father" (*The Singing Swan; An Account of Anna Seward and her Acquaintance with Dr. Johnson, Boswell, Others of their Time*, New Haven: Yale University Press, 1931, p. 32).

[48] Alexander recorded the legal age of marriage for girls as twelve. His research led him to view marriage as a human rather than a divine institution.

asserted that marriages could lead to happiness if firmly based on reciprocal esteem, especially of the mind, rather than on mere physical attraction.

Significantly, the progressives stressed that neither wifehood nor motherhood was instinctive; women had to be intelligently trained to be good companions as well as good mothers. Wollstonecraft cautioned women that, as mothers, they must uniformly act from the principle of reason rather than from momentary bursts of impulse. Years ahead of her time, she saw maternal affection as resulting "quite as much from habit as instinct" (p. 3). Furthermore, the insistence of progressives like Astell, Wortley Montagu, and Wollstonecraft that maternal affection accompany parental instruction seems a significant indicator of their genuine commitment to the emotional well-being of their sex.

The classic progressive example of the mother as educator in the late eighteenth century was perhaps de Genlis's learned baronne d'Almane, who wrote several volumes for her daughter's edification. Ironically, we see the baroness spend her entire day supervising Adèle's education, to the total exclusion of any time for her husband, a glaring social error that de Genlis, in her obvious identification with the paragon-instructor, failed to see. But the baroness's dedication to teaching cannot be doubted; she falls in the same category as the matronly, intelligent Madame de Clemire of de Genlis's *Tales* and such highly capable governesses as Murry's Mentoria, and indeed of the real-life women who strove to educate their sex through their own writings.

But prescription was not enough, as both Astell and Wollstonecraft were well aware. Gentlewomen had to desire changes in themselves, regarding both the familial as well as the more personal virtues. For those who honestly sought change, the progressives often recommended the more androgynous virtues. *Female Restoration* demanded that gentlewomen not be brought up from the cradle in "effeminacy," for "good sense" was of no gender (p. 23). Just as it was unfair to label traits like cowardice and weakness in men effeminate, it was unjust to call courage, strength, and intellectual capacity in women masculine.

Other progressives attempted to modify certain supposedly feminine virtues so as to make them serve women better. Thus, Drake rejected absolute simplicity as undesirable; both sexes, she advised, needed to act with caution, circumspection, and even a certain degree of dissimulation. Likewise, Lambert recommended that female docility, although necessary, was not to be cultivated at the expense of judgement and understanding. In de Genlis's *Tales*, the abbé Fremont teaches fortitude to Pulcheria, the younger daughter: "It is not required that she [woman] should be a heroine but absolute pusillanimity is unpardonable" (I, 268). Wollstonecraft too wanted women to cultivate the virtues of gentleness, courteousness, benevolence, studiousness, civility, sincerity, and meekness of spirit, but as a result of good sense and resolution and not from indolence and timidity posing as good nature.

The progressives did not, however, entirely reject the so-called feminine virtues. Even Wollstonecraft admitted that she was "quite charmed when I see a sweet young creature, shrinking as it were from observation, and listening rather than talking" and found "humble softness of manners" in women rather "bewitching" (pp. 20, 31).[49] De Genlis too saw gentleness and modesty, the traditional traits prescribed her sex, as their chief ornament. As for the men, Defoe asked for softness, sweetness, peace, love, wit, and delight; Locke for compliance and obedience; Knox for delicacy, sweetness, sense, and sensibility; Alexander for delicacy, which he described as "that unaffected timidity and shyness of manners," and, more importantly, for chastity (II, 1).

Although himself a man, Richardson was largely instrumental in redefining the patriarchal notion of chastity from the female point of view. His *Pamela* has often been cited as the classic eighteenth-century example of the equation of chastity with a purely technical virginity. But, innocently or otherwise, Pamela is shown as turning this patriarchal censor to her own benefit; by allowing Squire B— almost every sexual license but actual intercourse, the young servant girl ensures matrimony and wealth for herself instead of dishonorable dismissal and poverty.

In his next novel, *Clarissa*, Richardson developed a feminist and more organic notion of chastity, by making it depend on his heroine's mental and emotional rather than sexual purity. On the surface, however, the story reads like a sadistic male fantasy—through imprisonment, rape, and emotional degradation, the intelligent, beautiful, and sensitive heroine is completely trapped in the bonds of a misogynous, "loveless" rake. But the end of the novel is not tragic in the physical fact of Clarissa's death; rather, it is poetically just in the toll it takes on the seducer's mind and life. To Lovelace's amazement and

---

[49] One remembers with amusement Wollstonecraft as she was perceived by Godwin at their first meeting in 1792, at the radical publisher Joseph Johnson's. Godwin had come to hear the famous Thomas Paine; instead, he heard Wollstonecraft determinedly talk all evening, much in the nature of a *femme savante* and much to his own frustration.

chagrin, he finds he cannot erase in Clarissa's behavior the effects of a virtuous education; the rape of her body cannot effect a corresponding defilement of her mind. Therefore, he himself dies in a duel, fully conscious that his death is an expiation for his inhuman treatment of a virtuous woman. Misunderstanding the significance of Clarissa's strength, Robert P. Utter and Gwendolyn B. Needham, in *Pamela's Daughters*, point out that prior to 1748 (the year of *Clarissa's* publication) no heroine had died for the loss of her virginity.[50] However, the converse is also worth noting, that neither had a rake died before (at least in male-oriented literature) for his time-honored "right" to female seduction.

Seduction and passion were accepted by eighteenth-century society as natural to dissolute gentlemen. It has been seen in Chapter 1 that the conservatives saw passion as belonging to women too, although admittedly the examples they chose were from the lower classes, the dissolute aristocracy, or from gentlewomen with overexercised sensibilities. With a surprising degree of prudery (and unlike the radicals of the 1790s), the progressives in general anticipated the Victorians in professing that virtuous gentlewomen were either totally without passion or only reluctantly submitted to it. Drake declared outright that she felt her sex was not subject by nature to the passions; even Wollstonecraft, who in a few years was to shock England with her ideas on free love, asserted in her earliest work that it was quite sufficient for women to receive caresses but not to give them. Among the men, Defoe admitted to believing that women sometimes succumbed to sexual desires too and went astray but gallantly qualified his statement: "Yet I think, verily, custom, which we call modesty, has so far the ascendant over the sex that solicitation always goes before it" (p. 147). Woty and d'Holbach, on the other hand, lay all the blame on their own sex for dishonestly leading women to sexual folly and a consequent loss of reputation.

Aside from sexual passion, there were other qualities gentlewomen were warned to shun. Murry advised her pupils to avoid ignorance, prejudice, fear, superstition, envy, and everything that made them deviate from the path of duty. With lively female chauvinism, Drake presented a portrait gallery of beaux, bullies, pedants, sottish squires, and so on; her intention was to show that certain undesirable traits, traditionally attributed to women, were found in men too, such as vanity, impertinence, dissimulation, envy, levity, inconstancy, and intemperate passion.

---

[50] *Pamela's Daughters* (New York: Macmillan, 1936), p. 268.

Qualities of the heart, therefore, whether good or bad, seemed to the progressives to belong equally to both sexes. It became increasingly clear to them that the state of the mind and body in adults of both sexes was the product of nurture not nature. Feminists were fully aware of the significant role education could play in effecting changes for women, but they were also aware, if perhaps with less perspective, of the odds against which they were fighting. The eighteenth century was, by and large, a conservative century, especially before its final politically turbulent decade; as in all conservative societies, the politically powerless sections of the community were heavily repressed and displayed the problems and effects of that repression. An understanding of the situation and its solution, on the part of the progressives, did not guarantee any actual changes (and indeed, on some issues in the eighteenth century, no one was very enlightened), but it did prepare the ground for a future amelioration of the status of gentlewomen in English society.

## IV. Professionalism

The progressives were no doubt aware that the changes they envisioned in female education were far from realization in their time. But so long as projects and protests were freely allowed, they boldly expressed their opinions on the rights of women. They saw a better education for gentlewomen as leading not only to self-fulfillment but also to independence, whether in an unpaid or paid professional situation. The married and the single state continued to be the main unpaid professions considered; the fallen state was a way of life that could belong to either category. Existing paid professions were few and ill-remunerated, but projected professions seemed excitingly bold and often totally visionary.

As already seen in Section III, feminists from Astell to Wollstonecraft cautioned gentlewomen to marry wisely, since later repentance could prove bitter and often futile. Astell was also ahead of her time in realizing the economic basis of marriage: she understood that it was sometimes necessity rather than reason that kept women trapped in unhappy marriages.[51] In her novel *The Adventures of David Simple* (1744), Sarah Fielding was perhaps the first feminist to call such marriages a form of legal prostitution, an expression also used

---

[51] The conservative Chapone echoed this insight in "The Story of Fidelia," in her *Miscellanies in Prose and Verse* (1775).

by Chapone and later by Wollstonecraft. A few other progressives were also ahead of their time in not upholding the sanctity of unhappy marriages; instead, they suggested different measures of self-deliverance from undeserving husbands.

Acting on the principle that wives mistreated to the point of madness had a right to separate from their husbands,[52] Wortley Montagu and Wollstonecraft actually rescued their respective sisters, Lady Mar and Eliza Bishop, from their brutal husbands.[53] D'Holbach went further, at least in theory; he advocated not just separation but legal divorce. The radical nature of his plea is made clear when one remembers that at this time a married woman had almost no legal rights, not even to her own earnings, or, without a marriage settlement, to inherited property; the moment she married, Alexander pointed out, "her political existence is annihilated" (II, 486). In his Appendix, nevertheless, Alexander tried to educate women about their legal status in marriage. He exposed the ironic truism that only a widow with an independent fortune "can be called free"; otherwise, men, in their capacity as fathers and husbands, had a perpetual guardianship over women and their money (II, 505).

But guardianship did not always ensure protection. Some of the progressives, therefore, were particularly sensitive to the needs and feelings of single women, as the patriarchal-minded conservatives, who found such women an undesirable burden to a man's immediate family, seldom were. Astell and Wollstonecraft were especially sympathetic to the condition of the single woman of good family, fallen into financial decay: she was often indelicately forced into an undesirable marriage, either to escape the mocking title of "old maid," or, worse still, to obtain a means of economic support. One of the specific intentions of Astell's seminary was to provide a home for such unprotected gentlewomen, giving them both security and a feeling of their own usefulness to society. The possession of financial security, however, entirely changed the picture for single women. Like two conservatives of the next generation, namely, Chapone and Fordyce, Astell believed that the monied single gentlewoman could lead a useful existence on her own, for her very freedom from family life allowed her to be beneficial in the larger social sphere.

---

[52] Chapone advocated this measure too.

[53] Alexander noted that, according to European laws, a mother was not regarded as the guardian of her children, nor was she endowed with any authoritative power over them. Eliza Bishop therefore lost the right to her baby girl (who died the following year); she never forgave her sister for the loss.

*Female Restoration* lamented that gentlewomen were allowed a social but not a political existence. The anonymous author argued that it was because of their legally inferior status, especially their debarment from the two grand instruments of political control, namely, wealth and power, that gentlewomen made use of the more devious and private methods of rhetoric and caresses. She realized that this strategy often failed, sometimes resulting in seduction without marriage. Progressives like Defoe, Woty, and d'Holbach sympathized with the condition of the fallen woman; others, like Astell, ignored it altogether.

Only Cappe pleaded earnestly for sympathy for the seduced woman, especially of the servant class. Her account dated June 3, 1786, is worth quoting for its feminist assessment of the consequent personal and economic helplessness of such women:

Will it be said, that on complaint being made to a Magistrate, redress may be obtained for this as for any other offence? Let it be remembered, that independently of the general disadvantages under which oppression must always labour when opposed to power; that these are cases of such delicacy, that the very appeal to a Court of Judicature, would be ruinous to the character and future prospects of the unfortunate girl, who should be driven to make it; for, admitting the guilt of the Master, and the innocence of the Girl to be fully proved (a thing in itself almost impossible), yet would not something of disgrace still attach to her? What decent family would hazard taking as a servant, one who has been thus circumstanced? (p.111)

The answer was often unwilling prostitution (a fate the wily Pamela escapes), a subject of concern, surprisingly, for more of the conservatives than the progressives.

Familial protection, even in indigence, seems to have made some difference to the impoverished gentlewoman, even though the work available to her was insignificant and often ill-paid. Thus, we see the eponymous heroine Elfrida bravely supporting both herself and her family by turning her ornamental education to use: she cuts and paints watch cases and ribbons, draws valentines with elegant devices, and supplies a shop with artificial flowers. But although independence is as important to her as to the progressive theorists in general, she chooses to benefit by her ornamental rather than her learned education, perhaps because only the former would help her salvage her gentility with the utmost privacy.

The other paid professions were not closet-jobs, and invariably involved a loss of caste. As in Chapter 1, one is forced to look at the lives of some of the writers themselves for information on the subject. Wollstonecraft worked as a companion to a Mrs. Dawson, as a governess to the Kingsborough girls in Ireland (at forty pounds a year), and as a teacher and administrator in her own school at Newington Green from 1783–86. She wrote with bitterness about the humility of working in these positions, all of which included not just hard work and low pay, but a lonely life of anguished sensibility, further soured by the insolence of superiors.

Wollstonecraft's experienced assessment of the requirements of such professions appears more realistic than Astell's idealistic one. With the sanguinity of her contemporary, Locke, Astell demanded that the teachers of the religious boarders in her projected seminary be good (Anglican) Christians, who have "lived much," yet are of "irreproachable lives, of a consummate Prudence, sincere Piety, unaffected Gravity," clear comprehensive understandings, regular affections, controlled passions; possessing a full knowledge of human nature and of its defects and means of correction, total goodness, reasonable minds, authoritative ability, the best breeding, the best nature; and also that they be charming and happy in themselves, and agreeably beneficial to all (*Serious Proposal*, Part I, pp. 60–63). Then, as in ensuing ages, low pay and the best credentials seem to have often been the lot of the working woman.

A more private employment for indigent learned women was writing, where gentility could be protected by anonymity. But true gentlewomen did not write for remuneration. Secure in her comfortable private fortune, Wortley Montagu attacked the professional nature of writers like her cousins, Sarah and Henry Fielding: "The greatest virtue, justice, and the most distinguished prerogative of mankind, writing, when duly executed, do honour to human nature; but when degenerated into trades, are the most contemptible ways of getting bread" (Louvere, June 23, 1754, *Works*, IV, 268). "Contemptible" but tempting in the face of poverty and with dependents to support; Wollstonecraft used the ten guineas she earned for her first work from the kindly, encouraging publisher, Joseph Johnson,[54] to send her friend Fanny Blood's parents, whom she supported, to their son George in Ireland.

---

[54] Flexner attributes Wollstonecraft's consequent career as an important writer rather than a drudging hack to Johnson. He encouraged the poorer public to read, by printing in cheap formats, and talented, impoverished progressive authors to write, by buying their manuscripts, even if he did not always publish them. He lived in St. Paul's Churchyard from 1770 to his death in 1809.

Besides the pursuits outlined above, no other professions seem to have been available to gentlewomen. The progressives wanted more fields to open to women. Alexander, d'Holbach, and Gibbon pointed out the irony involved in allowing an Englishwoman to rule the country but to occupy no position in the government. Alexander further recorded that the law denied women positions in the church, the state, the senate, and the army, and even in middle-class commercial enterprises. Children of their time, some of the progressives concurred with these laws—Astell and "Sophia" (of the *Sophia Pamphlets*) agreed that women had no right to church ministry, Astell and Wortley Montagu that they had no business in government. But Poulain de la Barre and *Female Restoration* were not quite so meek. They boldly asserted that "women are suited for all kinds of vocations whatever," including the professional fields that patriarchal society denied them, namely, religion, law, government, politics, the army, business, and medicine (*Female Restoration*, p. 46). Their assessment of the phenomenon of female professionalism was both accurate and insightful—only the novelty of seeing women in all professions would at first seem strange, not the change itself. Given time to get over their initial awkwardness, women would begin to show themselves proficient in all these new fields.

In her tale of "Leonora," included in *A Journey through Every Stage of Life* (1754), Sarah Scott gave a rare fictional instance of the ability of determined women to make a living. Confronted with poverty, in a world prejudiced enough to deny women occupation even as a means of subsistence, Leonora supports herself, her cousin, and her old nurse by dressing up in male attire and working in a man's world. Her nurse says of her: "She was the only woman I have ever met with, who endeavoured to conquer the Disadvantages our Sex labour under, and who proved that Custom, not Nature, inflicts that Dependence in which we live" (quoted in Crittendon, p. 85).

Dependence was, of course, an upper-class prerogative; lower-class women were expected to toil for a living. With their genuine concern for the welfare of their sex, Drake and *Female Restoration* wrote on the working middle-class woman too. The former, especially, recommended that English tradesmen's wives help their husbands in their commerce, as the French and Dutch women did. This would not only free the lusty men who now worked in shops for the army or for jobs where physical strength was required, it would also prevent the ruin of families when the husband or father died because the wives and daughters would know how to carry on the business.

With regard to job conditions for the poor, Catherine Cappe put forward two options. One, the girls could be trained in schools to be efficient, honest, industrious servants. Concerning the Grey Coat School in particular, she further suggested that its benevolent supervisors place the pupils in good homes and make sure that they were not physically abused or sexually molested. Her second proposal was to train girls to teach in schools for the poor. She was aware of both the difficulty and the necessity of finding a proper mistress for the Spinning School and the Grey Coat School she helped supervise; she also knew that the orderly conduct, industry, and the improvement of the pupils would greatly depend on their instructor's good sense, firmness, self-command, forbearance, and kindness of disposition. Such kindly instruction and affectionate interest in the welfare of the female pupil seem to have been the concern of most of the progressives, from Astell, who wrote only for the upper classes (although she opened a school for the poor), to Cappe, who wrote and diligently worked only for the poor.

Until higher education and professionalism became actual possibilities for gentlewomen, the only answer seemed to be for them to educate themselves and each other. In the absence of public approval or adequate institutional instruction, gentlewomen could still read each other's works, whether or not in agreement, thereby forming a sort of "correspondence-course" floating university among themselves. It is clear that the suggested improvements of the progressives were heard and remembered, even if not actually implemented, in the course of the eighteenth century. For instance, Astell's project of an academy filtered down through the works of Defoe, Richardson, and Wortley Montagu to Clara Reeve towards the end of the century, finally materializing in 1848 as Queen's College for women. The progressives had dreams, and the consciousness of the eighteenth century regarding female status was imperceptibly raised through their works. That was enough, for the times. Makin had rightly pointed out as early as 1673: "To ask too much is the way to be denied all" (quoted in Reynolds, p. 281).

# CHAPTER 3

# The Radical Tradition, 1788–1799

"Man is born free, and yet we see him everywhere in chains."

Rousseau, *The Social Contract*, 1762

"And to what purpose did she rally all her energy?—Was not the world a vast prison, and women born slaves?"

Wollstonecraft, *The Wrongs of Woman, or Maria*, 1798

"Can man be free, if woman be a slave?"

Shelley, "The Revolt of Islam," 1818

## I. Political and Intellectual Background

Influenced by the political turmoil in both England and France from the years 1788 to 1799, the controversy about female education in England came to a head in the last decade of the eighteenth century. Like two of the major French feminists, the marquis de Condorcet (1743–94) and Olympe de Gouges (1748–93), the four major English feminists of the 1790s, namely, Catherine Macaulay Graham (1731–91), Mary Wollstonecraft (1759–97), Mary Robinson (1758–1800), and Mary Hays (1759 or '60–1843), all published their most important works on women's education and rights during this twelve-year period. Except for Macaulay Graham, who died in 1791, the Englishwomen wrote with a full awareness of each other's works. There is a steady ideological development from Macaulay Graham's polemic, *Letters on Education;[sic] With Observations on Religious and Metaphysical Subjects* (1790), to Mary Robinson's *Thoughts on the Condition of Women, and on the Injustice of Mental Subordination* (1799), just as there is a clear connection between the heroines in didactic fiction, from Wollstonecraft's Mary (*Mary, A Fiction*, 1788) to Hays's Mary (*The Victim of Prejudice*, 1799).

In many ways, Mary Wollstonecraft represented the radicals as the champion of the rights of women. Like the progressives before her, she believed that women's status could be improved only through a rational education; in fact, her ideas seem to have developed in a direct line from those of her progressive foremother, Mary Astell. And just as the progressives had struggled ideologically against the conservatives in the course of the eighteenth century, Wollstonecraft and her radical peers had to battle with their reactionary counterparts in the 1790s.

The educational controversy reached two peaks: from 1788 to 1793, under the influence of the political events taking place at home and in France, and from 1797 to 1799, as a result of Wollstonecraft's untimely death by septicemia in 1797, a few days after childbirth. In spite of the burst of energy in the last years of the decade, by the end of 1799, radical fervor was reaching an end. The major English and French feminists, Wollstonecraft, Macaulay Graham, Condorcet were dead and de Gouges beheaded; Robinson was dying; except for Hays, the surviving English radicals were turning away from the feminist struggle, disillusioned with the increasing socio-political repression of the times.

The year 1799 also saw the demise of the *Analytical Review*, the radical periodical started in 1788 by the publisher Joseph Johnson. During its twelve-year life span, the *Analytical* loyally supported feminism (especially in relation to the much-maligned Wollstonecraft), the new philosophy,[1] and English revolutionism. Johnson's bookshop in St. Paul's Churchyard, London, became the meeting place for diverse political liberals in the 1790s, from extremists like Thomas Paine (the American revolutionary cohort of English radicals),

---

[1] This was a new system of ethics, propagated by radicals like Godwin, Holcroft, Wollstonecraft, and Hays. They believed in the preeminence of Reason, in individual rights over social duties, as also in human perfectibility, free love, and self-sufficiency (sometimes to the point of atheism).

William Godwin, and Helen Maria Williams, to moderates like Elizabeth Inchbald and Amelia Alderson (later Opie).

A definition of terms is perhaps necessary at this point. In this chapter, the term "radical" is applied to writers of the 1790s who, following the progressive tradition, recommended a rational education for women as the first step towards redressing their social and familial wrongs. Although their main interest was in the education of gentlewomen, they improved on their forebears by showing a significant concern with the education of middle- and lower-class women also—probably because they themselves were upper middle class or borderline gentility. However, their commitment to improving female education is not to be confused with radicalism in politics, ethics, or even feminism: all the English radicals were not necessarily revolutionary democrats, new philosophers, or militant feminists, although the major theorists, Wollstonecraft, Hays, Macaulay Graham, and Robinson, were all three.

Many of the radicals were, in fact, only moderate feminists, as, for instance, the actress, novelist, and dramatist, Elizabeth Inchbald; the novelist and poet, Amelia Alderson; the physician, Erasmus Darwin; the philanthropist, Sarah Trimmer; and the theorists, Priscilla Wakefield, Clara Reeve, and the Anglo-Irish daughter and father team, Maria and Richard Lovell Edgeworth. Some, like Elizabeth Hamilton, were feminist in their views on women's education but reactionary in their politics; some, like the French baroness, Anne Louise Germaine de Staël[2] and the English poet and novelist, Charlotte Smith, were revolutionary in their politics but lukewarm in their feminism. All the English writers were influenced by the educational tradition that stretched from Astell to Wollstonecraft; surprisingly, however, none mentioned the former writer although many acknowledged the latter in their works. Personal association with Wollstonecraft was another matter. In the latter part of the decade, Hays loyally supported her friend, in spite of the moral opprobrium society attached to her name; Inchbald and some others prudishly gave up her acquaintance.

---

[2] Ellen Moers describes de Staël as very much a presence in the "great decade of English feminism, the 1790s" and also as a woman who impressed herself on all the important public events of her time—political, revolutionary, and literary (*Literary Women*, New York: Doubleday, 1977, pp. 151, 176). Yet in some of her works of this decade, unlike those of the next, de Staël acknowledged women to be inferior to men, as creatures made primarily for love, an assertion which alienated Wollstonecraft from her.

Aside from the feminism of Wollstonecraft, three important political movements influenced radical theories in the early 1790s. All three movements were for human rights of one kind or another, led, specifically, by slave-trade abolitionists in England, by Dissenters, and by the lower classes in France. The first two met with reverses early in the decade. William Wilberforce's bill for the abolition of the slave trade was defeated in 1788, giving added significance to the equation of women with slaves in the works of such sympathizers as Hays, Robinson, Inchbald, Smith, and the Bristol milkwoman-poet, Anna Yearsley.[3]

The defeat of the Dissenters' bill for the repeal of the Test and Corporation Acts in 1790 added impetus to an ongoing religious and political controversy in which radicals like Macaulay Graham, Hays, and Helen Maria Williams earnestly participated. (A century earlier, Astell too had taken part in the religious and political controversies of her period.) The sensitivity of major writers to the Anglican oppression of religious minorities stemmed either from their own Dissenting backgrounds or those of their philosophical mentors. Their sensitivity to women's oppression, however, reflected Dissenting attitudes to "mankind," not necessarily to women. Hays was a Rational Dissenter; Inchbald, a Roman Catholic (a minority); Hamilton, a Presbyterian; Wakefield, a Quaker; Alderson, a Unitarian (who later turned Quaker); and William Godwin, a Dissenting minister who turned atheist (under the influence of Thomas Holcroft). Macaulay Graham, Williams, and Wollstonecraft, for their part, applied to women the precepts they had learned from well-known Dissenting clergymen like Andrew Kippis, Joseph Priestley, and Richard Price. In her biography of Hays, Gina Luria points out that in the mid and late 1790s, the equation of Anglicanism with patriotism had led many religious Dissenters to be branded as Jacobin traitors desiring to undermine the government.[4] As such, the Dissenting sympathies of Wollstonecraft, Williams, Macaulay Graham, and Hays, added to their radical extremism in education, their feminism, and their revolutionary politics, did nothing to better their reputation in society.

---

[3]  Among the radicals, only Clara Reeve supported the slave trade. Seemingly giving in to the pressure of the times, she turned from a political liberal, in her *School for Widows: A Novel* (1791), to a classist, racist political reactionary, in her *Plans of Education* (1792).

[4]  "Mary Hays: A Critical Biography," Diss. New York University 1972 p. 99.

The term "Jacobin" was, however, a misnomer, deliberately applied by the reactionaries to the new philosophers or "levellers" who supported the democratic ideals of the French Revolution. In actual fact, the English democrats were closer in their philosophy to the moderation of the Girondins than to the anarchism of the Jacobins. But the reactionary periodical, *The Anti-Jacobin Review and Magazine*, comprehensively defined Jacobin as "whoever is the enemy of Christianity and natural religion, of monarchy, of order, subordination, property, and justice."[5] Radical feminists like Wollstonecraft and Hays, who sought to upset the existing religious, political, social, and familial hierarchy that subordinated woman to man, were naturally included under this head. But if these writers were not Jacobin, neither were the French Jacobins themselves (and Napoleon after them) feminist; the declaration of the rights of man, made by Lafayette on July 11, 1789, did not include the rights of woman.[6]

De Gouges and Condorcet in France and Wollstonecraft and others in England therefore attempted to broaden the generic term "man," so narrowly defined by the French revolutionary leaders, to include the other half of the human species. Not content with merely exposing the wrongs of women, they began now to demand their rights. De Gouges went so far as to write up her own *Déclaration des droits de la femme et de la citoyenne* (1791) in which she applied the seventeen original articles on the rights of man to her own sex. Like man, woman was a fundamentally free being, she declared, possessing "les droits naturels et imprescriptibles . . . de la liberté, la propriété, la sureté, et sur-tout la résistance ã l'oppression" (article II, p. 7).

De Gouges cannily argued that women ought to have equal political rights with men since they were equally subjected to the guillotine; Wollstonecraft posited that women ought to have civic rights because they fulfilled their duties as citizens in the private roles of daughter, wife, and mother, just as men fulfilled their public duties in the world outside the home. Both Wollstonecraft and de Gouges agreed with Condorcet that the government could improve conditions for women by first improving their education. As it was, the sole rights granted Frenchwomen by the revolutionary leaders were familial rather than educational: in 1792, they were freed from the authority

---

[5] Vol. I, August 1798, quoted by Mitzi Myers in "Aspects of William Godwin's Reputation in the 1790s," Diss. Rice University 1969, p. 223.

[6] In *Du contrat social* (1762), Rousseau had awarded all citizens the same political rights of liberty and equality.

of tyrannical parents and also given the right to divorce. Although French-women were not accorded any of the original rights of man, the significance of this particular piece of legislation is not to be underrated either, since the independence of women rested almost entirely on their marital status.

Feminist radicals in England, who often compared the unhappily married woman to the slave or the prostitute, applauded the marital rights granted their French sisters. Their reactionary opponents, however, viewed these rights with alarm, as a threat to the existing social and familial hierarchy. They pointed to the deviant lives of some of the major radicals as proof of the inevitable demoralization that befell Englishwomen who acted on French principles. Had not Macaulay Graham, at the mature age of forty-seven, married a man twenty-six years her junior; Robinson become for a while the mistress of the Prince of Wales (later, George IV); Hays made sexual and marital overtures (unsuccessfully) to her male friends; and Wollstonecraft and Williams (like de Staël) openly lived with their lovers? Of course, what the reaction refused to see was that except for the seduced Robinson, the above-named women were acting on a belief in the sacredness of love rather than out of sexual promiscuity.

These radicals were all well aware that the freedom of their lives took its toll on the effects of their sound educational precepts, yet they also understood that pioneers must often suffer for the novelty of their principles. Accordingly, the heroine of Hays's semi-autobiographical novel, *The Memoirs of Emma Courtney*, writes to her adopted son: "Those who have the courage to act upon advanced principles, must be content to suffer moral martyrdom."[7] Nevertheless, Emma also asserts that the true dignity and virtue of the human mind consists in being free rather than fettered by the chains of prejudice and that, in a more perfect future state, such early moralists would be applauded by society for their lessons to humanity.

As with the progressives and the conservatives, such didacticism played a very important part in the educational works of the radicals. Since the lives and principles of major writers like Hays were often closely related, their fictional works sometimes tended to be autobiographical, with the explicit intention of reminding their readers of the wrongs of women. In *A Room of One's Own*, Virginia Woolf declared that "it is fatal to her artistry for a woman to lay the least stress on any grievance; to plead even with justice any

_______________________________

[7] *Emma Courtney* (1796; rpt. New York: Garland, 1974), II, 86.

cause; in any way speak consciously as a woman."[8] But she was applying a twentieth-century concept to earlier women's literature. The eighteenth century believed it perfectly legitimate, even imperative, for literature to teach, so long as it combined entertainment with instruction. The overt didacticism of most of the radicals led their works to be intentionally topical; they deliberately manipulated the written word to disseminate feminist and philosophical messages among the reading public. Fortunately for them, because of the increasing literacy among upper- and middle-class women in the course of their century, the radicals could be reasonably sure that a significant part of their audience would be female.

Since they were able to assume a larger female audience than that of their progressive predecessors, these writers felt free to divert their energies to matters of literary style too. They used different ones for non-fictional and fictional literature. The major stylistic concern of theorists like Wollstonecraft (who wrote hurriedly, in spite of her good intentions), Macaulay Graham, Maria Edgeworth, and Mary Ann Radcliffe[9] was to convey their message in as clear a language as possible. Hence, their prose attempted to be both precise and energetic, deliberately avoiding the euphemistic and metaphorical fogginess used by conservatives like Fordyce to conceal their patriarchal intent. Hamilton and Wollstonecraft prescribed the same care to other writers that they desired in their own productions: women who took their work seriously were to regard good writing as a duty, to be performed with the same conscientiousness as their gender-related tasks. As with some of the progressives, Hamilton's and Wollstonecraft's first attack was on the self-deprecating preface, a convention that so-called modesty demanded from women writers. In the preface to her *Letters of a Hindoo [sic] Rajah; Written Previous to, and During the Period of his Residence in England* (1796), a fictitious translation styled on Montesquieu's *Lettres persanes* (1721), Hamilton declaimed against the female tradition of excusing poor artistry by humbly pleading ignorance. Using a similar argument, but with greater bluntness, Wollstonecraft admonished Hays to change the apologetic preface to her *Letters and Essays, Moral and Miscellaneous* (1793):

---

[8] *A Room of One's Own* (1929; rpt. New York: Harcourt, Brace, and World, 1957), p. 108.

[9] Mary Ann Radcliffe published her *Memoirs* in 1810; these included her earlier feminist tract, *The Female Advocate* (1799). To avoid confusing her with the popular gothic novelist, Ann Ward Radcliffe, all future references to both writers will be by their full names.

Disadvantages of education etc. ought, in my opinion, never to be pleaded with the public in excuse for defects of any importance, because if the writer has not sufficient strength of mind to overcome the common difficulties which lie in his way, nature seems to command him, with a very audible voice, to leave the task of instructing others to those who can. This kind of vain humility has ever disgusted me—and I should say to an author, who humbly sued for forbearance, 'if you have not a tolerably good opinion of your own production, why intrude it on the public? We have plenty of bad books already that have just gasped for breath and died.'[10]

Like Wollstonecraft, the female editors of the *Lady's Monthly Museum, or Repository of Amusement and Instruction*, a periodical started in July 1798, were concerned with improving women's self-confidence and the quality of their writing. Well aware of the often-genuine diffidence of women conditioned from birth to believe in their own inferiority, these editors urged shy but respectable female writers to submit articles to them, promising to correct minor stylistic errors. The anonymous reviewer of Priscilla Wakefield's *Leisure Hours* (3rd edition, 1798) recommended the work to beginners as a model of good style, worthy of emulation for its vigor, correctness, ease, expressiveness, conciseness, flowing eloquence, simplicity without vulgarity, and elegance without prudery (Nov. 1, 1798, 402). In a more comprehensive attempt to encourage as well as celebrate female authors, Robinson added a long list of well-known fiction and non-fiction writers to the end of her *Thoughts on the Condition of Women*.

When it came to their own fiction, the styles of most radical writers generally differed from those of their non-fiction. Although the radical emphasis on rationality made clarity and precision important in polemical tracts, the fiction of writers like Smith and Robinson succumbed to the maudlin sentimentality of novels of sensibility. Other novelists such as Hays and Eliza Fenwick drew on the inflated emotionalism but better-controlled artistry of pre-romantic novels like *La Nouvelle Héloïse* and *Werther*, to slightly better effect. In spite of her concern with adequate expression, even Wollstonecraft's prose had its defects; it combined patches of fine writing with lamentable stylistic weaknesses.

---

[10] Wollstonecraft's letter is dated "Store Street, November 20, 1792," and is quoted in *The Love-Letters of Mary Hays (1779–1780)*, ed. A. F. Wedd (London: Methuen, 1925), pp. 224–25.

If the styles of many of the fiction writers left much to be desired, it was because a percentage of them were upper middle class, whose women had hitherto been proscribed intensive learning, unless they were destined to be teachers and assistants in schools. What is surprising, however, is that in their educational works, many of the writers concentrated largely on gentlewomen, even if they paid greater attention to the lower classes than had ever been done before. Yet in spite of theoretical class-related proscription and prescription, in real life these writers shared a limitation with their better-born peers: not a dearth of literary talent but a lack of formal education. Their consequent collective awareness of the reasons for their own professional inadequacies, added to what Woolf would have called their "autobiographical impulse," must have contributed to their determination that others of their sex, the younger generation of the upper classes in particular, should receive a worthwhile education that would teach them to be not just elegant dilettantes but rational human beings.

## II. Works, Theories, Places of Education

According to the baronne de Staël, the scope of literature included "everything that involves the exercise of thought in writing, except for the physical sciences."[11] In the 1790s in particular, literature was used as a political, philosophical, and educational tool in England. The radicals made no secret of the fact that their main purpose in writing was to impress their own ideas on the minds of their readers. The times also were on their side: It was a decade for polemical writing in both fiction and non-fiction; as already seen, even publishers and periodicals sometimes took sides in the educational controversy.

Pope's adage that "whatever is, is right" was finally demolished by a series of non-fictional educational works on the particular wrongs of women, all of which suggested the means of ameliorating these conditions. Two major treatises on the subject, Macaulay Graham's *Letters on Education: With Observations on Religious and Metaphysical Subjects* (1790) and its ideological successor, Wollstonecraft's *A Vindication of the Rights of Woman: With Strictures on Political and Moral Subjects* (1792), were both written at the beginning of

---

[11] Morroe Berger, *Madame de Staël on Politics, Literature, and National Character* (New York: Doubleday, 1965), p. 61.

this decade. There was some dearth of feminist polemics from late in 1792 to 1795, possibly because of the royal proclamation of 1792 against seditious writing[12] and Wollstonecraft's residence in France during these years. But after her death in 1797 and the publication of Godwin's misunderstood *Memoirs of the Author of a Vindication of the Rights of Woman* in 1798, England again saw a spate of works on women's grievances. Wollstonecraft's own *Wrongs of Woman, or Maria* appeared in 1798 as part of her *Posthumous Works*; the same year Hays published her *Appeal to the Men of Great Britain in Behalf of Women*, as Wakefield did her *Reflections on the Present Condition of the Female Sex*, and the Edgeworths, their *Practical Education*. The next year, Robinson presented the public with her *Thoughts on the Condition of Women, and on the Injustice of Mental Subordination* and Mary Ann Radcliffe published her *Female Advocate, or an Attempt to Recover the Rights of Women from Male Usurpation*.

The concern of the radicals with the plight of women is also seen in their fiction. Since their aim was didactic, many of these writers chose the form of the *tendenz* novel (the novel of purpose), believing as they did that "fictitious histories, in the hands of persons of talents and observation . . . become a powerful and effective engine of truth and reform."[13] They wrote with the specific intention of exposing the effects on women of different types of education; the novels of Wollstonecraft, Williams,[14] Hays, Holcroft, Fenwick, Inchbald, and Alderson were all therefore *Bildungsroman* of a kind, testing their heroines' early education against the varied vicissitudes of female life.

Children's books also became a popular form of radical propaganda. Some representative works include Wollstonecraft's *Original Stories from Real Life; with Conversations . . .* (1788), Wakefield's *Mental Improvement or the Beauties and Wonders of Nature and Art in a Series of Instructive Conversations* (1794), Smith's *Rural Walks: In Dialogues* (1795) and *Rambles Farther* (1796), Maria Edgeworth's *Parent's Assistant; or, Stories for Children* (1796), and Mary Elizabeth Jackson's *Botanical Dialogues between Hortensia and her Four Children* (1797). These popular textbooks, thinly disguised as fictional

---

[12] Margaret Eliot MacGregor, *Amelia Alderson Opie: Worldling and Friend, Smith College Studies in Modern Languages*, 14 (Northampton, MA: The Collegiate Press, Oct. 1932-July 1933), p. 15.

[13] Mary Hays, *Monthly Magazine*, 4 (Sept. 1797), 180–81, as quoted in Burton R. Pollin's "Mary Hays on Women's Rights in the *Monthly Magazine*," *Études Anglaises*, 24, No. 3 (1971), 279.

[14] Williams's historical works on the French Revolution and Wollstonecraft's accounts of her travels in Scandinavia and Germany, both regarded in the 1790s as well-informed, first-hand reports, also included discussions on the conditions and education of women in various European countries.

works, used the methods of dialogue and/or narration to convey moral and rational instruction, especially to their young female readers. Wollstonecraft, Smith, Jackson, and Wakefield all employed the central figure of a matronly, well-educated, moral preceptor, modelled much along the lines of the progressive Ann Murry's fictional governess, Mentoria.

Through such works, as well as through reviews in magazines, the radicals attempted to inundate the reading public with their views on female education. As a regular reviewer for the *Analytical* from 1788–92 and a more sporadic one from 1795–97, Wollstonecraft advised her readers on the worth of several contemporary women's and children's educational works.[15] Her employer, Joseph Johnson, was not the only publisher to support feminists and their works on female instruction. J. J. and G. Robinson did likewise; the notorious William Lane of circulating-library fame perhaps did better. Because of the second- or third-rate nature of his publications, Lane's contribution to women's literature has not been fairly gauged. Whether or not he exploited them as hack-writers, he provided indigent women with a source of income by publishing their works; although he published on both sides of the controversy,[16] he contributed to the radical effort through such novels as the anonymous *Twin Sisters, or the Effects of Education* (1788–89), Eliza Parsons' *Errors of Education* (1791), and Robert Bage's *Hermsprong, or Man as He Is Not* (1796). That Lane often seemed to be benefiting from the controversy cannot be doubted, but neither can the obvious interest of even his less serious readers and writers in the pressing need for an improved education for women.

What the publishers, the periodicals, and the individual writers were actually attempting to do was to reform conditions for women through the efforts of Reason, the new god of the progressives and the radicals (as well as the new philosophers). The radicals put forward various theories to improve female education by rational means. Unfortunately, as Wakefield pointed out, the influence of reason was undermined by the reactionaries, who gave the word "reform," with which it was connected, a decidedly negative connotation by associating it specifically with the new philosophers. More concerned

---

[15] In a letter dated December 5, 1786, she exulted to her sister Everina that as a periodical reviewer, she would become "the first of a new genus" (quoted in Kenneth Neill Cameron's edition of *Shelley and his Circle 1773–1822*, Cambridge, MA: Harvard University Press, 1961, I, 61).

[16] Among the reactionary works he published was Jane West's *The Advantages of Education, or the History of Maria Williams* (1793).

with bringing about changes in women than in public opinion, Wollstone-craft argued against women's continuing to deny themselves for the preservation of the latter, for "where were the rules of accommodation to stop?"[17]

If anyone was to make accommodations in his thinking, she insisted, it was the educated man: his elaborate schooling was worth nothing if his mind continued to be warped and narrowed by prejudices against the natural rights of the other sex. Further, truth itself would be devalued if man's bias in his own favor led him to deny woman an equal education:

> Contending for the rights of reason, my main argument is built on this simple principle; that if she be not prepared by education to become the companion of man, she will stop the progress of knowledge and virtue; for truth must be common to all, or it will be inefficacious with respect to its influence on general practice. (Preface, *Rights of Woman*, n.pag.)

Importantly, besides teaching people to shed gender-related prejudices, Reason, in conjunction with virtue and right action, would necessarily lead them to happiness. Godwin, especially, based his famous theory of human perfectibility on his doctrine of necessity and his faith in man's basic rationality (Myers, p. 78). The result of this striving for perfection, he felt, would be both private and public felicity: "The true object of education, like that of every other moral process, is the generation of happiness. . . . If individuals were universally happy, the species would be happy."[18] But in the course of his *Enquirer*, Godwin seems to be speaking only of men; Hays, who was a disciple of Godwin as well as Wollstonecraft, went a step further in asserting that God intended the right of happiness for women too. In fact, in her *Appeal to the Men of Great Britain in Behalf of Women*, she accused man and not God of deliberately fashioning woman to be a slave rather than an equal human being, capable of reason and worthy of happiness.

Unlike Hays, the practical Edgeworths opposed the theory of equality, although they too believed in the necessity for human happiness. Professing themselves concerned only with (the unequal) existing conditions, they defined happiness as entirely different for both sexes. Hence their aim was "to

---

[17] *A Vindication of the Rights of Woman* (1792; rpt. New York: Norton, 1967), p. 155.

[18] "Of Awakening the Mind," *The Enquirer, Reflections on Education, Manners, and Literature,* Part 1 (London: Robinsons, 1797), p. 1.

educate women so that they may be happy in the situation in which they are most like to be placed" (that is, in the home and in an inferior position) than to delude them with "speculative rights."[19]

Notwithstanding the Edgeworths, many of the other radicals believed that women had equal rights with men to the interrelated triad of Reason, Virtue, and especially Happiness. Yet on the issue of class, specifically as it related to education, not all the radicals were levelers. Only democratic radicals like Robinson, Holcroft, and Hays came to see women as a class, equally oppressed with the laboring class by the existing patriarchal, social, and political structure. They theorized that neither mind nor virtue had a class or a sex; given the same education, women and the poor would both equal upper-class men in their intellectual and moral capabilities.

## Mary Hays (1759-1843)

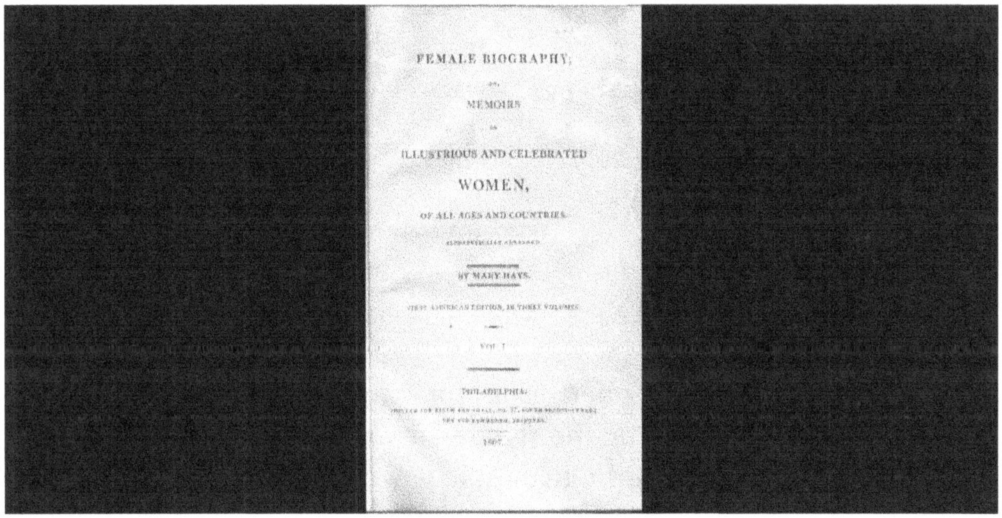

"Mary Hays." American ed. Wikipedia.

---

[19] *Practical Education* (1798; rpt. London: Garland, 1972), I, 168.

**Olympe de Gouges (1748–guillotined 1793) Mary Wollstonecraft (1759-97)**

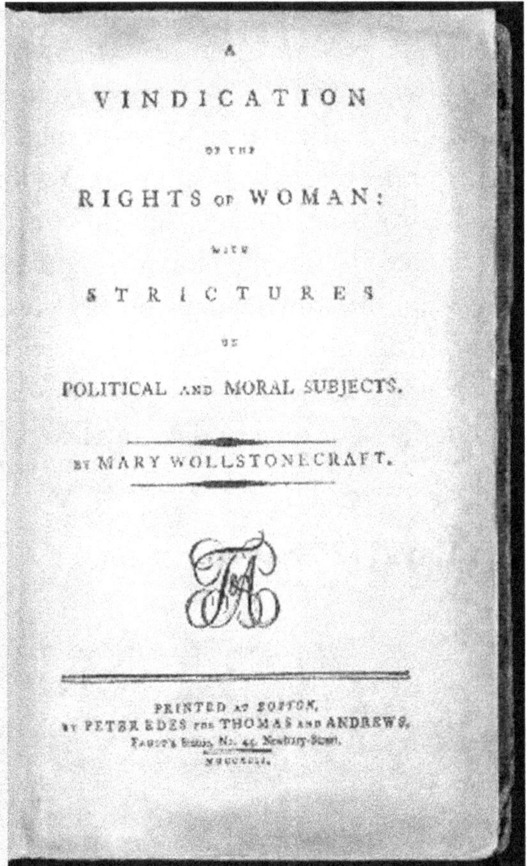

"Olympe de Gouges." First p. of
*Déclaration*. Wikipedia.

*A Vindication . . . .* American ed.
Wikipedia.

Democratic radicals therefore gauged nobility by virtue and talents, not by class and birth, especially on the question of marriage, where women traditionally had had very little voice. Radical fiction triumphantly portrayed a series of socially unequal but morally compatible marriages, as, for instance, in Holcroft's novel, *Anna St. Ives* (1792),[20] Smith's novel, *The Old Manor House* (1793), and Inchbald's most feminist work, *Lover's Vows*, a translation of Kotzebue's controversial play, *Das Kind der Liebe* (1791). But, writing at the end of a decade which saw the increasing suppression of the ideals of feminism and of democracy, Hays was more realistic than the others in her novel, *The Victim*

---

[20] Unlike the Cinderella (or Pamela) pattern of social climbing, Holcroft's upper-class heroine marries the son of her father's steward because she loves him as her moral equal.

*of Prejudice* (1799). The heroine Mary's kindly guardian-preceptor (fashioned much along the lines of *Evelina*'s Mr. Villars) reminds her of the unbridgeable social gap between her, a natural-born child, and her higher-born lover: "The beauty, the virtue, the talents, of my child, in the eyes of philosophy, are an invaluable dowry, but philosophers are not yet the legislators of mankind."[21]

And until they became so, the more class-conscious Wakefield cautioned, lower-class women were not to receive an education above their station. In its realism, her argument sounds more rational than biased:

> The injudicious practice of bringing up girls above their expectations originates in a common opinion that a good education is more valuable than a dowry; the sentiment is a just one, the error consists in a misapprehension of what constitutes a good education: No system of instruction can properly be denominated good, which is not appropriate to those who receive it.[22]

Accordingly, she carefully differentiated among the education of daughters of the nobility, the upper middle class, the lower middle class, and the laboring poor. Similarly, Reeve warned against any instruction beyond the degree of necessary female knowledge in each particular station as akin to physical "curvature" and "deformity."[23]

Wakefield was not alone in her practical class differentiation. Even Wollstonecraft and Macaulay Graham, who both preached equal education for all elementary-school-aged children, directed their major educational works at the middle and the "opulent" classes, respectively. Likewise, Macaulay Graham, Smith, and Condorcet argued that although social class prejudice was effete, at least in theory, economic class distinctions must continue to exist—the rich man exchanging his property, which was money, for the poor man's property, which was time. On a more social level, the philanthropist Catherine Cappe accepted class-related inequality yet encouraged rich women to concern themselves with the welfare of poor women.[24] Believing women related to one

---

21  *The Victim of Prejudice* (London: Johnson, 1799), I, p. 75.

22  *Reflections on the Present Condition of the Female Sex* (1798; rpt. New York: Garland, 1974), p. 61.

23  *Plans of Education* (London: Hookham and Carpenter, 1792), p. 196.

24  In *An Account of Two Charity Schools for the Education of Girls* (1800). Cappe's tract is included in this chapter because it largely consisted of extracts written during the late 1780s and in the 1790s. The preface too is dated 1799, although the work was published early the following year.

another as a sex if not by class, Cappe felt it the duty of the more privileged to assist their less privileged sisters in their right to a proper education.

If not all the radicals opposed class distinctions for women, many more of them opposed the distinctions made on the grounds of Nature by the conservatives. Following the progressives, they asserted that existing female physical and mental inferiority was no criterion for evaluating actual capability, since it was a result of nurture, not nature. This deliberate conditioning in weakness, acting on the precepts of Custom and Prejudice, was responsible for making gentlewomen into trifling and inconsequential instead of virtuous human beings. But matters could be improved. Believing that virtue was not innate in either sex but the effect of a rational education, Wollstonecraft, Hays, Darwin, and the Edgeworths urged parents to begin early such an instruction for their young children; for, said Inchbald in *A Simple Story*, "education is called second nature" and is sometimes more powerful than nature itself.[25] Accordingly, in 1789 (before her contact with the new philosophy), Wollstonecraft asserted that an early instruction in virtue could stand a woman in good stead in later life if she conscientiously acted on rational principles.[26] Eight years later, Darwin expressed a similar faith in the life-long effects of a good, well-rounded education, that is, one based on an adequate attention to the mind, body, and morals:

> A good education furnishes us with this inestimable treasure; it accompanies us at home, *travels* with us abroad, delights us in solitude, graces us in society, comforts us in misfortune, guards us in prosperity, contributes to the happiness of others, and ensures our own.[27]

---

[25] *A Simple Story* (1791; rpt. London: Frowde, 1908), I, 65.

[26] *The Female Reader; or Miscellaneous Pieces in Prose and Verse . . . for the Improvement of Young Women* (1789), by "Mr. Cresswick, Teacher of Elocution." According to Godwin's *Memoirs of Wollstonecraft*, she had assumed the pseudonym for this collection. It contains extracts from her earlier works; moreover, the style of the introduction resembles that of her *Thoughts on the Education of Daughters* (1787) and her *Original Stories* (1788). These earlier works have a "religious school-marm" quality about them, one that Wollstonecraft gradually shed as she reviewed increasingly challenging works for the *Analytical Review* and became associated with Johnson's circle. Thereafter, her steadily growing militancy is apparent from her *Vindication of the Rights of Men* (1790) to her posthumously published *Wrongs of Woman* (1798).

[27] *A Plan for the Conduct of Female Education, in Boarding Schools* (Derby: Johnson, 1797), p. 118.

In its implications, Darwin's theory was the same as Hays's in *The Victim of Prejudice*: a virtuous education did not often serve as a dowry to a good marriage, but it certainly ensured peace and a sense of self-worth to its possessor in the face of all circumstances, good and evil.

But certain writers, including the later Wollstonecraft and Hays, believed the effectiveness of an early virtuous education to be not entirely within the instructor's control. They hypothesized that sometimes even the most affectionate parental instruction in virtue could prove powerless against accidental circumstances, which were capable of modifying the child's moral character. Carrying this theory to an extreme, Holcroft and Godwin asserted that people's characters originated only in their external circumstances. Furthermore, according to Godwin in *The Enquiry Concerning Political Justice* (1793), education by modifying circumstances could go on all through a person's life, while formal instruction itself often ended in youth. Like Wollstonecraft, Hays applied Godwin's theory especially to women in *Emma Courtney*, lamenting the negative effects of chance circumstances on unwary young girls. Wollstonecraft's fears for her infant daughter Fanny, expressed in her *Letters Written During a Short Residence in Sweden, Norway, and Denmark* (1796), is echoed by Hays:

> We are the creatures of education, but in that education, what we call chance, or accident, has so great a share, that the wisest preceptor, after all his cares, has reason to tremble. (*Emma Courtney*, I, 4)

In opposition to Hays's and Wollstonecraft's fears, a few of the radicals actually regarded adverse circumstances as the best conditions to nurture virtue in the pupil. Caroline, in Alderson's *Dangers of Coquetry* (1790); Lady Mathilda, in Inchbald's *A Simple Story* (1791), the two Henrys, in her *Nature and Art* (1796); and Marchmont, in Smith's eponymous novel (1796) all turn out to be good, principled people because they are educated in what Inchbald called the "school of adversity." Disciplined in the severity and poverty of this so-called school, these fictional characters escape the errors, vices, and degradations that were supposed to result from an overindulged, unregulated education. The latter type of education was seen as concomitant with wealth; undisciplined heirs and heiresses in the novels of Inchbald, Smith, Alderson, and Parsons all suffer variously for their early mistaken indulgence. For the female characters, the result was often seduction and/or death, horrors that

Goldsmith had so authoritatively foretold in his lovely-woman-stoops-to-folly formula in *The Vicar of Wakefield* (1766). In equating ultimate female virtue with mere sexual chastity, such novelists were subscribing to a patriarchal rather than a feminist system of values. Little wonder, then, that the increasingly reactionary reading public of the 1790s appreciated their novels more than they did those of outspoken militants like Wollstonecraft and Hays.[28]

In direct contradiction to her theories on character-formation by adverse circumstances or parental dignity, Inchbald, in *Nature and Art* (1796), followed Smith in *Emmeline* (1788) and Williams in *Julia* (1790) in insisting that certain individuals had an innate knowledge, dignity, elegance, and understanding that had nothing to do with the superimposition of education or art. In the case of Inchbald's lowborn heroine, Hannah Primrose, one is tempted to scoff, with Hays, that the notion of such inborn powers is "monstrous and hypothetical."[29] Smith's delineation of such wonderfully endowed heroines was slightly less ridiculous than Inchbald's, for she ensured that her paragons, natural or otherwise, were later instructed through the affectionate care of mother-surrogates or lover-tutors. The former were generally older, literary gentlewomen, wronged by either profligate husbands and/or unscrupulous lawyers, much as Smith herself was; the latter stemmed in a more or less direct line from Rousseau.

Especially in her last novel, *The Young Philosopher*, Smith seems to have closely followed the concept of the lover-tutor as seen in *Émile*. Accordingly, the heroine Medora's lover Delmont, in spite of being a "young philosopher," boasts to his friend that his fiancée is "brought up exactly as I should wish a wife to be educated for *me* [emphasis mine]."[30] Like Rousseau's Sophie, Medora is also a "child of nature," that is, ironically, a young woman brought up in complete and *unnatural* retirement by her parents until she can be handed over to her husband's safekeeping. In her *Lettres sur ouvrages et le caractère de Jean-Jacques Rousseau* (1788), de Staël shrewdly pointed out the flaw in his theory: Sophie's ultimate infidelity to Émile disproved his hypothesis that education in complete retirement from the world was the best way to ensure good behavior in women.

---

[28] This statement needs to be qualified, for both Inchbald and Smith were likewise attacked for the revolutionary politics expressed in their novels.

[29] *The Monthly Magazine*, 1 (June 1796), 385–87, as quoted in Pollin's article on Hays, p. 275.

[30] *The Young Philosopher* (1798; rpt. New York: Garland, 1974), I, 245.

Rousseau himself seems to have amended this error in his next novel, *La Nouvelle Héloïse*, by pointing to Julie's secluded upbringing, away from worldly norms (and prudery), as the cause of her passionate nature and consequent sexual freedom. Improving on his lead, Eliza Fenwick, in *Secresy [sic], the Ruin on the Rock* (1795) and Hays, in *Emma Courtney*, insisted that some knowledge of worldly affairs was absolutely essential in the education of a young woman, otherwise she would be the innocent dupe of her own "passions" when interacting with the more worldly sex. She would let her emotions overrule her reason; such behavior, according to the radical correlation of reason, virtue, and happiness, could only lead to mistaken morals and, consequently, misery. More importantly, according to Hays, Fenwick, and Wollstonecraft, direct experience of the ways of the world would allow women to make moral judgements on their own, instead of having always to depend on male protection.[31] Women would then be able to act from strength of mind rather than from the weakness of ignorance, which trait, Wollstonecraft objected, had been so speciously named "innocence" by conservatives like Rousseau. Above all, such women would have been educated not for society ("the world"), not for a husband, but for themselves.

The radicals' concern to improve education extended to their discussions on the issue of home versus school education, as with all the theorists. In spite of the fear of adverse circumstances, even radical feminists like Macaulay Graham and Wollstonecraft regarded private instruction at home, under the affectionate and zealous guidance of enlightened parents, as the best system of instruction for young women. They were aware, nevertheless, that parents did not always fulfill their obligations to their children, and, if of the upper classes, often left them to the care of illiterate and perhaps immoral servants. Although most eighteenth-century educators castigated the influence of servants, Hays spoke up for the many nurses who affectionately carried out their duties where fashionable mothers had failed. Going farther, the Edgeworths, along with Cappe and other philanthropists, reminded their readers that the vices and ignorance of servants stemmed from their illiteracy rather than from innate depravity; one could not, they argued in *Practical Education*, reasonably expect a waiting maid to enter into the views of a Locke or a Barbauld.

---

[31] These three women came to be close friends; in fact, Hays and Fenwick attended Wollstonecraft at her deathbed in 1797.

But the problem of inadequate home education still remained, so the radicals variously projected an elaborate hierarchy of schools for girls: from nurseries and elementary schools; through day, vocational, or secondary schools; to institutions of higher learning. Of course, class-related biases still continued among some of the radicals, who therefore outlined separate plans for the middle and lower segments of society, who were not, above all else, to receive a boarding school education.

Boarding schools apparently flourished in the 1790s as they had earlier in the century. Except for a letter in the *Lady's Monthly Museum*, which testified to the existence of some excellent female seminaries (Aug. 1, 1798, 138), they were as much denigrated by the radicals as by the progressives and the conservatives before them. Reeve, Hamilton, and Inchbald objected to boarding schools on the old grounds that they provided an immoral and frivolous education. Others found new grievances. The anonymous author of *The Twin Sisters* accused them of turning out a mindless, faceless regiment of young ladies who all talked, walked, behaved, and dressed with a uniform artificiality of manner. In her *Rights of Woman*, Wollstonecraft objected to boarding schools as giving girls "nasty or immodest [personal and sexual] habits" which undermined what she considered the three main effects of a good education, namely, a healthy mind, a healthy body, and sound moral habits (p. 193). Her solution was that boarders be kept away from the influence of ignorant servants and from the close physical proximity enforced in the dormitories. For health, beauty, and modesty, she further recommended frequent ablutions, insisting that the girls wash and dress alone and not in the company of their peers.

In his *Plans for the Conduct of Female Education, in Boarding Schools*, written specifically for the Misses Parkers' school, Darwin was more constructive than many of the above-mentioned radicals. Instead of merely attacking the abuses of boarding schools, he systematically presented a plan for their improved management and instruction. Wakefield also had a plan to improve boarding-school education, one that was by no means new in the century. She suggested that wealthy parents who did not themselves care to educate their children should pay enlightened governesses of schools a handsome enough sum so they could afford to restrict the number of their charges. In this way, the governesses could give the girls more individual attention, especially regarding their morals; such an arrangement would combine the good effects of both public and private instruction, at the same time benefiting both the pupil and the instructor.

A step above the progressives, democratic radicals like Macaulay Graham, Wollstonecraft, Price, and Condorcet were concerned not so much with already extant boarding schools as with projects for national, coeducational schools that would do away with all distinctions of class and sex, at least in the formative years.[32] Influenced by the politics of the French Revolution, Condorcet insisted that the curriculum in such schools include just ideas of the rights and duties of all citizens and also the main points of the country's laws,[33] to which Godwin strongly objected as propaganda training. On the social as opposed to the political level, Wollstonecraft agreed with Condorcet that coeducation would allow young children to grow up naturally in relation to one another, which would prevent false expectations in the later interaction of the sexes.[34]

On the basis of the above ideals, the democratic radicals variously proposed a graded system of schooling for children of different ages. On the primary level, Macaulay Graham suggested public nurseries for infants of all classes; Paine advocated that every child under fourteen be educated in the basics of reading, writing, and arithmetic. Condorcet and Wollstonecraft recommended that the government establish free elementary day schools for all children;[35] thereafter, according to the former, desirous students were to be directed to colleges, and later, to places of even higher learning. Borrowing from Talleyrand's views on public education, Wollstonecraft specified the ages of elementary day scholars as being from five to nine; significantly, the children were all to wear uniforms in order to avoid class distinctions. However, economic if not social class distinctions were to come into effect after age nine: students of either superior abilities or fortune were to go to schools offering a more liberal curriculum, while boys and girls intended for domestic employments and mechanical trades were to be sent to vocational schools. At the latter schools, coeducational instruction was to continue in the mornings, the sexes separating in the afternoons for gender-related education, which, for girls, would include learning such useful arts as plain work, mantua-making, and millinery.

---

[32] The anonymous author of *Elfrida* (1786) was the only progressive novelist to give her heroine coeducational instruction.

[33] "Essai sur la constitution et les fonctions des assemblées provinciales," Part II (1788).

[34] In her free translation of the German educator Christian Gotthilf Salzmann's *Elements of Morality*, as well as in her *Rights of Woman*, Wollstonecraft even recommended sex education for children, an idea far ahead of her time.

[35] Hamilton too recommended the continuation of Scottish coeducational day schools, a system she felt was beginning to die out in her time.

Wollstonecraft did not outline a specific plan of higher education for women; Reeve, Wakefield, and Robinson did. Their plans for a female academy, a teachers' college, and a women's university, respectively, were alike not only in the sound education they recommended for women but also in the professional ends they all envisioned. All three systems suggested that the teachers initially or eventually be female, drawn, if possible, from among their own scholars. The three plans are important enough to be discussed separately.

Reeve's project, as outlined in her *Plans of Education; with Remarks on the Systems of Other Writers* (1792), was for a Protestant convent, intended as both an asylum and a seminary for women of all ages.[36] She professed herself primarily a disciple of Mme de Genlis and gave her opinion on other systems she had read; for instance, she dismissed Macaulay Graham's as impractical. In fact, however, she seems to have plagiarized largely from the system of Astell, and, to some extent, from those of Defoe and Richardson. She referred to the existence of a real school at Tottenham (where Bathsua Makin had opened her progressive school in 1673), started by a Mrs. M. Scriven in 1788. This school was run on lines similar to her own plan, except that it allowed private instruction to older, and therefore perhaps shy, female students.

Like Astell, Reeve saw her school as an asylum for single gentlewomen with unsettled plans in life and for older women of small fortunes, cultivated minds, and benevolent hearts, who would choose to retire from the bustle of the world and devote their time and talents to the benefit of others. Like Richardson, she included among her proposed boarders ladies with their husbands abroad, as also women recently widowed. Such older lodgers were to be women of unspotted character; they would pay handsomely for their board and be admitted for not less than a year (Defoe's system had suggested payment for the whole year even if the boarders chose to leave before then).

The scholars for the seminary were to be drawn from children of the rich and of the gentility, who, like the older lodgers, would pay handsomely for their board. But this seminary would also serve as an asylum-cum-school for young motherless upper-class girls, for those who came suddenly into good fortunes, for those whose fathers remarried, and for those whose parents were in the East or West Indies. In addition, unprovided daughters of indigent or

---

[36] She acknowledged the success of the school run at St. Cyr by Mme de Maintenon in the seventeenth century and that opened by her own contemporary, the Empress of Russia, in the eighteenth century.

dead clergymen, army or navy officers, and placemen were to be taken into the academy too. Like Wollstonecraft, Reeve intended the students to wear school uniforms so as to make no distinction for children of birth, fortune, or other accidental advantage. The poorer scholars, however, were also to receive a seven-year practical training in some future business or employment, such as millinery, mantua-making, and clear-starching. The richer students too could learn the arts of clear-starching, pastry-making, confectionery, and cookery, if their parents or guardians so stipulated. But regardless of future projects, all students would receive instruction in moral, mental, and personal improvements, and in every branch of useful and domestic knowledge.

The teachers for this school were all to be female, even for the fields of dancing, drawing, music, and languages, traditionally taught by masters. The teachers' assistants were to work for the benefit of the community; the money arising from their efforts was to be pooled to settle them in trade or marriage when they left. Below them in rank would be the female servants, who were likewise to work, especially to spin, for both the community and themselves— in their case, to create savings for old age and sickness. They were to be chosen from the deserving poor and from the unfortunate (as in Richardson's plan).

The community was to be entirely female, lodging in a large, commodious house in a convenient situation, renting its own land, growing its own food, and keeping its own cows, hogs, and poultry. As in Defoe's plan, no men would be allowed to reside in the house, although a chaplain was to visit on Sundays and on holidays. Every morning, prayers from the Church of England liturgy would be read, presumably by the ladies themselves. Male servants would be lodged in a separate house, within hearing distance of the house bell. The seminary was to be superintended by a group of twelve dedicated ladies under a main governess, all contracting to support the community for three years at a time (as in Cappe's plan for the Grey Coat Charity School). All in all, Reeve's project for a female academy, as well as the actual school she referred to in Tottenham, showed that Astell's idea of an Anglican seminary was very much alive in the eighteenth century, even though its instigator's name was surprisingly not mentioned or acknowledged by any of the radicals in the 1790s.[37]

---

[37] There were apparently no reprints of Astell's work in the latter half of the eighteenth century, although Myra Reynolds records that Judith Drake's work was reprinted in 1791 (p. 396). Neither reactionaries nor radicals referred to either work in the 1790s; in 1803, however, Hays's *Female Biography* included a chapter on Astell, ascribing Drake's (anonymously published) work also to her.

Reeve's ambitious plan did not seem to have been intended for immediate implementation. With perhaps greater practical intent, Wakefield suggested a teachers' college for young women of small means, in her *Reflections on the Present Condition of the Female Sex.* She intended these scholars to be trained to teach every useful science, with the use of books, globes, and other apparatus of instruction.[38] At first, they would necessarily be taught by masters since no body of women was yet proficient in teaching, but after a certain number of years, only women would serve as instructors in this college. Such an institution would provide England with a constant succession of teachers, properly prepared for their profession not only by a regular course of study but also by a "thorough initiation into the philosophical principles of education" proposed by the most eminent writers on the subject (p. 56). Ranking above the teachers would be the higher-born governesses; both groups would together give their pupils a sound intellectual and moral education based on philosophical principles.

Aspiring higher than either Wakefield or Reeve, Robinson boldly proposed a "UNIVERSITY FOR WOMEN," becoming the first feminist in the eighteenth century to do so.[39] At this institution, she envisioned that women would receive both a "polite" and a classical education, their studies proportionate to their mental powers. After a fair trial, the incompetent would be allotted to the humbler paths of life, such as domestic and useful occupations. Like Wakefield and Reeve, Robinson showed a concern for poorer scholars also: wealthy parents who neglected to educate their daughters would have to pay fines, which would then be used for the maintenance of such scholars. Echoing Wakefield's assurance, she promised her readers that in time, specifically half a century, there would be enough learned women to fill all the university departments creditably. Finally, and in agreement with Reeve and Wakefield, Robinson surmised that in taking over the task of educating one another, women would at last be independent of men for their higher education.

---

[38] According to Nicholas Hans, two well-known schools (among others) in the 1790s gave a solid and well-taught scientific education to their female pupils. These were the mathematics scholar Mrs. Bryan's school at Blackheath and Mrs. Florian's school at Epping Forest (*New Trends in Education in the Eighteenth Century* [London: Routledge and Kegan Paul, 1951], p. 203).

[39] *Thoughts on the Condition of Women*, 2nd ed. (1799; rpt. London: Longman, Rees, 1799), p. 92.

These proposals for higher education for gentlewomen made provisions for scholars on the bases of needs, means, and intelligence. Some of the radicals also made class-related provisions for daughters of tradesmen and of laborers. Wakefield, for instance, did not believe in denying middle-class girls some form of rational education but insisted it be given in day schools only, to include the effects of domestic and maternal tutelage. On a narrower plan, Reeve allowed school education to daughters of tradesmen and mechanics, that is, of the lower middle class, but restricted it to knowledge useful to their rank in life.

On a similar class-related principle, Reeve expressed preference for schools of Industry over Sunday schools for daughters of the poor: the former taught them some useful trade as well as a sense of their duty to God, their neighbors, and themselves, every day, instead of just on the Sabbath. Like Reeve, Godwin too objected to Sunday schools, but on atheistic and democratic principles: the chief lessons Sunday schools taught the poor were a "superstitious veneration for the Church of England, and to bow to every man in a handsome coat. All this is directly contrary to the true interests of mankind."[40]

With greater philanthropy than Reeve and less philosophizing than Godwin, the educators Wakefield, Cappe, and Trimmer[41] followed Paine in demanding a more "liberal" education for the poor, one which would include the three R's, instead of just reading and church catechism. Trimmer proposed an escalated system of instruction, to be based on the circumstances of the students' parents and on their own bent and capacity. She democratically refuted the objection that learning raised the poor above their station, by arguing that if learning were made more general, it would cease to give preeminence to any class. Like Cappe, she also attempted to raise the feminist consciousness of affluent young ladies by encouraging them to assist in the education, welfare, and employment of girls in Charity schools.[42] Even more importantly, like

---

[40] *Political Justice* (1793; 3rd ed. rev., 1798; rpt. Toronto: University of Toronto Press, 1946), II, 299.

[41] In *Reflections upon the Education of Children in Charity Schools* (1792). The information on Trimmer is also from Edward H. Reisner's *Nationalism and Education since 1789* (New York: Macmillan, 1923), pp. 236–40.

[42] At this stage, none of these female theorists seems to have been influenced by Andrew Bell's and Joseph Lancaster's popular monitorial systems, launched in 1797 and 1798, respectively. These systems attempted to make up for the lack of qualified instructors for the poor by substituting student-teachers instead.

Robinson, Wakefield, and Reeve, both Trimmer and Cappe seemed aware that women's education could be improved most effectively by women themselves.

In contrast to the more class-conscious progressives, the radicals showed greater interest in the rational instruction, albeit in different degrees, of women of all classes. To a large extent, their concern with the improvement of the whole sex, as expressed in their projected schools, their educational theories, and their individual works, was colored by the feminist and democratic activism of the times. Women and the poor, minorities oppressed for centuries by the existing political, social, and religious structure, had finally found themselves a body of champions who launched a rigorous campaign to inform the public of their grievances. No longer was better education for women and the poor proposed by isolated individuals of liberal inclinations; many of the feminist radicals and the political democrats of the 1790s were acquainted with and consulted one another about their causes. If, in actual fact, the radicals were scarcely more successful than their progressive forebears in effecting changes in female education, it must be remembered that both were at least instrumental in creating an increasingly positive climate for future reforms to take place.

## III.  Education of the Head, the Heart, the Person, and the Physique

𝔉or the radicals, as for the progressives, the education of the intellect was the most important of the four main types of instruction suggested for gentlewomen in the eighteenth century. Their theories were largely constructed on the foundation laid by the earlier feminists, although the influence of the new philosophy gave them a greater sophistication. First, and most important, they drew an intimate parallel between instruction of the intellect, which concentrated on reason, and that of the heart, which concentrated on virtue, by positing an essential connection between reason and virtue: the former necessarily led to the latter (barring the influence of accidental circumstances), while both directed the person in particular, as well as society in general, closer to a state of perfection. Significantly, while virtue did not preclude an appropriate sense of duty in the individual, it included the idea of personal happiness; the radical concept of woman was therefore at opposite poles from that of Rousseau's selfless Sophie, brought up only to please others, especially men.

In her *Letters on Education*, Macaulay Graham decisively stated her aim (and, incidentally, that of her peers):

> As I intend to breed my pupils up to act a rational part in the world, and not to fill up a niche in the seraglio of a sultan, I shall certainly give them leave to use their reason in all matters which concern their duty and happiness, and shall spare no pains in the cultivation of this only sure guide to virtue.[43]

Along with Wollstonecraft and the Edgeworths, however, Macaulay Graham also suggested that children implicitly submit to parental authority until they reached the age of reason and could be accountable to themselves. The Edgeworths emphasized the need for the child's active industry in the process of learning to reason; knowledge was not to be given children only in the form of play, as Locke and disciples like Hays advocated for the very young. Wollstonecraft believed it was also the duty of the parents to "set the child's understanding in motion before the body arrives at maturity" so that, in her adult years, she would have merely to continue and not initiate the "important task of learning to think and reason" (*Rights of Woman*, pp. 51–52). Given such an upbringing, the Edgeworths added, the adult woman would be trained to trust her own judgement when it differed from that of an authoritarian father or husband; they advised her, nevertheless, to assert herself "with all the graces of female gentleness" rather than aggressively or with "any of that debasing cunning which Rousseau recommends" (*Practical Education*, I, 167). Through its connection with virtue, knowledge would thus give woman a power over her own actions that cunning never quite could.

The knowledge demanded for gentlewomen by radicals like Wollstonecraft and Macaulay Graham was not merely the erudition and classical learning given upper-class men; rather, it began with mastering the *tools* of learning itself. Like Astell, these writers wanted women to enlarge their minds by developing their capacity to think, to organize and combine ideas, and to draw logical generalizations from individual premises. As a result, women would be able to reach a clear understanding of themselves and their relationship to the world around them, including its civic and social structure. Such knowledge, the theorists argued, would rationally convince women of their rights and duties and allow them mental as well as economic independence.

---

[43] *Letters on Education* (1790; rpt. New York: Garland, 1974), p. 220.

The basis of such independence was a thinking mind; hence, like the progressives, the radicals also laid great emphasis on training women to think for themselves instead of through men and society. De Gouges demanded freedom not just of thought but also of expression: "La libre communication des pensées et des opinions est un des droits les plus précieux de la femme" (*Déclaration des droits*, article XI, pp. 9–10). Furthermore, added Hays, such mental freedom would improve the relationship between the sexes, while its lack would result in discord in family life and society. In her *Letters and Essays*, No. 3, Hays argued that women whose studies were narrowly confined only to Mrs. Glasse's *Art of Cookery* (a popular eighteenth-century cookbook) turned into domestic drudges or scolds; they made life miserable for everyone around them, whereas a little well-directed learning would have made these same women into affectionate, intelligent companions to their husbands.

The heroines of most of the *tendenz* novels of Wollstonecraft, Bage, Hays, Inchbald, Fenwick, Holcroft, and Hamilton were therefore all thinking women, who chose to associate with men for their rational capacities and not for their looks or social status. Conversely, intelligent, sensible male characters, like the hero Grandby in *The Twin Sisters*, also preferred rational, intelligent women rather than mere pretty faces for their wives. In *Political Justice*, Godwin probably made the classic statement of the 1790s on such a relationship: "I shall assiduously cultivate the intercourse of that woman, whose moral and intellectual accomplishments strike me in the most powerful manner" (II, 511). And in truth, Godwin and Wollstonecraft's love-relationship seems to have been one of the most perfect models of an equal and happy union between intellectuals in the 1790s.

Learning could therefore be an asset rather than a defect, even in the marriage market. Smith and Hamilton, who scoffed in their novels at certain single women as undesirable "bluestockings"[44] and "new philosophers," respectively, agreed, however, with the other radicals that not all literary gentlewomen were necessarily unkempt slatterns, ugly hags, or pedantic bores who abused their learning. In her *Letters for Literary Ladies*, a far more feminist work than *Practical Education*, which she had co-authored with her father,

---

[44] The term had already developed disparaging connotations by the 1790s. A noteworthy exception is the well-known Irish couple known as the "Ladies of Llangollen [in Wales]," Lady Eleanor Butler and Sarah Ponsonby. They were an upper-class probably lesbian couple much visited by many of the major Romantic poets in the next century.

Maria Edgeworth sensibly pointed out that if women grew undesirably vain from a little learning, "they will be sobered into good sense when they shall have learnt more."[45] Likewise, echoing Astell, Darwin added that the truly advanced scholar would be humbly aware of her deficiencies instead of vain of her acquisitions; moreover, learning would keep women away from the far greater danger of dissipation. As a protector of rather than a threat to virtue, learning was surely one of the most positive attributes gentlewomen could possess.

The radicals had to answer one more traditional accusation against learning, namely, that it unsexed women and made them masculine. Hays, Robinson, and Smith followed Wollstonecraft in smoothly turning the argument around: if by "masculine women" was meant women who, like men, cultivated their understanding, virtue, and talents, that is, exercised the faculties that ennobled the human character, then indeed, all philosophical people would agree that masculinity in women was a very good thing (*Rights of Woman*). But if, added Hays, being masculine meant aping men's negative qualities, that is, their unrestrained passions and improprieties, as well as their inhumane activities, such as hunting, shooting, war, gaming, and cruelty to animals, then it was truly reprehensible—in both sexes (*Appeal to the Men of Great Britain*). As her feminist consciousness grew, Wollstonecraft replaced the epithets "masculine" and "manly," used in her reviews as sexless terms of approbation for mental capability, with the epithet "sound" (adopted in the *Rights of Woman* to evaluate Macaulay Graham's understanding).[46] What the radicals sought for women, after all, was an equality of opportunities with men, while retaining their own uniquely positive attributes, and not a mere single-sex kind of uniformity.

In spite of its continued inferiority to the curriculum prescribed for upper-class men, the scope of a "sound" education for gentlewomen had greatly increased by the 1790s, in both the arts and the sciences. In their arts curriculum, the radicals made changes in the existing fields. For instance, they

---

[45] *Letters for Literary Ladies* (1795; rpt. New York, Garland, 1974), p. 56.

[46] It is probably symptomatic of her increasing feminism that Wollstonecraft followed up her *Vindication of the Rights of Men* (1790), an answer to Burke's reactionary *Reflections on the Revolution in France* (1790), with *A Vindication of the Rights of Woman* two years later. She also began to prefer the term "woman" to "lady" when speaking of members of her own sex. Her friend Eliza Fenwick followed her in this preference, being (to my knowledge) the only eighteenth-century novelist to sign her work as "By a Woman" instead of "By a Lady."

generally accepted that gentlewomen should be taught not merely to read and write, but also to study the rules of English grammar, a point much debated at the beginning of the century. Likewise, although practical sense had earlier dictated that gentlewomen learn arithmetic and household economy, those who loved learning were now prescribed simple geometry and algebra. More specifically, to the polite languages of French and Italian, Wollstonecraft, Robinson, Macaulay Graham, Hays, and Mary Ann Radcliffe, like some of the progressives, added the classical languages of Greek and Latin; to the study of history and geography, Darwin and Macaulay Graham added "heathen" mythology; to the study of polite literature, Hays, Wakefield, Macaulay Graham, Wollstonecraft, and the Edgeworths variously added criticism and logic.

Opinions differed regarding certain other types of reading. For instance, the effects of novel-reading continued to be debated in the 1790s as they had throughout the previous few decades. Wollstonecraft declared her impatience with what she called the "trash" which she sometimes had to review for the *Analytical*'s literary section but acceded in the *Rights of Woman* that, for idle gentlewomen, even novel-reading was better than no reading at all. Some radicals attacked specific types of novels, while recommending others: Reeve and Hamilton objected to sentimental novels, Smith (herself a prolific novelist) to "bad" ones, Macaulay Graham and Darwin to romantic ones. On the other hand, Darwin allowed women serious novels, and Smith, following Rousseau and Fanny Burney, permitted "good" novels which gave a true representation of life but did not corrupt the heart and morals. For those who enjoyed more serious reading than the novel generally offered, Condorcet recommended the study of local jurisprudence; Bage and Macaulay Graham, metaphysics; Hays, Wollstonecraft, Macaulay Graham, Wakefield, and the Edgeworths, philosophy. Lastly, for those who were interested in more practical study, Wollstonecraft, Condorcet, and Darwin variously suggested shorthand and even mechanics.

Like the arts, the sciences also found champions among the radicals. Macaulay Graham, Hays, Darwin, and the Edgeworths sweepingly prescribed them all, the Edgeworths cautioning young girls to view them as rational and permanent objects of study and not as mere sources of excitation. Other writers showed a bias for particular sciences; for instance, Smith encouraged the study of botany, of which she herself was passionately fond. Yet others suggested zoology, astronomy, physics, and (following de Genlis) chemistry, Maria Edgeworth declaring that a good cook was an "empirical chemist" (*Letters for*

*Literary Ladies*, p. 66). Like the militant progressives Poulain de la Barre and the anonymous author of *Female Restoration*, Hays and Wollstonecraft also believed a study of anatomy and medicine appropriate for women. Darwin went so far as to include minerology, electricity, hydrostatics, optics, and magnetism, his philosophy being that male education (especially of the Dissenting academies) was replacing the ancient languages with the more useful sciences; if women were to be rational companions of men, their education must necessarily follow similar guidelines.

Among all the subjects open to upper-class women, two, in particular, had been viewed by eighteenth-century conservatives as highly improper for women: religious and political controversy. But in the 1790s, radical women themselves took an active part in such disputes; it was only natural, then, that many of them should recommend the study of religion and politics to their own sex. Hays prescribed religious study because it could work with reason to form the basis of a good system of education. With Wollstonecraft, Hamilton, Macaulay Graham, and Inchbald, and like the earlier progressives, she further stressed the necessity for women to become Christian by conviction instead of through unquestioning faith. Furthermore, to the consternation of her reactionary counterparts, Macaulay Graham followed Rousseau in suggesting that religious instruction be delayed until the student had reached the age of reason. With characteristic non-commitment, the Edgeworths refused to comment on religious instruction in *Practical Education*; however, Maria Edgeworth's biographer, Marilyn Butler, records that evangelical critics rebuked them for this neglect.[47] Among the radicals, only Darwin suggested that women's minds had better not be perplexed with religious controversy, even though he allowed them all manner of secular learning.

Participation in and the study of political controversy were likewise much-debated issues. In France, de Gouges, Condorcet, and de Staël recommended that women be allowed equal places in government, since they had been allowed the equal honor of losing their heads on the block. Improving on their lead, Wollstonecraft demanded for Englishwomen the right to vote. As such, she may rightly be called the first of the English suffragettes. Less radically, Robinson and Smith urged that women be allowed at least a study of the contemporary political situation, since they were intimately involved with it as the daughters, wives, and mothers of the active male participants.

---

[47] *Maria Edgeworth: A Literary Biography* (Oxford: Clarendon Press, 1972), p. 172.

With less temerity, perhaps because she was writing towards the end of an increasingly hostile decade, Hays admitted that women were rightfully excluded from political science, even if they had the capacity to equal men in their understanding of it (*Appeal to the Men*). Repressive political circumstances perhaps forced even so radical a feminist as Hays to speak conservatively on this issue.

This cautionary conservatism showed itself in the curriculum prescribed for the lower classes too, even by Wollstonecraft, the leader of the feminists and border-genteel herself. Along with Wakefield, she recommended a different knowledge for middle-class girls from that given to their higher-born contemporaries. Thus, their curriculum was first to include useful knowledge, as of arithmetic, book-keeping, and kitchen physic, and of the domestic arts pertaining to child-care and family-management. Thereafter, however, in keeping with the principles of democracy, these writers allowed middle-class girls a degree of rational instruction, in such basic fields as literature, history, biography, experimental philosophy, and simple mathematics. But above all, Wakefield insisted, again conservatively, middle-class girls were to be given a sound religious education (non-controversial, of course) to teach them to accept their God-ordained place in society.

In the 1790s, as in the previous decades, theorists also continued to prescribe dogmatic religious instruction for the poor, especially recommending the works of Sarah Trimmer and of the reactionaries Hannah More and Anna Laetitia Barbauld. Unlike Reeve, the philanthropists Cappe, Trimmer, and Wakefield proved their liberalism by adding writing and the four rules of arithmetic to reading and the church catechism. In general, however, domestic knowledge ranked high in the list of subjects for the female poor; Cappe specified washing, ironing, cleaning house, cooking, bleaching linen, carding, spinning, quilting, sewing, and knitting. Like Trimmer and unlike the reactionaries, her aim was not so much to keep laboring women at the bottom of the social ladder as to train them to be well-qualified members of the economic workforce.

The insistence of the radicals on a rational and useful education for all women, albeit according to class, was a practical improvement on the sometimes-visionary curriculum suggested by some of the progressives for upper-class women only. Although radical theories were built as much on past progressive idealism as on contemporary political revolutionism, the joint emphasis on rationality, usefulness, as well as independence was a particularly new phenomenon. Wollstonecraft gave a representative definition of rational education as understood by radical thought:

> The most perfect education, in my opinion, is such an exercise of the understanding as is best calculated to strengthen the body and form the heart. Or, in other words, to enable the individual to attain such habits of virtue as will render it independent. (*Rights of Woman*, p. 52)

The emphasis on virtue intimately connected the education of the intellect with the education of the heart, next in importance in the theories of the radicals. They believed that virtue alone could give a woman the fortitude to lead her life on principles of rational morality; accordingly, fortitude, as popularized by de Genlis's educational philosophy, became the specific trait most approved of by all these writers. In Wollstonecraft's *Original Stories from Real Life; With Conversations, Calculated to Regulate the Affections, and Form the Mind to Truth and Goodness*, the mentor Mrs. Mason informs her young female charges:

> The term *virtue*, comes from a word signifying strength. Fortitude of mind is, therefore, the basis of every virtue, and virtue belongs to a being, that is weak in nature, and strong only in will and resolution.[48]

Wollstonecraft believed that weakness was inherent in the human species, yet it was not incurable, for both sexes were capable of reason and therefore of virtue. At the same time, the qualities of reason and virtue themselves, as already seen, were inherently sexless. If virtue was sexless, however, duties were not; Wollstonecraft agreed with the conservatives that in general men fulfilled their duties outside the home and women inside it. She did not deny the necessity of women's duties, but neither did she forget the importance of their rights; both together made the composite rational being, the free yet patriotic citizen.

Like Wollstonecraft, the other radicals recognized that in the system of moral education, that is, of the heart, women's traditional duties as daughters, wives, and mothers were important, but like the progressives, their emphasis, for the most part, was on women's duties to themselves. There were, of course,

---

[48] *Original Stories* (1788; rpt. London: Johnson, 1791), p. 77.

some major dissidents on this issue. Wakefield followed Rousseau in advocating that women cheerfully submit to the caprice of parents and husbands because "from the first dawning of reason [a girl] should be impressed that she lives not for herself, but to contribute to the happiness of others" (*Reflections*, p. 36). Refusing as usual to question the validity of a sexist system, the Edgeworths advised that, conditions being what they were, women should early be inured to restraint and good temper since they would need to exercise these qualities all their lives. Yet in spite of being recognized in their time as respectable educators of women, Wakefield and the Edgeworths were only a minority voice among the radicals in their conservative insistence that woman was a creature of duties more than rights.

Traditionally, filial duty was the first in the series of women's obligations within the family. Except for Wakefield and the Edgeworths, the radicals followed Astell and Wortley Montagu in emphasizing the rational mutuality of the parent-child relationship: "The ties of blood are weak, if not the mere chimeras of prejudice, unless sanctioned by reason, or cemented by habits of familiar and affectionate intercourse" (Hays, *Emma Courtney*, I, 47). If any, their pressure was on the parents, especially in their important role as preceptors of their children. Wollstonecraft was aware of the difficulties involved in overcoming in the grown woman the effects of an improper education given in infancy; likewise, the novelists Inchbald (*A Simple Story*), Parsons (*The Errors of Education*), and Alderson (*The Dangers of Coquetry*) demonstrated the ineffectiveness of even a naturally good disposition against harmful childhood instruction. Only the anonymous author of *The Twin Sisters* insisted that a wayward young woman, falsely educated, could be redeemed, if repentant: Under the affectionate guidance of her parents, the co-heroine Amelia conquers the dissolute propensities encouraged in her by her childhood guardian, a fashionable and wealthy aunt.

On the important question of marriage, too, major theorists like Wollstonecraft, Hays, Robinson, Holcroft, Condorcet, and de Gouges and novelists like Bage, Fenwick, Parsons, and Ann Ward Radcliffe opposed parental tyranny in the choice of a partner.[49] Following Astell, *The Twin Sisters* assured

---

[49] Marthe Severn Storr points to Wollstonecraft's *Mary, A Fiction* as showing the harmful effects of forced marriages, in terms of their consequent barrenness, extramarital affairs, and emotional void ("Mary Wollstonecraft et le mouvement féministe dans la littérature anglaise," Diss. Paris 1931, p. 286).

parents that few daughters, if properly educated, would make dishonorable choices. Even when affianced, according to Holcroft, the young woman was not to pass merely from her parents' authority to that of her lover's, but to remain under the true authority of Reason: "Husband, wife, or lover, should all be under the command of reason; other commands are tyranny. Reason and not relationship alone can give authority."[50]

Reason and self and not the husband were also supposed to be the priorities when the young woman was actually married. Most of the radicals saw wives as having not just duties but also rights—including (for Godwin and Condorcet) the right to control their own bodies through contraception. Opinion was divided on the question of marital infidelity in women; not believing in double standards, Wollstonecraft, in *The Wrongs of Woman*, and Robinson, in *The False Friend* (1799), felt it justified if the husband were also unfaithful and/or a brute; conversely, Inchbald, in *A Simple Story*, and Alderson, in *The Dangers of Coquetry*, condemned it as punishable with disgrace, remorse, and death. Alderson, however, also affirmed that both partners in a marriage owed duty to one another; consequently, her hero dies lamenting not that his wife had sullied his "honor" by her coquetry, but that he himself had neglected his duty to correct her of her fault. Both Inchbald and Alderson traced their heroines' errors to an initial source, namely, their loss of maternal instruction early in life.

On the question of maternal duty, at least, the radicals were in unison, not only with each other, but also with the progressives and the conservatives of earlier decades. Even Wollstonecraft, in her pioneering work on the *Rights of Woman*, agreed with the conservatives that "whatever tends to incapacitate the maternal character takes a woman out of her sphere" (qtd. in the Introduction, n.pag.). She further suggested that all young girls be educated in the practical art of childrearing because their frequent ignorance of such matters increased the infant mortality rate. Given such a practical, as well as a rational education, young mothers would then be capable of bringing up their children according to the dictates of reason instead of through thoughtlessness and caprice.

The radicals also believed in the primacy of maternal love over all a woman's affections. Herself a mother of twelve children, Smith declared such love

---

<sup>50</sup> *Anna St. Ives* (1792; rpt. New York: Oxford University Press, 1970), V, 284.

to be the "strongest passion the female heart can feel."[51] Likewise, considering a mother's love for her children superior to that which she felt for her husband, in 1792 Wollstonecraft posited that neglected wives made the best mothers; she also advised widows to curb their sexual feelings and refrain from remarriage, so they could devote their lives to their children's education.[52] But if she demanded that mothers spend most of their time and efforts on their offspring, she was, nevertheless, already ahead of her time in asserting that wives and not husbands should therefore have the natural rights to the children.[53]

In spite of the insistence on the mother's importance in her daughter's education, radical fiction, like that before the 1790s, frequently portrayed motherless heroines. Smith, however, offered her heroines substitutes in the form of kindly mother-surrogates or even prospective mothers-in-law; on the other hand, following her own preference (like that of Wollstonecraft and de Staël), Hays provided her heroines with kindly, older male philosopher-friends, such as Mr. Francis (modelled on Godwin) in *Emma Courtney*. These men were affectionate, intelligent father-figures, a more common phenomenon in earlier fiction than similar female mentors. Perhaps Hays preferred men because she felt they could educate her heroines in the ways of the world and not just in female virtues, as mother-surrogates would.

But whoever their mentors, all the heroines in radical fiction commonly shared one moral trait—their rationality.[54] According to the degree of their rational self-control, these heroines fell into two categories—the ineffably good and the not-so-good. The best of the ineffably good heroines—in terms

---

[51] *Montalbert* (London: Booker, 1795), II, 180.

[52] Closer to her position in *Thoughts on the Education of Daughters* (1787) and differing from that of *The Wrongs of Woman* (1798), Wollstonecraft was unwilling to accept the legitimacy of women's sexual feelings in the *Rights of Woman* (1792). Anna Seward, whose letters show her to be a sympathizer of Wollstonecraft, nevertheless agreed with less charitable critics that Wollstonecraft's own actions often detracted from the influence of her sound educational theories. For instance, after being deserted in France by her lover Gilbert Imlay, Wollstonecraft twice attempted suicide, instead of determining to live for the sake of her infant daughter, Fanny.

[53] In her introduction to Wollstonecraft's *Mary, A Fiction*, Janet Todd records that women were not given any rights over their own children until 1839 (1789; rpt. New York: Schocken Books, 1977, p. xv).

[54] Rationality was so dear to the radicals that even in her gothic novels, Ann Ward Radcliffe ultimately offered rational explanations for all the supposedly supernatural events in them (E. B. Murray, *Ann Radcliffe*, New York: Twayne, 1972, p. 14).

of their rationality, virtue, and ultimate happiness—were those of Holcroft and the gothic novelist Ann Ward Radcliffe; they were gentlewomen of self-respect, independence, intelligence, and an unwavering fortitude in the face of all danger, human or supernatural. Smith's and Robinson's heroines equaled Radcliffe's in their moral rectitude; but unlike hers, their characterizations suffered because of their authors' sentimentality about them. Smith and Robinson portrayed most of their heroines as the epitome of womankind, and boringly described them as such. For instance, the latter says of Elvira, the beautiful fifteen-year-old heroine of *Vancenza; or, the Dangers of Credulity*: "Her mind [was] the perfection of intellect! . . . She was everything that fancy could picture, or conviction adore!—Perfection could go no further!"[55] The perfection Robinson exclaimed about seemed closer to the pseudo-romanticism of sentimental novelists than to the philosophical idealism of Godwin, more like the innocence of angels before the fall than the goodness of real but fallible human beings. In her preface to *The Wrongs of Woman*, Wollstonecraft lamented that the double standards inherent in sentimental fiction demanded such early unerring perfection from the heroines, while the heroes were allowed to mature at the normal pace of mortals.

This fault was remedied in the *tendenz* novels and plays; except for Holcroft's consistently good Anna, the not-so-good heroines were all portrayed along the lines of Aristotelian tragic figures—they suffered for some hubris or ruling passion that controlled their lives, in spite of their inherently good dispositions (and rational education). Their errors were those of mistaken judgement rather than of conscious depravity; their characterization, therefore, was more true to life than that of some of Smith's and Robinson's heroines. Thus, Fenwick's Sibella, Hays's Emma, Alderson's Louisa, Inchbald's Miss Milner, Williams's Julia, as well as Sophia Lee's Cecilia (*The Chapter of Accidents, a Comedy*, 1796), and Inchbald's Miss Dorrilon (*Wives as They Were, Maids as They Are, a Comedy*, 1797) were all human types, with both the good points and the failings of normal mortals.

In the eighteenth century, sexual passion, in particular was seen as reprehensible in women. However, unlike the conservatives and even the progressives, Hays, Fenwick, Williams, Godwin, Holcroft, and the later Wollstonecraft did not condemn it as a failing, provided it was the result of a philosophical

---

[55] *Vancenza* (Dublin: Wogan, Byrne, Grueber, et al, 1792), I, 23.

belief in free love and not looseness of principles.[56] Before their own marriage in 1797, Wollstonecraft and Godwin specifically preached as part of their new philosophy that true love was more sacred and binding than the formal institution of marriage. Such new principles effected a radical change in fiction, not only in terms of the relationship between the sexes but also with regard to the notion of chastity.

Like Richardson in *Clarissa*, the feminist radicals believed that a woman's chastity depended on her own self-image and the cleanness of her moral conscience, not on her reputation in the eyes of the world. This organic notion of chastity carried over into the arena of rape too, attempted or perpetrated. Instead of tears or fainting fits, we see Smith's Emmeline and Medora, Holcroft's Anna, and Fenwick's Sibella all rationally talk their abductors out of rape. But perhaps class-status and male protection had something to do with their escape also, for without these assets, Hays's natural-born Mary (*The Victim of Prejudice*) and Wollstonecraft's servant-girl Jemima (*The Wrongs of Woman*) find themselves less fortunate. Yet except for Jemima, who is not brought up on rational principles, none of these heroines is demoralized or considers herself defiled, not even Mary, who, unable to seek redress in a court of law, is victimized by society after her rape. Experience and a belief in their own morality teach these heroines that a man can defile a woman's body, society can punish her to the point of starvation, but demoralization can come only from within herself. This realization was a moral triumph for radical fiction; chastity, which for the conservatives had encompassed all of a woman's virtue, and consequently controlled her social acceptance, had finally been presented by an entire body of literature as a mental and not a gender-related virtue.

In their theoretical works too, radicals like Hays and Robinson objected to the double standards in morality which caused an unnatural bifurcation between so-called masculine and feminine virtues. In her *Appeal to the Men*, Hays pointed out that what was called laudable ambition in men became vanity and pride in women; Robinson objected that high spirits in men were termed vindictiveness in women (*Thoughts on the Condition of Women*).

---

[56] In France (1792–95), Wollstonecraft did not associate with the feminist revolutionaries, Olympe de Gouges, Etta Palm, and Théroigne de Méricourt because of the freedom of their sexual lives. She radically changed her views during her passionate liaison with the American adventurer Gilbert Imlay, with whom she had a daughter, Fanny, in 1794.

Robinson further protested that while a man was allowed "nobly" and "bravely" to defend himself against physical attack, a woman defending herself on the same terms was scorned as a "Zantippe." Except for Darwin, most of the other radicals did not believe physical or moral helplessness in gentlewomen a laudable virtue. Following Wollstonecraft, Hays declared that such deliberate weakness, speciously termed "innocence," was encouraged only by men who wished to keep women in a state of "perpetual babyism" and thereby to stunt their overall growth. In general, the radicals considered double standards unfair; weakness was a failing in women as it was in men because both sexes were capable of the same moral and mental perfection.

Reeve was among the few radicals who insisted on a gender-related differentiation of human behavior. She condemned what she saw as effeminacy in men as much as she did so-called masculinity in women of the upper classes, theorizing that the unisexual and dissipated manners of the youth of England pointed to a major defect in their educational systems. Like Hamilton, however, she admitted that dissipation in gentlewomen signified a radical defect in their upbringing rather than in their sex.

Dissipation was, of course, a recognized fashionable vice among the eighteenth-century *ton*. The ills stemming from dissipation were the lamentable prerogatives of only the better-born, especially men, societally punishable in women if *exposed*. Although radical theorists regretted its prevalence among the nobility and the gentility, they took great care (like the progressives and conservatives before them) to forbid it absolutely to all the lower classes. Instead, they sternly advised daughters of the middle and laboring classes to cultivate the more practical virtues of industry, frugality, and simplicity of behavior. In spite of the above class distinctions, however, the radicals insisted that virtues arising out of rationality were common to *all* women.

None of the eighteenth-century writers on female education approved of female dissipation, even if their views differed on the system which directly fostered it. The radicals were especially scornful of the excesses of the education of the person, which system included a detailed attention to physical appearance, dress, and the accomplishments. By encouraging such an education, argued Wollstonecraft, male writers from Rousseau and Gregory to Edmund Burke (whom she opposed in the 1790s as a monarchist) attempted to ensure that women remained artificial, weak creatures, whose sole interest in early life was to secure a husband through the arts of a mistress rather through reason and virtue.

According to Wollstonecraft and Macaulay Graham, this English system of instruction resembled that of the supposedly uncivilized Turks, in degrading women, even wives, to the role of a mistress; Hamilton likewise compared it to that of the Hindus. Hence the radicals felt it incumbent on themselves to expose the defects of this system. Wollstonecraft began by denigrating it for teaching girls to behave like calculating women in their childhood and like silly children in their womanhood, a role reversal which did nothing to fit them for the serious duties of life. Moreover, by concentrating only on externals, it sharpened women's senses; it also made them "the mere objects of sense" (Macaulay Graham, *Letters on Education*, p. 61). With such women, brought up only to please men, Wollstonecraft warned, when the initial ardor of a husband cooled, the urge to please—other men—would continue. Hays drew on the metaphor of slavery instead of seduction to make her point: the complete bondage to physical appearance demanded by this system would stultify a woman's body as well as her mind. The body would eventually take over the mind and render the gentlewoman dissipated, possibly immoral. In no way, therefore, could excessive attention to external appearance be deemed beneficial.

Macaulay Graham sweepingly declared that so long as both women and men proved unable to assess the appearance of the female body properly, especially with regard to physical beauty, no perfect plan of education could be devised for either sex. Not that she intended good-looking women to deny their attractiveness; like the progressive Wortley Montagu, she too believed that a correct idea of beauty as well as of chastity would keep women from falling prey to adventurers and coxcombs. But like Wollstonecraft, and, indeed, like many of the pre-1790s theorists, Macaulay Graham also stressed the importance of moral over physical beauty as ultimately more lasting.

Moral beauty, however, was to be its own reward; Wollstonecraft was upset with sentimental novelists who recompensed such virtue with external wealth as well. Thus, in her review of an anonymous novel, *The Mental Triumph: A Sentimental Tale* (1789), she approved of the author's portrayal of an artless, well-educated woman, destitute of beauty, as attracting the attention of a worthy man but objected to the novel's conclusion: "So far, so good; but why is virtue to be always rewarded with a coach and six?"[57] To Wollstonecraft, moral behavior lost some of its value if its fruits were to be counted in such materialistic terms.

---

[57] *Analytical Review*, 5 (Oct. 1789), 216.

Smith, on the other hand, followed the conservative novelists not only in rewarding moral beauty with unforeseen wealth but also in equating its physical counterpart, ugliness, with wickedness, coarseness, and an undesirable masculine boldness. She habitually described ugliness in terms of a red face, carroty red hair, often accompanied by pseudo-intellectualism, in which last she was joined by Hamilton. Smith's Mrs. Manby in *The Old Manor House* and Lady Llancarrick in *Montalbert*, like Hamilton's Miss Ardent in *The Hindoo Philosopher*, were all portrayed as older, ill-favored women, who consequently sought male approval by overemphasizing mental beauty.

Wollstonecraft and Hays were aware that conservatives like Rousseau, as well as radicals like Smith, who sometimes subscribed to his values, based their attitude to female attractiveness on the shaky foundation of external appearance. In her *Appeal to the Men*, Hays reminded her readers that youth and beauty were neither external nor universal; moreover, she felt it was unfair to judge the worth of old women and ugly women by merely physical standards. She advised readers not to scoff at the interest of the latter types in mental cultivation; instead, the young and the beautiful among them were to feel encouraged to follow their lead.

Hays further warned attractive women that they would pay in later life for the habits of flightiness and the neglect of mind they had allowed themselves in their youth. Possessing minds, in spite of themselves, and therefore being capable of reflection of some kind, in old age they would find their reflections turning only into a source of vexation: thinking would reveal their injuries to them but not the ways of redress; this would lead them to turn, in despair, to increased vanities and follies. Society would now turn a scornful rather than an indulgent eye on them for they would no longer have the twin pleas of youth and beauty to excuse their giddy behavior.

So Hays and other radicals urged gentlewomen to dress their minds rather than their bodies in youth and thereby prepare themselves for a rational and peaceful old age. Hays also cautioned women against over-attention to dress, by reminding them that the human mind must be occupied, whether in a good or evil way: "Turkish" education harmfully stuffed a woman's head with ribbons, fringes, gauzes, flounces, and furbelows instead of useful knowledge, thereby misdirecting her talents and industry into trifles.

Hamilton too warned her female readers against an excessive interest in dress, especially in French fashions, which she considered highly immodest. Using satire instead of direct exhortation, she made Sheermal, her travelling

Hindu priest, innocently praise boarding schools for giving women a lifelong taste for the feminine "science" of dress. Finding that, after years of studying French, English girls neither read nor spoke it fluently, Sheermal assumes that the only advantage of learning the language was that it "enabled them to understand the terms belonging to the particular articles of dress imported from that country France, which had its acknowledged right of imposing its fashions on other nations in Europe."[58] Like Hamilton, Reeve too did not approve of emphasis on fashion and recommended simplicity and neatness instead. All in all, the radicals showed more practical concern with dress than the progressives had done, the consensus being of course, that considerations of dress were external to a gentlewoman's moral and mental attractiveness.

As with dress, the radicals considered the accomplishments external to mental charms. If Robinson, Bage, Hays, Darwin, Hamilton, and the Edgeworths recommended them at all, it was for purposes of private solace or enjoyment and not as a passport to marriage or from a fear of idleness in women. Gentlewomen were therefore to be indulged in singing, dancing, music, and drawing, only if they had an inclination for these arts. For those further interested, Wakefield also recommended statuary; Smith, herself an artist, drawing;[59] Darwin was unique in suggesting chess as a means of both strengthening the understanding and providing recreation. He also allowed cards as a family pastime although Hamilton objected to them as possibly addictive.

As always with the radicals, educational theories were based on a view of gentlewomen as individuals, rather than as only familial and social beings; thus, knowing gentlewomen's lives to be passive, the utilitarian Edgeworths encouraged every sedentary occupation as valuable to them. Less enthusiastic about artistic pursuits, Hamilton cautioned young ladies against devoting too much time and energy to the accomplishments at the expense of their intellectual and moral development. Least enthusiastic of all, the feminist Mary

---

[58] *Hindoo Rajah* (1796; 2nd ed, rpt. London: Robinsons, 1801), I, 133. However, the *outré* fashions of the revolutionary French women did not become as popular in England as those of their more frivolous upper-class predecessors had done.

[59] Except for Monimia in *The Old Manor House*, all Smith's heroines were endowed with various artistic skills. Monimia was possibly the only heroine in sentimental eighteenth-century fiction to be totally without a knowledge of the ornamental accomplishments; even her servant-girl predecessor, Richardson's Pamela, was given such a genteel training by her mistress.

Ann Radcliffe dispensed with the ornamental accomplishments altogether, in favor of some knowledge of a trade which might later prove financially useful.

In keeping with their rational utilitarianism, the radicals paid more attention to needlework than to any of the other accomplishments, although not always with favor. Following Dr. Johnson, Macaulay Graham recommended this skill as helping to preserve female virtue and happiness, insisting at the same time, like Rousseau, that boys too learn some handicraft such as drawing to employ their leisure hours. Wollstonecraft departed from Macaulay Graham on the question of ornamental (as opposed to useful) needlework: it contracted women's faculties by confining their thoughts to the adornment of their persons.[60] Ever a disciple of Wollstonecraft, Hays too condemned needlework—it not only cramped the minds of young ladies, it also cramped their bodies by keeping them constantly in the same position. Moreover, needlework was as useless in the next life as this: "I doubt whether there will be any sewing in the next world," she joked (*Letters and Essays*, No. 4, p. 33).[61]

Matters were different for girls of the middle class. In their case, the radicals encouraged plain needlework as a useful, indeed, necessary skill. Following a century-old argument, Wakefield denied the more ornamental accomplishments to middle-class girls, unless intended for the teaching profession; otherwise, these arts would only give the girls ideas above their station in life and make them susceptible to seduction and prostitution. Nonetheless, she allowed them drawing as a useful and amusing qualification, and further suggested rational conversation and reading as occupations for leisure hours.

As seen earlier, radical theorists prescribed reading even to women of the poorer classes, but for purposes of religious enlightenment rather than for rational entertainment. They recommended needlework too, but as a useful rather than an ornamental art. Aside from these two employments, labor-class girls were not to indulge in any of the accomplishments or receive any training in the adornment of the person. Thus, in spite of the professed democratic principles of some of the radicals, when it came to education of the person, all of them gave priority to class instead of to sex.

---

[60] Objecting to Fordyce's sentimental, exhortatory style, she wrote: "It moves my gall to hear a preacher descanting on dress and needlework" (*Rights of Woman*, p. 150).

[61] Hays's youthful humor, seen in her love letters to her fiancé John Eccles before his untimely death in 1780, was almost eradicated as she became a philosophical writer in the early 1790s.

On the fourth system of education for women, that of the physique, the radicals were on the whole as much in favor of it for the upper classes as they were against that of the person. Following Macaulay Graham, Wollstonecraft urged parents to strengthen their daughters' bodies, at least so as not to destroy their constitutions by mistaken notions of beauty (as dictated by the education of the person) or of feminine delicacy (as dictated by the conservative method of education of the heart). A stronger constitution, she continued, would help gentlewomen through both childbearing and child-rearing, at the same time keeping them from the enfeebling nervous diseases to which upper-class women were often subject. Finally, she concluded, it would give gentlewomen the energy to seek their own living, if circumstances called for it.

Followers of Locke, such as Wollstonecraft and Macaulay Graham, understood that the energy needed by women either to support themselves financially or to carry on their traditional duties in the home depended on the simultaneous soundness of their physical and mental constitutions. But Robinson, herself an invalid in the 1790s, denied a necessary relationship between mind and body, supporting her position with an argument straight out of the anonymous progressive tract, *Female Restoration*. She affirmed that mental powers could not be estimated by corporeal powers, otherwise the uncultivated ploughboy would surpass the man of letters in mental capacity. Similarly, superior physical strength in men was no indication at all that their mental abilities were greater than those of the other sex.

If Robinson did not agree with some of the other radicals on the intimate relationship between a strong mind and body, she was totally in agreement with the more feminist among them that weakness, at least, was not inherent in gentlewomen. It was the result of nurture not nature and could therefore be overcome, first by dismissing all negative ideas and practices based on the theory of female physical inferiority, next by replacing them with healthier concepts and exercises.[62]

Among the first practices to be attacked were those which early conditioned gentlewomen to a sedentary life, thereby weakening their muscles, relaxing their nerves, and destroying their digestion in later life. Responding to Rousseau, Wollstonecraft insisted that indoor confinement and not natural

---

[62] Robinson praised Wortley Montagu for introducing the system of smallpox inoculation to England from Turkey, thereby helping to combat a disease that was rampant in England in the eighteenth century.

inclination forced little girls into dressing their dolls instead of participating in their brothers' sports. In addition, she continued, it was the false notion of female delicacy and its correlative idea of the weaker female frame, rather than a natural lack of stamina, that undermined female health. Even in her reviews, she lashed out at novels of sensibility which included a predilection for fevers, fainting, and tears among the heroine's charms.

Among others, Smith, especially, was guilty of this offense. She celebrated the "delicacy of frame" of her heroines, although the improbabilities of some of her narratives ironically implied in these women the robustness of peasants rather than the fragility of fairytale princesses. The best (and most comic) example is the eponymous Ethelinde: she nearly drowns in a lake, suffers a severe illness, gets drenched in thunderstorms, falls violently from a horse, and is struck by a bolt of lightning, yet lives through it all, her beauty unimpaired, to marry the hero at the end of the novel.

Of course, conservative precept and actual practice were both responsible for encouraging debility in gentlewomen. However, Rousseau, believing that healthy women made healthy babies, had condemned the restrictive blocks, tight stays, stiff collars, and other artificial constrictions used to distort women's bodies into fashionable shapes. In spite of their many differences with him, Wollstonecraft, Macaulay Graham, Darwin, and Wakefield acknowledged the soundness of his plea for the free development of the female body. But in place of these restrictions and the distortions they caused, Wollstonecraft countered with the idea of physical health, assuring her sex that a healthy bloom gave more charm to the female physique than the half-formed limbs and the real or affected delicacy of women of fashion.

Her suggestion was that both men and women change their attitudes to the female form and grant women the right to develop their bodies normally. In agreement with her own mother, as well as with Locke, Macaulay Graham, Wakefield, Hays, Darwin, and Robinson, she urged that young girls be allowed to romp around in childhood as freely as boys and be given plenty of fresh air, exercise, and cold baths to strengthen their constitutions and to immune them to all types of weather. For the young children who attended school, she recommended a large playground for adequate exercise.

Even by today's standards, the sports encouraged by some of the radicals seem vigorous, although cautious theorists like Darwin advised gentlewomen to prefer exercises that promoted physical growth to those that rendered the body robust and muscular. With some confusion of intent, Wakefield urged girls to develop strength, agility, and health the same way as boys did but reassured them that their natural physical inferiority and such female indispositions as those resulting from childbearing would keep their bodies in the appropriate degree of "feminine delicacy" (*Reflections*, p. 14). Any strength beyond that required to be a good wife and mistress of a family, she firmly concluded, was unnecessary in gentlewomen.

In spite of her concession to the conservative idealization of female delicacy, Wakefield suggested exercises like weightlifting, which were as physically demanding as those recommended by the other radicals. Alongside the traditional exercise of walking, Wollstonecraft, de Genlis, Wakefield, Darwin, Robinson, Hays, and Macaulay Graham variously proposed gymnastics, dumbbells, jumping, swimming, battledore, swinging, fencing, pulley exercises, playing ball, skipping rope, trundling the hoop, marching like soldiers (a popular exercise of the time), and what Hays called "horsewomanship."

Wollstonecraft and Hays applied this vigorous system of physical education to their novel heroines as well, who consequently enjoyed a refreshingly sound constitution. For instance, by age ten, aside from having a cultivated understanding and a well-developed intellect, Hays's Mary could leap fences, ride horses bareback, climb the highest trees, and wrestle and dance with the village children.* Significantly, in later life, this same robustness of mind and body not only helped her survive her imprisonment and physical and mental suffering, it also kept her from the demoralization that undermined her weaker mother. Thus, Hays implied, a sound mind in a sound body might not always ensure a woman's happiness in society, but it could at least protect her morals and give her peace in her own heart.

Matters were different for lower-class women: no one had ever objected to a robust constitution in women of the middle and laboring classes. In fact, as Wollstonecraft pointed out in both her *Letters from Sweden* and her *Wrongs of Woman*, the latter were given tasks befitting beasts of burden rather than the so-called weaker sex, even in the supposedly civilized nations of Europe. Benevolent radicals like Cappe therefore concerned themselves with the physical well-being of labor-class girls too. In 1797, Cappe noted with approval the visible improvement in looks, the greater activity and exertion, and the more regular attendance of the girls of the Spinning School she supervised, af-

---

* How much did Hays contribute to Catherine Morland's boisterous childhood romping?

ter the plain tea they had at home for breakfast was replaced at school by milk. With similar charitable intent, the gentlewomen who supervised the Grey Coat School with Cappe stipulated that the children should quit their work at six every evening, regardless of whether their tasks were finished or not, for nothing was to intrude on their playtime. It was a great step forward in the movements in behalf of women and the poor when good people, however few, began to insist that the daughters of the poor—the lowest of the low by reason of both class and sex—also enjoy good health and play.

In the 1790s, radical theorists about all four educational systems fought a fierce battle against the forces of reaction, even though the latter rested on whole centuries of social, political, economic, and religious prejudice against women. In spite of overwhelming opposition, these writers continued to demand changes in the status of women through a rational education. The more revolutionary among them even envisioned a Utopia on earth—a state where women and men would be equally free and rationally educated to become full-fledged, self-supporting human beings, rather than mere dolls or minions who acted according to the specifications of a sexist and classist political system.[63]

# IV. Professionalism

Themselves self-supporting women and men, the radicals encouraged professionalism in indigent gentlewomen as befitting rational, independence-loving, self-respecting citizens. The idea of genteel dependence, with all the humiliation it involved, seemed particularly repugnant to the female writers. In a poem entitled "To Dependence," Smith made a declaration in favor of economic independence, one that was often echoed by her own fictional heroines as well as those of Wollstonecraft, Hays, and Robinson:

> DEPENDENCE! heavy, heavy are thy chains,
> And happier they who from the dangerous sea,

---

[63] Sick of conditions in England, novelists like Smith and Inchbald sometimes sent their heroines and heroes to America or Africa to live in peace in a free new nation or among "noble savages," far away from the inequalities and oppression of their own civilized homeland. The "pantisocratic" scheme projected by the Romantic poets Coleridge and Southey was also a part of this restlessness among English liberals.

Or the dark mine, procure with ceaseless pains
An hard-earned pittance—than who trust to thee.[64]

More encouragingly, Wakefield assured upper-class women (as Smith did some of her heroes) that working, when the situation so demanded, did not detract from their gentility but rather gave them the true dignity of a free human being. To her, work was an honorable matter of economics; considerations of neither class nor sex were to preclude women from fulfilling their social duty through work, when imperative. She clearly understood not only the relationship between professionalism and a rational female education but also the legitimacy of women working. In fact, the opening line of her *Reflections* begins with a syllogism on this issue. The first premise is a statement made by the economist, Adam Smith (author of *Wealth of Nations*). Smith had declared every unproductive individual a burden to society; in this category, according to Wakefield, he must have included women, "since the female sex is included in the idea of the species, and as women possess the same qualities as men, though perhaps in a different degree"; therefore, women, like men, could not be free from the claims of the public for their portion of economic usefulness (p. 2).

Such glorification of the work-ethic penetrated even the consciousness of the nouveau-genteel gothic novelist Ann Ward Radcliffe (herself the daughter of a haberdasher), who shuddered at the thought of being known as a professional.[65] Her comment on the secrecy with which her heroine Ellena Rosalba supported herself and her aunt, by selling beautifully embroidered silks through a convent, stemmed directly from the philosophical jargon of the times: Ellena's mind was not yet strong enough or her views sufficiently enlarged to teach her to ignore the sneer of the rich at poverty or to "glory in the dignity of virtuous independence."[66] Significantly, as Ellena's moral judgement grows in the novel, so does her self-respect; she prefers independence by industry to clandestine marriage into a noble family, until the latter is finally willing to accept her.

---

[64] *Elegiac Sonnets and Other Poems* (1784; 9th ed, London: Cadell and Davies, 1800), p. 57.

[65] *The Posthumous Works of Anne Radcliffe . . . To which Is Prefixed a Memoir of the Authoress, with Extracts from her Private Journals* (London: Colburn, 1833), I, 13.

[66] *The Italian, or the Confessional of the Black Penitents* (London: Cadell and Davies, 1797), I, 12.

Less fortunate in real life than her financially secure, happily married, and childless namesake, Mary Ann Radcliffe realized that not all gentlewomen of her generation were or could afford to be in favor of economic independence. In her *Female Advocate*, she pleaded from men the "protection which they themselves vow to be the real rights of women. . . . All women possess not the Amazonian spirit of a Wolstonecraft [*sic*]," she admitted; most were "so perfectly tame either through custom or compulsive submission" that if economically protected, they would contentedly give up their rights as rational beings.[67] However, as she showed herself so amply aware in both her *Memoirs* and her feminist pamphlet, male protection often failed. She therefore urged that rational education for gentlewomen include a training in practical employment rather than in mere unproductive idleness. Wollstonecraft herself condemned not only idleness but also debility in gentlewomen. Following *Female Restoration*, she encouraged gentlewomen to acquire the physical strength necessary to work, assuring them that the true definition of independence was the ability to earn one's own subsistence.

In spite of all this insistence on independence, it must not be forgotten that like all the other radicals, Wollstonecraft was realistic enough to intend paid professionalism only for exceptional or indigent gentlewomen; the primary sphere for all other women was the home. The women who needed to work were impecunious single women and widowed, separated, or unsupported wives. Of course, the need to work and the availability of work were not one and the same thing; accordingly, de Gouges demanded that society equally admit women to "toutes dignités, places et emplois publics, selon leurs capacités, et sans autres distinctions que celle de leurs vertus et de leurs talens" (article VI, pp. 8–9). Not all the English radicals were as intrepid as de Gouges; reality made some of them propose professions for women that were class-related and therefore socially acceptable.

Unlike Hays, Robinson, Wollstonecraft, and sometimes Smith, Wakefield insisted that upper-class women engage only in employment that was "neither laborious nor servile," but since indigence alone would have driven them to work, the work itself was to be economically productive, without requiring capital. Aside from the few professions already open to gentlewomen, she followed de Genlis in proposing the fine arts, under which she included painting; miniature portraiture; sketches and pictures for books, for instance

---

[67] (1799; rpt. New York: Garland, 1974), pp. 398–99.

on natural history; agriculture, especially the management of ornamental gardening; coloring maps and globes; making patterns for music composing; and making designs for draperies, landscapes, printers' windows, needlework, and ornamental work. In opposition to Wakefield, but like Mary Ann Radcliffe, Hamilton actually advocated trade as an honorable enterprise, although she was aware that it was considered taboo as a form of employment for gentlewomen. More practically, the other radicals discussed professions already extant; these included the traditionally unpaid ones of the single or married woman and the paid ones of writing, teaching, acting, and, most unfortunately, prostitution.

Since the ideal of working for job satisfaction alone had not yet been current in the eighteenth century, the radicals were mostly concerned with the plight of the single, working gentlewoman, under which head one might also include widowed, separated, or even married women. (Women like Smith and Mary Ann Radcliffe, married to shiftless husbands, worked to provide for their several children and often their spouses.) Especially concerned with the economic helplessness of single women forsaken by relatives and by society, Reeve made provisions for them in her projected female seminary. She upbraided not only the brothers and kinfolk who shunned such women as encumbrances, but also the dramatists who held them up to ridicule as Aunt Deborahs and Mrs. Malaprops. In her own Mrs. Darnford, heroine of both *The School for Widows* and *Plans of Education*, Reeve presented the reader with the positive example of a virtuous woman who separates from her husband to work at various jobs to keep herself solvent. Mrs. Darnford acts as a companion to a temporarily deranged foreign woman (whom she cures of madness), as steward to a sea captain's estate, as instructor to his ward and her own adopted daughter, as governess of a school, and so on. Most importantly, she has the strength of mind to ignore the coldness of erstwhile friends and relatives and to seek satisfaction within herself. In actual fact, life seems not to have been easy for single women, even such strong fictional examples as Mrs. Darnford. A private legacy made a difference; the single and the widowed state were among the very few conditions under which gentlewomen had a legal right to their own property.

Except for the wealthy, then, the single state was far from an economic blessing in the eighteenth century; hence, like the conservatives and the progressives before them, the radicals too saw marriage as the profession most applicable to gentlewomen. They readily admitted that a marriage between two rational beings, based on reciprocal affection and esteem, could lead to happiness for both partners. After his ideal marriage to Wollstonecraft, even Godwin, who had attacked the institution of marriage as the worst of monopolies (in *Political Justice*), accepted the idea that marriage was a viable alternative to cohabitation (*St. Leon*, 1799).

Other philosophical radicals, such as Condorcet, de Gouges, Wollstonecraft, Hays, and Holcroft defined marriage as a civic contract rather than as an indissoluble and sacred bond. Aside from the social aspects of the marriage contract, all the radicals were especially aware of its economic nature—that women often married to ensure themselves future support but that as wives they also legally forfeited their rights to their own property and even to themselves. Independent-minded heroines like Smith's Rosalie in *Montalbert* refused to sell themselves into undesired marriages, but many women in real life must have been forced to do so. In the 1790s, Wollstonecraft popularized a metaphor that had been first used by the progressive Sarah Fielding, then by the conservative Hester Chapone, and even by the reactionary John Bennett, namely, that marriage entered into for purely financial purposes was a form of legal prostitution for the woman. Husbands even had the power to prostitute their wives, according to the novels of Reeve (*School for Widows*, 1791), Smith (*Desmond*, 1792), Gilbert Imlay (*The Emigrants*, 1793), and Wollstonecraft (*Wrongs of Woman*, 1798). Or they could incarcerate them as madwomen for refusing to give up their personal valuables, as in the novels of Smith (*Old Manor House*), Maria Edgeworth (*Castle Rackrent*, 1800),[68] and Wollstonecraft (*Wrongs of Woman*). Little wonder then, that most of the radicals refused to regard such marriages, which violated all the laws of decency and humanity, as either sacred or binding.

Following progressives like d'Holbach, some of the feminists campaigned through their works for better divorce laws. In actual fact, divorce was not easily obtainable; hence, wronged heroines like Reeve's Mrs. Darnford and Wollstonecraft's Maria, considering themselves divorced emotionally if not legally, take the initiative to separate from their husbands. Separation itself needed great moral strength since it automatically involved social ostracism for the wife, whether or not she was to blame. Not all women could have this strength. In Maria Edgeworth's *Letters for Literary Ladies*, the practical Caroline finds herself advising her flighty friend Julia not to leave her

---

[68] Chronologically, this novel belongs to Chapter 5.

husband, for socio-economic rather than ethical reasons: a separated woman had no resources, unless she was of the higher classes and was allowed a separate maintenance; even in the latter case, she suffered as a social outcast while her husband was freely admitted everywhere. An unfailing practicality, as well as lack of personal experience, was perhaps responsible for Maria Edgeworth's advocating passivity, instead of the active redress suggested by Wollstonecraft.

In spite of their differences on the question of marriage, all the radicals agreed that it was economic desperation as also an initial overemphasis on the education of the person that made some women the victims of seduction and, sometimes, prostitution. They offered statistics on the issue. In 1796, Hamilton's Sheermal records that "thousands and ten thousands, of these Christian women, [are] being yearly suffered to perish in the streets of their great metropolis, under the accumulated misery of want, disease, and infamy" (*Hindoo Rajah*, I, 142). In 1799, Mary Ann Radcliffe more modestly estimated that there were at least five to ten thousand prostitutes in England, a large enough number. Whatever the figures, the radicals showed more interest in the plight of the fallen woman than the progressives had done, perhaps because of the greater importance of the question of the rights of women—all women—in their decade. This concern appears especially concentrated towards the end of the 1790s, as is seen in Inchbald's *Lovers' Vows* and Wollstonecraft's *Wrongs of Woman* in 1798; and Hays's *Victim of Prejudice*, Mary Ann Radcliffe's *Female Advocate*, and Robinson's *Thoughts on the Condition of Women* in 1799.

The theorists made several suggestions to keep seduced women from prostitution, especially through governmental and social measures. Condorcet and Mary Ann Radcliffe started with prevention, the former suggesting homes for unmarried pregnant women and institutions for teaching illegitimate children a trade (in "Sur l'instruction publique," 1791–92), the latter pleading for an Asylum of Prevention to keep young, unprotected, virtuous women from seduction. It was generally agreed that even better ways to root out the evils of seduction were to devise an ethical, useful, and enlightening system of education for women, to apply equal standards of morality to the behavior of both sexes, and to place less value on a woman's technical virginity.

In most cases, however, social forgiveness, not prevention, seemed the answer. Like their peers, Wollstonecraft, Inchbald (who lost a beloved sister to the streets), and Hays were especially aware that the first false step often proved irrevocable because society immediately ostracized fallen, even raped women. Their concern, therefore, was to allow such women re-entry into society and/

or redress before they were forced by circumstances into confirmed prostitution. In their novels, these three writers vividly portrayed the hardships of unprotected, seduced, or raped women to whom society denied self-support, even through menial jobs. They lamented that such women were driven by hunger and an instinct for self-preservation to the demoralizing lifestyles of prostitution, thieving, or begging. More actively, they followed some of the conservatives in demanding that society treat seduced women with humanity. Further, they also sought justice for such women, both in and out of court. De Gouges asserted that the seducer should be forced by law to marry his victim or pay her an indemnity proportionate to his fortune. Wollstonecraft recommended that the case be considered a "left-handed marriage," the man being made to support the woman and his children so long as she remained faithful to him and until she felt capable of working for her own independence.

For women who had actually given in to prostitution, the radicals emphasized the need for rehabilitation, particularly with the help of the state and through social work by members of their own sex. First, they suggested that the state create more Magdalen homes to keep such women off the streets. Rehabilitation would halt the inevitable deterioration of seduced women; next, the benevolent concern of the government, of society, and of individuals would collectively help to convert these hapless women into useful, worthy citizens again. The reformed prostitutes would then be able to earn a living by decent means, rather than by selling themselves.

Not that there was an abundance of paid professions open to women. By the 1790s, one of the few accepted employments for gentlewomen was writing, especially of novels, educational works, children's books, and periodical articles. Some of these writers even assured other women that no modesty would be lost by publishing through subscription. Actually, most of the radical women were themselves self-supporting writers, driven to the profession through financial want or through the insolvency of male relatives. The *Lady's Monthly Museum* supported such female effort, particularly praising Charlotte Smith for rising so nobly above her well-known misfortunes: "And happy were it for every woman in narrow circumstances, if they [*sic*] had the same resources in talents as well as cultivation, and exertions as indefatigable" (May 2, 1799, 341).[69]

---

[69] For almost thirty years, Smith's children were deprived by unscrupulous lawyers of their grandfather's ample legacy. During most of this time, weighed down by court battles, she supported her nine surviving children, sometimes her husband, and even some of her grandchildren. Her novels were full of lamentation for her unfortunate condition.

Writing for profit may not have been a social asset, but in the 1790s, at least, it was proving to be a marketable business. This was so even in the case of minor women novelists, thanks to William Lane's Minerva Press, started in 1790. Lane mostly published novels for light reading, although occasionally a good writer like Robert Bage also came his way. Alderson too started her novel-writing career as what was known as a "Minerva Lady." In *The Minerva Press 1790–1820*, Dorothy Blakely records that from 1763 to 1784, Lane had paid five, ten, or twenty guineas for minor novels, while the average for the sixty or so novels published by his new Press between 1790 and 1792 had risen to thirty pounds each. Lane's circulating libraries likewise became popular all over the country, with agents as far away as New York and Bombay [Mumbai].[70] Even though it had become fashionable to decry Minerva publications, the Press showed itself woman-oriented in allowing indigent writers like the prolific Eliza Parsons a living through the pen. The works of better-known fiction writers, such as Inchbald and Mary Ward Radcliffe, were issued through more respectable publishers like the Robinsons and Cadell and Davies, often greatly to the writer's profit; Radcliffe received eight hundred pounds for her gothic novel, *The Italian*. Joseph Johnson also provided a ready market for the educational and feminist non-fictional works of new philosophers like Wollstonecraft and Hays.

For women with a good education but no writing talent, teaching was often the answer. Specific teaching positions and their salaries were class-related in the eighteenth century, upper-class women serving as private or public-school governesses, middle-class women as the teachers under them at school. Both governesses and teachers were ill-paid; the Edgeworths made a radical plea in behalf of the former in suggesting that private governesses be given a compensation of three hundred pounds a year; this would enable them to retire comfortably when their charges grew up and no longer needed their services. (This sum must have seemed outrageous to their contemporaries; one remembers that even Wollstonecraft had earned only forty pounds at the Kingsboroughs', although she seems to have been better treated socially than most governesses were.)[71] The radicals asked not only for better pay but also

---

[70] Blakely, *The Minerva Press 1790–1820* (London: Oxford University Press, 1939), p. 26.

[71] Wakefield recorded that upper-footmen earned fifty pounds a year; on the basis of sex, then, lower-class men at this level had a higher earning capacity than even better-born and better-educated women.

for more respect from employers, especially of the upper classes, for those entrusted with the important task of educating their daughters. Most optimistically of all, Robinson envisioned a university for women where members of her sex would be not just governesses but esteemed university professors in the various departments.

Robinson herself had been a well-known actress before she turned to the writing of poems and novels. Unfortunately, she succumbed to the temptations offered by the Prince of Wales and became for a time his mistress, before taking up professional writing. Other actresses, like the well-known Sarah Siddons and Elizabeth Inchbald (who gave up acting for a profitable play- and novel-writing career), maintained unblemished characters, thereby partially redeeming their profession from the reputation given it by their freer counterparts of the Restoration and early 1700s. In her *Social Life in England and France, from the French Revolution in 1789, to that of July 1830,* their contemporary Mary Berry credited the blameless conduct of Siddons and her brother John Kemble with placing the acting profession on a far higher footing than it had ever attained in any country.[72] Nevertheless, acting was still a public profession which required free interaction between the sexes; hence, except by example, the radicals did not actually encourage gentlewomen into it.

As with acting, the radicals showed themselves more cautious than the progressives in suggesting that gentlewomen attempt entry into certain male professions. Rational pragmatism perhaps kept them from making impossible demands, conditions being as repressive as they were in the 1790s. Hence, Reeve argued against women becoming philosophers, doctors of theology, and professors of the arts and sciences. Even so militant a feminist as Hays disapproved of law, theology, and politics as suitable fields for women. Wollstonecraft, Smith, and Robinson, however, agreed that women should be allowed some degree of political participation, as did de Gouges, Condorcet, and de Staël. Wollstonecraft followed the progressives Poulain de la Barre and *Female Restoration* in suggesting that women participate in military service in times of war, although she did not recommend it as a peacetime profession for her sex.

If they were less visionary than the progressives about professional possibilities for upper-class women, the radicals (often coming from Dissenting, middle-class backgrounds themselves) proved themselves more liberal than their predecessors in the sizeable list of trades they proposed for women of

---

[72] *Social Life* (London: Longman, Rees, Orme, et al., 1831), p. 37.

the middle class. Concerned writers like Wakefield, Reeve, Wollstonecraft, Hays, and Mary Ann Radcliffe variously recommended not only teaching in schools, but also practical trades such as millinery, perfuming, haberdashery, spinning, knitting, darning, mantua-making, clear-starching, lacemaking, stay-making, florist's work, professional housekeeping, embroidery and plain work, and stationery- and book-selling. Following a progressive tradition, Wollstonecraft, Wakefield, and Hays further proposed that middle-class girls serve as surgeons and physicians as well as midwives and female undertakers (in the last case to protect female modesty in death).[73] But Hays cautioned that women were not fit for certain male jobs: for example, those of masons, carpenters, blacksmiths, and farmers.

Shopkeeping was by far the most preferred profession for middle-class women. Like Drake in the 1690s, Wakefield, Mary Ann Radcliffe, and others were especially insistent that men vacate women's jobs behind the counter; conversely, they encouraged upper-class women to give their trade only to female employees and to guard the latter's morals against the advances of gentlemen-rakes. Wakefield expressed resentment at the inequality in pay between the sexes, recognizing it as "an injustice which pervades every species of employment performed by both sexes" (*Reflections*, p. 151).

Wollstonecraft and Wakefield were similarly aware of the inequality of both pay and labor in jobs available to the lowest classes, particularly with regard to domestic help. Wakefield quoted specific differences in the salaries of domestic servants of both sexes: an upper-footman received fifty pounds with perquisites, while a cook-maid got less than twenty pounds, "though her office is laborious, unwholesome, and requires a much greater degree of skill than that of a valet" (*Reflections*, p. 151). This inequality seemed to have continental parallels; Wollstonecraft recorded that even in Scandinavia, servant women performed the most menial and arduous tasks, such as washing clothes in winter in icy river water which cut and bled their hands, while their male fellow servants would not deign to "disgrace their manhood by carrying a tub to lighten the burden."[74] She shrewdly pointed out that the notion of female physical inferiority completely fell apart when it came to female

---

[73] Wollstonecraft insisted on midwives for her own two deliveries.

[74] Letter No. 3, *Letters from Sweden, Norway, and Denmark* (1796; rpt. Fontwell, Sussex: Centaur Press, 1970), p. 27.

servants—their jobs demanded far greater drudgery and vigor than those of male servants.

Along with Robinson, Trimmer, and Cappe, Wollstonecraft and Wakefield also suggested other work for lower-class women, such as employment on the land as field laborers, in manufactories as spinners and weavers, and in Charity schools as teachers and assistants. As in the case of middle-class tradeswomen, they also urged the employers, especially of their own sex, to watch over the moral, emotional, and financial well-being of their female domestics. In addition, Wakefield reminded upper-class women that it was their duty to inspect conditions for lower-class women in workhouses, in Schools of Industry, and in cottages, as well as to aid them in times of sickness and childbearing. All these recommendations showed a feminist concern with the welfare of laboring women, a significant recognition on the part of the radicals that subsistence was not the only requisite that met the needs of the poor.

This urging for women to bond and help others of their sex was perhaps one of the most significant aspects of the feminism of the 1790s. The female radicals themselves reached out through their writings to all classes of women and advised them on all aspects of their education, especially as they related to professional possibilities. Although some of the writers still adhered to class-related distinctions, their essential ideal with regard to women as a class was to encourage independence of mind, body, and soul through an appropriately rational education.

If the radicals did not always agree on the equality of all women, even as a class, they certainly believed that women were equal to men, as a sex. Following revolutionary philosophy, some of them affirmed the rights and duties of each sex in both familial and professional life to be equal in importance since both sexes were equally to be regarded as citizens of the state. Democratic feminists like Condorcet and Wollstonecraft also considered it the duty of the state to give women a threefold education in understanding their rights and duties: as members of the human race; as rational beings, developing their God-given faculties; and as economically productive agents, turning their talents and education to profitable use, when necessary.

Unlike the militant Judith Drake and the anonymous author of *Female Restoration*, who had written towards the beginning and the end of the progressive period, respectively, the feminist radicals of the 1790s were not female chauvinists. Following the more moderate reasoning of progressives like Astell, who believed in the equality of both sexes rather than the superiority of the female sex, and checked, perhaps, by the governmental oppression of their times, the radicals moderated their demands and made them practical rather than visionary. Conservatives like Rousseau had cautioned women against pleading their rights, warning them that an equal education with the other sex would make them lose their indirect power over men. Wollstonecraft's answer to him, as expressed in the *Rights of Woman*, spoke both for herself and for the feminism of the 1790s: "I do not wish them [women] to have power over men, but over themselves" (p. 107).

# CHAPTER 4

# The Reactionary Tradition, 1788–1799

"From Liberty, Equality, and the Rights of Man, good Lord deliver us."

Hannah More[1]

"Let her [More] however, go on in her career, and she may probably soon be at the head of a petticoat gang, united against levellers and Republicans, for the *preservation of grievances* [emphasis mine]."

Charles Pigott, *The Female Jockey Club* (1794)

"'It is no compliment in my mind [that women are capable of men's employments],' said Miss Sumelin; —'and so will ladies think the remainder of the century, let Mrs. Wolstonecraft [*sic*] say what she will.'"

Robert Bage, *Hermsprong* (1796)

## I.  Political and Intellectual Background

If Mary Wollstonecraft's *A Vindication of the Rights of Woman* (1792) best symbolized the educational radicalism of the 1790s, Reverend Thomas

---

[1] Quoted in Joyce Horner's *The English Women Novelists*, p. 9.

Gisborne's *An Enquiry into the Duties of the Female Sex* (1797) best summed up its reactionary opposition. The reactionaries of the 1790s were a body of militant writers who based their educational theories on the belief that woman was inferior to man, according to the decrees of God, Nature, Custom, and sometimes even Reason (the God of the new philosophers). As such, she was to be systematically trained to perform her familial and social duties rather than to believe in her personal rights.

In accepting this premise, the reactionaries were only continuing the conservative tradition that had preceded them for over a hundred years, but in light of the political turbulence of the times, they felt it even more imperative than their predecessors to uphold that "whatever is" was more right than ever in England. Their major difference from the conservatives was in their reaction to three ideologies particular to their decade: militant feminism, with its radical educational theories; the new philosophy, with its revolutionary ideas in ethics; and so-called Jacobinism, with its democratic tenets. Hence, in this chapter, the term "reactionary" is applied to these writers more to show their opposition to the radicals than to differentiate them from the conservative tradition.

Notable among the reasons which contributed to the closeness of the relationship between the conservative and the reactionary traditions was that both shared certain common leaders in the last quarter of the eighteenth century. The most influential of these educators was the evangelist Hannah More. According to her biographer, Mary Gwladys Jones, from 1789 onwards, More rejected her earlier gay secular life and became increasingly pious.[2] She kept up her association with the upper classes, however, not by social contact so much as through the moral and educational works she directed specifically at them. From 1788 to 1799, she published three major treatises, each of which ran into several editions: *Thoughts on the Importance of the Manners of the Great to General Society* (1788), *An Estimate of the Religion of the Fashionable World* (1791), and *Strictures on the Modern System of Female Education, with a View of the Principles and Conduct prevalent among Women of Rank and Fortune* (1799). Threatened as they were by the forces of democracy, the upper classes read her works with the same enthusiasm in the 1790s that they had shown for her elegant and over-estimated *vers de société* and plays in more peaceful

---

[2] *Hannah More* (Cambridge: Cambridge University Press, 1952), p. 129. Much of the information on More is from this work.

times. Like More, the educator Anna Laetitia Barbauld and the novelist Fanny Burney were as widely read on the subject of female upbringing in this decade as they had been in the two preceding ones, their established literary and social standing giving them a decided edge over the newer, bolder, and therefore far-from-decorous reputations of their radical peers, Wollstonecraft and Hays.

This continuity of tradition between conservative and reactionary influence was also apparent in the unabated popularity, at least with regard to prescription, of earlier non-feminist texts like those of Drs. Fordyce and Gregory. Lastly, although the word "Bluestocking" itself had become a term of opprobrium by this time, prominent conservatives of Bluestocking fame (other than More and Burney), namely, Elizabeth Montagu, Hester Chapone, and Hester Piozzi, continued in the public eye, commanding the affection, if not always the total respect, of their peers and of the younger generation.

In the 1790s, as earlier, Burney, More, and Barbauld continued to share a significant trait with the older Bluestockings—operating according to double standards, they followed one in their own lifestyles and recommended another for the rest of their sex. They are labelled "reactionary" solely for their educational views; even their contemporaries were aware that they themselves generally lived by radical standards. Their behavior in the 1790s amply demonstrates this fact. Thus, Burney, who had earlier denounced her benefactor Hester Thrale (Piozzi) for marrying, at the "advanced" age of over forty, a man who was both a foreigner and a Catholic, did likewise in 1793, marrying a penniless French *emigré*, Alexandre d'Arblay (Hemlow, pp. 167–172, 299).

More and Barbauld, for their part, lived continually in the public eye, at the same time prescribing that other women embrace the hearth and home. They even took part in such exclusively "male" spheres as politics and religion (especially with regard to the abolition of the slave trade), much to the ire of right-wing extremists.[3] For instance, among other projects, More directed the monumental task of educating the poor in their duties to King and Country through her *Cheap Repository Tracts* (1795–98), two million copies of which sold in the first year of their publication (Jones, p. 142).

Barbauld became known as one of the leading defenders of the rights of Dissenting men to positions in the church and state; her sympathies with the rights of men in general even made her join Joseph Johnson's revolutionary

---

[3] In the 1790s, Walpole satirized Barbauld as "Deborah" and "the virago Barbauld," while William Cobbett later styled More, "the old bishop in petticoats."

circle in the early 1790s (Ellis, I, 178–82, 114). But she did not side with the feminist Dissenters. In spite of her religiopolitical liberalism and recognized public activism, she totally opposed the rights of her own sex, especially with regard to a solidly intellectual education. Hence, whatever labels her so-called humanitarianism might induce other critics to give her, she has been included among the reactionaries in this chapter, expressly because of her retrogressive effect on educational theories about women. Not that she lost favor with the conservative public for these views; she, and especially More, remained the most respected, and probably most solvent, female reactionary voices on the subject in the 1790s.

New reactionaries also rose to prominence in this decade, notable among whom were the novelist, Jane West; the poets, Richard Polwhele and Thomas Mathias; and the theologian-theorists, John Bennett and Thomas Gisborne. They were typical products of the 1790s, combining their educational reactionism with a corresponding support of the Anglican church; all showed their patriotism by a fierce loyalty to the prime minister, William Pitt, and to the king, George III (a man of exemplary domestic habits, unfortunately given to bouts of madness from the 1780s on).

A stroke of luck for reactionary politics was Edmund Burke's monarchist hostility to the French Revolution, in marked opposition to his liberal attitude towards reform in general and the American Revolution in particular.[4] He no doubt had the beheading of the Stuart King Charles I in the previous century in mind, when, as early as 1790, in his *Reflections on the Revolution in France*, he accurately predicted the murder of the French royal pair and the consequent anarchy in France. The years between the first publication of the *Reflections* and the royal murders in 1793 saw a growing sympathy among certain circles in England for the emigrant French clergy.[5] Even Burney, now Madame d'Arblay, turned political advocate. But in her highly rhetorical and typically self-approving *Address in Behalf of the French Emigrant Clergy*, she excused her public interference as arising from an appropriately feminine

---

[4] The term "reactionary" in this chapter refers specifically to education. However, perhaps except for Barbauld, most of the reactionary educators were anti-revolutionary in their politics too.

[5] According to John Derry, not all patriots supported the French emigrants. The general political paranoia in England in the 1790s led emigrants to be suspected of being disguised revolutionaries, fear of whom made the government pass the Aliens Act in 1792 to control foreign immigration (*A Short History of Nineteenth-Century England* [London: Blandford Press, 1963], p. 19).

tenderness and humanity for the oppressed upper classes, rather than from an undesirable masculine boldness in herself.

The possibility of political oppression in England was a major source of concern to both the reactionaries and the radicals—with an important difference. D'Arblay and her peers were largely interested in the continuation of things as they were, that is, in upholding the rights of upper-class men. The political radicals, on the other hand, were concerned with the rights of all men (especially the poor), as preached by Tom Paine; the feminist radicals were more concerned with the rights of women, as championed by Mary Wollstonecraft. Furthermore, unlike the radicals, the reactionaries affirmed that in education as in politics, women and the poor were to be prescribed only their duties on this earth, with the promise of enjoying their rights in the life hereafter. Nor were women and the poor, both politically unrepresented groups, to be allowed to think for themselves; Burke, More, and others taught their readers that the church and the state, as well as leaders like themselves, would do the thinking for these groups.

The reactionaries were especially insistent that women were not to think about their own rights—at best, these were considered as purely speculative, at worst, as morally harmful. In her first novel, *The Advantages of Education, or, the History of Maria Williams* (1793), Jane West made a clever analogy between contemporary feminists and ogres of yore. Her comic female narrator, the "old-maid" Prudentia Homespun, tells her readers that in their times, there are no dragons, enchanters, or giants for heroes to combat: "the evils most dangerous to the damsels of the present age, lurk in the bosoms of their pretended champions."[6]

As the main champion of the rights of women, Wollstonecraft became the target of prolonged attack, an attack that increased in venom in the course of the 1790s. Initially, around 1792, only her educational precepts and feminist concepts were refuted. Thus, in a poem on the rights of women, Barbauld followed Rousseau, smilingly asserting that the real "right" (she meant "purpose") of women was to love. Similarly, More's primary response to Wollstonecraft's feminism was not entirely serious. With an attempt at feminine frivolity, the evangelist wrote to her friend, Horace Walpole, in 1793:

---

[6] *Maria Williams* (1793; rpt. New York: Garland, 1974), II, 204.

> I have been much pestered to read the 'Rights of Women,' but I am invincibly resolved not to *do* it. Of all jargon, I hate metaphysical jargon: besides there is something fantastic and absurd in the very title. How many ways there are of being ridiculous! I am sure I have as much liberty as I can make good use of, now I am an old maid; and when I was a young one, I had, I dare say, more than was good for me.[7]

Influential, militant, and therefore as "masculine" as the leader of the radicals, More ironically saw herself as at opposite poles from the "unsexed" Wollstonecraft. The essential difference between the two women, of course, lay not in their personalities but in their ultimate aspirations for their sex and in their private and public conduct.

As already seen in Chapter 3, Wollstonecraft's liaisons and the posthumous publication of Godwin's misunderstood *Memoirs* of her did much to interfere with the general acceptance of her sound educational proposals. In the last two years of the decade, the reactionaries triumphantly drew moral parallels among her life, principles, and death. For instance, in one of the many notes to his poem, *The Unsex'd Females*, Polwhele gloatingly noted that Wollstonecraft's death (from puerperal fever) strongly marked the distinction between rather than the equality of the sexes: "The hand of Providence [was] visible in her life, her death, and in the *Memoirs* themselves."[8] Similarly, the *Anti-Jacobin Review and Magazine*, started in 1798 specifically to combat the principles of democracy and of the new philosophy, called her a buoy rather than a beacon to her sex.[9] Even the *Lady's Monthly Museum*, generally conducted on feminist principles, opposed Wollstonecraft as an enemy instead of a champion of her sex. "The Old Woman," a serial writer for the magazine, exulted at the waning influence of Wollstonecraft and her disciples towards the end of this decade:

> A WOLLSTONECROFT [*sic*], who squared her principles to her conduct, no longer stimulates the vain and the bold, nor stuns the sensible and the mild. The champions of female equality, who were as inimical to the happiness and

---

[7] Qtd. in Luther Weeks Courtney's *Hannah More's Interest in Education and Government*, *The Baylor Bulletin*, 32, No. 4 (Dec. 1929), 38.

[8] The Unsex'd Females (1798; rpt. New York: Garland, 1974), pp. 29-30.

[9] In a review of Godwin's *Memoirs*, 1 (July 1798), 94.

interest of the sex as those who preached up the doctrine of liberty and equality to the men, are no longer regarded as sincere and politic friends, but as base and insidious enemies. For they must be the most bitter enemies who would try to rob women of the influence derived from their beauty, their temper, and their worth; and substitute in their room a contention for power, and an emancipation from restraints which are imposed by society, and sanctioned by God.[10]

Quite in keeping with this antipathy to Wollstonecraft, the opening article in the first volume of the *Lady's Monthly Museum* praised Hannah More, leader of the opposition. In her *Strictures* of 1799, More herself attacked Wollstonecraft far more spitefully than she had done in her letter to Walpole in 1793. Ironically, in light of this attack, her major educational precepts, as expressed in this work, frequently paralleled those in the *Rights of Woman*, a point that their contemporary, the social historian Mary Berry, noted with great amusement (Jones, p. 115). Nevertheless, ever if the leaders demanded many of the same improvements in women's education, their aims, as noted earlier, were entirely unrelated. Wollstonecraft intended women to use their education for personal and civic benefit; More intended it for the glory of the spirit and of God.

The two leaders also differed in the social classes they attempted to reach. Wollstonecraft directed her *Rights of Woman* mainly at the middle class; More wrote her *Strictures* for gentlewomen. In its capacity as reactionary monitor, the *Anti-Jacobin* praised More's treatise but instructed her to address herself to middle-class women as well, to prevent them from aping the education of their social superiors (Oct. 4, 1799, p.199). But she also found herself a champion. An article in the *Lady's Monthly Museum* defended More's class-bias, arguing that an aversion to democratic principles forced reactionaries like her to concentrate only on the education of the privileged classes (May 2, 1799, p. 397).

More's class-bias and pietist emphasis, although not her inconsistently radical precepts on education, were echoed by the other reactionaries with varying degrees of agreement. There was, however, no disagreement among them in their first premise about female education: It was to be used to keep woman in her inferior place so that the male-oriented church and state could

---

[10] *Lady's Monthly Museum*, 1 (Sept. 1798), 186. This magazine is discussed in both Chapters 3 and 4 because its articles included both radical and reactionary viewpoints.

continue to maintain their joint supremacy, a supremacy that seemed dangerously threatened in the 1790s by the atheism and democracy advocated by the French revolutionaries.[11] This fear colored the theories of the reactionaries on all the essential points of female education: regarding women's capabilities, their systems of instruction, and their professional possibilities; nothing, in short, was to free women from the bastille to which conservative theory had attempted to commit them throughout the eighteenth century.

## II. Works, Theories, Places of Education

In *The Pursuits of Literature*, James Mathias stated: "Literature, well or ill conducted, is the great Engine by which all Civilized States must ultimately be supported or overthrown."[12] In keeping with this political view of literature, the reactionaries launched an extensive campaign to remind women, especially of the upper classes, of their gender-related duties and also to combat the subversive influence of feminism, democracy, and the new philosophy. Like other eighteenth-century conservative theorists, they believed that regulating female behavior was best effected by controlling the limits of their education. To this purpose, they wrote different types of didactic literature, warning their female readers against whatever they regarded as harmful in current systems of instruction.

They were especially fond of the genres that had become common to women's literature by the 1790s: children's stories, courtesy books, poems, plays, novels, and even periodicals. Well-known educators of children, Barbauld and her brother John Aikin collaborated on a popular six-volume collection, called *Evenings at Home* (1792–96), which instructed children through entertaining dialogues, fables, and tales in principles of gender-related virtue, as well as in subjects such as natural history, chemistry, mineralogy, and geography. These six volumes were so popular for children ages seven to ten that they continued to be reprinted until 1891.[13]

---

[11] Abolishing religion, the militant French revolutionaries had exalted the Goddess of Reason in its place by 1793.

[12] From "Dialogue the Fourth and Last" (1794–97; rpt. London: Becket and Porter, 1812), p. 212.

[13] Betsy Rodgers, *Georgian Chronicle: Mrs. Barbauld and her Family* (London: Methuen, 1958), pp. 122, 125.

Like the conservatives before them who wrote mainly for gentlewomen, the reactionaries also wrote courtesy-book-cum-educational treatises geared at improving the morals and manners of young ladies.[14] For instance, Isabella Howard, Countess of Carlisle, wrote *Thoughts in the Form of Maxims, addressed to Young Ladies, on their First Establishment in the World* (1789); John Bennett published *Letters to a Young Lady* (1789); and John Burton, *Lectures on Female Education and Manners* (1793). In a heavier strain and with a far greater religious emphasis were Thomas Gisborne's *Enquiry into the Duties of the Female Sex* (1797) and Hannah More's *Strictures on the Modern System of Female Education* (1799).

In response to her growing evangelicalism, More gave up poetry and play-writing in the 1790s, but others, like the poets Richard Polwhele and James Mathias and the dramatist Joanna Baillie, used these literary genres to teach female virtues to their readers. The two men wrote long, satirical poems, with even longer explanatory footnotes, in weak imitation of Pope's *Dunciad*. Baillie's moralistic *Plays of the Passions* are boring to today's reader, although they were much appreciated in their time. Apparently in the 1790s, as before, the conservative section of the reading public judged literature more by its didactic intent than its intrinsic merit. But even so moral-oriented a critic as Barbauld acknowledged in her introduction to Mark Akenside's *Pleasure of the Imagination* (1795) that didacticism did not make great literature.

As a genre, the novel, in particular, suffered because of the heavy educational intent of writers in the 1790s. Yet the continued attacks on this form resulted from its supposedly immoral influence and not from its literary weaknesses. Except for Barbauld and the Countess of Carlisle, all the reactionaries attacked the novel, including its two major *exponents*, Fanny d'Arblay and Jane West. With the double standards typical of both reactionary and conservative women, the two novelists condoned their own use of the form as educational and moral. D'Arblay further attempted to circumvent the issue by refusing to label as a novel her third fictional work, *Camilla, or a Picture of Youth* (1796). She had two explicit reasons for this refusal. First, she felt a novel "gives so simply the notion of a mere love story that I recoil a little from

---

[14] Joyce Hemlow points out that after *Émile*, courtesy books tended to merge into educational treatises (*The History of Fanny Burney*, p. 164).

it. I mean it [*Camilla*] to be *sketches of character and morals, put in action.*"[15] Second, and more important, she was aware that Queen Charlotte had long resisted allowing the princesses to read her second fictional work, *Cecilia*, because it had the word "novel" in its title. D'Arblay's ruse worked. As Bridget MacCarthy sarcastically states:

> Her Majesty allowed the three older princesses, aged respectively thirty, twenty-eight, and twenty-six, to read *Camilla* without first censoring it. If Madame d'Arblay sold her genius for a mess of patronage, verily she had received her reward.[16]

But the end must have been well worth the means to d'Arblay, for her reward also included the high acclaim of her peers and of her beloved father, who described the work as "the best system of Education I ever saw, particularly for females."[17]

Although as highly respected as d'Arblay by the end of the century, West began her novel-writing career as a Minerva Lady. Her first novel, *The Advantages of Education, or, the History of Maria Williams* (1793), was a very readable piece of fiction, both instructive and entertaining. As her fame grew, however, both she and her comic narrator, Prudentia Homespun, lost some of their initial liveliness. West now claimed that she used the novel form purely to expose the new philosophy through one of its own vehicles. Yet in terms of her anti-leveling principles, it is ironic that in her novel-cum-poem, *A Gossip's Story and a Legendary Tale* (1796), the poetic tale is the story of a brave but low-born crusader who loves and marries an earl's daughter, on the basis of his virtue and personal worth (new philosophical principles) rather than his newly acquired knighthood.[18] A host of lesser novelists also capitalized on reactionary hatred of the new philosophy and of feminism, especially after

---

[15] Letter to her father from Bookham, June 18, 1795, in *Journals and Letters* (Oxford: Clarendon Press, 1972), III, 117.

[16] *The Later Women Novelists 1744–1818* (New York: Salloch, 1948), p. 126.

[17] Quoted in Hazel Mews, *Frail Vessels*, p. 36.

[18] Only Burton and the nobly-born Countess of Carlisle openly subscribed to the radical theory that virtue was more important than birth. Burton taught that dignity of birth was worthless without dignity of conduct; Carlisle asserted that dignity of birth and rank were not things to be vain about for "they are accidents, not always acquired by merit" (*Thoughts in the Form of Maxims* [1789; 2nd ed. rpt. London: Cornell, 1790], p. 106).

Wollstonecraft's death in 1797 and the publication of Godwin's *Memoirs* of her in 1798. Even a sixteen-year-old like Sophia King found an audience for her trite, badly written novel, *Waldorf, or the Dangers of Philosophy*. All these novels, however, only concentrated on what they deemed the abuse and absurdly impractical applications of radical ideals, refuting them by deliberate distortion rather than through rational argument.

The *Anti-Jacobin Review and Magazine* expressly attacked radical ideals in education, women's rights, and ethics. In the preface to Volume III, it exulted over the dissolution of "this democratic viper," namely, its educational, political, and literary opponent, the *Analytical Review* (May-August 1799, p. v). In its vitriolic abuse of the radicals Wollstonecraft, Robinson, Inchbald, Smith, Williams, Hays, Holcroft, and Godwin, the *Anti-Jacobin* was consistently uncivil and often even crude. Moreover, like some other journals of this period, it praised the literary efforts of only those writers who agreed with its own political stance. Thus, Polwhele's indifferent versification in *The Unsex'd Females* was applauded as "good poetry" because he had employed his poetical talents on the side of Britons and Christians (May 3, 1799, p. 33). Conversely, Charlotte Smith's *Young Philosopher* was criticized for its politics rather than its intrinsic defects, the reviewer reminding his readers that the best English female novelists, d'Arblay, for instance, did not interfere with church and state (1 August 1798, 190).

The *Anti-Jacobin* had accurately assessed d'Arblay's reactionary principles, even though on one significant occasion her "femininity" prevented their propagation. According to her biographer, L. B. Seeley, she modestly declined a Mrs. Crewe's proposal to start and direct a weekly anti-Jacobin paper, to be called *The Breakfast Table*.[19] Equally reluctant, Barbauld rejected Maria and Richard Lovell Edgeworth's offer to start a *Feminead*, a literary paper which was to be written entirely by gentlewomen, accepting all the articles submitted to it. She wrote to Maria Edgeworth, declining to participate in the project (as she had earlier refused Elizabeth Montagu's offer to direct a female academy), saying:

There is no bond of union among literary women any more than among literary men; different sentiments and connections separate them much more than the joint interest of their sex could unite them. Mrs. Hannah More, [*sic*] would

---

[19] *Fanny Burney and Friends* (New York: Scribner and Welford, 1890), p. 307.

not write alongside you or me, as an evangelist, and we probably should hesitate at joining Miss Hays or—if she were living—Mrs. Godwin.[20]

Instead of herself, she suggested Joanna Baillie, Amelia (Alderson) Opie, Lucy Aikin (her niece), and Samuel Rogers, whom she thought might join the scheme. For the second time in half a century, Barbauld had turned down a major proposal that would have intellectually benefited her sex. Apparently the Edgeworths, themselves turning conservative toward the end of the decade, did not pursue the scheme any further either.[21] With d'Arblay's rejection of Mrs. Crewe's proposal, the *Anti-Jacobin* remained the chief periodical to represent reactionary views on women's roles and on politics.

In conjunction with *Anti-Jacobin* propagandizing, the four major writers, More, Gisborne, Barbauld, and d'Arblay, also presented the public with various reactionary theories on female education. Religion and morals were the basis of all their theories; More, Gisborne, and Barbauld, however, often generalized about both sexes, whereas d'Arblay wrote mostly about (upper-class) women. In her *Strictures*, More divided a human being into three parts—the spiritual, the intellectual, and the physical—insisting that education be geared to these three parts in decreasing degrees of importance. According to her, the grand end of female education, in particular, was moral excellence through religious piety, of which domestic life was the proper sphere. In opposition to Rousseau's theory (advocated even by radicals like Macaulay Graham) that children should not receive religious instruction until they were capable of thinking and judging for themselves, More, Gisborne, and Barbauld stressed the absolute need for parents to indoctrinate children's minds with what they called legitimate religious "prejudices."[22] They believed this early inculcation would ensure not only a principled adult life but also happiness in the hereafter.

---

[20] A. I. Thackeray, *A Book of Sybils* (London: Smith, Elder, 1883). p. 41.

[21] The French entry into Ireland and the peasant revolt of 1798 directly affected the Anglo-Irish Edgeworth family. A Catholic mob rose against them as they took shelter from home in Longford; at the same time, Richard Lovell was accused of being a French spy. The family was deeply affected by the Longford incident (Butler, pp. 138–39). Perhaps it helped to further cool R. L. Edgeworth's earlier enthusiasm over the French Revolution, as well as his general radicalism.

[22] Wollstonecraft and the new philosophers believed that a rational education would necessarily lead a person to virtue; the reactionaries believed that only a religious education, early inculcated, could do so.

Their reasons for demanding an early education in religious principles were, however, different. The severe evangelist More, subscribing to the doctrine of original sin, condemned children as beings with a corrupt nature and an evil disposition, which it was the prime end of education to rectify.[23] Thus, the purpose of education for her was to weed out this original evil with which a child was supposedly born. Such early cleansing of the soul would have salutary secular and religious effects on the female sex in particular—it would train the girl to lay up "rich resources" for the "sober season of life" and teach the woman to age gracefully, thereby leading the sex to "as much perfection as was possible in this corrupt earthly frame."[24] (In essence, her theory that God is good but humans, innately evil, was not so very different from Rousseau's in *Émile*.)

On the question of the nature of the child's mind, Gisborne did not revert to the theory of original sin, as More did, although with regard to life after death for sinners on earth, his *Enquiry* was as full of threats of hellfire and damnation as were More's *Strictures*. In an argument that closely resembled Barbauld's (in "On Prejudices") and also that of Hays, he pointed out that Locke's comparison of the human mind to a blank sheet of paper failed in the material point that "the sheet of paper deposited on a shelf, or locked up in a drawer, continued a blank," while this was not the case with the youthful mind. He warned that if parents forbore to improve the child's mind with their own ideas and sentiments, it would receive harmful impressions from the influence of others:

The mind, be it assumed, is originally an unsown field, prepared, it may be, for the reception of any crop. But if those, to whom the culture of it belongs, neglect to fill it with good grain, it will speedily and spontaneously be covered with weeds.[25]

---

[23] Anna Seward indignantly attacked More for denying the innocence of children, in a letter to Mr. Whalley, dated from Lichfield, November 19, 1801 (*Letters* [Edinburgh: Constable, 1811], V, 412–13).

[24] *Strictures* (1799; rpt. New York: Garland, 1794), I, 58.

[25] *Enquiry* (1797; 11th ed. rpt. London: Cadell, Davies, 1816), p. 46. This image is originally from a parable of Christ's. However, the simile of the mind as a field or garden to be lovingly cultivated by parents was popular in the second half of the eighteenth century, beginning in the novel with *Pamela*, Part II.

It was therefore imperative that, above all, parents give their children a religious instruction, which, in turn, would give them the principles of conduct that could ensure some happiness in this life and complete joy in the future state. Gisborne believed it was only the secondary aim of education to give gentlewomen a training in ornamental acquisitions, which would provide for some of their comfort and usefulness on earth.

Barbauld's theory of the nature of education, as outlined in "What is Education?" was more comprehensive than More's or Gisborne's.[26] It seemed to be drawn from the eighteenth-century idea greatly popularized by Godwin that the educational process goes on throughout a person's life and not merely in the period of youth. She defined education as "the whole process by which a human being is formed to be what he is, in habits, principles, and cultivation of every kind" (*Works* II, 306). Like More, she differentiated among three types of education: direct education, apparent education or "the education of circumstance—insensible education," and the "education of events." Direct education was formal, given by precept and in keeping with one's social rank. According to Barbauld, it was far less influential than the "education of circumstance." This process, she felt, insensibly began the moment the child was able to form an idea and to observe, consciously or otherwise, his social standing and the example of his parents, their company, their friends, and their servants. Unlike de Genlis, Barbauld did not find it necessary for the parents to use fancy apparatus or retire from society for this second type of education—the child was best brought up in its parents' social world. "Education of events" corresponded to what Inchbald called "the school of adversity": It was given by Providence through the teaching of "faded beauty, humbled self-consequence, disappointed ambition, loss of fortune" to ameliorate the temper and bring out all the energies of the finished character (p. 318). Such an education would cure everything if life were long enough, she wrote, piously concluding with the hope that God would "renew the discipline in another state, and finish the imperfect man" (p. 320).

Barbauld's, Gisborne's, and More's theories were based on their strong religious beliefs. D'Arblay's theory of female education, as outlined in *Camilla*,

---

[26] In the *Monthly Magazine*, 5 (1798), 167–71. She was writing here largely on the education of the male child, although the principles seem general enough to include in a discussion on theories of female mental processes. This essay was published as "On Education" in the second volume of her collected *Works* (London: Longman, Hurst, Rees, et al., 1825).

was more secular. Following the conservative tradition from Halifax to Rousseau, she envisioned the purpose of female education as molding a woman to suit her husband's status and temper. In accordance with this, Mr. Tyrold writes to his daughter Camilla that he has brought her and her sisters up without any specific expectations, but rather with as much simplicity as is compatible with instruction, with invariable principles, and with an ability to accommodate to the world at large. Since his educational aim is secular, his fears are temporal instead of other-worldly. No parent, he continues, can foresee the situation in life to which his daughter will belong by marriage and therefore educate her for it. Even if no outward vicissitudes appear, "the proper education of a female, either for use or for happiness, is still to seek, still a problem beyond human solution; since its refinement, or its negligence, can only prove to her a good or an evil, according to the humour of the husband into whose hands she may fall." But through her heroine's example, d'Arblay showed that it was not enough for parents merely to give their daughters virtuous principles. Their duty also consisted in superintending the girls' first entry into society, to prevent the contagion of dissipated or immoral example.[27] Gisborne gave another warning for this danger-prone stage between the close of formal education and a young lady's first "coming out." Insightfully, he pointed out that when domestic education was drawing to a close, the shackles of instruction were to be gradually not abruptly dropped, so that the student would retain the habit of steady application, instead of suddenly finding a large amount of time on her hands. There was no need for him to descant on idleness. Conservatives like Fordyce had amply discussed the negative effects of idleness and free time on the female character.

The rigid regulation of a gentlewoman's free time implied daily, even hourly, supervision; hence the next question on female education was where it should take place. The old controversy between home and school education was as much an issue for the reactionaries as it had been for preceding educators. Like most eighteenth-century theorists, they agreed that home education under the mother's supervision was the ideal situation for young ladies; mothers best understood their daughters' dispositions and could teach them habits of virtue, orderliness, and domesticity.

Unlike most novelists, and even unlike their own other works, both d'Arblay and West presented their heroines with mothers, in *Camilla* and

---

[27] *Camilla* (1796; rpt. London: Oxford University Press, 1972), III, 356.

*Maria Williams*, respectively. Camilla's mother, Mrs. Tyrold, is adored by her family, yet she is a stern, matronly figure; like Wollstonecraft's Mrs. Mason in *Original Stories*, she inspires distant respect rather than affection in the reader. On the other hand, Maria Williams is blessed in being perhaps the only eighteenth-century English heroine to have a loving mother-preceptor, a mother who remains by her side throughout the novel,[28] singlehandedly giving her a virtuous education, protecting her from a would-be seducer, and marrying her to a good man of whom both approve. Maria and her mother are as fully devoted to each other as Adèle and the baroness d'Almane are in de Genlis's fictional treatise, *Adèle et Théodore*. But there is an important difference. While Madame d'Almane continues to supervise her daughter's education even after her marriage, West follows Rousseau's conservative tradition of transferring the heroine's education to her lover. Because they both love her, mother and lover adequately fulfill their roles as Maria's preceptors. As Gisborne said in his *Enquiry* (following Locke): "That instructor who is loved the best will commonly prove the most efficacious" (p. 59).

Unlike these fictional examples, not all mothers, apparently, were leisured, dedicated, or educated enough to instruct their own daughters. The reactionaries recognized that in the case of upper-class women, social duties or even a husband's prohibition sanctioned their giving up this important maternal duty. In such cases, they could either hire a private governess or send their daughters to boarding school. Unlike the radicals and the progressives, they did not propose any other school system for gentlewomen: "Whatever is" might not always be right in the case of boarding schools, but, as an established source of upper-class female education, they earned cautious acceptance from some of the reactionaries. In *Maria Williams*, Prudentia Homespun debates the pros and cons of boarding school education, using arguments that myriad theorists had discussed before her. For her, the drawback of such an education was its superficiality and over-emphasis of the accomplishments. Its advantages, on the other hand, were that it removed local prejudices, inculcated habits of industry, and excited emulation in the student. But emulation, at best, was considered a mixed asset for women; Gisborne agreed that it was one of the few beneficial consequences of school education yet warned that it was to be exercised only in the Christian virtues and not in schoolwork. A competitive spirit in schoolwork could lead only to negative traits like pride,

---

[28] Camilla's mother is absent in Lisbon at a critical time in her daughter's life.

envy, detraction, malevolence, contempt, and self-conceit, "some of the darkest passions of the human mind" (p. 71).

Class-differentiation was as important to reactionary educators as was morality; like the conservatives, therefore, most of them strongly advised that middle-class girls be kept away from boarding schools for young ladies. The passing concern of the reactionaries with the education of middle-class girls was expressed chiefly in a negative: they were not to ape the education of upper-class women. Home was the best place of instruction for them, unlike the female poor, whom social workers like More believed could be profitably institutionalized; in their case, More followed up her precepts with action; for her, the education of the poor was entirely a matter of benevolence—it was to be the concern of social superiors like herself, and not of the government, as Wollstonecraft had suggested.

More was further encouraged in this belief by the evangelical reformer, William Wilberforce. In 1789, she and her sister Martha defied local landowners and farmers, opening Sunday schools (on the Raikes and Trimmer plan) in the district around Cheddar in the Mendip hills. Their scheme included not just Sunday-school instruction but also industrial education for girls on weekdays, as well as religious education for adults in the evenings. For the girls, reading and religious knowledge were the only curriculum, besides spinning, weaving, and the domestic arts. More believed the poor should be given no further education and considered even instruction in writing as potentially seditious.[29] She encouraged morality, nevertheless, by holding annual feasts where she made a present of five shillings, a pair of white stockings, and a Bible to girls who had married during the year and kept a reputation for chaste behavior and good works (Courtney, p. 124). Like the radicals Cappe and Trimmer, the More sisters too were concerned with the welfare of the poor; they organized women's clubs, closely connected to the schools, and helped their widowed and sick members.

Their purpose was not entirely apolitical. Hannah More believed that contentment and morality would make the poor appreciative of conditions in England as compared to the turmoil in revolutionary France. As Jack Anvil the blacksmith teaches Tom Hod the mason, in her marvelously successful piece of propaganda, *Village Politics* (1792), the English poor enjoyed the "true rights of man" which consisted of the natural right to use one's limbs

---

[29] Josephine Kamm, *Hope Deferred*, pp. 99–100.

and liberty, the civil right to use the laws, and the religious right to use the Bible; all else is "nonsense, madness, wickedness."[30] With greater honesty, More pointed out in her *Strictures* that although equal rights existed in the books, in reality the poor had no right to complain against abused laws. Her solution was social rather than legal—the rich were to do their duty by their inferiors, instead of reforming the legal system and making it more equitable.

Instruction and politics were therefore closely associated in the theories of the reactionaries on women's education. All their efforts were aimed at silencing women and the poor on the question of their rights: their lot was to consist of duties in this life and rewards in the next. Like the radicals, the reactionaries emphasized virtue, but unlike the former, they defined virtue in terms of cheerful submission rather than rational independence. It is not surprising then, that of the four main systems of female education prevalent in the eighteenth century, these writers preferred the one that concentrated on morality and good behavior—the system better known as the education of the heart.

## II. Education of the Heart, the Head, the Person, and the Physique

With their emphasis on duty, it was natural that the reactionaries stressed the education of the heart and not of the head, the person, or the physique. Like other eighteenth-century moral theorists, they especially condemned the system that concentrated entirely on personal adornment. For instance, More began the introduction to her *Strictures* thus: "It is a singular injustice which is often exercised towards women, first to give them a most defective education, and then to expect from them the most undeviating purity of conduct" (I, ix).

Her statement echoed a well-worn progressive argument made from Astell to Wollstonecraft; her emphasis, however, was even more pietist than Astell's. She objected that girls were educated only for the transient period of youth, for a crowd rather than for living at home, for the world and not for themselves (that is, spiritually), for show and not for use, for time and not for eternity. Moreover, her evangelicalism led her to believe that the entire

---

[30] *Works* (1835; rpt. New York: Harper, 1855), I, 366.

regulation of a woman's heart and affections depended not on the individual alone but on the operation of divine grace. To Godwin's theory of human perfectibility, More opposed the Christian theory of human frailty. Moral perfection was beyond human attainment, yet it was the duty of every Christian to cleanse her or his heart by extinguishing sin, subduing a worldly temper, and controlling irregular desires.[31]

The Reverend John Bennett's aim was far more secular than Hannah More's, continuing in a straight line, in both style and content, from the conservatism of men like Rousseau, Fordyce, and Gregory. He saw in woman's charming serviceability to man her primary reason for existence:

> The softer sex, it is certain, are exceedingly injured by their education. If they were what they should be, they are those lights in the picture of human [men's] life, that are intended to cheer all its darkness and its shades.[32]

In her critique of Bennett's *Letters* for the *Analytical Review*, Wollstonecraft pointed out that male-oriented systems like his, which couched their sexism in gallant euphemisms, debilitated rather than strengthened female character and worked against women rather than for them.[33]

The aims of most of the other reactionaries were not as intentionally enervating as Bennett's nor as entirely pietist as More's—but neither were they liberal. For what they feared more than the learned woman, or the frivolously dissipated woman, was Wollstonecraft's new ideal of the assertive woman, who, believing in her rights to her own mind and body, to independence of thought and of subsistence, and to a civic and political existence, refused to accept the status of woman as it then was. Wollstonecraft had insisted

---

[31] *Thoughts on the Importance of the Manners of the Great to General Society* (1788; 6th ed. London: Cadell, 1788). p. 19.

[32] *Letters to a Young Lady* (1789; rpt. New York: Clusman, 1830), p. 7. The anti-feminism of conservatives and of reactionaries like Bennett is symbolized by their inability to call or accept women as women, that is, as human beings like men. Instead, they always called women "the fair sex" or some such corresponding term, with its connotations of imbecile beauty and gender-related enervation.

[33] She described his entire *Letters* as consisting of nothing that Gregory, Chapone, Pennington, and Fordyce had not already said more elegantly. She found his taste artificial and his style too imitative of the novels for which he had so much contempt. Trying to adapt himself to what he saw as inferior female capacity, she wrote, "he sometimes softens his tone into a whine," while his supposedly friendly and rational precepts are "interlarded with pretty periods and absurd epithets" (January 4, 1790, 104–05).

that such a woman, intelligently aware of her rights, would also be more efficient in the performance of her duties. The reaction preferred to oppose the whole question of the rights of women and concentrate solely on their gender-related duties.

Gisborne, More, Barbauld, and others were fully aware that such duties involved many petty trials and sacrifices, which could well breed a spirit of dissatisfaction and unrest. So, like the conservative Rousseau and the pragmatic radicals, the Edgeworths, they advised that women be early habituated to the female virtues of restraint and patience. In the same letter to Walpole in which she had refused to read the *Rights of Woman*, More applauded such restraint: "There is perhaps no *animal* [emphasis mine] so much indebted to subordination for its good behavior, as woman" (quoted in Courtney, p. 38).

So the education of the heart was to consist of a systematic training in subordination, the prime quality that would make women perform their duties uncomplainingly. In this system alone, all women were to receive a common education in usefulness, while ornamental or intellectual education was to be given strictly according to class. The main duties of the entire female sex were to be good daughters, wives, mothers, companions, friends, and, if of the upper classes, mistresses of families (that is, of household servants). As West put it, in *Maria Williams*, a good heart, regular temper, and proper conduct were as necessary for a mechanic's daughter as an earl's. Polwhele presented Queen Charlotte as an example to his readers; she was "thoroughly skilled in the cultivation of the heart" and had given her daughters a virtuous education "whose high example must surely have a benignant influence on the British ladies unless the example of the great hath ceased to attract imitation" (p. 35).

Like the conservatives, the reactionaries affirmed that God and Nature had not only prescribed these duties to women as members of the inferior sex but had also implanted in women a willingness to perform them. According to Gisborne,

> Providence, designing from the beginning that the manner of life to be adopted by women should in many respects ultimately depend, not so much on their own deliberate choice, as on the determination, or at least on the *interest and convenience* [emphasis mine] of the parent, of the husband, or of some other connection; has implanted in them a remarkable tendency to conform to the wishes and example of those for whom they feel a warmth of regard, and even of all those with whom they are in familiar habits of intercourse. (pp. 122–23)

In the 1790s, writers like Gisborne stressed filial and conjugal duties as examples of natural womanly behavior, especially to combat the new philosophy of free love, equal rights in marriage, and the right to divorce. West's Prudentia Homespun affirmed that posterity would specifically blame the new philosophers for the calamities at the end of the eighteenth century. She considered gender-related virtues to be not the "remnants of feudal barbarism" but rather happy institutions that promised domestic peace.[34]

Because of their interest in guarding property rights, the reactionaries first impressed filial piety on gentlewomen, especially with regard to the choice of a marriage partner. On this important question, Mr. Tyrold, Camilla's father, purports to understand that it is custom and not theory, nature, or common-sense that denies equality to women in the free disposal of their affections. With the double-standards typical of reactionary women, d'Arblay, who herself had married an impecunious *emigré* against her father's wishes, made Mr. Tyrold acquiesce to this custom, even though he recognized its falsity. In keeping with such conservative forerunners as Fordyce and Moore, Bennett alone, surprisingly, insisted on a woman's rights to marry the man of her choice, agreeing with Sarah Fielding, Hester Chapone, and even Wollstonecraft that forced marriage was a form of legal prostitution.

Unlike Bennett, but in the tradition of the sentimental novelists, West, Charlotte Lennox,[35] and Eliza Parsons[36] inculcated the importance of implicit filial obedience, even at the risk of perjury at the church altar. In West's *Gossip's Story*, Louisa's supposedly affectionate father attempts to extricate himself from financial difficulties by forcing her, through guilt, to accept Sir Milton's marriage proposal. He then sentimentally descants on the sale of his virtuous daughter, praising "the sweet and candid partner he [Sir Milton] has *purchased* [emphasis mine] with his liberty and fortune" (I, 65).[37] Likewise, Parsons's heroine Emily in *Woman as She Should Be, or the Memoirs of*

---

[34] *A Tale of the Times* (1799; rpt. New York: Garland, 1974), I, 4.

[35] Lennox, who had written popular novels in the 1750s, took up fiction again in the 1790s. Like d'Arblay and West, her first pleasantly comic and preeminently readable novel was followed by increasingly sentimental and didactic works.

[36] A Minerva Lady, Parsons wrote on both sides of the controversy in the 1790s.

[37] In contrast, none of Charlotte Smith's radical heroines allows her parents or guardian to sell her into a loveless match. In this case, West uses a device from Frances Sheridan's *Sidney Biddulph* to extricate her heroine from the engagement, by a note accusing Sir Milton of a prior duty to a woman he has supposedly seduced.

*Mrs. Menville* (1793) and Lennox's eponymous heroine in *Euphemia* (1790) are forced by their parents into undesired matches. Neither Emily nor Euphemia is shown as happy in wedlock, yet the authors applaud their patient and martyred submission to filial and conjugal duty.

If parents in sentimental novels were often coercive, heroines themselves also willingly performed their duties, filial or conjugal, whichever they felt the more important. Thus, in the anonymous novel, *Agatha: or a Narrative of Recent Events* (1796), a tale that takes place in both England and France, a mother disobeys her own mother's injunction to become a nun then forces her daughter to become one in expiation. After this, even at the dissolution of her French nunnery, the heroine Agatha holds sacred her vow of celibacy and her mother's wish and refuses to marry her erstwhile lover. On opposing lines of reasoning, Camilla's sister, Eugenia, refuses her mother's advice to annul her marriage to Bellamy even though it is the result of abduction: she has made vows at the altar which she considers irrevocable, even under maternal sanction. But this is not the end of her story; d'Arblay rewards Eugenia's dutiful martyrdom and patient suffering with the opportune, if accidental, suicide of her unscrupulous husband and with her consequent marriage to her first choice, a man of sensibility who had initially rejected her for her deformity. D'Arblay's purpose, after all, was to reward virtue and punish vice; in keeping with her secularism, she leaves Eugenia with happiness on this earth rather than make her anticipate it in the hereafter.

After filial piety came the gender-related duty of conjugal obedience. The admired model, held up for emulation by Gisborne, Bennett, More, and others was a submissive rather than an equal spouse, namely, Milton's self-effacing Eve before the fall. Among their favorite lines were these of Eve to Adam:

My author, and disposer, what thou bidd'st,
Unargu'd I obey; so God ordains;
God is thy law, thou mine: to know no more
Is woman's happiest knowledge, and her praise.

*Paradise Lost* 4, 635–38 (Quoted in Bennett's *Letters*, p. 243)

In opposition to radical theory, reactionary theology saw Man as the all-important link between woman and God. In *A Gossip's Story*, West's heroine Louisa celebrates her marriage to her lover Pelham in the following verse:

Talk not of restriction, the bond I approve,
'Tis sanctioned by reason, religion, and love. (II, 224)

Thus, in fiction as in theory, writers made exemplary wives, like exemplary daughters, willingly embrace their apparently God-ordained duties.

Even the reviewers of reactionary periodicals presumed to dictate to their female readers about the sanctity of marriage. The disapproving *Anti-Jacobin* reviewer of Godwin's *Memoirs* of Wollstonecraft defined marriage as a positive institution, conducive to virtue and private happiness (July 1, 1798, 101). In a later issue, the reviewer lashed out at the new philosophical principles in Godwin's *St. Leon* but professed himself delighted at finding Godwin finally placing social and domestic virtues in their proper sphere (February 5, 1800, 152). Similarly, a review in the *Lady's Monthly Museum*, while praising Anna Seward's poetry, went so far as to censure her *celibacy*: "We still presume to think, that all her productions are very inferior to what she might have yielded in a conjugal state, and as a mother of a family" (March 2, 1799, 171).

In spite of upholding the institution of marriage, the reactionaries were realistic enough to see its defects. In keeping with the theory of subordination, of course, their answer was for wives to bear all patiently. "Prepare yourself to bear inequalities," counselled the Countess of Carlisle, and "attempt every sacrifice in your power in married life" (pp. 88, 91). Similarly, on the eve of her wedding day, Maria Williams's mother gives her the common conservative advice not to expect the lover in the husband but rather to discipline herself to be a helpmate and not an encumbrance. More in keeping with radical theory, however, she tells Maria that connubial felicity is based on mutual esteem, confidence, and reciprocal acts of tenderness since wedlock calls for social equality.

Of course, none of these writers advocated separation or divorce in the case of marital discord; neither did any of them advocate free love as the new philosophers did. What they refused to acknowledge, with regard to the last outlet, was that the modern philosophers were advocating what they considered a new virtue rather than an old vice—a monogamous sanctity of the affections rather than a licentious promiscuity of the flesh. Social stability was of prime importance to the reactionaries, and marriage provided the basic unit of society. Thus, the radical concept of rational and mutual independence within a union appeared far too threatening for West and others to face honestly. Instead, it was safer for them to turn from conjugal duty to maternal duty.

Like most eighteenth-century theorists, they stressed the importance of the mother's role in educating her daughters until their marriage and her sons in their infancy, which latter duty More deemed a "mighty privilege" (*Strictures*, II, 52). Aside from presenting two fine fictional examples of dutiful mothers in Mrs. Tyrold and Mrs. Williams, reactionary writers did not have anything new to say on this subject.

Hence, after the specific virtues attached to the three major roles of women, these writers gave a detailed list of general gender-related virtues that gentlewomen were to cultivate. Chief among these were the qualities necessary to a subordinate being, such as piety, self-denial, acceptance, docility, industry, prudence, fortitude, and cheerfulness. Complemented by graceful manners, benevolence, and an appropriate femininity, these characteristics became the mark of a well-bred gentlewoman.

Besides virtues, the heart was also considered susceptible to a long list of gender-related as well as human vices and errors, which More, using medieval terminology, called "the world, the flesh, and the devil" (*Strictures*, I, 238). Along with inculcating virtues, it became equally the duty of education to guard the heart against such traits as impiety, artfulness, dissipation, vanity, coquetry; against emotions conducive to insubordination, such as anger, hatred, discontent; and against a desire for independence. On the grounds of both gender and class, gentlewomen were especially warned to avoid so-called masculine traits and habits; in Lennox's *Euphemia*, Harley, the hero of the subplot, declares: "Women should always be women; the virtues of our sex are not the virtues of theirs."[38] Gisborne and More condemned masculine deportment and habits of address in women, the latter reminding her sex that masculine manners did not necessarily indicate similar strength of virtue or vigor of intellect.

The male trait found most objectionable in women was sexual passion. Using Christian terminology, Gisborne described sexual desires as God-given trials of fortitude rather than sources of gratification. Others continued in his vein. With their emphasis on marriage and their antagonism to free love, writers like More specifically warned women against "adultery." Like the conservatives, More believed adultery to be a crime only in women; in her *Strictures*, she attacked Wollstonecraft for supposedly recommending it to her betrayed heroine in her novel, *The Wrongs of Woman, or Maria*. Besides condemning her

---

[38] *Euphemia* (London: Cadell and Evans, 1759), II, 165.

influence on young women, Polwhele and the *Anti-Jacobin Review* also harshly attacked Wollstonecraft personally. The index to Volume I of the *Anti-Jacobin* says: "Prostitution. See Mary Wollstonecraft" (Appendix, p. 859). Ugly.

Moreover, the reactionaries considered women guilty under conditions of both sexual acquiescence and assault. Unlike Hays's self-respecting heroine Mary, West's Geraldine believes herself defiled after being raped by her new-philosopher lover; her only solution is to repent and die. Unlike the radical feminists Wollstonecraft and Robinson, West did not agree that marital infidelity was equally a woman's right if her husband proved a philanderer. Men had rights and women had duties; the more readily women accepted this fact, the easier would be their lot. Finally, if the education of the heart were administered properly, in keeping with women's inferior status, the sex would be trained neither to question nor analyze their state—to their own benefit, as well as that of their families in particular and of society at large.

If in the education of the heart gentlewomen were mostly instructed according to sex, in the system of the intellect, they were educated as members of a class. In an article in the *Lady's Monthly Museum*, entitled "Admonition of a Father to his Daughter at a Boarding School, in the Best Means of Acquiring Knowledge," the father reminds his daughter that people of superior birth and fortune should maintain their superiority by their intellectual acquirements (February 2, 1799, 110). Yet knowledge had to be given gentlewomen in just the right degree; it was as ungenteel for them to be highly proficient in learning as it was in the accomplishments.

The reactionaries disagreed among themselves on the degree of learning appropriate in a gentlewoman. At one extreme, Bennett and d'Arblay believed that intellect could be properly combined with qualities of the heart to make a well-rounded gentlewoman; at the other, Polwhele professed to prefer a modest blush to sparkling intelligence in women. Along more radical lines, "An Essay on Education" in the *Lady's Monthly Museum* objected that female ignorance resulted from the superficial rather than intensive knowledge young ladies were given on various subjects, and that, unlike boys, they were taught to use their memory instead of to exercise their reason or judgement (July 1, 1798, 55).[39]

---

[39] This essay echoes many of Wollstonecraft's ideas as expressed in *Thoughts on the Education of Daughters*.

On the other hand, Barbauld, herself a classically educated scholar, recommended just this sort of "smattering" to others of her sex: "In no subject is she [a gentlewoman] required to be deep—of none ought she to be ignorant."[40] Echoing the metaphoric language of conservatives like Fordyce and reactionaries like Bennett, she continued: from books, conversations, and learned instruction, a woman must learn "the flower of every science, and her mind, in assimilating everything to itself, will adorn itself with new graces" (p. 286). The end she envisioned for this half-knowledge was an outright lesson in hypocrisy: modesty would both prevent a woman from unnecessarily displaying what she knew and "cause it to be supposed that her knowledge is deeper than in reality it is . . . her silence will seem to proceed from discretion rather than a want of information" (pp. 286–87). Head and heart would therefore operate together in gentlewomen; men meanwhile would be none the wiser about which had the ascendancy.

As superiorly educated as Barbauld, Hannah More lacked the other's certainty on the gender-necessitated degree of female learning, yet, in *Strictures*, argued against female capacity. Outrageously regardless of her own achievements and God-given gender, she reminded other women that they were incapable of "close reasoning on a subject," that their judgement was "naturally incorrect," and that after all their efforts (in the words of Swift) they could never aspire to the learning of even a schoolboy (*Strictures*, I,167). Moreover, she believed it was according to God's plan that woman was inferior to man in mental capacity.

This inferiority manifested itself in woman's inability to compare, analyze, or separate ideas, which proved she lacked a "wholeness of mind" (II, 26). Quite contrarily, More also declared in the same work that education must teach women to think, compare, combine, and methodize, as well as give them judgement and discernment because knowledge would eminently qualify them for the performance of their duties. This was exactly what the radicals, following Astell, were arguing for in the 1790s, yet More misunderstood them as merely filling women's heads with "imaginary rights" and false ideas of intellectual equality, at the same time attempting to take them away from their allotted stations in life.

There were other viewpoints on the question of female capacity. Burton allowed equality to both sexes in mental capability, genius, judgement, taste, and imagination but cautioned that women must direct their capacities

---

[40] "On Female Studies, Letter II," *Memoir, Letters, and a Selection*, II, 279.

to subjects proper to their sex and not despise their duties. On more traditional, gender-related grounds, Bennett argued that gentlewomen were better suited to develop their sentiment and taste than their reasoning or intellectual powers:

> The prominent excellencies of your mind are taste and imagination, and your knowledge should be of a kind that assimilates these faculties. . . . Machiavel, Newton, Euclid, Malebranche, or Locke, would lie with a very ill grace in your closets. They would render you unwomanly indeed. . . . Elegant studies . . . do not require so much time, abstraction, or comprehensiveness of mind—they bring no wrinkles [and will polish your manners and expand your understanding]. . . . Whilst men, with solid judgement and a superior vigour are to combine ideas, to discriminate and examine a subject to the bottom, you are to give it all its brilliancy and all its charms. (pp. 98–99)

Ironically, More, who had elsewhere agreed with Bennett's last statement, opposed him on this point in the *Strictures*, insisting that female reading should not include works of the imagination but should concentrate instead on books that "exercise the reasoning faculties" (I, 164). To this end, she recommended Duncan's logic book, parts of Locke's *Essay on the Human Understanding*, and Bishop Butler's *Analogy*; after which, she declared, with an illogicality of argument that matched her confused hypotheses: "Far be it from me to desire to make scholastic ladies or female dialecticians" (I, 168). Rather, she suggested that gentlewomen use their knowledge for practical purposes and with religious intent.

In spite of her confusion about female capacity, More sided with Carlisle, West, and even Bennett, as also with the progressives and the radicals, in defending truly learned or "scholastic" ladies (perhaps remembering her earlier association with the learned Bluestocking coterie): it did not inevitably make them slatternly, pedantic, undomestic, masculine, or overly fond of male company. In her *Strictures*, More spiritedly pointed out that a larger number of families were disoriented by a mother's passion for gaming than for books, and that for every one literary slattern who neglected care of her person, thereby showing indifference to her husband, there were scores of elegant spendthrifts who ruined him by excessive decoration.

Not all the reactionaries could quite brush aside the old prejudices. For instance, in *Euphemia*, Lennox maliciously satirized an ugly Lady Cornelia

Classick for turning desperately to learning to attract male attention. Other reactionaries acknowledged the prevalence of prejudices but attempted to soften them. The story of d'Arblay's learned, virtuous, but misshapen heiress Eugenia showed that even in the fictional world, learning was as great a defect in the marriage market as actual physical deformity (a lesson that Wortley Montagu had taught her daughter over three decades previously). But in spite of d'Arblay's protests to the contrary, *Camilla* was, after all, a sentimental novel; hence, as already seen, Eugenia's patience, virtue, and suffering were ultimately rewarded with a husband who appreciated her for herself, learning and deformity included. Similarly, through a real-life example, an article in the *Lady's Monthly Museum* vindicated learning by coupling it with virtues of the heart: It represented Barbauld's exemplary conjugal and social life as giving the lie to the prejudice that female writers ignored the important duties of life (September 1, 1798, 175).

Having variously proved that learning was acceptable in gentlewomen if subjected to their domestic duties and gender-related virtues, the reactionaries next discussed the subject of curriculum. First and unanimously on the list was religious instruction. Even diehard non-feminists like Bennett, Gisborne, More, and West conceded to the progressive and radical theory that women needed not only to be good Christians but also to understand the principles of Christianity, so as not to be led astray in conduct. (It must be remembered that atheism was one of the vices of the new philosophy much feared by the reactionaries.) Religious controversy was another matter; the *Anti-Jacobin* rightly pointed out to More that she herself indulged in such polemics, although condemning them in her sex. The reviewer put her in the same category as Wilberforce's school, pronouncing their errors to be as much a threat to the national church as that of "avowed separatists" (October 4, 1799, 495).

In keeping with such paranoia regarding church and state, the curriculum recommended by the reactionaries in the 1790s was far more repressive than that of even their conservative predecessors. Among the generally accepted subjects were French, Italian (often together classified as polite accomplishments), history, biography, geography, natural history (believed especially conducive to arousing admiration of the Creator), the modern English classics, and belles-lettres, including voyages and travels. Unlike the curriculum of the radicals, the sciences were less unanimously urged, as were even accounts, moral poetry, moral drama, and English grammar. Individually, Burton suggested philosophy; Bennett recommended the theory of the fine arts of painting, sculpture, architecture, and heraldry, as also the study of male poets like Homer and Virgil in translation, and of contemporary female poets like More, Barbauld, Seward ("a star of the first magnitude in the hemisphere of [the] imagination," p. 124), and Smith (whose "little sonnets . . . [are] soft, pensive, sentimental, and pathetic, as a woman's productions should be," p. 125). The dual responses of many of the reactionaries to female perfection in learning, as indeed to female achievement of any kind other than in the submissive virtues, is hilariously seen in Carlisle's urging women, on the one hand, to keep applying themselves to "profitable studies" and not to be discouraged by initial difficulties, and, on the other, advising them with regard to orthography, "Spell well if you can" (pp. 123, 126).

With a curious mixture of liberal curriculum and illiberal theory, Barbauld recommended Latin, at least the grammar, if the pupil had no inclination to learn the language itself, and sciences like astronomy (as did Burton, Bennett, and *The Female Aegis*), experimental philosophy, chemistry, and physics. She saw such a study of science as a learning of "the great laws of the universe . . . [which] it is unpardonable not to know" because they aroused gratitude to God. Yet, she continued, "In these you will rather take what belongs to sentiment and to utility than abstract calculation or difficult problems. [And, in direct opposition to radical theory] You must often be content to know a thing is so, without understanding the proof" ("On Female Studies," p. 184).

According to such writers, then, a gentlewoman's learning was to be regulated by both her class and gender, but these, among other factors, sometimes debarred her altogether from certain subjects. Fear of revolution led many of the reactionaries to forbid political, theological, and metaphysical controversy with even greater vehemence than their predecessors. Further, on the grounds of gender, Bennett prohibited mathematics for women; Polwhele objected to botany as an indelicate subject, since it involved sexual studies, including the "prostitution* of a plant" (p. 8). He condemned Wollstonecraft for prescribing sex education for youth, sarcastically commenting that botanizing girls were in a fair way of becoming "worthy disciples of Miss W" (p. 9). Even literature did not escape proscription. Like others of their century, most of the reactionaries, except for Barbauld and Carlisle, denounced the novel; More went further in banning what she called works of English sentiment, French philosophy,

---

* Polwhele seemed rather fixated on the term; one remembers he agreed with the definition of prostitution . . . "see Wollstonecraft").

Italian poetry, and German fantasy. Thus, although given the permission to study, gentlewomen were not to overstep the various bounds set them by the reactionaries; after all, these writers preferred to do the thinking for women rather than to encourage them, as the radicals did, to think and act for themselves.

If the reactionaries disapproved of Wollstonecraft's model of the independent, thinking woman, they equally disapproved of the frivolous, unthinking woman of fashion. The latter type was educated in the system that concentrated on the person, which laid emphasis on the externals of physical beauty, dress, and the ornamental accomplishments. According to theorists, this system seemed especially connected to a woman's wealth—to either an abundance or a lack of it, since it was given as much to heiresses like West's Marianne Dudley in *A Gossip's Story* as to impoverished beauties like d'Arblay's Indiana in *Camilla*. Both types of gentlewomen were supposed to suffer from insufficient training in the education of the heart, the grand controller of the female propensities to instability and caprice, characteristics that More believed only too common in others of her sex.

Yet certain theorists encouraged attention to the person if it were complemented with suitably feminine traits, notably the ability to attract good men and the willingness to please them. For instance, Polwhele opposed to the "unsex'd [intellectual] females" those women refined in mind and shape by "modest luxury," women whose "limbs, figures [were] graced by fashion, beauty, and taste," and who learned the accomplishments. He described such an education as true to nature, because it was drawn from the feminine attributes of fancy and feeling rather than from "sceptic Reason" (p. 10). Along the same lines, Bennett, Gisborne, and Barbauld followed Rousseau in reminding women: "Your best, your sweetest empire is to please."[41]

The most obvious way to please the eyes of men was naturally through personal beauty. Unfortunately, such attention could go too far, with unhappy results. In West's *Tale of the Times*, the beautiful but moneyless Arabella's entire education is geared to avoiding what is bad for the eyes, the shape, and the complexion and in acquiring what is considered perfectly suitable and elegant for a young lady of the first fashion. Her aunt, Lady Madelina, spoils her even further by indulgence, instead of training her to restraint; as a result,

---

[41] Barbauld, "To a Lady, with some Painted Flowers" [poem], *Works* (London: Longman, Hurst, Rees, et al., 1825), I, 10.

Arabella lacks the qualities necessary to female subordination, engages herself abortively to a new philosopher, and ends up as a fast-living lady of fashion and questionable principles.

In agreement with many of the conservatives and progressives before them and even with their own radical contemporaries, moral theorists like More, d'Arblay, Carlisle, Burton, Bennett, Gisborne, and the anonymous author of *The Female Aegis*[42] therefore downgraded the importance of physical beauty, as at best transient and skin-deep, in favor of beauty of the mind and heart. Through the example of a beautiful but mad woman, Mr. Tyrold teaches his youngest daughter, the good-hearted, intellectual, but deformed Eugenia, the lesson that "beauty, without mind, is more dreadful than any deformity" (d'Arblay's comment, *Camilla*, II, 311). Good men would value women for their true worth, regardless of their looks; conversely, according to Bennett, only men like Pope and Chesterfield, who lacked mental beauty themselves, would insult members of the "fair sex." He defended women against the former's misogyny: "I would . . . retaliate his insults on the sex, and become the champion of their injured honour, I would insinuate, that the poet was little and deformed, and had experienced few of their caresses and attentions" (p. 13). Mental ugliness was beginning to be viewed as a deformity in both sexes; physical beauty was worth little, if unaccompanied by pleasing moral traits.

In the system of the education of the person, after beauty came dress, which could enhance the effects of or hide the defects in physical appearance. Following conservatives like Rousseau, West and Gisborne, the reactionaries declared that women had a natural propensity to self-adornment through dress. As such, this love was to be controlled rather than denied. Like their forebears, the reactionaries drew on qualities of the heart for their criteria on dress: Burton and Bennett recommended simplicity, neatness, and, along with the Countess of Carlisle, sufficient conformity to fashion to avoid "singularity." West, Bennett, and Gisborne particularly attacked female dress that aped male attire and gave its wearer "the unpleasing air of an Amazon or a virago" (Bennett, p. 138). "Amazon" continued to be a disparaging term for the reactionaries as it had been for the conservatives; strength could not be considered a trait congenial with subordination.

---

[42] This work is an almost complete plagiarism of Gisborne's *Enquiry*, but without his heavy religiosity, and therefore one-third the size of the original.

If masculinity was considered the undesirable mark of an Amazon or a virago, accomplishments were believed the necessary marks of well-bred femininity. The paradox is that while expensive masters were hired to teach these arts and the young lady practiced for long hours at them, gentility demanded that she be charmingly pleasing rather than brilliantly proficient in them, even though More herself had defined the original meaning of accomplishments to be "perfection" (*Strictures*, I, 61). In *Camilla*, Miss Margland, governess to the beautiful but empty-headed Indiana, believes that all a young lady needs for education is what she herself has had: a little music, a little dancing, and a little drawing, "which should all, she added, be but slightly pursued, to distinguish a lady of fashion from an artist" (I, 46).

And to distinguish her from a woman of the middle class, she might have further added—even more than their predecessors, the reactionaries were clamorous that accomplishments were a prerogative only of young ladies of rank and fortune. West's increasing anti-democratic leanings are manifested not only in the escalating ranks of her three heroines of this period, but also in the gradation of their musical instruments—her first heroine, Maria, plays the guitar; the second, Louisa, plays the harpsichord; the third, Geraldine, plays the harp.

Besides music, Bennett, Burton, and Gisborne also recommended that young ladies learn dancing as a healthful exercise but cautioned them against improperly mixing with the other sex in ballrooms. Drawing and painting were perhaps better suited to gentlewomen; Burton found them as agreeable in the privacy of the home as needlework and embroidery were serviceable. If the reactionaries were generally inclined to favor the accomplishments, it was precisely for this reason—these arts were believed to domesticate gentlewomen, encouraging them to spend their leisure hours at home rather than at public diversions.[43]

There was one accomplishment/activity that only the nobility among both conservative and reactionary theorists accepted as suitable to gentlewomen: card-playing, at home and in moderation. Thus, like Lord Halifax and others before her, the Countess of Carlisle allowed card-playing as a social pastime; even Gisborne permitted it as recreation for the old. Most other

---

[43] In John Aikin's allegory, "The Female Choice, a Tale," included in Volume III of *Evenings at Home*, the heroine Melissa chooses the companionship of industrious Housewifery to that of gay Dissipation, as promising her more solid and permanent contentment.

theorists, however, themselves often of borderline gentility, completely banned cards as leading to gaming, one of the major sources of dissipation in fashionable women. Hannah More warned her readers that an entire devotion among gentlewomen to cards and to the fine arts bespoke the corruption of society itself. On a more personal level, Gisborne added that it could bespeak the corruption of the heart; the accomplishments were to be used as methods of contemplating God's goodness and power, and not as a means of self-fulfillment or for public applause.

As with the education of the person, the reactionaries differed in the degree of participation believed necessary for gentlewomen in the fourth system of instruction, namely, physical education. If education of the person depended on class biases, education of the physique was controlled by gender-related considerations. Many of the reactionaries subscribed to the conservative theory of the inherent physical weakness of women, especially of the upper classes. In total opposition to the radicals, Bennett, Gisborne, Carlisle, and *The Female Aegis* asserted that female debility was more a result of nature than of cultural conditioning. Carlisle further warned women against assuming "masculine airs"; these were not merely contrary to nature but also to nobility of birth: "Real robustness, and superior force, is denied you by nature—its semblance, denied you by the laws of decency" (p. 103).

As seen earlier, Amazonian strength was considered unfeminine; Polwhele sarcastically warned that the day would come when women, following Wollstonecraft's advice, would be "No more by weakness winning fond regard" (p. 14). Instead, they would "nobly boast the firm gymnastic nerve," using it to replace what he considered the appropriately feminine artillery of blushes, languors, flutters, delicacy, and coy reserve (p. 15). Bennett informed women that, already weak by nature, they were further enervated by female diseases and by social conditioning. Like Diderot, he commented on the "numerous diseases to which you [women] are liable." Like Gregory, he pointed out that

the sedentariness of your life, [is] naturally followed with low spirits or ennui, whilst we are seeking health and pleasure in the field; and the many lonely hours, which, in almost every situation, are likely to be your lot, will expose you to a number of peculiar sorrows, which you cannot, like the men, either drown in wine or divert by dissipation. (p. 8)

But although believing in natural female delicacy, Gisborne, More, and sometimes even Bennett did not feel a need for its perpetuation by further conditioning. Instead, they lamented the unhealthiness of a forced sedentariness that kept gentlewomen indoors in heated, elegant rooms, and, together with a lack of exercise, caused nervous disorders, "pale cheeks, a languid aspect, and a feeble frame" (Gisborne, p. 94); of low spirits and fashionable complaints (Bennett); as well as such undesirable qualities as caprice, irritability, and discontent (More). Following Locke, Gisborne asserted that cure or prevention could come from wholesome food, early hours, pure air, and bodily exercise. He called these four the rudiments of health and knowledge, the "four indispensable requisites [needed] in every place and mode of education," especially in boarding schools (p. 94).

Open-air exercise was generally deemed important in developing a healthy constitution, yet, for most reactionaries, it had to be suitably feminine. Like Hays, the anonymous *Female Aegis* opposed violent field sports like fox-hunting; Bennett condemned archery. The latter, however, suggested horseback riding as an active cure for nervous dispositions. The most popular reactionary form of physical education was gardening, encouraged in the novels of West and others, as well as in the educational treatises of Carlisle, who included farming; Bennett, who called it an excellent restorative if combined with a taste for botany (which Polwhele had condemned as dealing with the prostitution of plants); and Gisborne, who asserted that the healthiness of the employment would amply compensate for a few "daggled frocks and dirty gloves"( p. 957). Next to gardening came walks, suggested especially by West, Burton, and Bennett. But Gisborne questioned the benefit of the stiff, regimental walks undertaken by boarding-school girls: "Is it exercise to pace once a day in procession down a street or round a square, or in regular arrangement to follow a teacher along the middle walk of a garden, forbidden to deviate to the right hand or to the left?" (p. 94).

Walking and gardening did not always require much expenditure of energy. Gisborne and More therefore urged even greater activity in the open air, as "daily recreations, one of their daily *duties* [emphasis mine]" (Gisborne, p. 95). Echoing Wollstonecraft, More went further than any of her peers in suggesting that young girls be allowed to play outdoors with unrestrained freedom, instead of being cooped up indoors to learn dancing steps. She and Gisborne coincided in their views that children's bodily recreations should be such as to promote health, enliven spirits, and strengthen and quicken the mind. Surprisingly, with all their emphasis on the domestic nature and duties of women, the reactionaries did not expand on the common conservative as well as radical notion that healthy women gave birth to healthier offspring and were more capable of carrying out their all-important familial duty than were enervated women of fashion.

So far, it has been seen that duties rather than rights regulated the opinions of these writers on the four systems of female education open to gentlewomen in the eighteenth century. These duties related to either class and/or gender; education of the intellect, physique, and person was mostly governed by class, that of the heart by gender. Hannah More had asserted that education ought to be a school to fit us for life, and life, a school to fit us for eternity. Yet, to the reactionaries, training gentlewomen for life meant training them to be dutiful subordinates in the already existing social and familial hierarchies rather than to be independent members of the economic workforce, even when necessary. Paid professionalism had not been the mark of a gentlewoman before the 1790s; whatever the radicals said, it could not be accepted as such during this decade either, regardless of the reactionary female theorists' own well-padded reticules. No revolutions in politics, society, economics, or family could be allowed to threaten the relation of the sexes as ordained by the sacred trinity of God, Nature, and Custom.

## IV. Professionalism

In the 1790s, as earlier in the century, gentility continued to frown on paid professionalism. It did not, however, deny women a gender-related vocation in life. More, Barbauld, Gisborne, and Burton neatly absolved their educational systems of professional outlets by calling women's combined gender-related roles a collective profession in itself. As Barbauld put it: "Men have various departments in active life; women have but one, and *all women* [emphasis mine] have the same, differently modified indeed by their rank in life and other incidental circumstances. It is to be a wife, a mother, a mistress of a family." Other than this, a woman is excused from all "unprofessional knowledge" which fits a man for employment ("On Female Studies," p. 278). No doubt the highly educated, childless Barbauld awarded herself a special dispensation since she not only earned good money for penning her voluminous works and running a boarding school but also secured social respect.

The great flaw in arguments like hers was that not all women could or did get married or have a personal source of income. True, Gisborne and West stated that marriage was not the only end of a woman's life, but neither did they point to any working alternatives for unprovided single women or widows. As already seen in earlier chapters, poverty or seduction and betrayal sometimes pushed women into prostitution, the profession always open to their sex. Unlike the radicals, their opponents were not very sympathetic with fallen women, seeing them as deviants who had resisted one of the prime virtues of the heart, namely, the *prudence* of retaining a technical virginity. In contrast with Wollstonecraft, who had suggested governmental rehabilitation for such women, More urged that society ostracize them, even though she acknowledged the seducers' guilt in leading them astray. But, to her credit, she advised that women of delicacy also shun such libertines and that relatives and friends of fallen women snatch them from continued vice, if possible.

The severe morality of the female reactionaries with regard to the fallen of their own sex is seen also in West's *Tale of the Times*. Geraldine is drugged and raped (like Clarissa) by Fitzosborne, yet though her husband (himself unfaithful to her) finally seeks a reconciliation, the female narrator declares that on reflection, his wounded honor would have demanded a separation. Unlike Holcroft's Anna St. Ives and Hays's Mary, Geraldine believes herself defiled by the rape, as her author believes her to have disgraced her husband by it. Like Mary, Geraldine too correctly determines it would be futile to accuse her rapist in court because the cross-examination of the lawyers would confuse and insult her and make her lose the case. With glaring inconsistency, West simultaneously condemned Geraldine as criminal, even though the victim of rape, yet praised her at her death as "the faithful friend, the dutiful daughter, the observant wife, the tender mother" (III, 266). (The panegyric seems even more hypocritical because in the course of the novel, West had shown Geraldine spurning her true friends, marrying her own rather than her father's choice, and preferring the companionship of a new philosopher to that of her intellectually inferior husband.)

For single women who kept their "virtue," the genteel means of subsistence was dependence instead of self-support through a profession. Carlisle, Gisborne, and West pleaded for better treatment of dependent female relatives; Gisborne suggested that rather than humiliate and debase such women, if unwanted in a household, it would be kinder to send them off with a small pittance to seek a maintenance in obscurity. The novelists dealt with the question of single women and dependence in a dual way—either ridiculing them as ageing, interfering, malicious, pedantic, half-literate, or class-conscious "old maids," or, in the case of sympathetic characters, commiserating with them as good women wronged by a money-conscious society, who bravely sought their sustenance in it. In West's first novel, Maria Williams's mother, as a young woman, chooses to marry a profligate, unprincipled man for his money and the security he offers her, rather than to continue as housekeeper to an erstwhile friend, in what she sees as a miserable position between servant and companion. Thus, in direct opposition to the radicals, writers like West encouraged dependence as less humiliating to gentlewomen than working.

By and large, these writers did not so much suggest professions for gentlewomen as occasionally portray women reduced by circumstances to work. As seen earlier in this chapter, teaching was a frequent recourse for such women. In *Camilla*, the governess, Miss Margland, is depicted as "a woman of fashion and family . . .reduced through the gaming and extravagance of her father" to support herself in the position of governess. Although dedicated to her beautiful pupil, she is unable to give her a good moral education. D'Arblay explains that, "neglected in her own education, there is nothing she could teach . . .born and bred in the circle of fashion, she imagined she has nothing to learn . . . while a mind proudly shallow kept her unacquainted with her own deficiencies" (I. ch 6, "Tuition of a young Lady").

The qualities preferred in a governess by More, West, and a writer for the *Lady's Monthly Museum* were those of the heart, before those of the intellect, since they laid greater stress on a moral education. Therefore, West recommended superior care and abilities, a correct taste, and a skillful hand at education (*Maria Williams*); More was in favor of piety and knowledge (*Strictures*); and a *Monthly Museum* writer, of gentle firmness and unbounded good temper (August 1, 1798, 108). Unlike the radicals, these writers did not concern themselves with advocating better conditions or higher pay; surrogate moral qualities were more important to them since governesses were to take over the duties of negligent upper-class mothers.

Along with teaching, by the 1790s, writing had also become an accepted profession for indigent gentlewomen, yet none of the reactionaries actively spoke up in its favor. Herself a highly successful writer, whose exhortations were obeyed even by the Queen,[44] More strongly discouraged literary

---

[44] The Queen obeyed More's injunction to women not to have their hair dressed on Sundays so that hairdressers could go to church (Jones, p. 109).

professionalism in other women on the old plea that women's work was never taken seriously. In 1791, Burney gave up her position as Second Keeper of the Robes to Queen Charlotte and her pay of two hundred pounds; subsequently, in 1793, she married Alexandre D'Arblay, supporting them through her writing and her annual income of £120 (a hundred-pound pension and twenty pounds from investments from *Cecilia*). *Camilla* cleared one thousand pounds by subscription (a genteel form of social patronage used after the system of noble patronage had died out in the mid-century); its author accepted another thousand from the publisher for the copyright.[45] Tremendously successful professionals, both d'Arblay and More built cottages for themselves and their families with their earnings. Yet it seems that even if such professionalism was tolerated as an extension of domestic duty, it was not always acceptable as a means of personal profit: Joanna Baillie modestly refused to acknowledge her anonymously published *Plays of the Passions* on their first appearance, although the publisher Cadell offered a thousand pounds for the author to reveal herself.[46]

Writing or teaching were both semi- or fully public professions. The only other employment discussed by reactionaries was needlework, which Burton recommended as both an accomplishment and as a financial asset for women in reduced circumstances. Gisborne alone lamented that unsupported women had so few means of providing for themselves and that female employments, especially of the middle class, were usurped by men. Following the feminist tradition from Drake in the 1690s to Mary Ann Radcliffe and Wakefield in his own time, Gisborne encouraged his upper-class female readers to support lower-class female labor, even suggesting that certain shops and occupations now in the hands of men, such as hairdressing, should, more properly, be transferred to women.

On the whole, the reactionaries were more vocal about what gentlewomen should not do professionally rather than what they should, even as a means of survival. Foremost among the proscribed positions were those connected with the church and state: politics, clergy, and the military. These were followed by "honorable" professions such as law, in which only gentlemen could engage,

---

[45] Hemlow, pp. 234, 269.

[46] Sarah Tytler and J. L. Wetson, *The Songstresses of Scotland* (London: Strahan, 1871), II, 21. As often happened with anonymous writers, Baillie was soon discovered as the author and feted by her friends.

*God* having assigned them these jobs on the basis of class- and gender-related superiority. Even further down the ladder, gentlewomen were not to engage in trade or commercial enterprises, the prerogatives of middle-class men. Collectively, the reactionaries concurred that women were to be kept from working in professions long denied them, for instance, as physicians, surgeons, scientists, orators, painters, historians, naturalists, mathematicians, geographers, astronomers, philosophers, or even as connoisseurs or virtuosos of any kind. By thus closing off most of the new avenues that the radicals had envisioned as bringing independence to women, by advocating a rigorous system of education of the hearth and heart, the reactionaries hoped, at least in theory, to enclose women meekly in the fold.

On the question of female professionalism, as of female education and capabilities, the battle of feminism versus femininity had therefore come to a head in the 1790s. Ironically, all the denial, ridicule, hatred, and rancor of the reactionaries helped keep knowledge of radical and feminist theory more securely in the public eye than if they had ignored it. Their self-righteous, zealous, didactic works strove to expose the monster, but although they successfully stifled it for a while, they could not kill it. Even if not yet an actual movement, feminist thinking was still in the air. Ellen Moers optimistically describes this period:

> In the 1780s, 1790s, and 1800s, feminism touched them all, from those who supported, to those who opposed its doctrines, with all the range of possible attitude (including apparent indifference to controversy) that lie between; the elitism of Mme de Staël, the Evangelicalism of Hannah More, the conservatism of Maria Edgeworth, the cautious prudery of Fanny Burney, the pedagogical hauteur of Mme de Genlis, the Americanism of Susanna Rowson, the escapism of Mrs. Radcliffe, the irony of Jane Austen. (p. 125)

To all appearances, nevertheless, at the close of the eighteenth century, the reaction seemed very much in the ascendant. Wollstonecraft and Robinson were dead at 39 and 42 respectively, whereas the influence of the long-lived More (88), Barbauld (83), d'Arblay (88), and West (92) increased from that of previous decades. Politically too, the English government had become severely repressive; in France, the revolution died with Napoleon's coup in November 1799, and with it died the democratic dreams as well as the terrorist atrocities of a stormy decade. On the English throne, Queen Charlotte proved a stabilizing influence to her countrywomen, providing them with a shining example of the devoted wife and mother, bearing her otherwise loving spouse's bouts of madness and the Prince of Wales's dissolute behavior with the unfailing stoicism and patient tolerance demanded of all her sex.

But notwithstanding the appearance of status quo, changes were taking place in the minds of gentlewomen. Ultimately, it is symbolic rather than ironic that although at opposite poles, More's educational precepts often closely resembled those of Wollstonecraft, and her example showed that women could earn a living by the pen even while urging others to mind their needles and their housekeys. Double standards undoubtedly existed, not only between women and men, but among women themselves. In light of this fact, it is significant that some of the reactionary writers agreed with many of the progressives and radicals that young women could be allowed friends of their own age and sex, a bonding that the earlier conservatives had strictly forbidden. Many of these writers, for instance, More, d'Arblay, and Baillie, also had close ties with their own sisters, proving to the public that women could live amicably together with others of their sex. Through radical theory, this sense of sisterhood also permeated the relationship between women of different classes. Divided as they were from their better-born sisters by class barriers, middle- and lower-class women still had gained the attention of certain sympathetic educators; the idea of the equality of women as human beings was beginning to emerge, even if the idea of women as a gender- and class-regulated sub-species was still universally accepted.

All these internal rumblings began to influence women's thinking in the 1800s, even if actual changes in female education took place far more slowly. The victory of the reactionary educators at the end of the 1790s was only temporary; influential writers like More and Barbauld continued to prescribe restrictions to others of their sex, but their ostensible example, like that of the radicals, must have taught many women something quite different—to desire similar power—over themselves.

# CHAPTER 5

# Merging Traditions, 1800–1820

Women are much better educated now [1808] than they were a century ago; but they are by no means less remarkable for attention to the arrangements of the household, or less inclined to discharge the offices of parental affection. It would be very easy to show that the same objection has been made at all times to every improvement in the education of both sexes, and all ranks—and been as uniformly and completely refuted by experience.

Sydney Smith, *Essays Social and Political*[1] (1882)

## I. Intellectual Background

The eighteenth century has generally been considered a conservative century, complacently accepting, as already seen, that "Whatever is, is right." "Whatever is," of course, had comprised a socio-political hierarchy, with upper-class Anglican men at the top and politically impotent groups beneath, prominent among whom were women, the poor, the middle class, and Dissenters. The imperial British governing system of "divide and conquer" had especially been applied to the status and corresponding education

---

[1] Critique on Thomas Broadhurst's *Advice to Young Ladies on the Improvement of the Mind*, in *Essays* (1882, rpt. New York: Ward and Locke, 1888), p. 95. The *Essays* included reprints of articles published in the *Edinburgh Review* in the early nineteenth century; this particular review appeared in 1808. In this chapter, Sydney Smith will be referred to by his full name, to distinguish him from the novelist and poet, Charlotte Smith.

of women; society had made clear demarcations between the rights of upper-class men and the duties of all women and among the privileges of ladies and the duties of middle- and lower-class women. As seen in previous chapters, the conservatives and the reactionaries had been particularly concerned with enforcing the subordination of women through educational theory. On the other hand, and also in theory, the progressives had attempted to narrow gender-related distinctions between the sexes, while the radicals, themselves often of the upper-middle class and with Dissenting backgrounds or connections, had sought an improvement in rational education for all women, albeit according to their socio-economic status.

Radicalism and the reaction to it were, however, phenomena particular only to the 1790s. Hence, in this chapter, the tradition from Astell to Wollstonecraft as it emerged in the 1800s is again labelled "progressive," while its opposing trend reverts to "conservative." As in previous chapters, both labels necessarily refer to educational theories only. The emphasis, however, is not on emergence so much as on *merging*. Ironically, the reactionary Hannah More now became the indirect propagator of progressive thought from Astell to Wollstonecraft, following the latter's death in 1797 a few days after giving birth to daughter Mary (of *Frankenstein* fame). Although More's aims for and attitudes towards her sex continued a variance with theirs, some of the educational precepts expounded in her works from the *Strictures* of 1799 on, as well as in those of her peers, sometimes closely paralleled those of the radical leader, albeit with a pious veneer.

Viewed in a historical context, the increased progressivism of theories on women's education in this period reflects the general move towards reform in all areas in the nineteenth century. In their more immediate context, however, the old issues and conflicts seemed to continue in the first two decades of the new century, as before, although with an increasing number of paradoxes and a growing confusion in conservative theory. (Since this chapter is largely concerned with the effects of eighteenth-century theories on early nineteenth-century thinking, it concentrates on presenting an immediate rather than a historical perspective.) One of the paradoxes of the first decade of the nineteenth century was that while feminist educational principles were gradually seeping into conservative theory, feminists themselves continued to be decried as they had been in the 1790s. Jane West, in particular, grew shriller than ever, especially against Wollstonecraft, misrepresenting the latter's theories in her *Letters to a Young Man* (1801). In her subsequent *Letters to a Young Lady*

(1806), she recorded what she saw as the defeat of the feminists, beginning with an attack on the *Rights of Woman*:

> It was a book of supereminent absurdity and audacity. . . . It, indeed, amazed and confounded for a day; . . . It was soon found, however, that the times were *not sufficiently illuminated* [ironic emphasis mine] to bear such a strong doctrine; and the disciples of the school of equality have since found it more convenient to gloss, and soften, and misrepresent.[2]

Indeed, on the surface, West seemed to be right because in the early nineteenth century, the radical party appeared much depleted. By 1800, Wollstonecraft and Mary Robinson were dead; by the end of 1810, Charlotte Smith, Anna Seward, Thomas Holcroft, Joseph Johnson, and Sarah Trimmer too were gone. In these first two decades, Amelia Alderson Opie, Maria Edgeworth, and, to a lesser extent, Elizabeth Hamilton, toned down their occasional forays into progressiveness; Elizabeth Inchbald concentrated on editing dramatic collections; even William Godwin, Charlotte Smith, and Priscilla Wakefield quietly turned to children's books and to non-controversial literature. Broken in fortune and spirit, Eliza Fenwick emigrated to America; deeply disillusioned with her own censorious country, Helen Maria Williams accepted French citizenship. Following Wollstonecraft's death, Mary Hays's friendship with Godwin cooled; reactionary hatred, moreover, left her chastened and subdued for a while, even if not so silent as most of the others. A year after the publication of her wonderfully feminist *Female Biography*, Hays privately admitted both defeat and hope to Henry Crabb Robinson:

> The ill treatment I received in the world of literature made an indelible impression on my mind which was too delicate to sustain undeserved reproach. I have quitted it. . . . I aim at nothing striking or original, I aspire not to shine. Yet I flatter myself I shall have done something towards enlightening & liberalising the rising generation, more especially those of my own sex.[3]

---

[2] *Letter to a Young Lady*, 2nd ed. (1806; rpt. New York: Garland, 1974), I, 199. All further reference to West's *Letters* will be to this work.

[3] Letter dated September 1804 and quoted in Gina Luria's "Mary Hays," pp. 465.

If in the first decade of the nineteenth century, many of the surviving ex-radicals were thus subdued in mind, work, and spirit, the members of the opposition, for the most part, continued in health, respectability, friendship, and comfortable solvency. Anna Laetitia Barbauld, Hannah More, Fanny d'Arblay (politically stranded *en famille* in France from 1802–12), Joanna Baillie, Hester Thrale Piozzi, and Jane West (as also the neo-conservatives Amelia Alderson Opie and Maria Edgeworth) all lived to be eighty or over, keeping in touch with one another in varying degrees of intimacy, and forming acquaintances with the new generation of male romantic writers, such as Sir Walter Scott, William Wordsworth, Samuel Taylor Coleridge, and Charles Lamb.

In spite of this association with the romantics, the works of the above educators continued to bear the marks of eighteenth-century conservatism. More's first and only novel, *Coelebs in Search of a Wife* (1808), symbolized the ideologies of the whole group, at the same time that it incorporated certain progressive educational principles. It seemed to have been written as an answer to the only romantic novel written in this decade by a major controversialist of the 1790s, namely Baronne de Staël's *Corinne, ou Italie* (1807).[4] Both More's Lucilla and de Staël's Corinne are well-educated, accomplished women, with the difference that the former heroine turns her talents back to the home, the latter uses hers to shine professionally outside it. Although both novels celebrated Englishwomen to a greater or lesser extent, the heroines themselves incorporate French ideals of the previous century: à la Rousseau, Lucilla plays an evangelical Sophie to Coelebs's anglicized Émile, whereas Corinne epitomizes the professionally acclaimed artiste envisioned by de Genlis in the 1780s.

The difference between Corinne's and Lucilla's motivations also symbolized the difference between the concepts of nineteenth-century progressives and conservatives regarding a woman's capabilities and roles. The base of this disagreement rested on what they saw as the natural rights of the individual versus her duties to society. In her biography of Wollstonecraft's life and times, Hays stated the progressive position: "The laws of nature are paramount to the

---

[4] More's heroine Lucilla was perhaps named after the part-Italian Corinne's English half-sister Lucille, both Englishwomen being shining examples to their sex of obedience and virtue. It is typical of the double standards of conservative women that More presented her readers with a model of the ideally domesticated woman, while in 1819, at the death of the last of her four sisters who had managed her housekeeping for her, she proved totally incompetent, was robbed by her servants, and had to be rescued by friends (Jones, pp. 226–27).

customs of society; its dictates will not be silenced by factitious precepts."[5] On the other hand, in her *Letters to a Young Lady*, West called herself a "staunch advocate for all the rights of my sex" because she recommended to women what they ought to do, not dare: "No one (unless, like Mrs. Wolstonecraft's [*sic*] lawless planets, they rush madly from their sphere) lives for himself. We are formed for society; and in society we must act or be wretched" (II, 197–98). Because she acted only according to her own nature, Corinne's talents and passionate intensity made her an outcast in conservative British society; her domestic and insipid half-sister Lucille, along with More's more intelligent but equally tame Lucilla, on the other hand, was regarded as an ornament to it.

In the first decade of the nineteenth century, as in the 1790s, this conflict between the rights of individuals and the duties to society was also seen in various assessments of Wollstonecraft and her influence on female education. While uncharitable attacks like West's continued, vindications of her life and works also found their way into print, with varying degrees of approval. Thus, Hamilton, in *Memoirs of Modern Philosophers* (1800), and Opie, in *Adeline Mowbray, or the Mother and Daughter* (1804), lamented that Wollstonecraft's sensible educational precepts had been marred by her rejection of social norms of behavior.

With greater understanding, Sir Charles Aldis explained the nature of her mistake, in his highly supportive *Defence of the Character and Conduct of the late Mary Wollstonecraft Godwin* (1803): she had acted on her own principles, believing herself justified in the eyes of God, but she had unfortunately ignored her justification in the eyes of society. Yet he found not the woman but society at fault, declaring that the world, with its absurdities, vices, prejudices, and vanities, was unworthy of her intelligence, independence, goodness, and greatness. Similarly, if along more traditional lines, the anonymous author of *Eccentric Biography, or Memoirs of Remarkable Characters, Ancient and Modern* (1804) praised Wollstonecraft for simultaneously fulfilling her social and familial duties as a wife, mother, companion, and friend, as well as acting as an "enlightened advocate" of the rights of her sex.[6] It seems, then, that in the early

---

[5] In the *Annual Necrology 1797–98* (Phillips, 1800), as quoted by Luria, pp. 409–10.

[6] (Worcester: by Thomas, 1804), p. 14. Luria points out that this essay on Wollstonecraft was a direct plagiarism of Hays's obituary of her friend in the *Monthly Magazine*, September 1797 (p. 439).

1800s, at least, such partial or total vindications of Wollstonecraft appeared as readily as did satires and execrations against her.

As Astell's name, but not her ideas, had been apparently forgotten in the last quarter of the eighteenth century, so, according to Flora Tristan had Wollstonecraft been forgotten by the 1830s (Moers, p. 21). But this amnesia about the radical leader did not last long. As Wollstonecraft's biographer, Eleanor Flexner, points out, the *Rights of Woman* influenced Victorians late into the nineteenth century in both Britain and America, feminists whose names are as well-known today as hers: Frances Wright, Margaret Fuller, Lucretia Mott, Elizabeth Cady Stanton, and Millicent Fawcett (p. 265).

But this is anticipating. From 1800 to 1820, the progressive tradition as epitomized by Wollstonecraft continued to thrive in educational theories, not because it had outspoken radical exponents, as in the 1790s, but because much of it had entered the mainstream of conservative thinking. The chief mistake of the conservatives was in believing that by reviling or silencing the feminists they could also suppress their theories. This attempted suppression of both the progressives and their views might have worked, if the conservatives had not themselves imbibed some of their opponents' ideas, having critically appraised them—and silently found them valid.

## II. Works, Theories, Places of Education

In the first two decades of the nineteenth century, the continued interest of writers in women's education was demonstrated by the host of treatises, novels, magazines, letters, biographies, and children's books published during this period. Unlike the democratic radicals of the 1790s, most writers now conservatively catered to upper-class women only. Two major fiction writers of the 1790s in particular, namely Hamilton and West, turned their attention largely to pedagogical works for gentlewomen. Thus, Hamilton wrote *Letters on the Elementary Principles of Education* (1801–02) and *Letters Addressed to the Daughter of a Nobleman* (2nd ed., 1806); West published *Letters to a Young Lady, in which the Duties and Character of Women are Considered* (1806). Likewise, More, disregarding the *Anti-Jacobin*'s advice to her to write on the education of middle-class women, went several steps higher in her *Hints towards Forming the Character of a Princess* (1805). Barbauld's contribution consisted of a collection of prose and poetry for young ladies entitled *The Female Speaker* (1811).[7]

Aside from such overtly instructive works, educators also advised their readers through didactic fiction. The two criteria of amusement and instruction remained important to writers who had started their careers in the previous century; Richard Lovell Edgeworth in particular warned Maria that "to be a mere writer of pretty stories and novelettes would be unworthy of his partner, pupil, and daughter."[8] Her father's literary as well as personal approval was important to Maria Edgeworth. Consequently, she created *Moral Tales* and other fictional stories to illustrate (as her father pointed out in the prefaces) their joint opinions on education, first outlined in *Practical Education*.

Like Richard Lovell Edgeworth, other writers felt the need to justify their use of fiction by combining it with an overt didactic purpose. Following the lead of the *Anti-Jacobin*, educational novels of this period took a political stance as well, attacking the 1790s' ideals of democracy and the new philosophy. Prominent among these were Hamilton's *Memoirs of Modern Philosophers* (1800),[9] Dubois's *St. Godwin* (1800), West's *Infidel Father* (1802), Opie's

---

[7] In the first decade of the century, she worked on voluminous critical and editorial projects. However, devastated by the *Quarterly Review*'s abusive attack of her long poem, *Eighteen Hundred and Eleven* (1812), she gave up her plan to collect her own works, expecting posterity to vindicate her talents (Ellis, I, 279).

[8] Maria Edgeworth's letter to Sophy Ruxton, dated February 26, 1805, as quoted in Butler, p. 209. Richard Lovell Edgeworth has often been regarded as a pompous, egotistical father who curbed his daughter's literary talent by his own didactic preferences. He married four times; Maria, his second child, often looked after his numerous brood of twenty-one other children, helped him run the estate, and remained unmarried herself. Significantly, her best work, *Castle Rackrent* (1800), an Irish novel as well as the first regional novel in British literature, was written in secret and therefore escaped paternal interference. It is to her father's credit, however, that he encouraged his daughter to become a writer; de Genlis, de Staël, and other women had often lamented men's deliberate suppression of artistic aspirations in their female relatives.

[9] This novel included vicious personal attacks on the new philosophers: Hays was satirized as [see next p] [9 contd]. Bridgetina Botherim and Godwin as Mr. Myope. Both Gina Luria and Mitzi Myers see Mr. Glib as Holcroft, but I tend to think Mr. Vallaton, who rises to be a philosopher from the lowly social origins of a street urchin and finally elopes with a French whore, is Holcroft, who started life as a shoemaker's son and whose fourth wife was a young Frenchwoman. Mr. Glib, the bookseller who gives dinners to his philosophic friends, buys seditious French literature, and is imprisoned for revolutionary principles, seems to represent the radical publisher, Joseph Johnson. Mr. Glib's wife and family in the novel were artistic fabrication; after all, Hamilton had blatantly asserted in her preface that she made no personal attacks.

*Adeline Mowbray* (1804), Sophia Lee's *The Life of a Lover* (1804), More's *Coelebs* (1808),[10] and d'Arblay's *The Wanderer, or Female Difficulties* (1814). Progressive novels, on the other hand, were not produced quite so prolifically. Among the few noteworthy examples were the anonymous (I suspect Hays) *Julietta, or the Triumph of Mental Acquirements over Personal Defects* (1802), and de Staël's *Delphine* (1802) and *Corinne*, the latter two presenting forceful examples of the fate of strong, aspiring women in a repressive society.

Unlike de Staël's *Corinne*, professional pride was not a major characteristic of early nineteenth-century conservatives, as seen in their self-deprecating prefaces and in Edgeworth's, Opie's, and d'Arblay's reluctance to call their novels by their proper generic names. Instead, these three writers used moral-sounding circumlocutions in their fiction to emphasize their didactic intent. In sharp contrast, a few novelists, notably Jane Austen and James Sand (in *Monckton; . . . To which is Prefixed, a General Defence of Modern Novels,* 1802), were finally beginning to profess pride in their own art, emphasizing amusement over overt instruction in their works. Although an apparent conservative who incorporated important educational issues in her novels, Austen yet exercised superb artistic control over her material. Her works therefore possess a comparative and refreshing detachment from the heavy-handed didacticism of her peers. Like Wollstonecraft and a very few writers before her, she also defended her art:

> I will not adopt that ingenious and impolitic custom, so common with novel writers, of degrading, by their contemptuous censure, the very performances to the number of which they themselves are adding. (*Northanger Abbey*, p. 107)

Furthermore, she objected to the second-class status that even the reviewers accorded fiction,

> while the abilities of the nine-hundredth abridger of the History of England, or of the man who collects and publishes in a volume some dozen lines of Milton,

---

[10]  It is ironic that although More meant her heroine Lucilla, trained along the lines of Milton's Eve, to be the perfect example of the well-educated evangelical woman, Sydney Smith compared *Coelebs* to a Minerva novel in his article on it for the *Edinburgh Review*. Moreover, even the evangelical *Christian Observer*, not recognizing More as the author, criticized the novel as vulgar, wanting in taste, and lacking in strict moral delicacy (Jones, p. 197). Both More and Hamilton wrote their anti-Jacobin novels under assumed male editorship.

> Pope, and Prior, with a paper from the *Spectator*, and a chapter from Sterne, are eulogized by a thousand pens. (*Northanger Abbey*, p. 21)

Austen specifically condemned uninspired compilations, but there were other collections that must have proved useful to those who actually instructed young ladies. Notable among these was probably Sarah Trimmer's *Guardian of Education* (1802–06), a five-volume collection of her critiques of various educational works. Sydney Smith, a progressive critic for the *Edinburgh Review*, also wrote a number of similar critiques for it; these were collectively published later in the century as *Essays Social and Political* (1882). Likewise, magazines written for and often by women played their part in propagating views on education; prominent among these were the *Lady's Monthly Museum*, which had already won positive recognition by the end of the eighteenth century, and a new magazine, *La Belle Assemblée*, started in 1804. According to Cynthia White's *Women's Magazines 1693–1968*, in the first decade of the nineteenth century, women's magazines were generally mentally stimulating, representing the opinions of both sexes and dealing with a wide spectrum of issues. Their prime aim was to cultivate women's minds, not beautify their bodies, as later magazines attempted to do (pp. 35, 39).

The liberal interest of the magazines in encouraging female mental development was echoed in Hays's preface to her *Female Biography* (1803), one of the first works by an Englishwoman to celebrate famous European women of ancient and modern times. Female biography was yet a comparatively new form; George Ballard's collection of 1752 had been the first of its kind in England. Hays's example immediately caught fire: the anonymous *Eccentric Biography* and Mathilda Betham's *Biographical Dictionary of the Celebrated Women of Every Age and Country* appeared only a year after her own publication (Luria, p. 439). A few years later, Barbauld's liberal-minded niece, Lucy Aikin, published her poetical *Epistles on Women Exemplifying their Character and Condition in Various Ages and Nations* (1810).

Through the example of others, writing women could goad their sex on to desire mental improvement, yet some of them were restrained by so-called modesty from presenting themselves as good models for their sex. Hence while biography was becoming a legitimate form for women, autobiography often was not (although scandalous memoirs had been published as early as the late seventeenth century). Even a former radical like Inchbald destroyed her memoirs, as the progressive writer Lady Wortley Montagu and others had done before her. Similarly, according to Vineta Colby, in later life Maria Edgeworth flatly refused to write an autobiographical preface to a collected edition of her novels, although she had been lionized by London society in the first two decades of the nineteenth century. Her reason was that "as a woman, my life, wholly domestic, can offer nothing of interest to the public."[11] Only Mary Ann Radcliffe, struggling to provide for herself and her seven children, after her lazy husband had spent her entire fortune, published her own *Memoirs* in 1810, desperately seeking subsistence through subscription. Besides remuneration, her specific intention was to remind young women of the connection between their happiness and their financial condition, warning them, through her own example, of the misery resulting from an imprudent early marriage.

Unlike Mary Ann Radcliffe, the more famous Bluestockings, Montagu, Carter, and Chapone, had always been solvent enough to afford literary modesty and genteel enough to decry professionalism. As seen in Chapter 1, there had been a discrepancy between their supposedly conservative published works and their unconventional private lives. Montagu died in 1800, Chapone in 1801, Carter in 1806; now, for the first time, with the posthumous publication of their letters, readers were given first-hand accounts of their private feminism and progressivism. The letters finally placed these women, who had lived by double standards in their lifetime, in their proper perspective as members, after all, of the progressive tradition.

Along with letters, novels, magazines, and educational treatises, children's books also continued as popular forms of instruction for the daughters of the upper classes. They were an especially popular genre with some of the erstwhile radicals. Hurt by adverse criticism and by adverse circumstances, Hays and Charlotte Smith (as well as the latter's sister, Catherine Ann Dorset), turned their attention to histories and other non-controversial works for the young. In her biography of Smith, Hays feelingly repeated what was by now becoming a common complaint of women writers:

The penalties and discouragement attending the profession of an author fall upon women with a double weight; to the curiosity of the idle and the envy of the malicious, their sex affords a peculiar incitement: arraigned, not merely as writers, but as women, their characters, their conduct, even their personal

---

[11] *Yesterday's Woman* (Princeton: Princeton University Press, 1974), p. 89.

endowments, become the subject of severe inquisition. . . . Wanton malice, in the failure of facts, amply supplies defamation, while, from the anguish of wounded delicacy, the gratification of demons seems to be extracted.[12]

Thus, even at a time when more and more women were using literature to educate their own sex, writing women, including the respected ones, were not exempted from social censure. Society demanded that women had to be women first, in all aspects of life; in the first part of the nineteenth century, therefore, educators patiently had to reiterate earlier theories in pleading for a better education for gentlewomen, based on greater respect for their intrinsic as well as social worth.

Hence, in the first two decades of the nineteenth century, educational theories regarding women largely represented a cross-section of theories of the previous century. First of all, theorists believed that women should be educated according to their destination in life, their rank, constitution, ability, and natural disposition. The major writers of this period were especially concerned with the education of gentlewomen, although philanthropists like Trimmer and More continued to write and work for the enlightenment of labor-class women. Whatever the class-biases, most of the theories on female instruction centered on the belief that education was a means, not an end in itself. As such, women were to be trained not entirely for themselves, but for their usefulness to society and/or to men.

Nevertheless, influenced by a century of progressive thought, most of the major writers of this period agreed that women were capable of thinking and reasoning for themselves. Yet conservatives like West as well as feminists like Lucy Aikin (almost thirty years later) repeated the old lament that gentlewomen were seldom taught to think—either along proper (moral) lines or at all. In her *Letters on the Elementary Principles of Education*, Hamilton, like others before her, regretted that the only mental power exercised in women was memory. But she felt this situation could be amended, to the satisfaction even of society. So, like Wollstonecraft and others, she gave a social basis to the theory of female self-improvement: if gentlewomen cultivated their reason and judgement, they would be more efficient in carrying out their gender-related duties.

---

[12] *Public Characters of 1800–1801* (London, 1807), as quoted in Luria, p. 443.

Certain other theorists regarded the gentlewoman solely in Rouseau's terms. For instance, in his *Enquiry into the Best System of Female Education*, J. L. Chirol declared that women were "created for the domestic comfort and felicity of man" and should be educated accordingly.[13] Moreover, he grandly asserted, like others before him, that the end of such a "virtuous" education for women would be repercussive: besides the felicity of husbands, it would lead to the advancement of families, the progress of the arts and sciences (he does not explain this claim), the improvement of society, and the general prosperity of the state. Conversely, in *De la littérature considérée dans ses rapports avec les institutions sociales*, de Staël affirmed that if women's education affected society, society itself determined female instruction: "On a dirigé l'éducation des femmes, dans tous les pays libres, selon l'esprit de la constitution qui y etait établie."[14] She supported her argument with a contemporary example: revolutionary French leaders had thought it politically and morally useful to reduce women to "la plus absurde médiocrité" instead of granting them the rights of (hu)mankind (p. 305). But this policy had proved unsound, since the best foundation for lasting political and social relations was the equal education of men and women:

> Éclairer, instruire, perfectionner les femmes comme les hommes, les nations commes les individus, c'est encore le meilleur secret pour tous les buts raisonnables, pour toutes les rélations sociales et politiques auxquelles on veut assurer un fondement durable.
>
> (*De la littérature*, pp. 303–04)

This idea of the social nature of female education was connected to other theories. For instance, like de Staël and Wollstonecraft, Hamilton believed that boys and girls should receive an identical education, at least in their early years, but like most other theorists, she emphasized the absolute necessity of a virtuous education for members of her own sex. West and More, for their part, insisted that education in itself was not all; it could not counter the effects of divine grace (West) or of original sin (More). Hamilton and Trimmer were less deterministic, believing that a good education, that is, a religious and

---

[13] *Enquiry* (London: Cadell and Davies, 1809), p. 16.

[14] In *Oeuvres complètes* (1800; rpt. Genève: Slatkine Reprints, 1967), I, 305.

moral one, could prevent the growth of evil principles in women and in the poor (whose education they respectively dealt with) and teach them to translate moral precepts into principles of right action. In his essay on Broadhurst, Sydney Smith gave a secular slant to Hamilton's and Trimmer's views, defining a "good" education as one that would give women not only principles but also active resources, habits, and occupations, which would all benefit them in this life by rendering sickness tolerable, solitude pleasant, age venerable, life more dignified and useful, and death less terrible.

The above were largely general theories. Perhaps the most specific, or at least the most practical reason now offered for educating gentlewomen was John Locke's from the previous century: women needed adequate instruction because, as mothers, they were primarily responsible for the children's education. Their sons were under their charge up to seven or eight years of age, their daughters until they married. Sydney Smith, Lee, West, Hamilton, and Chirol, in particular, thoroughly agreed on the mother's need for a sound education, so she could transmit it to her children. Lee, Hays, Hamilton, and More also stressed that it was the duty of both parents to give the children, especially girls, a sound (moral) education. Even if a mother failed in her duty, having never been educated to think or reason for herself, Hamilton considered it the father's responsibility to take over the education of his children. But men could not always be depended upon; like the earlier Wollstonecraft, she therefore reassured well-educated women, married to autocratic husbands, that maternal duties and filial gratitude would compensate for their spouses' lack of esteem and respect. In effect, nothing short of illiteracy could free a woman from her maternal duty: even if she were married to a man who despised female intellect and instead of a friend and companion, "merely wishes in his wife to find the qualities of a housekeeper and the virtues of a spaniel; even then the wife is without excuse, who does not endeavour to qualify herself for fulfilling the duties of a mother."[15]

In *Adeline Mowbray*, Opie followed Barbauld in stating that a mother's responsibility for the education of children of both sexes began from the moment of their birth; therefore, a wise mother would use every circumstance as a tool to fashion their minds. West opposed this theory, believing the mother to have sufficiently carried out her duties to her daughters if she led them to

---

[15] *Letters on the Elementary Principles of Education* (1801–02; rpt. Bath: Robinsons, 1803), II, 251. All further references to her *Letters* will be to this text.

the age of adolescence with healthy bodies, docile tempers, just notions, benevolent hearts, and firm minds; all other education was a superaddition to this "sure foundation" (*Letters*, III, 199).

Like many of the other conservatives, West also stressed the need to indoctrinate children in stereotypical behavior. Girls were to be brought up in habits of docility, contentment, prudence, and domesticity, while boys were to be encouraged in habits of activity, courage, and enterprise. To her credit, however, she agreed with Hamilton that mothers were to teach their sons to respect their sisters' feelings instead of selfishly acting on a belief in their own superiority. The benefits of such behavior to women would be three-fold, in terms of their relation to men as daughters, wives, and mothers: boys taught to behave fairly with their sisters (and consequently with their own mothers) would later turn out to be just instead of tyrannical husbands and fathers. Mothers would thereby be responsible for assuring peace within the home for both sexes.

The primary importance attached to the role of mother as teacher made the writers in the early nineteenth century, as in the previous one, prefer a home rather than a school education for girls. Among others, More, Lee, Chirol, West, and Hamilton especially advocated home education because it fostered domestic sentiments, provided knowledge of domestic economy, and gave the girls better health, individual attention, and the possibility to develop at their own pace. Hamilton and Austen, in particular, expatiated on the healthful effects of a home education given in the country rather than in the city, for daughters of both the rich and the poor. Another advantage of home education, according to Hamilton, was that it helped maintain sympathetic affections between parents and their daughters, which feelings became extinct in cases where girls were early separated from parents for educational purposes (*Letters*, I, 161). But although young ladies were to be brought up at home, Lee and More warned, as others had done before them, that "few girls brought up in absolute retirement make good wives"[16]; a certain amount of knowledge of the world and of society was necessary so girls' heads would not be turned at the first sight of urban, especially London, dissipation.

In spite of its many assets, home education could also prove defective; educators of this period therefore drew on a number of solutions that had become commonplace by the late eighteenth century. First, they considered it

---

[16] *Life of a Lover* (London: Robinsons, 1804), I, 164.

imperative that parental education be based on moral principles only. A father who painstakingly educated his daughter in ideas of religious infidelity, new-fangled principles of independence, natural perfectibility, and a disregard of filial piety, as Caroline's father does in West's *Infidel Father*, was considered as having failed in his parental duty. In the same novel, West had entitled a chapter "Necessary to be Read by All Mothers, as it Contains a Synopsis of Education on a Liberal Plan"; her specific aim was to point out the harm done by mothers who read modern educational works indiscriminately and tried outlandish instructors and systems on their children. She especially attacked equal education of the sexes, atheism, and theories of human perfectibility, seeing the last as a false system that taught vice while it professed virtue. But theorists realized that, wise or ill, parents could not or would not always carry out their duties to their daughters; hence, it seemed essential they hire governesses on the basis of their moral and religious traits to give the girls a correspondingly moral education. All in all, the system of home education demanded that the instructor, whether parent or governess, be virtuous in a Christian sense, in order to inculcate similar principles in the female charges.

In the early nineteenth century, boarding schools continued to be the chief alternative to home education, but, as with previous theorists, both the progressives and the conservatives found them severely defective in developing the morals and health of their scholars. Declaring himself to have researched the subject of female education for nineteen years, Chirol provided statistics he had read a few years before: twice as many girls aged five to eighteen died at school as at home, since schools were notorious for their poor attention to physical development and hygiene.[17] Following Wollstonecraft in one of her earlier prudish beliefs, Chirol condemned the "fatal" sexual indulgences schoolgirls often engaged in because of their enforced proximity to each other in beds and rooms.

There were other thread-bare arguments against these schools. For instance, the class-conscious conservative West attacked the pseudo-gentility and smattering of ill-learnt accomplishments that school education gave middle-class girls, which completely unfitted them for their station in life. In *Emma*, with characteristic humor, Austen satirized the inflated promises of contemporary boarding schools by presenting the comfortable, nourishing values of the homely country school:

---

[17] Chirol's work is subtitled *Boarding School and Home Education Attentively Considered.*

> Mrs. Goddard was the mistress of a school—not of a seminary, or an establish-
> ment, or anything which professes, in long sentences of refined nonsense, to
> combine liberal acquirements with elegant morality upon new principles and
> new systems—and where young ladies for enormous pay might be screwed out
> of health and into vanity—but a real honest, old-fashioned boarding-school,
> where a reasonable quantity of accomplishments were sold at a reasonable price,
> and where girls might be sent out of the way and scramble themselves into a
> good education, without any danger of coming back prodigies.[18]

Besides the fact that the school itself was set in a good, healthy location
in the country, Mrs. Goddard herself proved to be a motherly sort of woman
who gave her students wholesome food, good exercise, and maternal treatment, three essentials often lacking in many of the schools set up for profit.

Besides boarding schools, only two other types of schools were proposed
in this period, both deriving from eighteenth-century origins. Lee and, surprisingly, even Barbauld, borrowed Astell's plan in nostalgically envisioning
monastic institutions, without vows of celibacy or total seclusion, for single or
unprotected young ladies.[19] Chirol appropriated Wakefield's idea of a teachers' college, recommending the founding of a seminary to train governesses
and boarding-school teachers—an idea that finally materialized later in the
century.

In contrast to the systems they proposed for young ladies, theorists allowed only home education for middle-class girls, but encouraged daughters
of the poor to attend Sunday, Industry, or Charity schools. Through their
own school systems, publications, and even the social praise and censure they
received, Trimmer and More, especially, kept the idea of education for labor-
class girls well in the public mind.[20] Like Clara Reeve in the 1790s, Trimmer

---

[18] *Emma* (1815; rpt. New York: Norton, 1972), pp. 12–13.

[19] Apparently, non-educational institutions along such lines did exist. The Catholic Inchbald's biographer, S. R. Littlewood, records that she lived for a while at Annandale House, "a kind of convent
without vows, where married ladies without husbands or other inconveniences, and spinsters of
mature years, lived together in amity" (*Elizabeth Inchbald and her Circle* [London: O'Connor, 1921],
p. 101).

[20] In spite of her pro-church-and-state attitude, More was severely censured for her part in the Blagdon controversy (1800–03) by even the *Anti-Jacobin*. The ostensible reason for this controversy was a
quarrel between the schoolmaster and the curate of Blagdon. The real issue was whether or not and by
whom the poor were to be instructed. The Mores' efforts at instruction were regarded as subversive,
radical, and Jacobinical, but the sisters were finally acquitted of blame (Jones, p, 172).

recommended that Sunday and Industry schools supplement each other where possible, so that girls could be instructed every day of the week. In her *Oeconomy of Charity, or an Address to Ladies*, substantially revised in 1801 from the first edition of 1787, she provided statistics on the number of poor scholars: there were forty thousand children educated annually as Church of England members in Charity schools. Generously, she praised the efforts of the More sisters in their Mendip schools and of the Female Friendly Society's work with Charity schools, and recommended the Shakespeare's Walk School as a model for Charity schools.

Yet the education of the poor continued to be a controversial issue; hence, as in the 1790s, there were differences of opinion as to *who* should administer instruction. Hannah More considered it the social duty of the rich towards the poor; in *Coelebs*, the wealthy Astons patronize a village school, conducting it much along the lines of the Mores' own Cheddar schools. Trimmer believed that the education of poor children of both sexes should be a public concern; since social stability depended on the good behavior of the poor, their education was not to be left to ignorant and corrupt parents. Hamilton countered with an argument in favor of individual responsibility rather than patronage: it was of more service to train labor-class parents to educate their own children than to undertake this duty for them.

Following Wollstonecraft, Sydney Smith countered with an argument in favor of national education. In his critique of Trimmer's *Comparative View of the New Plan Promulgated by Mr. Joseph Lancaster*, he professed himself "disgusted" at her "patronizing and protecting air" toward Lancaster's plan of education (*Essays*, p. 50). He accused her of falsely claiming that, since the establishment of the Protestant Church in England, the education of the poor had been a national concern, and he noted that her only evidence was an appeal to the Act of Uniformity. Smith himself believed that no other Protestant country ignored the education of its poor as England did. He praised Lancaster for calling public attention to this fault and for presenting new and active remedies. Concerned as he was with the education of both the poor and women, Smith proved himself one of the major progressives of this period. The two traditions met in him, as in many of the other educators; this fusion was apparent in their various theories of female education in general, and also of the four main systems of female instruction in particular, of the person, heart, head, and physique.

## III. Education of the Person, the Heart, the Head, and the Physique

In the first two decades of the nineteenth century, the same basic theories about the four major systems of education for gentlewomen carried over from the latter half of the eighteenth century, although here, as elsewhere, the two traditions tended to merge as never before. In the eighteenth century, progressives and radicals had concentrated largely on the education of the head, and the conservatives and reactionaries on the education of the heart; both traditions had decried the excesses of the education of the person and approved of physical education, with varying degrees of agreement. Since no major innovations were now proposed, this section will largely depict a tenuous merging rather than a detailed account of each system as it evolved during this period.

If the theorists are to be believed, the education of the person continued, as before, to be more popular among the general public than the other three types. Like the radicals, many nineteenth-century progressives as well as conservatives described this system as undeniably "Turkish" in intent because it concentrated solely on the externals of dress, beauty, and showy accomplishments. Yet it was agreed that a certain amount of respect had to be paid to the person and to dress to keep gentlewomen from being slovenly and unkempt; conservatives, especially, felt that education of the person and heart could be profitably combined by conferring the good points of the latter upon the former—women were to adorn themselves only according to the dictates of purity, modesty, and decorum.

Similarly, physical beauty was believed of value only if combined with mental attractiveness. In sentimental novels, however, goodness and beauty were often seen as necessary correlatives; a woman who fell from virtue, like Opie's Adeline Mowbray (modelled on Mary Wollstonecraft), lost her beauty, in this case through an attack of smallpox. On the other hand, in keeping with the platonic equation, "good" heroines, from Pamela on, who contracted the disease in eighteenth-century novels, incredibly escaped with their beauty unimpaired and their faces unmarked.

Conversely, the question of ugliness and its moral repercussions was discussed at length in two novels of this decade, Hamilton's *Modern Philosophers* and the anonymous *Julietta, or the Triumph of Mental Acquirements over*

*Personal Defects.*[21] In spite of her denial of personal satire in her preface, Hamilton cruelly caricatured Hays as the squint-eyed, ugly, short, vulgar, crass, indecorous, oddly dressed, shrill-voiced, man-chasing pseudo-intellectual Bridgetina Botherim, whose conversation is a constant pastiche of the works of Godwin and of Hays herself. Hamilton pointed out that it was "Biddy's" poverty and ugliness and not her new philosophical principles that kept her from seduction, for she offered herself in vain to the hero, as Emma Courtney does in Hays's novel, and as Hays (acting on principles of equality) did in real life to some of her male friends. Hamilton showed the lovely Julia as "seduced" into erroneous beliefs, but the ugly Biddy as rushing headlong into them, haranguing meanwhile against physical beauty and against the social decorum that denied women the right to court. Clearly, Hamilton not only equated physical with moral loveliness, she also displayed personal malice towards a philosophical opponent. Bridgetina's words alone would have sufficed to render her ridiculous without the addition of poverty and grotesque physical defects. This novel says more about Hamilton's mental ugliness than it does Biddy's.

In sharp contrast to Hamilton's novel, *Julietta* was a vindication of ugliness. Here the heroine is a small, hump-backed, deformed, yet talented and well-educated heiress, much like d'Arblay's Eugenia in *Camilla*. The anonymous author feelingly exposes the cruelty of satire like Hamilton's, in making the heroine say to her mother, who expresses abhorrence of her daughter for her misshapenness: "'Deformity of body,' she said, 'is an evil, but it is most painful to those who bear it; but where is a deformity of mind—Ah, how cruelly I feel that another must be its victim!'"[22] Yet Julietta is fortunate in her mentor, Lord Marsham, who encourages her to be wise, independent, estimable, and happy in order to counter her sense of her own deformity.

---

[21] Supposedly following A. Block, in *The English Novel*, the NUC wrongly ascribes this novel to William Parnell. Block himself records *Julietta's* author as anonymous. Could the novel perhaps have been written by Hays as a self-vindication for Hamilton's malicious caricature of her? The strongly feminist elements in the novel, the vindication of ugliness if combined with moral principles and mental excellence, and the system of separate apartments and separate friends that Julietta and her husband initially decide on, which recalls the arrangement between Hays's close friends Wollstonecraft and Godwin in the brief six months of their marriage, all temptingly point to Hays as author.

[22] *Julietta* (London: Johnson, 1802), p. 26.

The change in Julietta's "good" husband, who marries her for mercenary reasons (a paradox with which the author unsuccessfully struggles), from abhorrence to pity to love of his wife's virtue, talents, finally even of her physical appearance, was a triumphant enactment of the eighteenth-century dictum that the beauty of virtue was more durable and worthwhile than that of the body. The best-known nineteenth-century example of this tradition was perhaps Charlotte Bronte's *Jane Eyre*, who is small, short, and plain, yet wins the love of her passionate, intelligent employer.

As with the question of physical appearance and dress, for almost a century, moral theorists had decried an overemphasis on a purely "ornamental" education, that is, one based only on the accomplishments. Conservatives, however, acknowledged the propriety of studying these arts to a certain extent. Since class-biases still prevailed in the early nineteenth century, More, West, Chirol, and others insisted that accomplishments were meant strictly for the gentility and nobility. Here, as everywhere with women, time was an all-important factor: these arts were therefore to be developed only if the individual had an inclination for them. In *Coelebs*, More's evangelicalism led her to desire that girls be trained to be good Christians rather than to spend all their time at the piano or the harp, in drawing and gilding flowerpots, and in netting gloves and veils. In a different vein, the eighteenth-century progressive insistence on developing the female intellect had also left its mark on early nineteenth-century thought; Sydney Smith argued for a more profitable employment of women's time on the basis that "it takes quite as many years to be charming as it does to be learned" (on Broadhurst, *Essays*, p. 99). He emphasized that knowledge could prove a useful resource in all stages of one's life while the numerous accomplishments, as taught in his time, were useful only in youth, a period which he felt had too many charms of its own to need such laborious external enhancements.

Indeed, the list of accomplishments seems to have grown with the years. Far more were (satirically) mentioned in these decades than the standard earlier ones of drawing, dancing, music, needlework, and the modern languages, the last often being considered as part of a gentlewoman's ornamental rather than intellectual education. For instance, Amelia Rattle, a giddy young lady in *Coelebs*, is fashionably educated in French, Italian, German, painting flowers and shells, drawing ruins and buildings, varnishing, gilding, japanning, modelling, etching, engraving in mezzotinto and aquatinta, dancing Scotch Irish steps, singing, and harp- and piano-playing[23]—all of which constitute her "principal" education, while she gives only her "odd moments" to the cultivation of her intellect. More practically, Hamilton and West both preferred girls to spend their time at the needle than in the other arts, considering needlework as an occupation at once useful and elegant.

The elegant, the useful, the moral—these traits which gave a woman habits of gentility, domesticity, and Christian conduct—had come by the end of the eighteenth century to be regarded as the essence of upper-class female behavior. Consequently, the education of the heart continued to be the system of instruction most emphasized by the conservatives. As with the reactionaries, Milton's Eve before the fall remained their ideal of womanhood, especially Coelebs's. The protagonist's mother defines her idea of such an education for women:

> For my own part I call education, not that which smothers a woman with accomplishments, but that which tends to consolidate a firm and regular system of character; that which tends to form a friend, a companion, and a wife. I call education not that which is made up of shreds and patches of useless arts, but that which inculcates principles, polishes taste, regulates temper, cultivates reason, subdues the passions, directs the feelings, habituates to reflection, trains to self-denial, and, more especially, that which refers all actions, feelings, sentiments, tastes, and passions to the love and fear of God.[24]

In keeping with the progressive tradition, Hamilton emphasized the need to combine the education of the heart with that of the head. Such an education, consisting of the development of virtuous principles of both thought and action, would arise from a purity of heart that was not based "solely on innocent ignorance" (*Letters*, I, 262). Combining both traditions, More insisted that a woman thus educated would possess the "truest independence" because she would derive her "principles from the Bible and her amusement from intellectual sources, from the beauties of nature, from active employment [of her time] and exercise." In other words, she would "live on her own stock" since her resources would come from within rather than from outside herself (*Coelebs*, II, 421). Such a woman would be truly virtuous.

---

[23] The piano replaced the harpsichord in the nineteenth century.

[24] *Coelebs in Search of a Wife* (1808; rpt. Cadell and Davies, 1809), II, 421.

In spite of all these benefits, for certain writers the education of the heart was not a fool-proof system. With Christian pessimism, More and West asserted that men and women were, at best, fallen creatures, so could never attain perfection of virtue in this life. In contrast, Hamilton's faith in the efficacy of virtue was more active: it was the duty of humans at least to cultivate virtue to the highest degree of perfection possible in this life. She also believed that there was no distinction of sex in the cultivation of virtue, for the end of a moral education for both sexes was "to render virtue the object of love, and vice the object of hatred" (*Letters*, I, 75).

Hamilton and, surprisingly, the conservative-minded Chirol were among the few writers of this period to follow the progressives in recommending certain common virtues to both sexes, as, for instance, industry, temperance, compassion, fear of God, and love of truth. (At the other end, Hamilton condemned certain vices, for example, licentiousness, as criminal in both sexes and not just in women.) In general, however, although some of the conservatives agreed with the progressives that female moral frailty was the result of pernicious education and not of gender, they also subscribed to the theory that certain virtues were specifically female, in particular those that trained upper-class women in habits of subordination and gentility.

Consequently, gender-related duties were of supreme importance; Opie, More, West, Edgeworth, and also Hamilton all agreed that active virtue in a gentlewoman implied cheerful compliance with her God-given social and familial duties, especially those of the daughter, the wife, and the mother. The novels of Opie, Hamilton, West, More, Austen, and even de Staël stressed the primacy of duty to one's parents (or parent substitutes), although Hamilton, Opie, and Hays,[25] in the liberal tradition, recognized the parent-child duty as reciprocal too. On the question of conjugal duty, the conservatives Chirol, More, and West expatiated on the necessary Eve-like qualities in a wife: obedience, submission, chastity, and blindness to the husband's faults. Furthermore, Chirol cited the Bible, Nature, experience, and, uniquely, Jeremy Bentham's *Treatise on Legislation* as proof that man was the obvious and proper head of the household (even if it was more particularly the woman's realm of operation).

De Staël was almost alone among all these writers to challenge the blanket submission and passivity expected of all women by non-feminist thought. Like Wollstonecraft, her heroine Corinne passionately declares:

---

[25] In *Harry Clinton* (1804), a reworking of *Henry Brooke's Fool of Quality* (1766–70).

Narrow spirits and mediocre people attempt in the name of Duty to impose silence on talent. . . . But is it true that Duty prescribes the same rules for all? . . . Every woman, just like every man, must forge her own path according to her character and talents. (Quoted in Moers, p. 205)

Significantly, de Staël makes it clear that Corinne meets her downfall only in renouncing her passionate convictions for her faithless but demanding English lover. In contrast, de Staël's contemporary conservatives roundly censured all such "masculine" aspirations and behavior as unsexing gentlewomen. Maria Edgeworth especially held up a host of masculine women to ridicule, for instance, Araminta in "Angelina, ou l'amie inconnue," Lady Di Spanker in "Mademoiselle Panache" (*Moral Tales*), and Miss Luttrell in *Belinda,* to name only a few. Aside from masculine behavior, other theorists denounced vices they regarded as innately female, such as cunning, curiosity, vanity, levity, and caprice. (Did they see themselves as exempt?)

Among the moral educators, only Hamilton asserted (like Hays and the earlier radicals) that the so-called female vices were not gender-related but the vices of slaves, the result of systematic conditioning.[26] Her answer to the question of female depravity was to educate (instead of denying) women's intellects as well as hearts, and vice would correspondingly diminish. Like More, she further asserted that a liberal Christian education was not based on ignorance; as the former stoutly put it, "ignorance may be the safety of an idiot, and seclusion the security of a nun" (*Coelebs*, II, 415). Christian behavior, on the contrary, was the result of active principles and not of mechanical rules.

Despite some remaining prejudices, in the education of the intellect, as of the heart, ignorance rather than learning had by now become generally subject to attack. In the preface to her *Memoirs of Queens* (1821), Hays recorded this improvement in thinking:

The powers and capacity of women for rational and moral advancement are, at this day, no longer a question. . . . We live in an age of great events, vicissitudes, and innovations: the invention of printing, the consequent diffusion of literature and extension of education, necessarily lead to a new order of things: it is

---

[26] The slave trade was finally abolished in England in 1807 (but not fully enforced until 1833) although the metaphor of slavery continued to be used by women to describe the subjugation of their sex.

in the nature, and of the essence, of man and mind to be active and progressive: much is to be feared; more perhaps to be hoped. Knowledge, virtue, happiness, are inseparably connected: wisdom must be the mean, moral improvement the end. (pp. iv–v, vii–viii, quoted in Luria, p. 445)

The accent was still on moral improvement; liberals like Hays and Hamilton agreed on the necessary correlation between education of the heart and of the intellect in contributing to right action in women. On the other hand, West, More, and Edgeworth, who understood virtue only in the traditional sense, condemned their contemporary female philosophers for supposedly disgracing their talents by their conduct.

This distinction between the proper use of reason and its abuse had been one of the most common eighteenth-century issues regarding the female intellect. In these two decades, Sydney Smith, Hamilton, and More opted for female learning on the by now familiar grounds that the truly learned woman (or man) was humble rather than pedantic or vain; furthermore, such a woman would effectively carry out her familial duties because she understood them better than the illiterate woman did.

Yet old prejudices against female learning were by no means dead. Still using Molière's worn-out terms, writers like Opie, Hamilton, West, and Lewis Stewarton (in *The Female Plutarch*) derided the *précieuse* or the *femme savante*, that is, the woman who supposedly "abused" her learning, as a failure in family and social life. The new generation of romantic writers—Keats, Hazlitt, and Byron in particular—were no different. In the character of Donna Inez in *Don Juan*, Byron satirized learned women as henpeckers who read deeply into the sciences, mathematics, romances, and contemporary women's works. In describing Donna Inez, he laughingly took a swipe at More's Lucilla too along the way:

In short, she was a walking calculation, Miss Edgeworth's novels stepping from their covers, or Mrs. Trimmer's books on education, or "Coelebs' Wife" set out in quest of lovers. (Canto the First, st. xvi)[27]

---

[27] *English Romantic Writers*, ed. David Perkins (New York: Harcourt, Brace & World, 1967), p. 834. Donna Inez's portrayal represented Byron's bitter attitude to the intellectualism of his own moral wife, a mathematician betrayed by his affairs (capped by his supposed incest with his half-sister), which caused the poet to flee England.

With such romantics, as with younger generations of nineteenth-century writers, the English term "bluestocking" was now beginning to replace the older French terms of ridicule. Whatever the epithet, the learned woman was still regarded in certain circles as an undesirable oddity, a monstrous mistake of nature and of instruction.

In spite of censure of this kind, the scales were now definitely on the side of female learning. Throughout the eighteenth century, a host of very convincing reasons had been slowly gathered in its favor. A novel argument used by More was a curious twisting of Swift's famous cynical remark: there is no danger in cultivating a woman's intellectual powers, she seriously insisted, for "after all, it is a hackneyed remark, that the best instructed girl will have less learning than a schoolboy" (*Coelebs*, II, 231). Similarly, Sydney Smith turned Swift's statement to a feminist purpose: "It is not easy to imagine that there can be any just cause why a woman of forty should be more ignorant than a boy of twelve years of age." He further pointed out that learning would profit the "perhaps 50,000 females in Great Britain, who are exempted by circumstances from all necessary labour" (on Broadhurst, *Essays*, pp. 93, 97). Yet he made it clear that gentlewomen's knowledge was to be used for passing the time, not to turn them into professionals.

A battery of other arguments was variously repeated on the pro-learning side by Sydney Smith, Hamilton, Lee, and others: an intellectual education would give a woman mental resources within herself; keep her away from folly, dissipation, and trashy novels; strengthen her judgement; enlarge her sympathies; and develop her faculties of perception, attention, conception, abstraction, taste, and imagination. Importantly, they continued, it would make her an intelligently companionable wife (since God had designed her to be man's helpmate), an instructive parent, and an efficient manager of her time and of her household; as a corollary, it would encourage *men* to develop their minds so as not to be outshone by women.

Alongside these rational, sober pleas was juxtaposed Corinne's passionate declaration of intellectual deprivation, in its intensity looking back to the aspirations of Wollstonecraft's heroine Mary and forward to Bronte's Jane Eyre:

For what is happiness, I asked myself, if not the development of our faculties? Is not mental suicide as bad as physical? And if I must repress my mind and my spirit what's the use of preserving the miserable rest of my life, which begins to drive me wild? (Quoted in Moers, p. 205)

But it was Coelebs's rather than Corinne's voice that seemed to clinch the argument for female learning. Like others before him, he affirmed that general knowledge was the stamp of the gentlewoman (who, one remembers, apparently could not even sign her own name in Swift's time); it raised her above the middle-class woman whose knowledge was still to pertain to the purely useful.

The positive literary arguments in favor of learning seem to have influenced the minds of upper-class women in real life too. In a letter from Hampstead, dated 1800, to her friend Mrs. Kenrick, Barbauld did a *volte face*, stating with obvious satisfaction:

> I went a few mornings ago to hear Dr. Garnet, who is at present the only lecturer [at the Royal Institution], and was very much pleased to see a fashionable and very attentive audience, about one-third ladies, assembled for the purpose of science and improvement. How much is taught now, and even made a part of education, which, when you and I were young, was not even discovered! It does some credit to the taste of the town, that the Institution and the Bishop of London's lectures have been the most fashionable places of resort this winter. (Ellis, I, 266)

The interest of both gentlewomen and of theorists in improved female education led to the prescription, in the early nineteenth century, of a curriculum that seems far from modest. After a century of heated and often negative debate, the study of religion, politics, classical languages, and sciences such as botany and medicine was finally being considered, at least in theory, and even by certain conservatives, as perhaps suitable for the female mind. Paradoxically, with regard to rational religious instruction, the conservatives proved as feminist as the progressives in refusing to believe that a gentlewoman need only act on the tenets of religion without first understanding them. It was fear of atheism, with its connections with Jacobinical thought, that prodded even diehards like Chirol and West to insist that women be rationally instructed in the articles of the Anglican faith. Although disapproving of the earlier radicals for daring to assert female equality with men, More and West followed certain conservatives in pronouncing women as "superior" to men in their "peculiar fitness" to obey the precepts of the Gospel (West, *Letters*, II, 264).

The radical desire in the 1790s for female participation in politics was cautiously toned down by writers like Maria Edgeworth and West into a belief that women could study, although not take part in, political activities. By the 1820s, Edgeworth, in particular, had begun to abandon the feminine distaste of politics that characterized her in the 1790s. By 1834, a leading character in her novel *Helen* could actually declare:

> "Let me observe to you, that the position of women in society, is somewhat different from what it was a hundred years ago, or as it was sixty, or I will say thirty years since. Women are now so highly cultivated, and political subjects are at present of so much importance, of such higher interest, to all human creatures who live together in society, you can hardly expect, Helen, that you, as a rational being, can go through the world as it now is, without forming any opinion on points of public importance. You cannot, I conceive, satisfy yourself with the common namby-pamby little missy phrase, 'ladies have nothing to do with politics.'" (*Helen*, II, p. 233, as quoted in Butler, p. 451)

Contrarily, adopting the double standards typical of the conservatives, the erstwhile radicals, de Staël, Opie, and Hamilton, now agreed with statesmen like Napoleon and educators like Chirol that women should have nothing to do with politics. Dr Staël, especially, was guilty of deceit, for Napoleon had actually banished her from Paris because of her political interference. Both before and after his rule, however, she exerted direct political influence in Europe through her associations with emperors and statesmen (Berger, p. 17). Thus, in spite of double standards, through such lives if not through precept, prominent women were gradually familiarizing the public with the idea of at least some women in politics.

If the study of religion and politics was now being cautiously suggested for women, even by certain conservatives, metaphysics was still viewed as dangerous to them by writers like West, Chirol, and Opie; only *Julietta* continued the radical tradition of including it among female studies. Of the other newly accepted fields, More agreed with Aikin and most of the progressives that gentlewomen like Lucilla with a "strong, inquisitive mind" might be allowed to learn Latin as an accomplishment (*Coelebs*, II, 230). Similarly, Seward and Chirol followed de Genlis, Wollstonecraft, Hays, and others in recommending that women learn practical medicine; under this term Chirol included dressing wounds, stopping hemorrhages, bleeding with leeches, treating scalds, and even assisting in childbirth (p. 229). Further, West, Chirol, Charlotte Smith, and Seward urged the study of botany; the last humorously dismissed the reactionary argument against it by refusing to believe that a virtuous young woman could be induced by reading Erasmus Darwin's *Botanic Garden* "to imitate the involuntary libertinism of a fungus or a flower."[28]

Other liberal subjects also found surprising encouragement in this period. For instance, under the influence of French writers from Fénelon to de Genlis, the study of accounts became linked with the even more practical suggestion that gentlewomen study laws relating to property, children, parents, matrimony, and succession. Further, under the English influence of Wollstonecraft, writers like Chirol, Hamilton, and West urged that such learning would prove particularly useful to widows without business knowledge, who were generally left helpless at their husband's death. Like the revolutionary Condorcet, and with a similar patriotic purpose, Chirol also proposed to gentlewomen the study of common jurisprudence and of laws pertaining to justice and to the country's constitution. The other subjects variously suggested by different writers were the more usual ones of reading, writing, arithmetic (although mathematics was still frowned on, until later on in the century), the English language, as well as French, Italian, German,[29] grammar, spelling, morality, ethics, geography, logic, rhetoric, history, natural/ moral/experimental philosophy, natural history, astronomy, and general literature such as poetry, good novels, moral plays, travels, and biographies.

The gap between the subjects recommended for the upper- and those suggested for the working class continued unbridged in these decades, as one means of maintaining the political and social status quo. Of course, the middle class had always been allowed useful knowledge; now, the concept of some degree of intellectual education for the poor was also being generally accepted, however grudgingly. In her *Oeconomy of Charity*, Trimmer quoted the Edgeworths in *Practical Education*: "Let the Poor be well-educated, and the difference in their conduct will repay society for the trouble of educating them."[30] But, as in the eighteenth century, More repeated that good education for the poor meant only the rudiments of religion, reading, and arithmetic, while Trimmer, as before, added writing, although only to Charity as opposed to

---

[28] Letter to Mrs. Childers from Lichfield, dated March 30, 1804, in *Letters*, VI, 144.

[29] German was a comparatively new language suggested as part of the curriculum, in spite of or perhaps because of the increasing translations of (supposedly immoral) German plays and novels in the 1790s. Luria points out that Anna Plumtree made herself known as one of the first introducers of German plays, especially Kotzebue's, to English readers (p. 455), as did Inchbald.

[30] *Oeconomy of Charity* (1787; rev., rpt. London: Johnson, Rivingtons, Robinsons, et al., 1801), I, 118.

Sunday and Industry schoolgirls. Both More and Trimmer agreed that, above all, the curriculum should include useful arts such as spinning wool and flax, knitting, plain work, and making and mending clothes. Even more important, the latter, with feminist generosity, suggested the girls should work not only for their mothers but also for poor women in the neighborhood. Like the radicals in the late eighteenth century, Trimmer was acting on the belief that women's lot and education could best be improved by women themselves, and that poor women, as human beings, even if of a lower social status, had a right to a little learning, just as their richer counterparts had a right to more.

Old prejudices against female learning were breaking down in these two decades. Similarly, progressive theory was gaining ground in the fourth type of education recommended for gentlewomen, namely, of the physique. Juvenal's perception of the intimate relationship between a healthy mind and body, popularized by Locke in the eighteenth century, was generally accepted by the first decade of the nineteenth, while Wollstonecraft's, Hays's, and More's insistence in the 1790s that little girls be allowed to romp freely was also repeated by writers like Hamilton and Austen.[31] Hamilton affirmed that "any little girl in high health and spirits" would prefer to be at the drum and whip tops with her brother rather than dress dolls. Following progressive and radical theory, she recognized that "here, as in many other instances, we find the inclinations which we have inspired by means of early association, ascribed to original instinct" (*Letters*, I, 381). In her liveliest novel, *Pride and Prejudice*, Austen makes Elizabeth Bennet energetically walk three miles over wet fields, "jumping over stiles and springing over puddles" to visit her sick sister at Netherfield.[32] Likewise, as a child, her comic heroine Catherine Morland has no taste for the more sedentary pursuits of gardening or dressings dolls; instead, she prefers cricket, baseball, horseback riding, and running about the country: "She was, moreover, noisy and wild, hated confinement

---

[31] Some decades later, Lucy Aikin wrote to Dr. Channing, somewhat rosily, about the improvement in women's health. Forty or forty-five years previously, women were tight-laced, with pinched figures, weak nerves, and miserable health; physicians prescribed exercise, but to no avail. But in the French Revolution, Frenchwomen emancipated themselves from stays; Englishwomen followed their example, and further learnt to march "and bid fair defiance to dirt and foul weather. We have now well-developed figures, blooming cheeks, active habits, firm nerves, and vigorous constitutions" (Letter dated from Hampstead, August 9, 1842, in *Memoirs, Miscellanies, and Letters* [London: Longman, Green, Roberts, et al., 1864], p. 435).

[32] *Pride and Prejudice* (1813; rpt. New York: Norton, 1966), p. 22.

and cleanliness, and loved nothing so well in the world as rolling down the green slope at the back of the house" (*Northanger Abbey*, p. 2).

In spite of their lip-service to adequate exercise, the specific physical pursuits approved by West, the anonymous *Julietta*, and even More (during this period) were not very strenuous. At the top of the list was gardening, a favorite prescription of the reactionaries of the 1790s; in *Coelebs*, Mr. Stanley goes overboard in describing it as an almost religious pursuit. More to the purpose, Chirol and *Julietta* agreed on riding as a healthful exercise. Lastly, with the inconsistency typical of the conservatives, Chirol, following Gisborne, condemned the "crocodile" walk of boarding-school girls as not supplying free and proper exercise, at the same time that he recommended that gentlewomen should be weak and delicate because their debility pleased the men.

Chirol's conflict was perhaps symbolic of the general conflict in conservative theory during the early part of the nineteenth century: while it sometimes honestly sought improved conditions and happiness for women, it was still constricted by considerations of sex, class, and existing conditions. Significantly, whenever actual merging of the traditions took place, it was almost always in favor of the feminist side. What is important about theories on the four systems of a gentlewomen's education in this period, therefore, is not that the education of the heart continued in preeminence but that those of the head and body were finally being accepted as a matter of course, while that of the person was given less importance than some of the conservatives of the eighteenth century had believed its due. If the radicals of the 1790s were subdued in this period, perhaps it was in part because they had already served their purpose: progressive thought had taken firm root; it now needed nurturance, not rhetoric, to further perpetuate itself.

## IV. Professionalism

In spite of the detailed attention paid by writers to the four systems of female education, the general end envisioned for gentlewomen was moral and social, not economic. At the beginning of the nineteenth century, the mark of a gentlewoman (as indeed, of a gentleman) continued to be her economic idleness. So the primary non-paying professional states for her were, as before, the married and the single, while the tireless efforts of More, Trimmer, and others encouraged her to do social work as a vocational outlet. These vocations were, however, the privilege of respectable women; for the woman fallen from virtue, if unkept, there often seems to have been no hope—as always, prostitution allowed her a meager subsistence, with its concomitants of social ostracism and personal misery.

Aside from this ancient means of subsistence, gentlewomen had made no overall professional strides by the end of the eighteenth century. Nevertheless, the few paying positions into which they had forced their way were now grudgingly accepted by society as a means of self-support, all else, including dependency, failing. Among the handful of paid jobs, writing and teaching were definitely becoming feasible options for the unprovided gentlewoman; although they involved a drop in social respectability, they presented alternatives lacking to gentlewomen a century and a half previously. Of course, the list of professional vetoes persisted in being much longer than the list of job options; a gentlewoman's place was still essentially in the home, unless economic necessity forced her to work. Working for job satisfaction alone was unthinkable.

As in the eighteenth century, marriage was the most respectable non-paying profession for gentlewomen, even if, as said earlier, it sometimes involved what Sarah Fielding, Chapone, Bennett, and Wollstonecraft, in the second half of the century, had called a form of legal prostitution. The most clear-eyed expression of this economic barter is seen in Charlotte Lucas's reason for marrying the pompously unbearable Mr. Collins in *Pride and Prejudice*:

> Without thinking highly either of men or of matrimony, marriage had always been her object; it was the only honourable provision for well-educated young women of small fortune, and however uncertain of giving happiness, must be their pleasantest preservative from want. (p. 86)

Yet like the reactionaries, the nineteenth-century conservatives encouraged marriage, not as a matter of economic necessity but as a way to form the basis of society, apparently threatened by the new philosophical principles of free love. Like Frances Sheridan's *Sydney Biddulph*, some of the important social novels of the first decade, such as Edgeworth's *Leonora* and Opie's *Adeline Mowbray*, even chose to deal with the life of the patiently suffering married woman, rather than with the vicissitudes of the sentimental young woman in love. Except for *Julietta*, which uniformly opted for an equal marriage, the message in such novels was partly traditional, namely, that the wife was to submit cheerfully to her husband, and partly progressive, in that she was always to preserve her own moral integrity. As with the reactionaries, the answer to unhappiness in marriage was patient resignation, not divorce (attainable for women only through her own marital infidelity or the proven impotency of her husband). Both Edgeworth in *Leonora* and de Staël in *De l'Allemagne* (1813) vehemently spoke against divorce, even though the latter openly flaunted her own extramarital affairs.

A social deviant like Opie's Adeline Mowbray, after an ironically happy life with her new-philosopher lover and an unhappy one with her socially acceptable husband, is made to die recanting her earlier views on free love; she finally accepts the goodness of age-old customs and the necessity of the marriage institution as the "dearest of all monopolies."[33] Like Julia in Hamilton's *Modern Philosophers*, she also dies affirming that the laws of society are to be submitted to, not questioned, if a woman is to be happy. Significantly, Opie asserted, as Charlotte Lucas realized, that often the real reasons for marriage were social and mercenary rather than religious. They included personal acceptance in society by other women, respectful treatment by men, as well as inheritance of paternal property (as dowry), legitimacy of the children, and the setting of good examples to inferiors, such as maids.

Marriage was undoubtedly the first and most honorable of professions, yet a percentage of gentlewomen continued to remain single, for whatever reason. If without a private income, they formed what had become a largely expendable section of society. Like the earlier conservatives, writers like West, Hamilton, and Trimmer ignored the possibility of indigence and emptily expatiated on the joys of the single state for women with comfortable incomes and good morals. According to them, such single women could be useful both in society, as charitable benefactors of the poor, and also in families, as helpful daughters, sisters, aunts, and friends. More practically, in her *Letters*, West urged women to develop a knowledge of business and monetary transactions, so they would be less dependent on men and less open to chicanery if left in the single state. Further, although she had piously censured female

---

[33] In *The Works of Amelia Opie* (1804; rpt. Philadelphia: Crissy, 1843, I, 126). Opie seems to have become less of a radical after her own marriage in 1798 to a well-known Cornish painter. In *Amelia Alderson Opie*, MacGregor quotes her as declaring: "Wives are not all free-agents, and I am more a wife of the *old*, than the *new* school" (p. 27). Like Wollstonecraft, and unlike Robinson, Inchbald, Charlotte Smith, Mary Ann Radcliffe, Fenwick, and other radicals, Opie had a happy (although childless) marriage.

independence in *The Infidel Father*, she now asserted, like the progressives, that the pride of self-dependence would prevent gentlewomen from rushing into unsuitable marriages, for fear of being ridiculed as old maids. But all the above were merely theories. With greater realism, Trimmer and Baillie pointed out that in actual fact, the self-respect of the single woman could not always equal the social respect accorded the married woman. In Baillie's comedy, *The Country Inn*, Lady Goodbody advises a headstrong young woman: "A married woman is always more respectable than a single one, let her be married to whom she will."[34]

And finally, with regard to the "fallen" woman (before she succumbed to ultimate debasement), the conservatives' interest in maintaining the male-dominated status quo now led them to concentrate more on the possibilities of her moral regeneration than on the actual prevention of rape or seduction.[35] Like More in her *Strictures*, West adhered to the notion that women who had lost their virtue should be allowed to repent in private but otherwise be banished from society. (In Austen's *Mansfield Park*, too, Maria Rushworth is banished, comfortably if not contentedly, from her family and from "polite" society.) In a more liberal strain, Opie made the heroines of both *The Father and Daughter* and *Adeline Mowbray* fallen women; yet her moral itself was conservative: such women, even if repentant and forgiven by friends, could never forgive themselves. The only way out for them, as for Goldsmith's "lovely woman who stoops to folly" was to die, although in the former novel, Opie followed Richardson's *Clarissa* in portraying the suffering and death of the seducer too. More practically, Hays in *Harry Clinton* and Hamilton in *Modern Philosophers* proposed the founding of asylums for such repentants to save them from prostitution.[36] In the latter novel, Mrs. Fielding, a respected single woman, sets up an Asylum for the Destitute, creating a haven to save seduced women from infamy, to give them independence through industry, and to lodge old or sick servants without jobs, as well as women rejected by

---

[34] In Miscellaneous Plays (London: Longman, Hurst, Rees, et al, 1804), p. 185.

[35] Only Lee, in *The Life of a Lover*, followed the radical advice of the 1790s in suggesting that her heroine Cecilia seek legal redress for an attempted rape; yet, like her fictional sisters, Cecilia decides not to do so, recognizing the futility of self-vindication in a patriarchal court and society.

[36] In her *Oeconomy of Charity*, Trimmer recorded that there were twenty thousand prostitutes in London and ten thousand servants without jobs. An increasing interest in statistics is apparent in this decade, as with the radicals in the 1790s, showing perhaps that theories were now being measured against actual social conditions.

families and the wretched outcasts from prison. "I cannot dictate to the government, but I can relieve them myself," she declares, at once upholding the system of personal benevolence and exposing the failure of the government to carry out its duty to the unprotected portion of its female citizens (III, 81).

The private interest taken by philanthropical gentlewomen in the welfare of the downtrodden of their sex as well as of the poor led reformers like Trimmer and More to reinforce an idea already prevalent in the eighteenth-century, namely, that upper-class women engage in active social work.[37] As More's biographer Jones put it, "Charity, said Miss More, unwittingly inserting the thin edge of the wedge into masculine preserves, was the calling of a lady; 'The care of the poor is her profession'" (p. 195). But in her *Oeconomy of Charity*, Trimmer testified that parish relief had for long been and was still considered in some places as "a concern with which women had no business" (II, 54). Nevertheless, in spite of pressure from certain clergymen, Trimmer proved herself a practical feminist, exhorting the more privileged members of her sex to set up schools for the poor, to spread religious knowledge among them, to support these schools by selling their own drawings, embroidery works, and so on, and to help lying-in women and the inmates of Magdalen hospitals. Social work, after all, was part of the duty the rich owed the poor, in return for the latter's grateful subservience to the former in all matters. And as a duty, it became an integral part of the unpaid professionalism expected of gentlewomen, along with their other tasks as daughters, wives, and mothers.

Among the few paid professions, writing was by now proving a financial outlet for gentlewomen, although society, and even a feminist like Sydney Smith, still sanctioned publication only for purposes of sustenance, not profit. On the other hand, in *De la littérature*, de Staël followed de Genlis in lamenting the deliberate withholding of encouragement by men and even by women to talented female writers. Charles Lamb joined the discouraging tribe, even though his sister Mary had coauthored their well-known *Tales from Shakespeare* (1807): he castigated all women writers, except Inchbald, as "impudent, forward, unfeminine, and unhealthy in their minds" (Rodgers, *Georgian*

---

[37] The socio-religious nature of social work and its connection to improved female education is recorded in Lucy Aikin's letter to Dr. Channing: "*Ladies* are, no doubt, much superior now in education, tastes, and manners, to that generation [Swift's]; then they played quadrille; now they read theory, and attend lectures, and gather pence for missions and Bible Societies" (Letter from Hampstead, dated April 18, 1838, *Memoirs*, p. 370).

*Chronicle*, p. 149). Yet popular and moral women writers won either open or the grudging respect of their contemporaries. As Sydney Smith expressed it:

> It may be an evil for ladies to be talked of; but we really think those ladies who are talked of only as Miss Edgeworth, Mrs. Barbauld, and Mrs. Hamilton are talked of, may bear their misfortune with a very great degree of Christian patience. (On Broadhurst, *Essays* p. 98)

Certainly, for such women, writing brought much fame. Edgeworth, in particular, was the most celebrated novelist in England from 1800 to 1814, before Austen and especially Sir Walter Scott replaced her in the second decade of the century.[38] To certain other writers, their works brought both fame and profit. Hamilton was awarded a pension by the Scottish government, while More, who for decades staunchly refused professionalism for other women, netted over thirty thousand pounds by her writings and continued to retain the respect of the government, which approached her even in her seventies to write tracts against the liberal MP William Cobbett (Jones, p. 186). Yet it must be repeated here that the female writers who succeeded in their profession were generally considered women of unimpeachable moral character, in contrast with the earliest forerunners like Behn and Manley. Such moral women helped influence society's opinion about their sex by winning its regard for themselves, if not quite for their profession; further, they won greater respect for women in fiction too, by creating moral characters of both sexes and by generally decrying male libertinism.

Yet the story of most early-nineteenth-century women writers, especially of the Minerva type, was perhaps closer to that of Mary Ann Radcliffe than to that of "literary aristocrats"[39] like More and d'Arblay. In her *Memoirs*, Radcliffe described the heartbreaking series of petty jobs she undertook to support herself and her seven children—working in small private businesses like pastry-making and shoe-selling, working as a governess and at other temporary jobs, and finally selling her "life" by subscriptions for her novels. The last few

---

[38] Austen humorously wrote to her novel-writing niece Anna Austen that Scott, with his poetic reputation, had no business to encroach on the novel form and thus deprive people of their livelihood (letter from Chawton, dated Wednesday, September 28, 1814, in Jane Austen's *Letters to her Sister Cassandra and Others* [Oxford: Clarendon Press, 1932]), I, 38.

[39] A term used in *Julietta*.

pages were a poignant testimony of her courage in the face of subscription-lists filling far too slowly and therefore of imminent homelessness for her children and herself.

Radcliffe's real-life difficulties were mirrored in fiction by those of d'Arblay's *Wanderer*, who sought self-support not through writing but through needlework, music lessons, millinery, mantua-making, and acting as governess and as companion. Influenced perhaps by the radical emphasis on work ethics, the concept of the working heroine attracted writers in these two decades more than ever before. Opie also introduced the working heroine in some of her novels—the repentant Agnes, in *Father and Daughter*, supports herself through shawl work, fancy work, making artificial flowers, and painting needlebooks and workbags, while Adeline Mowbray teaches school for a while until the discovery of her past forces her to move away.

The climactic example of the professional woman, was, of course, de Staël's Corinne—a poet, improviser, painter, musician, and dancer (all the accomplishments Sydney Smith and others had warned gentlewomen not to turn into professions)—highly appreciated in sunny Italy. Moers speaks of the "enormous [inspirational] influence" of the novel, which she sees as the first instance in fiction of the suffering of the gifted woman, on nineteenth-century literature.[40] She also quotes the Victorian writer, Fanny Kemble, as saying that the novel gave girls from Yorkshire to New England "a wild desire for an existence of lonely independence" (Moers, pp. 174, 203). But Corinne's professional success was directly at odds with the domestic success of her fictional opponent, More's Lucilla. In their decade, as later on in the century, both heroines represented the tension between home and (paid) work that was soon to become so integral a part of the lives of many women in both real life and in fiction.

Not surprisingly, Corinne was the only fictional instance of overwhelmingly successful professionalism in this period. For other gentlewomen, especially those without obvious literary or ornamental talents, becoming a governess seems to have been one of the few resources. Yet Chirol, like others before him, lamented that most governesses were ill-qualified to teach, not only because they were inadequately educated themselves, but also because some of them were former chambermaids, servants, and kept women; apparently

---

[40] Moers also cites Elizabeth Barrett Browning's *Aurora Leigh* (1857) as one long plea for the recognition of the woman artist and poet (p. 199).

widows and women in embarrassed circumstances undertook this profession too, for economic rather than vocational reasons. But in real life as in fiction, there were also examples of self-respecting women like Mary Ann Radcliffe and heroines like Lee's Cecilia and later, Bronte's Jane Eyre, who likewise toiled at this demanding, often degrading job. Mary Ann Radcliffe spoke feelingly of the long list of female "want-ads" in newspapers; in *Emma*, Mrs. Elton speaks of places in town called "advertising offices" for the "sale—not quite of human flesh—but of human intellect," which she calls "governess-trade" (p. 204).

It was apparently an unprofitable trade. Chirol agreed with the Edgeworths (in *Practical Education*) that qualified private governesses be given a salary of three hundred pounds a year as opposed to the real-life average, which he quoted as thirty to forty pounds, and, in rare cases, a hundred guineas. He pointed out that school education cost eighty pounds per annum per student, yet governesses received far less than this amount, "to the disgrace of the age in which those who cultivate the understanding, receive less than is given to certain classes of servants," specifically cooks, butlers, head gardeners, housekeepers, and lady's maids (p. 76). The disgrace of the age was two-fold—not only did it downgrade the importance of schooling, its upper-class also paid certain lower-class workers better wages than it did its own economically depressed peers, thus creating conditions for social imbalance.[41] Aware of this situation, West advised the readers of her *Letters* that the poor should *not* be well paid so as to keep them away from dissipation. The idea of increasing wages for gentlewomen seems not to have crossed her mind.

In these two decades, as before, jobs and often salaries were generally class- as well as gender-related. The few jobs suggested specifically for the middle-class woman—mainly teaching, millinery, mantua-making—seem to have been as badly remunerated as those for upper-class women. As in the previous century, the positions of school governesses (that is, headmistresses) were often filled by impoverished gentlewomen, but under them were the middle-class teachers, even more financially and personally abused than private governesses were. Chirol eloquently exposed the poverty and ill-treatment of teachers, suggesting social relief for and attention to their miserable

---

[41] In *Women Workers and the Industrial Revolution 1750–1850*, Ivy Pinchbeck writes about jobs for the working-class woman in this period, beginning with agriculture and cottage industries and leading to factory work, with the coming of the Industrial Revolution. Unlike the radicals, the writers discussed in this chapter did not display much concern for these issues.

state. He quoted their salaries as being fifteen to twenty pounds a year, out of which they had to pay for their laundry, as well as their board and necessities for the three-month vacation period. He felt it an adverse comment on the age that (male) dancing and music masters made ten times more than the (largely female) teachers of languages, geography, history, and religion. Other writers were similarly concerned with the lot of teachers. Hamilton pleaded for more respectful treatment for them by both parents and pupils, instead of the ill-usage they received as mere "hirelings" (*Letters*, I, 206). With respect to the shortage of instructors in Charity schools for the poor, Trimmer now followed Bell's and Lancaster's monitorial systems in proposing that female head scholars teach the younger children by means of the first volume of her *Teacher's Assistant*. This training would qualify them to teach school themselves, educate their own children, and make better-instructed nursery maids for children of the affluent classes.

Aside from the above-mentioned jobs, theorists did not display much interest in middle- or lower-class working women. In general, they agreed that the middle-class woman should marry a man of her own social standing and stay at home making clothes, pies, and jellies and instructing her children. Their advice seems somewhat ironic, for the availability of servants, governesses, and boarding schools, even for women of this class, had made the bourgeois housewife an expendable or expensive item—except in the matter of procreation and unless adequately trained to supervise the details of home management.

It has been seen that like the reactionaries of the 1790s, most of the conservative writers of this decade were more concerned about the upper- than the middle-class woman. Moreover, they were more vociferous about what professions unprovided gentlewomen should not engage in, than in what they could, to support themselves in reasonable comfort and dignity. Hamilton chided what she called the champions of female sexual equality for contending that equality in education would prepare women for equal public employments and vocations. Like Sydney Smith and even Wollstonecraft, she considered women's duties at home to be as important as men's professions outside the home, and agreed with West and Chirol on the necessity to separate the two. But unlike Wollstonecraft, she considered the home to be woman's only sphere, leaving no room for either female aspirations or for financial necessity. More specifically, West and Chirol prohibited certain fields outside the home, together pronouncing women totally unfit to be politicians, statesmen, legislators, generals, warriors, university professors, religious ministers, advocates, lawyers, physicians, and merchants. Unlike Wortley Montagu and certain other eighteenth-century progressives, West even denied the fitness of women to be queens, attributing the strengths of successful examples like Elizabeth I to their undesirable masculinity and their weaknesses to their inherent femininity. Carrying her point to an extreme, she condemned female *robbers* as being more dangerous than their male cohorts, curiously arguing that their gender-related cowardice made them murderers, not just thieves. It is ironic that a woman who had such a low opinion of her sex should pronounce herself its champion, glorying in her (lucrative) attempts to reconcile it to its inferior position in the socio-familial hierarchy.

In spite of writers like West, aspirations and talents, like murder, will "out," especially when cornered by financial difficulties. The consequent history of women's education and professionalism in the nineteenth century must have resulted partly from the previous century's plea, as well as the reaction to it, for women's self-improvement along lines traditionally seen as male. A brief synopsis will show how nineteenth-century developments rested largely (although not directly) on progressive ideas propagated in the previous century.

According to Lee Holcombe in *Victorian Ladies at Work*, women in the nineteenth century started to make serious inroads into the job market, especially in teaching, hospital work, and shopkeeping. Significantly, women now began to bond together for professional benefit; for instance, capable, well-to-do Victorians organized to help their less fortunate sisters: in 1859, the feminists known as "the Ladies of Langham Place" founded the Society for the Employment of Women.[42]

The expansion of the job market for women was related to their (somewhat) improved education. This connection was particularly seen in the case of governesses, who, after the founding of the Governesses' Benevolent Institution in 1841 and the opening of Queen's College for women in 1848 (Astell's dream come true at last!), received both an asylum when jobless and better training for their profession, even though job satisfaction itself was still not a reality. The idea of a teachers' college, voiced by Wakefield in the 1790s, thus actually came into being in the next century.

---

[42] *Victorian Ladies at Work* (Hamden, Conn.: Archon Books, 1973), p. 5. Information on later nineteenth-century education is mostly from Holcombe's work and from Josephine Kamm's *Hope Deferred*.

Both students and teachers began to receive better instruction as new institutions were founded for them through the efforts of devout feminists. Of the four main educational systems of the eighteenth century, the education of the heart continued to be the most important in the next century, but, following the progressives, dedicated Victorian educators like Emily Davies (1830–1921), Frances Mary Buss (1827–94), and Dorothea Beale (1831–1906) laid increasing stress on the development of women's intellects and bodies, while de-emphasizing the importance of purely ornamental instruction. From 1863 on, female academic achievement was measured by public high school exams, through the efforts of Davies. The general tendency was largely towards separate schools, although co-education was slowly coming into practice.

Perhaps more importantly, what Condorcet and Wollstonecraft had hoped in the 1790s came to pass in the next century: following the example of dedicated individuals, the state finally began to take on responsibility for educating women and the poor. The passage of a series of acts signalized its interest in improved schools and curricula for these two groups. In 1856, the government actually formed a Department of Education; earlier, from 1833 on, it had begun to supply grants for societies that educated the poor. In 1869, the Endowed Schools Act became the first acknowledgement by the state of women's claims to a liberal education; in 1870, the state passed the Education Act for England and Wales, thereby laying the foundation of a national system of public education. Furthermore, an act passed in 1880 made elementary education compulsory for all social classes of both sexes, while an act of 1891 made this education free in board and voluntary schools. Significantly, the Bryce Commission set up by the government in 1894 declared that the joint impetus of the report of the Schools' Inquiry Commission, the action of the universities in admitting women to higher education, and the creation of good secondary schools had proceeded

> 'an effect which is gradually pervading all classes of the community; and through this and other causes, the idea that a girl, like a boy, may be fitted by education to earn a livelihood, or, at any rate, to be a more useful member of society, had become widely diffused.' (Quoted by Kamm, p. 225)

Lastly, by 1914, England had developed a national system of public education, although it was not yet completely democratic or classless. By the early twentieth century, then, much that Wollstonecraft and her radical peers had envisioned in the 1790s had come into being: (cautious) equal education, national education, co-education, compulsory education, and increased professionalism for women. After two whole centuries of agitation by feminist thinkers, earlier theories were finally on their slow way to becoming a reality.

Improved education and career possibilities had their legal and social repercussions too. Later Victorian women saw a steady if far from satisfactory improvement over their eighteenth-century predecessors, in such respects as property rights, marriage rights, contraception, and divorce laws, which, according to Moers, "made the nineteenth century the greatest period of female social progress in history" (p. 19). Yet the overall picture was not entirely rosy. As in the previous century, feminists like John Stuart Mill wrote tracts for women, others fought for an equal recognition of women as human beings and citizens, yet, in practice, social and legal discrimination continued against the sex. Near midcentury, in a letter to Dr. Channing, Lucy Aikin acknowledged that even if her age was more favorable to women than former times, society continued to wrong her sex where the laws did not. Social and legal abuses against women, such as seduction, wife-beating, and loss of child custody, even if the father was "brutal and unfaithful," continued apace, as did the teaching to brothers to scorn their sisters as inferior beings, the meting out of more capital sentences to women than to men for lesser offenses, and the presence of different laws for the sexes regarding crime and felony.

Aikin made the wrongs of women even more apparent when she confessed that she spoke only of gentlewomen (whom, as socially superior, one might have expected to be treated with more respect) and admitted to knowing nothing personally of the lives of the "miserable drudges; the beaten and half-famished wives," and of prostitutes.[43] Yet, on an ultimate appraisal, on comparing the Code Napoléon with English laws, she considered Englishwomen to be better off than their French counterparts. What she might have acknowledged at this point, with much relevance, is that if Englishwomen were comparatively well off currently, it was because of earlier liberal French influence as well as that of like-minded Britons.

Overall, it must be recognized that women's education in the nineteenth century owed as much to French as to English tradition, as much to progressive and radical theorizing as to conservative and reactionary thinking of the previous century. In the early part of the new century, the two sides were

---

[43] Letter from Hampstead, dated April 18, 1838, *Memoirs*, pp. 368–69.

politely beginning to shake hands, even if the conservatives still maintained a cautious and sometimes disapproving reserve. Similarly, through practice if not precept, the conservatives were often passively responsible for propagating progressive ideas, while feminist idealists were actively inciting women to assume greater control over their own lives and happiness.

Although still separated by class boundaries and tied down by gender-related duties, women were becoming more and more aware that rational education and sisterly bonding could improve their status both within society and within the family. (In fact, the bonding seen between educated women in the eighteenth century became a particularly significant phenomenon among Victorian feminists.) Even more important, women were learning that instead of passively accepting their inferiority, they could claim the rights of human beings, not just as creatures with equal souls but as equally capable and intelligent members of the species. Not that all women were actively up in arms in the first part of the century—far from it, but women's consciousnesses were being touched, if not actually raised, to realize their wrongs. The educational literature of the times, both fictional and non-fictional, both liberal and traditional, testified to this fact, over and over again.

In spite of overt differences, then, the aspirations of feminist thinkers from Astell to Wollstonecraft and Hays, as well as the lives of unconventional conservatives from Montagu to More and d'Arblay, both played their part in the gradual improvement of women's socio-familial status. Ultimately, it was their joint or individual pains over the question of female education that were responsible for putting the pen—and consequently power—in the hands of British women of all succeeding generations.

# Primary Sources

## [Original spellings and punctation maintained]


Addison, Joseph (1672–1719), and Richard Steele (1672–1729), et al. *Guardian.* 1713; rpt. In 2 vols., London: Tonson, Draper, 1751; in 1 vol., London: Jones, 1829.

—. *Spectator.* 8 vols. 11th ed. 1711–72, 1714; rpt. London: Tonson, 1733; in 1 vol., London: Jones 1840.

*Agatha; or, a Narrative of Recent Events. A Novel.* 3 vols. London: The Author, 1796.

Aikin, Lucy (1781–1864). *Memoirs, Miscellanies, and Letters of the Late Lucy Aikin: Including those Addressed to the Rev. Dr. Channing from 1826 to 1842.* Ed. Philip Hemery Le Breton. London: Longman, Green, Roberts, et al., 1864.

Aldis, Sir Charles (1775?–1863). *A Defence of the Character and Conduct of the Late Mary Wollstonecraft Godwin, Founded on Principles of Nature and Reason; as Applied to the Peculiar Circumstances of her Case; in a Series of Letters to a Lady.* London: Wallis, 1803.

Alexander, William (1726–82). *The History of Women, from the Earliest Antiquity to the Present Time, Giving some Account of almost Every Interesting Particular concerning that Sex, among all Nations, Ancient and Modern.* 2 vols. 3rd ed. 1779; rpt. London: Dilly, Christopher, 1782.

*Amusement Hall; or, an Early Introduction to the Attainment of Useful Knowledge.* By a Lady. London: Gardiner, et al., 1794.

*Analytical Review, or History of Literature. Domestic and Foreign, on an Enlarged Plan.* 29 vols. London: Johnson, 1788–99.

*Anti-Jacobin; or Weekly Examiner.* 1797–98; rpt. New York: AMS Press, 1968.

*Anti-Jacobin Review and Magazine; or, Monthly Political and Literary Censor.* 61 vols. London: by Whittle and Chapple, 1798–1821.

Astell, Mary (1666–1731). *Letter Concerning the Love of God.* NP: J. Noris, 1697.

—. *A Serious Proposal to the Ladies, for the Advancement of their True and Greatest Interest.* By a Lover of her Sex. 4th ed. Part 1, 1694; Part 2, 1697; rpt. London: Wilkin, 1701.

—. *Some Reflections upon Marriage.* London: John Nutt, 1700.

Austen, Jane (1775–1817). *Emma.* 1815; rpt. New York: Norton, 1972.

—. *Jane Austen's Letters to her Sister Cassandra and Others*. 2 vols. Ed. R. W. Chapman. Oxford: Clarendon Press, 1932.

—. *Mansfield Park*. 1814; rpt. 1906; rpt. New York: Dutton, 1923.

—. *Minor Works*. In *The Works of Jane Austen*. London: Oxford University Press, 1954. Vol. VI.

—. *Northanger Abbey*. 1818; rpt. New York: Dutton, 1907.

—. *Persuasion*. 1818; rpt. Boston: Houghton Mifflin, 1965.

—. *Pride and Prejudice*. 1813; rpt. New York: Norton, 1966.

—. *Sense and Sensibility*. 1811; rpt. New York: Caldwell, 1907.

Bage, Robert (1728–1801). *The Fair Syrian. A Novel*. 2 vols. 1787; rpt. Louisville: Lost Cause Press, 1961.

—. *Hermsprong, or Man as He Is Not*. 1796; rpt. New York: Library Publishers, 1951.

—. *James Wallace, a Novel*. 3 vols. London: Lane, 1787.

Baillie, Joanna (1762–1851). *The Bride;*[*sic*] *a Drama. In 3 Acts*. London: Colburn, 1828.

—. *Fugitive Verses*. London: Moxon, 1840.

—. *The Martyr: A Drama, in 3 Acts*. London: Longman, Rees, Orme, et al., 1826.

—. *Miscellaneous Plays*. London: Longman, Hurst, Rees, Orme, 1840.

—. *A Series of Plays: In which it Is Attempted to Delineate the Stronger Passions of the Mind: Each Passion being the Subject of a Tragedy and a Comedy*. Vol. I. London: Cadell, Jr., and Davies, 1798.

Barbauld, Anna Laetitia Aikin (1743–1825). *Memoir, Letters, and a Selection from the Poems and Prose Writings of Anna Laetitia Barbauld*. Ed. Grace Atkinson Ellis. 2 vols. Boston: Osgood, 1874.

—. *The Pleasures of the Imagination. By Mark Akenside. To which is Prefixed a Critical Essay on the Poem by Mrs. Barbauld*. London: Cadell and Davies, 1795.

—. "What Is Education?" *Monthly Magazine*, 5 (1798).

—. *The Works of Anna Laetitia Barbauld. With a Memoir by Lucy Aikin*. 2 vols. London: Longman, Hurst, Rees, et al., 1825.

—, and John Aikin. *Evenings at Home: or the Juvenile Budget Opened. Consisting of a Variety of Miscellaneous Pieces, for the Instruction and Amusement of Young People*. 6 vols. 2nd ed. 1792–96; Philadelphia: Dobson, 1797.

Beckford, William (1760–1844). *Modern Novel Writing* (1796) *and Azemia* (1797). 4 vols in 1. Rpt. Gainesville, FL: Scholars' Facsimiles and Reprints, 1970.

Bell, Andrew (1753–1832). *An Analysis of the Experiment in Education, made at Egmore, near Madras. Comprising a System, alike Fitted to Reduce the Expense of Tuition, abridge the Labour of the Master, and Expedite the Progress of the Scholar; and Suggesting a Scheme for the Better Administration of the Poor-Laws, by Converting Schools for the Lower Orders of Youth into Schools of Industry*. 3rd ed. 1797; rpt. London: Cadell and Davies, 1807.

Benger, Elizabeth Ogilvy (1778–1827). *The Female Geniad; a Poem*. London: Hookham and Carpenter, Kearsley, 1791.

Bennett, Agnes Maria (d. 1808). *Anna, or Memoirs of a Welch Heiress*. 4 vols. 4th ed. 1785; rpt. London: Lane, at the Minerva Press, 1796.

—. *De Valcourt. A Novel.* Dublin: Wogan, Byrne, Browne, et al., 1800.

Bennett, John (na). *Letters to a Young Lady, on a Variety of Useful and Interesting Subjects, Calculated to Improve the Heart, to Form the Manners, and Enlighten the Understanding.* 9th American ed. 1789; rpt. New York: Clusman, 1830.

—. *Strictures on Female Education; Chiefly as it Relates to the Culture of the Heart, in Four Essays.* London: The Author, 1787.

Berry, Mary (1763–1852). *A Comparative View of the Social Life of England and France, from the Restoration of Charles the Second, to the French Revolution.* London: Longman, Rees, Orme, et al., 1828.

—. *Social Life in England and France, from the French Revolution in 1789 to that of July 1830.* London: Longman, Rees, Orme, et al., 1831.

—, and Agnes Berry (1764–1852). *The Berry Papers. Being the Correspondence Hitherto Unpublished of Mary and Agnes Berry (1763–1852).* Ed. Lewis Melville, New York: Lane, MCMXIV.

Bonhote, Elizabeth (1744–1818). *The Parental Monitor.* 1788; rpt. of 3rd ed. [1796], Boston: By Cotton, n.d.

Boswell, James (1740–95). *Life of Johnson.* 6 vols. 1791; rpt. Oxford: Clarendon Press, 1934.

Brontë, Charlotte (1816–55). *Jane Eyre.* 1847; rpt. London: Oxford University Press, 1973.

Brunton, Mary Balfour (1778–1818). *Self-Control. A Novel.* 1811; rpt. New York: Garland, 1974.

Burke, Edmund (1729–97). *Reflections on the Revolution in France, and on the Proceedings in Certain Societies in London relative to that Event.* London: Dodsley, 1790.

Burney, Charles (1726–1814). *Recollections of Dr. Johnson* (n.d., on Anna Barbauld).

Burney d'Arblay, Frances (1752–1840). *Brief Reflections Relative to the Emigrant French Clergy: Earnestly Submitted to the Humane Considerations of the Ladies of Great Britain.* London: Cadell, 1793.

—. *Camilla, or a Picture of Youth.* 1796; rpt. London: Oxford University Press, 1972.

—. *Cecilia, or Memoirs of an Heiress.* 5 vols. 4th ed. 1782; rpt. London: Payne, Cadell, 1784.

—. *Edwy and Elgiva.* [Produced at Drury Lane, March 21, 1795.] Skidmore College: n.p., 1957.

—. *Evelina, or the History of a Young Lady's Entrance into the World.* 1778; rpt. London: Oxford UP, 1968.

—. *The Journals and Letters of Fanny Burney.* Eds. Joyce Hemlow, Curtis D. Cecil, and Althea Douglas. 6 vols. Oxford: Clarendon Press, 1972.

—. *The Wanderer, or Female Difficulties.* London: Longman, Hurst, Rees, et al., 1814.

Burton, John (1745/6–1806). *Lectures on Female Education and Manners.* 3rd ed. 1793; rpt. New York: Gaine, 1794.

Cappe, Catherine Harrison (1744–1821). *An Account of Two Charity Schools for the Education of Girls: And of a Female Friendly Society in York: Interspersed with Reflections on Charity Schools and Friendly Societies in General.* York: sold by Johnson, Hatchard, Mawman, et al., 1800.

Carlisle, Isabella Byron Howard, Countess of (d. 1795). *Thoughts in the Form of Maxims Addressed to Young Ladies, on their First Establishment in the World.* 2nd ed. 1789; rpt. London: Cornell, 1790.

Carter, Elizabeth (1717–1806). *Letters from Mrs. Elizabeth Carter, to Mrs. Montagu, between the Years 1755 and 1800. Chiefly upon Literary and Moral Subjects.* 3 vols. 1817; rpt. New York: AMS Press, 1973.

—. *Memoirs of the Life of Mrs. Elizabeth Carter, with a New Edition of her Poems; to which are added some Miscellaneous Essays in Prose, together with her Notes on the Bible, and Answers to Objections Concerning the Christian Religion.* Ed. Montagu Pennington. 2 vols. 4th ed. 1807; rpt. London: Cawthorn, 1825.

—. *A Series of Letters Between Mrs. Elizabeth Carter and Miss Catherine Talbot, from the Year 1741 to 1770. To which are added Letters from Mrs. Elizabeth Carter to Mrs. Vesey, between the Years 1763 and 1787.* 2 vols. London: Rivingtons, 1808.

Catlow, Samuel (na). *Observations on a Course of Instruction, for Young Persons in the Middle Classes of Life.* London: Johnson and Knott, 1793.

Chapone, Hester Mulso (1727–1801). *Letters on Filial Obedience,* and *Matrimonial Creed.* In *The Posthumous Works of Mrs. Chapone. Containing her Correspondence with Mr. Richardson. A Series of Letters to Mrs. Elizabeth Carter, and some Fugitive Pieces, never before published. Together with an Account of her Life and Character, Drawn up by her Own Family.* 2 vols. London: Murray; Edinburgh: Constable, 1807.

—. *Letters on the Improvement of the Mind.* In *The Female Repertory; or, Young Lady's Guide to Virtue.* Vol. I. 1772; rpt. Edinburgh: M'William, 1808.

—. *Letter to a New-Married Lady,* bound with Dr. Gregory's *A Father's Legacy to his Daughters,* and Miss Talbot's *Education: A Fairy Tale.* London: Sharpe, 1821.

—. *Miscellanies in Prose and Verse.* 2nd ed. 1775; rpt. London: Dillys, Walter, 1775.

Charlton, Mary (fl.1794–1830). *The Wife and the Mistress. A Novel.* 4 vols. London: Lane and Newman, at the Minerva Press, 1802.

Chesterfield, Philip Dormer Stanhope, Earl of (1694–1773). *The Art of Pleasing; or Instructions for Youth. In A Series of Letters . . . to his Nephew. . . . To which are now added, Lord Burleigh's Advice to his Son.* 3rd ed. with considerable additions. London: Kearsley, 1783.

—. *Letters to his Son: On the Fine Art of Becoming a Man of the World and a Gentleman.* 2 vols in 1. 1774; rpt. New York: Tudor Publishing, n.d.

Chirol, J. L. (na). *An Enquiry into the Best System of Female Education; or Boarding School and Home Education Attentively Considered.* London: Cadell and Davies, 1809.

Cibber, Colley (1671–1757). *Womans [sic] Wit; Or the Lady in Fashion.* London: Sturton, 1697.

Cleland, John (1707–89). *Genuine Memoirs of the Celebrated Miss Maria Brown. Exhibiting the Life of a Courtezan in the most Fashionable Scenes of Dissipation.* 2 vols. 1766; rpt. New York: Garland, 1975.

—. *Memoirs of a Woman of Pleasure.* (1748–49); rpt. New York: Putnam's, 1963.

Condillac, Étienne Bonnot de (1714–80). [*Essai sur l'origine des connaissances humaines,* 1746.] *An Essay on the Origin of Human Knowledge,* Tr. Thomas Nugent. 1756; rpt. Gainesville, FL: Scholars' Facsimiles and Reprints, 1971.

Condorcet, Marie Jean Antoine Nicolas de Caritat, Marquis de (1743–94). [*Esquisse d'un tableau historique du progrès de l'esprit humain*, 1795]. *Sketch for a Historical Picture of the Progress of the Human Mind.* Tr. June Barraclough. Rpt. New York: Noonday Press, 1955.

—. "Essai sur la constitution et les fonctions des assemblées provinciales." *Oeuvres de Condorcet.* 1788; rpt. 1847; rpt. Stuttgart-Bad Constatt: Fromman Verlag (Günther Holzboog), 1968. Tome VIII.

—. "Lettres d'un bourgeois de New-Haven à un citoyen de Virginie, ou l'inutilité de partager le pouvoir entre plusieurs corps." *Oeuvres.* 1788; rpt. 1847, rpt. 1968. Tome IX.

—. "Project de déclaration des droits naturels, civils, et politiques des hommes." *Oeuvres.* 1793; rpt. 1847; rpt. 1968, pp. 417–22. Tome XII.

—. "Sur l'admission des femmes aux droits de cité." *Oeuvres.* 1790; rpt. 1847; rpt. 1968, pp. 121–130. Tome X.

—. "Sur l'instruction publique." *Oeuvres.* 1791–92; rpt. 1847; rpt. 1968. Tome VII.

*Cross Partners, a Comedy, in Five Acts.* By a Lady. London: Kearsley, 1792.

Darwin, Erasmus (1731–1802). *A Plan for the Conduct of Female Education, in Boarding Schools.* Derby: Johnson, 1797.

Day, Thomas (1748–89). *The History of Sandford and Merton: A Book for the Young.* 1783–89; rpt. London: Nelson, 1860.

Defoe, Daniel (1660–1731). *The Earlier Life and the Chief Earlier Work of Daniel Defoe.* Ed. Henry Morley. London: Routledge, 1889.

—. *An Essay upon Projects.* London: Cockerill, 1697.

—. *Moll Flanders.* 1722; rpt. Boston: Houghton Mifflin, 1959.

Dekker, Thomas (c. 1572–c.1632). *The Shoemaker's Holiday.* 1600; rpt. Berkeley: University of California Press, 1965.

Dickens, Charles (1812–70). *A Tale of Two Cities.* 1859; rpt. New York: Collier Books, 1974.

Diderot, Denis (1713–84). [*La Religieuse.* Written 1760; pub. 1796]. *Memoirs of a Nun.* Tr. Francis Birrell. New York: Brentano's, 1928.

—. "Sur les Femmes." *Oeuvres complètes.* Tome X. 1772; rpt. n.p.: Le Club Français du Livre, 1971.

—, and Jean Lerond d'Alembert (1717–83), eds. *Encyclopédie, ou dictionnaire raisonné des sciences, des arts et des métiers, par une société de gens de lettres.* Mis en ordre et publié par M. Diderot; et quant à la partie mathématique, par M. d'Alembert. Nouvelle ed. 1751–65; rpt. Geneve: Pellet, 1777–79. Tomes XIII, XXX.

[Drake, Judith] (1670s-123). *An Essay in Defence of the Female Sex, in which Are Inserted the Characters of a Pedant, a Squire, a Beau, a Vertuoso, a Poetaster, &C, in a Letter to a Lady.* London: Roper and Wilkinson, Clavel, 1696.

Du Bois, Edward (1774–1850). *St. Godwin: A Tale of the Sixteenth, Seventeenth, and Eighteen Centuries.* 1800; rpt. New York: Garland, 1974.

Duncombe, John (1729–86). *The Feminead. A Poem.* London: Cooper, 1754.

*Eccentric Biography: or Memoirs of Remarkable Characters, Ancient and Modern . . .* Worcester, England: By Thomas, 1804.

Edgeworth, Maria (1767–1849). *Belinda. In Tales and Miscellaneous Pieces*. 1801; rpt. London: Hunter, Baldwin, Cradock and Joy, et al., 1825. Vols. II, III.

—. *Castle Rackrent*. 1800; rpt. Coral Gables, Fl: University of Miami Press, 1964.

—. *Early Lessons*. 4 vols. 1801–03; rpt. London: Longman, Tegg, Hamilton, et al., 1848–53.

—. *Leonora. In Tales and Miscellaneous Pieces*. 1806; rpt. 1825. Vol. IV.

—. *Letters for Literary Ladies. To which is added, An Essay on the Noble Science of Self-Justification*. 1795; rpt. New York: Garland, 1974.

—. *Modern Griselda. In Tales and Miscellaneous Pieces*. 1805; rpt. 1825. Vol. I.

—. *Moral Tales. In Tales and Novels*. 1801; rpt. 1893; rpt. Hildesheim: Olms Verlagsbuchhandlung, 1969. Vol. I.

—. *The Parent's Assistant; or, Stories for Children*. 6 vols. 1796; rpt. 3rd ed,1800; rpt. in 2 vols, New York: Garland: 1976.

—, and Richard Lovell Edgeworth (1744–1817). *Practical Education*. 2 vols. 1798; rpt. London: Garland, 1974.

*Elfrida, or Paternal Ambition. A Novel.* By a Lady. 3 vols. London: Johnson, 1786.

*The Female Aegis, or, the Duties of Women from Childhood to Old Age, and in Most Situations of Life, Exemplified.* 1798; rpt. New York: Garland, 1974.

*The Female Patriot:* [Written as if] *an Epistle from C-t-----e M-c----y to the Reverend Dr. W-l-n on her Late Marriage. With Critical, Historical, and Philosophical Notes and Illustrations.* London: Bew, 1779.

*The Female Repertory, or Young Lady's Guide to Virtue.* 2 vols. Edinburgh: M'William, 1808.

*Female Restoration, by a Moral and Physical Vindication of Female Talents; in Opposition to all Dogmatical Assertions relative to Disparity in the Sexes.* London: Sold at MacGowan's, 1780.

Fénelon, François de Salignac de la Mothe (1651–1715). [*Les Aventures de Télémaque*, 1699.] *The Adventures of Telemachus, the Son of Ulysses.* Tr. William Henry Melmoth. London: Hogg, 1784.

—. [*Traité sur l'éducation des filles*, 1687.] *The Education of Girls.* Tr. Kate Lupton. Boston: Ginn, 1891.

Fenwick, Eliza (1766–1840). *Secresy* [*sic*]*, or the Ruin on the Rock.* By a Woman. 3 vols. 1795; rpt. New York: Garland, 1794.

Fielding, Henry (1707–54). *Amelia.* 1751; rpt. Oxford: by Blackwell, 1926.

—. *The History of the Adventures of Joseph Andrew and of his Friend Mr. Abraham Adams* [1742] and *An Apology for the Life of Mrs. Shamela Andrews* [1741]. Rpt. London: Oxford University Press, 1970.

—. *The History of Tom Jones.* 1749; rpt. Baltimore, MD: Penguin, 1971.

Fielding, Sarah (1710–68). *The Adventures of David Simple.* 2nd ed. London: Millar, 1744.

—. *The Governess; or Little Female Academy.* 1749; rpt. London: Oxford University Press, 1968.

—. *The History of Betty Barnes.* 2 vols. 1753; rpt. 2 vols in 1. New York: Garland, 1974.

Fordyce, James (1720–98). *The Character and Conduct of the Female Sex, and the Advantages to be Derived by Young Men from the Society of Virtuous Women.* 3 parts. 1775; Dublin: Price, Whitestone, Chamberlaine, et al., 1776.

—. *Sermons to Young Women*. 2 vols. 8th ed. 1765; rpt. London: Cadell, Dodsley, 1775.

Genlis, Stéphanie Félicité Ducrest de Saint-Aubin, Comtesse de, afterwards, Marquise de Sillery (1746–1830). [*Adèle et Théodore, ou lettres sur l'éducation . . .*, 1782.] *Adelaide and Theodore; or Letters on Education: Containing All the Principles Relative to Three Different Plans of Education; to that of Princes, and to those of Young Persons of Both Sexes.* 3 vols. London: Bathurst, Cadell, 1783.

—. [*Leçons d'une gouvernante à ses élèves ou fragments d'un journal*, 1791.] *Lessons of a Governess to her Pupils; or, Journal of the Method adopted by Madame de Sillery-Brulart (formerly Countess of Genlis) in the Education of the Children of M. d'Orléans,* London: Robinson, 1792.

—. [*Les Veillées du château*, 1784.] *The Tales of the Castle; or, Stories of Instruction and Delight.* Tr. Thomas Holcroft. 4 vols. new ed. 1785; rpt. London: Scatcherd and Letterman, Longman, Hurst, et al., 1819.

Gibbon, Edward (1737–94). *The History of the Decline and Fall of the Roman Empire.* 12 vols. 1776–88; rpt. London: Cadell and Davies, Johnson, et al., 1807.

Gisborne, Thomas (1758–1846). *An Enquiry into the Duties of the Female Sex.* 11th ed. 1797; rpt. London: Cadell and Davies, 1816.

Godwin, William (1756–1836). *The Enquirer. Reflections on Education, Manners, and Literature. In a Series of Essays.* London: Robinsons, 1797.

—. *Enquiry Concerning Political Justice and its Influence on Moral Happiness.* Ed. F. E. L. Priestley. 3 vols. 1793; 3rd ed. with revisions, 1798; rpt. Toronto: University of Toronto Press, 1946.

—. *Memoirs of the Author of a Vindication of the Rights of Woman.* 1798; rpt. New York: Garland, 1974.

—. *St. Leon: A Tale of the Sixteenth Century.* 1799; rpt. New York: McGrath, 1972.

—. [*Things as They Are, or, the Adventures of*] *Caleb Williams.* Ed. David McCracken. 1794; rpt. New York: Oxford University Press, 1970.

Goethe, Johann Wolfgang von (1749–1832). [*Die Leiden des Jungen Werther,* 1774.] *The Sufferings of Young Werther.* Tr. Bayard Quincy Morgan. New York: Frederick Ungar, 1968.

Goldsmith, Oliver (1728–74). *The Citizen of the World* [1762] and *The Bee* [1759]. Rpt. New York: Dutton, 1934.

—. *The Vicar of Wakefield.* 1766; rpt. New York: Lancer Books, 1968.

Gouges, Olympe de (pseud. of Marie Gouzes, 1748–93). *Déclarations des droits de la femme et de la citoyenne. (From the Bibliothèque Nationale),* 1791.

Gregory, John (1724–73). *A Father's Legacy to his Daughters.* New ed. 1774; rpt. London: Strahan, Cadell, 1784.

Halifax, George Savile, Lord Marquess of (1633–95). *The Lady's New Year's Gift: Or Advice to a Daughter.* In *Miscellanies,* 1688; rpt. 1700; rpt. Stamford, Conn: Overbrook Press, 1934.

Hamilton, Elizabeth (1758–1816). *Letters addressed to the Daughter of a Nobleman, on the Formation of the Religious and the Moral Principle.* 2 vols. 2nd ed. 1806; rpt. New York: Garland, 1974.

—. *Letters on the Elementary Principles of Education.* 2 vols. 3rd ed., 1801–02; rpt. Bath: Robinsons, 1803.

—. *Memoirs of Modern Philosophers.* 3 vols. 1800; rpt. New York: Garland, 1974.

—. *A Series of Popular Essays, Illustrative of Principles Essentially Connected with the Improvement of the Understanding, the Imagination, and the Heart.* 2 vols. 2nd ed. 1813; rpt. Edinburgh: Manners and Miller; London: Longman, et al., 1815.

—. *Translation of the Letters of a Hindoo Rajah; Written previous to, and during the Period of his Residence in England, to which Is Prefixed a Preliminary Dissertation on the History, Religion, and Manners, of the Hindoos.* 2 vols. 2nd ed. 1796; rpt. London: Robinsons, 1801.

Hanway, Mary Anne (c.1755-c.1823). *Ellinor; or, the World as It Is. A Novel.* 4 vols. (Minerva Press), 1798; rpt. New York: Garland, 1974.

—. *A Journey to the Highlands of Scotland. With Occasional Remarks on Dr. Johnson's Tour.* London: Fielding and Walker, [1776].

Hayley, William (1745–1820). *A Philosophical, Historical, and Moral Essay on Old Maids.* 3 vols. London: Cadell, 1785.

Hays, Mary (1759 or '60–1843). *An Appeal to the Men of Great Britain in Behalf of Women.* 1798; rpt. New York: Garland, 1974.

—. *Female Biography; or Memoirs of Illustrious and Celebrated Women of all Ages and Countries.* 6 vols. London: Phillips, 1803.

—. *Harry Clinton. A Tale for Youth.* London: Johnson, 1804.

— (?). *Julietta, or the Triumph of Mental Acquirements over Personal Defects.* London: Johnson, 1802.

—. *Letters and Essays, Moral and Miscellaneous.* 1793; rpt. New York: Garland, 1974.

—. *The Love Letters of Mary Hays (1779–1780).* Ed. A. F. Wedd. London: Methuen, 1925.

—. *Memoirs of Emma Courtney.* 2 vols. 1796; rpt. New York: Garland, 1974.

—. *The Victim of Prejudice.* 2 vols. London: Johnson, 1799.

Helvétius, Claude Adrien (1715–71). [*De l'homme, de ses facultés, intellectuelles et de son éducation. Ouvrage posthume, 1773.*] *A Treatise on Man; his Intellectual Faculties and his Education.* Tr. William Hooper. new, improved ed. 2 vols. 1777; rpt. London: Cundee, Vernor, Hoode, and Sharpe, 1810.

Hill, Elizabeth (fl. 1796–1815), ed. *The Poetical Monitor: Consisting of Pieces Select and Original, for the Improvement of the Young in Virtue and Piety: Intended to succeed Dr. Watts' Divine and Moral Songs.* London: sold by Longman, Johnson, Dilly, et al., 1796.

—. *Sequel to the Poetical Monitor: Adapted to Improve the Minds and Manners of Young Persons.* 2nd ed., nd; rpt. London: Longman, Hurst, Rees, et al., 1815.

Holbach, Paul Henri Thiry, Baron d' (1723–89). *Système de la nature, ou des lois du monde physique et du monde moral.* Nouvelle éd. 2 tomes. 1770; rpt. 1821; rpt. Hildesheim: Olms Verlagsbuchhandlung, 1966.

—. *Système social: ou principes naturels de la morale et de la politique. Avec un examen de l'influence du gouvernement sur les moeurs.* Trois tomes dans une tome. 1773; rpt. New York: Olms Verlagsbuchhandlung, 1969.

Holcroft, Thomas (1745–1809). *Anna St. Ives.* 1792; rpt. New York: Oxford University Press, 1970.

Imlay, Gilbert (b. 1754). *The Emigrants, or the History of an Expatriated Family, being a Delineation of English Manners, drawn from Real Characters, Written in America.* 1793; rpt. Dublin: 1794; rpt. Gainesville, FL: Scholars' Facsimiles and Reprints, 1964.

Inchbald, Elizabeth Simpson (1753–1821). *The Child of Nature.* 4 acts. *From the French of Madame the Marchioness of Sillery, formerly Countess de Genlis.* Dublin: Byrne, Colls, Jones, et al., 1789.

—. *Every One Has his Fault. A Comedy in Five Acts.* New ed. 1792; rpt. Dublin: Wogan, et al., 1793.

—. [*Das Kind der Liebe,* 1791.] *Lovers Vows, a Play in Five Acts, altered from the German of Kotzebue.* In *The British Theatre.* New ed. 1798; rpt. London: Hurst, Robinson, 1824. Vol 1.

—. *Nature and Art.* 2 vols. 1796; rpt. Philadelphia: Rice, 1796.

—. *Next-Door Neighbours: A Comedy, in Three Acts. From the French Dramas l'Indigent and Le Dissipateur.* London: Robinsons, 1791.

—. *A Simple Story.* [4 vols.] 1791; rpt. London: Frowde, 1908.

—. *Such Things Are; a Play, in Five Acts.* 3rd ed. 1787; rpt. Dublin: The Booksellers, 1790.

—. *The Wedding Day; a Farce, in Two Acts.* In *The New English Drama.* 1794; rpt. London: By Simpkin and Marshall, 1823. Vol. V.

—. *The Widow's Vow. A Farce, in Two Acts.* 1786; rpt. New York: by Gaine, 1787.

—. *Wives as They Were, and Maids as They Are, a Comedy, in Five Acts.* Dublin: Follingsby, 1797.

Jackson, Mary Elizabeth (1755–1829). *Botanical Dialogues between Hortensia and her Four Children, Charles, Harriet, Juliette, and Henry. Designed for the Use of Schools.* London: Johnson, 1797.

Johnson, Samuel (1709–84). *The Rambler.* 3 vols. 9th ed. 1750–52; rpt. Edinburgh: Donaldson, 1781.

*Julietta,* 1802. See Mary Hays.

Kames, Henry Home, Lord (1696–1782). *Loose Hints upon Education, Chiefly Concerning the Culture of the Heart.* Edinburgh: Bell; London: Murray, 1781.

Keir, Susanna Harvey (1747–1802). *Interesting Memoirs.* 2 vols. 2nd ed. 1785: rpt. London: Strahan, Cadell; Edinburg: Balfour, Creech, 1785.

Kenrick, William (1725–1779). *The Whole Duty of Woman.* By a Lady. 1753; rpt. New York: Borradaile, 1821.

King Fortum, Sophia (fl. 1798). *Waldorf, or the Dangers of Philosophy. A Philosophical Tale.* 2 vols. 1798; rpt. New York: Garland, 1794.

Knox, Vicesimus (1752–1821). *Essays Moral and Literary.* 2 vols. 6th ed. 1778–79; rpt. London: Dilly, 1785.

—. *Liberal Education: Or, a Practical Treaties in the Methods of Acquiring Useful and Polite Learning.* 6th ed. 1781; rpt. London: Dilly, 1784.

*The Ladies Advocate: or, Wit and Beauty a Match for Treachery and Inconstancy.* 1749; New York: Garland, 1974.

*Lady's Monthly Museum, or Polite Repository of Amusement and Instruction: Being an Assemblage of Whatever Can Tend to Please the Fancy, Interest the Mind, or Exalt the Character of the British Fair.* By a society of Ladies. 68 vols. London: Vernor and Hood, 1798–1832.

*The Lady's Poetical Magazine; or, Beauties of British Poetry.* Vols. II, III. London: Harrison, 1781, 1782.

Lambert, Anne Thérèse de Marguenat de Courcelles, Marquise de (1647–1733). [*Avis d'une mère à son fils et à sa fille,* 1728. Tr. W. Hatchett, 1729.] *Advice of a Mother to her Daughter.* In the *Young Lady's Pocket Library, or, Parental Monitor.* London: n.p., 1790.

Lee, Harriet (1757–1851). *Constantia de Valmont. A Novel.* Philadelphia: Carey, 1799.

Lee, Sophia (1750–1824). *The Chapter of Accidents. A Comedy.* London: Cawthorn, 1796.

—. *The Life of a Lover. In a Series of Letters.* 6 vols. London: Robinsons, 1804.

Lennox, Charlotte Ramsay (1720–1804). *Euphemia.* 4 vols. London: Cadell and Evans, 1790.

—. *The Female Quixote, or the Adventures of Arabella.* 2 vols. London: Millar. 1752.

—. *Henrietta.* 2 vols. 1758; rpt. New York: Garland, 1974.

Locke, John (1632–1704). *An Essay Concerning Human Understanding, in Four Books.* 1690; rpt. 5th ed., 1706; rpt. London: Dent, 1971.

—. *Some Thoughts concerning Education* and "Locke to Mrs. Clark, Feb. 1685." In *The Educational Writings of John Locke.* Ed. James L. Axtell. 1693; rpt. Cambridge: Cambridge University Press, 1968.

Macaulay Graham, Catherine Sawbridge (1731–91). *Letters on Education: With Observations on Religious and Metaphysical Subjects.* 1790; rpt. New York: Garland, 1974.

Mackenzie, Henry (1745–1831). *Julia de Roubigné, a Tale. In a Series of Letters.* 2 vols. 3rd ed. 1777; rpt. London: Strahan, Cadell; Edinburgh: Creech, 1782.

—. *The Man of Feeling.* 1771; rpt. New York: Oxford University Press, 1967.

—. *The Mirror.* 2 vols. 1779–80; rpt. 2 vols in 1, London: Parsons, 1794.

Makin, Bathsua (1600–75). *An Essay to Revive the Antient* [*sic*] *Education of Gentlewomen.* London, J. D., 1673.

Mathias, Thomas James (1754–1835). *The Pursuits of Literature, a Satirical Poem in Four Dialogues, with Notes to which Are added an Appendix; the Citations translated; and a Complete Index.* 16th ed. 1794-97; rpt. London: Becket and Porter, 1812.

Meeke, Mary (d. 1761-1826). "*There is a Secret, Find it Out!" A Novel.* 4 vols. London: Lane and Newman, at the Minerva Press, 1808.

Millar, John (1735–1801). *The Origin of the Distinction of Ranks; or, an Inquiry into the Circumstances which Give Rise to Influence and Authority in the Different Members of Society.* 3rd ed. 1779; rpt. Basil: Tourneisen, 1793.

Molière, Jean Baptiste Poquelin (1622–73). [*L'École des femmes,* 1663.] *A School for Women; a Comedy. The Works of Monsieur de Molière.* Tr. John Ozell. 1714 ed; rpt. New York: Blom, 1967. Vol. II.

—. [*Les Femmes savantes,* 1672.] *The Learned Ladies.* Tr. Curtis Hidden Page. New York: Putnam's, 1908.

—. [*Les Précieuses ridicules*, 1659.] *The Affected Ladies: A Comedy. The Works.* Tr. John Ozell. 1714; rpt. 1967. Vol. I.

Montagu, Elizabeth Robinson (1720–1800). *Elizabeth Montagu, the Queen of the Bluestockings, her Correspondence from 1720–1761.* Ed. Emily J. Climenson. 2 vols. New York: Dutton, 1906.

—. *An Essay on the Writings and Genius of Shakespear* [*sic*], *Compared with the Greek and French Dramatic Poets. With some Remarks upon the Misrepresentations of Mons. de Voltaire* [1769]. *To which Are now First Added Three Dialogues of the Dead* [in Lord George Lyttelton's *Dialogues,* 1760]. 4th ed. London: Dillys, 1777.

—. *The Letters of Mrs. Elizabeth Montagu, with some of the Letters of her Correspondents.* 4 vols. in 2 parts. 1809, 1813; rpt. New York: AMS Press, 1974.

Montagu, Lady Mary Pierrepont Wortley (1689–1762). *Letters from the Levant, during the Embassy to Constantinople 1716–1718, with a Preliminary Discourse and Notes Containing a Sketch of her Ladyship's Character, Moral and Literary.* By J. A. St. John. 1763; rpt. 1838; rpt. New York: Arno Press and the *New York Times,* 1971.

—. *Mary Wortley Montagu. Written by Herself.* New York: Athaeneum Press, n.d.

—. *The Works of the Right Honourable Lady Mary Wortley Montagu, including her Correspondence, Poems, and Essays.* 5 vols. 6th ed. 1803; rpt. London: Longman, Hurst, Rees, et al., 1817.

Montesquieu, Charles Louis de Secondat, Baron de la Brède et de (1689–1755). [*De l'esprit des lois,* 1748.] *The Spirit of the Laws.* Tr. Thomas Nugent. 2 vols in 1. 1750; rpt. New York: Hafner, 1949.

—. [*Lettres persanes,* 1721.] *Persian Letters.* Tr. John Ozell. 1722; rpt. New York: Garland, 1972.

Moore, Edward (1712–57). *Fables for the Female Sex.* In the *Young Lady's Pocket Library, or Parental Monitor.* 1744; London: n.p., 1790.

More, Hannah (1745–1833). *Address in Behalf of the Emigrant French Clergy.* In *The Works of Hannah More.* 1793; rpt. New York: Harper, 1855. Vol. V.

—. *The Bas Bleu.* London: Cadell, 1786.

—. [*Cheap Repository Tracts.*] *The Repository Tales.* In *Works.* 1795–98; rpt. 1855. Vol. I.

—. *Coelebs in Search of a Wife.* 2 vols. 3rd ed. 1808; rpt. London: Cadell and Davies, 1809.

—. *Essays on Various Subjects, Principally Designed for Young Ladies.* In *Works.* 1777; rpt. 1855. Vol. II.

—. *An Estimate of the Religion of the Fashionable World.* In *Works.* 1791; rpt. 1855. Vol. V.

—. *Florio: A Tale for Fine Gentlemen and Fine Ladies: and, the Bas Bleu; or, Conversation. Two Poems.* London: Cadell, 1786.

—. *Hints towards Forming the Character of a Princess.* In *Works.* 1805; rpt. 1855. Vol VII.

—. *Percy, a Tragedy.* In *Works.* 1777; rpt. 1855. Vol. V.

—. *Remarks on the Speech of M. Dupont, on the Subjects of Religion and Public Education.* In *Works.* 1793; rpt. 1855. Vol. V.

—. *Sacred Dramas: Chiefly Intended for Young Persons.* In *Works.* 1782; rpt. 1855. Vol. VI.

—. *The Search after Happiness. A Pastoral Drama.* 6th ed. 1773; rpt. Bristol: sold by Bonner and Middleton, Cadell, et al., 1775.

—. *Sensibility: An Epistle to the Honourable Mrs. Boscawen.* In *Works.* 1782; rpt. 1855. Vol. V.

—. "The Slave Trade." In *Works.* 1787. rpt. 1855. Vol. V.

—. *Strictures on the Modern System of Female Education, with a View of the Principles and Conduct Prevalent among Women of Rank and Fortune.* 2 vols. 1799; rpt. New York: Garland, 1974.

—. *Thoughts on the Importance of the Manners of The Great to General Society.* 6th ed. 1788; rpt. London: Cadell, 1788. Bound with Mary Wiseman's *A Letter from a Lady to her Daughter, on the Manner of Passing Sunday Rationally and Agreeably.* London: Marshall, 1788.

—. *The Works of Hannah More.* 7 vols. 1835; rpt. New York: Harper, 1855.

Murray, Judith Sargent (1751–1820. American). "On the Equality of the Sexes." *The Massachusetts Magazine,* 2 (1790).

Murry, Ann (1750–1818?). *Mentoria: or, the Young Ladies Instructor: in Familiar Conversations, on Moral and Entertaining Subjects. Calculated to Improve Young Minds in the Essential as well as Ornamental Parts of Female Education.* 8th ed. 1778; rpt. London: Dilly, 1796.

Opie, Amelia Alderson (1769–1853). *Adeline Mowbray; or the Mother and Daughter.* In *The Works of Mrs. Amelia Opie: Complete in Three Volumes.* 1804; rpt. Philadelphia: Crissy, 1843. Vol. I.

—. *The Dangers of Coquetry. A Novel.* 2 vols. London: Lane, 1790.

—. *The Father and Daughter.* In *Works.* 1801; rpt. 1843. Vol. I.

—. *Poems.* 3rd ed. 1802; rpt. London: Longman, Hurst, Rees, Orme, 1804.

Paine, Thomas (1773–1809). *Rights of Man; being an Answer to Mr. Burke's Attack on the French Revolution.* Part 1, 1791, Part 2, 1792; rpt. New York: Dutton, 1915.

Parsons, Eliza Phelp (1739–1811). *Errors of Education.* 2 vols. 1791; rpt. Dublin: Jackson, 1792.

—. *Woman as She Should Be; or, Memoirs of Miss Menville. A Novel.* 4 vols. London: Lane, at the Minerva Press, 1793.

Pennington, Lady Sarah (c. 1720–83). *An Unfortunate Mother's Advice to her Absent Daughter, in a Letter to Miss Pennington.* In *Young Lady's Pocket Library, or, Parental Monitor.* 1761; rpt. London: n.p., 1790.

Pigott, Charles (d. 1794). *The Female Jockey Club, or a Sketch of the Manners of the Age.* London: The Author, 1794.

Piozzi, Hester Lynch Salusbury Thrale (1741–1821). *The Intimate Letters of Hester Piozzi and Penelope Pennington, 1788–1821.* Ed. Oswald G. Knapp. New York: Lane, 1914.

—. *Thraliana: The Diary of Mrs. Hester Lynch Thrale (later Mrs. Piozzi), 1776–1809.* 2 vols. Ed. Katherine C. Balderstone. Oxford: Clarendon Press, 1942.

Plumptre, Anne (1760–1818), tr. *Sketch of the Life and Literary Career of Augustus von Kotzebue; with the Journal of his Tour to Paris, at the Close of the Year 1790.* London: Symonds, 1800.

Polwhele, Richard. (1760–1838). *The Unsex'd Females: A Poem, Addressed to the Author of The Pursuits of Literature.* 1798; rpt. New York: Garland, 1974.

Pope, Alexander (1668–1744). *An Essay on Man.* London: J. Wilford, 1733–34.

—. *Moral Essays.* In *Selected Poetry and Prose.* 2nd ed. 1721–35; rpt. New York: Holt, Rinehart, and Winston, 1972.

—. *The Rape of the Lock.* In *Selected Poetry and Prose.* 1712; rpt. 1972.

Priestley, Joseph (1733–1804). *The Proper Objects of Education in the Present State of the World: . . . To the Supporters of the New College at Hackney . . .* London: Johnson, 1791.

Radcliffe, Ann Ward (1764–1823). *The Italian, or the Confessional of the Black Penitents. A Romance.* 3 vols. London: Cadell and Davies, 1797.

—. *The Posthumous Works of Anne Radcliffe . . . To which Is Prefixed a Memoir of the Authoress, with Extracts from her Private Journals.* London: Colburn, 1833. Vol. I.

Radcliffe, Mary Ann (c. 1746–1818). *The Female Advocate, or an Attempt to Recover the Rights of Women from Male Usurpation.* 1799; rpt. New York: Garland, 1974.

—. *The Memoirs of Mrs. Mary Ann Radcliffe, in Familiar Letters to her Female Friend.* Edinburgh: The Author, 1810.

Reeve, Clara (1729–1807). *Plan of Education; with Remarks on the Systems of Other Writers. In a Series of Letters between Mrs. Darnford and her Friends.* London: Hookham and Carpenter, 1792.

—. *The Progress of Romance, and the History of Charoda, Queen of Aegypt.* 1785; rpt. New York: Facsimile Text Society, 1930.

—. *The School for Widows: A Novel.* 2 vols. Dublin: Wogan, Byrne, Colbert, et al., 1791.

Richardson, Samuel (1689–1761). *Clarissa or the History of a Young Lady.* Abridged and ed. by George Sherburn, 1747–48; Boston: Houghton Mifflin, 1962.

—. *The Correspondence of Samuel Richardson, Author of Pamela, Clarissa, and Sir Charles Grandison, selected from the Original Manuscripts, bequeathed by him to his Family. With a Biographical Account of that Author and Observations on his Writings by Anna Laetitia Barbauld.* 6 vols. London: Phillips, 1804.

—. *Familiar Letters on Important Occasions.* 1741; rpt. London: Routledge, 1928.

—. *The History of Sir Charles Grandison. In a Series of Letters.* 6 vols. 1753–54; rpt. Oxford: Blackwell, 1931.

—. *Pamela, or Virtue Rewarded: In a Series of Familiar Letters from a Beautiful Young Damsel to her Parents: Afterwards in her Exalted Condition, between her, and Persons of Figure and Quality, upon the most Important and Entertaining Subjects, in Genteel Life.* 4 vols. 1740, 1742; rpt. Oxford: by Blackwell, 1929.

Robinson, Mary Darby (1758–1800). *Hubert de Sevrac, a Romance, of the Eighteenth Century.* 3 vols. London: The Author, 1796.

—. *Lyrical Tales.* London: Longman and Rees, 1800.

—. *Memoirs of the Late Mrs. Robinson. Written by Herself. With Some Posthumous Pieces.* 4 vols. London: Phillips, 1801.

—. *Sappho and Phaon, in a Series of Legitimate Sonnets, with Thoughts on Poetical Subjects, and Anecdotes of the Grecian Poetess.* London: for the Author, 1796.

—. *Sight, the Cavern of Woe, and Solitude. Poems.* London: sold by Evans, 1793.

—. *Thoughts on the Condition of Women, and on the Injustice of Mental Subordination.* [By Ann Frances Randall (pseudonym) 1ˢᵗ ed., 1799.] 2ⁿᵈ ed. London: Longman, Rees, 1799.

—. *Vancenza; or, the Dangers of Credulity.* Dublin: Wogan, Byrne, Grueber, et al., 1792.

—. *The Widow, or a Picture of Modern Times. A Novel in a Series of Letters.* 2 vols. London: Hookham and Carpenter, 1794.

Rousseau, Jean-Jacques (1712–78). [*Les Confessions de J. J. Rousseau,* 1782.] *The Confessions of Jean-Jacques Rousseau.* Tr. W. Conyngham Mallory. 2 vols. rpt. New York: Brentano's, 1928.

—. [*Du contrat social, ou principes du droit politique,* 1762.] *The Social Contract.* 1791; rpt. New York: Hafner, 1951.

—. [*Émile, ou, de l'éducation,* 1762.] *Emilius; or, an Essay on Education.* Tr. Thomas Nugent. 2 vols. London: Nourse and Vaillant, 1763.

—. [*Julie ou la nouvelle Héloise,* 1764.] *Eloisa: or, a Series of Original Letters Collected and Published by J. J. Rousseau.* Tr. From the French. 4 vols. 3ʳᵈ ed. 1764; rpt. London: Becket and de Hondt, 1764.

—. *Memoir on the Education of the Prince of Wirtemberg's Infant Daughter, Sophie.* In *The Minor Educational Writings of Jean-Jacques Rousseau.* Selected and tr. by William Boyd. 1763; London: Blackie, 1910.

[Sand, James] (na). *Monckton; or, the Fate of Eleanor. A Novel. To which Is Prefixed, a General Defence of Modern Novels.* 3 vols. London: Robinsons, 1802.

Scott, Sarah (1720–95). *A Journey Through Every Stage of Life.* A. Millar, 1754.

Seward, Anna (1742–1809). *Letters Anna Seward: Written between the Years 1784 and 1807.* 6 vols. Edinburgh: Constable, London: Longman, et al., 1811.

—. *The Poetical Works of Anna Seward; with Extracts from her Literary Correspondence.* Ed. Walter Scott. 3 vols. Edinburgh: Ballantyne; London: Longman, et al., 1810.

Shaw, William (1749–1831). *Suggestions Respecting a Plan of National Education.* Bath: sold by Robinsons, 1801.

Sheridan, Frances Chamberlaine (1724–66). *Memoirs of Miss Sidney Biddulph. Extracted from her Own Journal.* 5 vols. 1761–67; rpt. London: Harrison, 1786.

Sheridan, Richard Brinsley (1751–1816). *The Rivals.* 3ʳᵈ ed. 1775; rpt. 1776; rpt. London: Oxford University Press, 1968.

Smith, Charlotte Turner (1749–1806). *The Banished Man. A Novel.* 4 vols. London: Cadell and Davies, 1794.

—. *Beachy Head with Other Poems.* London: Johnson, 1807.

—. *Celestina. A Novel.* 3 vols. Dublin: Cross, Wogan, Byrne, et al., 1791.

—. *Desmond. A Novel.* 3 vols. 1792; rpt. New York: Garland, 1974.

—. *Elegiac Sonnets and Other Poems.* 9ᵗʰ ed. 1784; rpt. London: Cadell and Davies, 1800.

—. *Emmeline, or the Orphan of Castle, a Novel.* 4 vols. 1783; rpt. London: Oxford University Press, 1971.

—. *Ethelinde, or, the Recluse of the Lake.* 5 vols. 2ⁿᵈ ed. 1789; rpt. London: Cadell, 1790.

—. *Marchmont. A Novel.* 4 vols. London: Low, 1796.

—. *Montalbert. A Novel.* 3 vols. London: Booker, 1795.

—. *The Old Manor House.* 1793; rpt. London: Oxford University Press, 1969.

—. *Rambles Farther: A Continuation of Rural Walks: In Dialogues. Intended for the Use of Young Persons.* 2 vols. 2nd ed. 1796; rpt. London: Cadell and Davies, 1800.

—. *Rural Walks: In Dialogues. Intended for the Use of Young Persons.* 2 vols in 1. 1795; rpt. Philadelphia: sold by Stephens, 1795.

—. *The Young Philosopher: A Novel.* 4 vols. 1798; rpt. New York: Garland, 1974.

—. *What is She? A Comedy, in Five Acts.* 1799; rpt. 1811; rpt. in *A Collection of Successful Modern Plays.* New York: Blom, 1968. Vol. V.

Smith, Sydney (1771–1845). *Essay Social and Political.* 1882; rpt. New York: Ward, and Locke, 1888.

Smollett, Tobias (1721–71). *The Expedition of Humphry Clinker.* 1771; rpt. Boston: Houghton Mifflin, 1968.

Southerne, Thomas (1660–1746). *Oroonoko; a Tragedy. In Five Acts.* In *The British Theatre.* Ed. Mrs. Inchbald. New ed. 1695; rpt. London: Hurst, Robinson, 1824. Vol. III.

Staël-Holstein, Anne Louise Germaine Necker, Baronne de (1766–1817). [*Corinne, ou Italie,* 1807.] *Corinne; or, Italy.* Tr. Isabel Hill. New York: Burt, 189–.

—. *De l'Allemagne. Première Partie.* Dans *Oeuvres complètes de madame la baronne de Staël-Holstein.* Tome I. 1813, rpt. Paris: chez Didot Frères, 1836.

—. *De la littérature considérée dans ses rapports avec les institutions sociales.* Dans *Oeuvres complètes de madame la baronne de Staël-Holstein.* Tome I. 1800; rpt. Genève: Slatkine Reprints, 1967.

Steele, Richard (1672–1729), et al. *Tatler.* 1709–11; rpt. rev. and corr., 4 vols, London: Nutt, Knapton, Sprint, et al., 1728; rpt. in 1 vol., London: Jones, 1829.

Sterne, Lawrence (1713–68). *The Life and Opinions of Tristram Shandy, Gentleman.* 9 vols. 1760–67; rpt. New York: Bobbs-Merrill, 1940.

Stewarton, Lewis. (na). *The Female Revolutionary Plutarch, containing Biographical, Historical, and Revolutionary Sketches, Characters, and Anecdotes.* 3 vols. 3rd ed. 1806; rpt. London: Murray, 1808.

Swift, Jonathan (1667–1745). "An Essay on Modern Education." In *The Works of Jonathan Swift. . . . With Notes and a Life of the Author by Sir Walter Scott.* 2nd ed. 1814; rpt. London: Bickers, 1883-84. Vol. IX.

—. *A Letter to a Very Young Lady on her Marriage.* In *Miscellanies.* Rpt. In *The Female Repertory; or, Young Lady's Guide to Virtue.* 1727; rpt. Edinburgh: M'William, 1808. Vol. II.

Talbot, Catherine (1721–77). *Education: A Fairy Tale.* Bound with Dr. Gregory's *A Father's Legacy to his Daughters,* and Mrs. Chapone's *A Letter to a New-Married Lady.* London: Sharpe, 1821–22.

Trimmer, Sarah (1741–1810). *The Guardian of Education, a Periodical Work, consisting of a Practical Essay on Christian Education . . . : Memoirs of Modern Philosophers, and Extracts from their Writings; Extracts from Sermons and Other Books Relating to Religious Education; and a Copious Examination of Modern Systems of Education, Children's Books, and Books for Young Persons.* 5 vols. London: Hatchard, 1802–06.

—. *The Oeconomy of Charity; or, an Address to Ladies; Adapted to the Present State of Charitable Institutions in England.* 2 vols. rev. ed. 1781; rpt. London: Johnson, Rivingtons, Robinsons, et al., 1801.

—. *Reflections upon the Education of Children in Charity Schools; with the Outlines of a Plan of Appropriate Instruction for the Children of the Poor; submitted to the Consideration of the Patrons of Schools of Every Denomination, supported by Charity.* London: Longman, Rivingtons, 1792.

*The Twin Sisters, or the Effects of Education. A Novel. In a Series of Letters.* 4 vols. London: Hookman, 1788–89.

Voltaire, François Marie Arouet de (1694–1778). [*Dictionnaire philosophique dans lequel sont réunies les questions sur l'encyclopédie*, 1ˢᵗ portable ed, 1764.] *A Philosophical Dictionary; from the French of M. de Voltaire.* 2 vols in 1. Boston: Adams, 1836.

—. *Épitre à madame la marquise du Chastelet, en Alzire, ou les Américains, une tragédie. En Oeuvres complètes de Voltaire.* First acted 1736; rpt. Kohl: De l'Imprimerie de la Société Littéraire-Typographique, 1784. Tome II.

Wakefield, Priscilla Bell (1751–1832). *Reflections on the Present Condition of the Female Sex.* 1798; rpt. New York: Garland, 1974.

Walker, Mary (np). *Letters of the Duchess de Crui and Others, on Subjects Moral and Entertaining, wherein the Character of the Female Sex, with their Rank, Importance, and Consequence, Is Stated, and their Relative Duties in Life Are Enforced.* 5 vols. London: Robson, Walter, and Robinson, 1776.

Wesley, John (1703–91). *Wesley's Letters to Young Women.* Ed. Frank G. Porter. Cincinnati: Cranston and Curtis, 1894.

West, Jane (1758–1852). *The Advantages of Education, or, The History of Maria Williams, a Tale for Misses and their Mammas.* By Prudentia Homespun. 2 vols. Minerva Press, 1793; rpt. New York: Garland, 1974.

—. *A Gossip's Story and a Legendary Tale.* 2 vols. 2ⁿᵈ ed. 1796; rpt. 1797; rpt. New York: Garland, 1974.

—. *The Infidel Father: A Novel.* 3 vols. London: Longman, Rees, 1802.

—. *Letters to a Young Lady: In which the Duties and Character of Women are Considered, Chiefly with a Reference to Prevailing Opinions.* 3 vols. 2ⁿᵈ ed. 1806; rpt. New York: Garland, 1974.

—. *A Tale of the Times.* 3 vols. 1799; rpt. New York: Garland, 1974.

Williams, Helen Maria (1762–1827). *Julia, a Novel; Interspersed with some Poetical Pieces.* 2 vols. 1790; rpt. New York: Garland, 1974.

—. *Letter from France.* 8 vols in 2. Introd. Janet M. Todd. 1790-96; rpt. Delmar, N.Y.: Scholars' Facsimiles and Reprints, 1975.

—. *A Tour in Switzerland; or, a View of the Present State of the Governments and Manners of those Cantons: With Comparative Sketches of the Present State of Paris.* 2 vols. London: Robinsons, 1798.

Wollstonecraft, Mary (1759–97). *The Female Reader; or Miscellaneous Pieces in Prose and Verse, selected from the Best Writers, and disposed under Proper Heads; for the Improve-*

*ment of Young Women. To which is prefixed a Preface containing some Hints on Female Education. With a Complete System of Geography, not in the London ed.* By Mr. Cresswick [pseudonym], Teacher of Elocution. 1789; rpt. Dublin: by Dornin, 1791.

—. *Four New Letters of Mary Wollstonecraft and Helen M. Williams.* Eds. Benjamin P. Kurtz and Carrie C. Autrie. Berkeley: University of California Press, 1937.

—. *Godwin and Mary: Letters of William Godwin and Mary Wollstonecraft.* Ed. Ralph M. Wardle. Lawrence, KS: University of Kansas Press, 1966.

—. *An Historical and Moral View of the Origin and Progress of the French Revolution; and the Effects it Has Produced in Europe.* Introd. Janet M. Todd. 2nd ed., 1795; rpt. Delmar, N.Y.: Scholars' Facsimiles and Reprints, 1975.

—. *Letters Written during a Short Residence in Sweden, Norway, and Denmark.* 1796; rpt. Fontwell, Sussex: Centaur Press, 1970.

—. *Mary, A Fiction.* 1788; rpt. New York: Schocken, 1977.

—. *Original Stories from Real Life; with Conversations Calculated to Regulate the Affections, and Form the Mind to Truth and Goodness.* 1788; rpt. London: Johnson, 1791.

—. *Posthumous Works of the Author of a Vindication of the Rights of Woman.* [Including *The Wrongs of Woman, or Maria, a Fragment.*] Ed. William Godwin. 4 vols. London: Johnson, Robinsons, 1798.

—. *Thoughts on the Education of Daughters: With Reflections on Female Conduct, in the More Important Duties of Life.* 1787; rpt. New York: Garland, 1974.

—. *A Vindication of the Rights of Men.* 1790; rpt. Gainesville, Fl: Scholar's Facsimiles and Reprints, 1960.

—. *A Vindication of the Rights of Woman: With Strictures on Political and Moral Subjects.* 1792; rpt. New York: Norton, 1967.

—. *The Wrongs of Woman, or Maria.* (posthumously published.) William Godwin, 1798.

Woty, William (1731?–91). *The Female Advocate, a Poem.* 2nd ed. corr. 1770; rpt. London: The Author, 1771.

Yearsley, Ann (1756 1806). *The Royal Captives: A Fragment of Secret History. Copied from an Old Manuscript.* Introd. Gina Luria. 4 vols. 1795; rpt. New York: Garland, 1974.

# Secondary Sources

Adams, Donald K. "The Second Mrs. Radcliffe." *Mystery and Detection Annual.* Ed. Donald K. Adams. Beverly Hills, CA, 1972, pp. 48–64.

Adams, M. Ray. "Helen Maria Williams and the French Revolution." *Wordsworth and Coleridge: Studies in Honor of George McLean Harper.* Ed. Earl Leslie Griggs. Princeton: Princeton University Press, 1939, pp. 87–117.

—. *Studies in the Literary Backgrounds of English Radicalism with Specific Reference to the French Revolution.* Franklin and Marshall College Studies, No. 5. Lancaster, PA, 1947.

Adamson, John William. *English Education 1789–1902.* Cambridge: Cambridge University Press, 1930.

Adburgham, Alison. *Women in Print: Writing Women and Women's Magazines from the Restoration to the Accession of Victoria.* London: Allen and Unwin, 1972.

Archer, R. L. *Rousseau on Education.* 2nd ed. London: Arnold, 1928.

Ashmun, Margaret. *The Singing Swan: An Account of Anna Seward and her Acquaintance with Dr. Johnson, Boswell, and Others of Their Time.* New Haven: Yale University Press, 1931.

Austen-Leigh, William, and Richard Arthur Austen-Leigh. *Jane Austen: Her Life and Letters. A Family Record.* London: Smith, Elder, 1913.

Berger, Morroe, tr., ed. *Madame de Staël on Politics. Literature, and National Character.* New York: Doubleday, 1965.

Blakely, Dorothy. *The Minerva Press 1790–1820.* London: Oxford University Press, 1939.

Blanchard, Rae. "The French Source of Two Early English Feminist Tracts." *Modern Language Notes.* 44 (1929), 381–83.

Block, Andrew. *The English Novel 1740–1850; a Catalogue . . .* London: Grafton, 1939.

Bouten, Jacob. *Mary Wollstonecraft and the Beginnings of Female Emancipation in France and England.* Amsterdam: Kruyt, 1922.

Bradbrook, Frank W. *Jane Austen and her Predecessors.* Cambridge: Cambridge University Press, 1966.

Brauer, George C., Jr. *The Education of a Gentleman: Theories of Gentlemanly Education in England 1660–1775.* New York: Bookman Associates, 1959.

Butler, Marilyn. *Maria Edgeworth: A Literary Biography.* Oxford: Clarendon Press, 1972.

Cameron, Kenneth Neill, ed. *Shelley and his Circle, 1773–1822*. Cambridge, MA: Harvard University Press, 1961. Vols. I, II, IV.

*A Catalogue of Books represented by Library of Congress Printed Cards*. Vols. 156–67. New York: Pageant Books, 1959–60.

Colby, Vineta. *The Singular Anomaly: Women Novelists of the Nineteenth Century*. London: University of London Press, 1971.

—. *Yesterday's Woman: Domestic Realism in the English Novel*. Princeton: Princeton University Press, 1974.

Collins, A. S. *Authorship in the Days of Johnson: Being a Study of the Relationship between Author, Patron,*

*Publisher and Public, 1726–1800*. London: Holden, 1927.

—. *The Profession of Letters: A Study of the Relation of Authors to Patron, Publisher, and Public, 1780–1832*. London: Routledge, 1928.

Costello, Louisa Stuart. *Memoirs of Eminent Englishwomen*. London: Bentley, 1844. Vols. II, III.

Cott, Nancy F. *The Bonds of Womanhood: "Woman's Sphere" in New England, 1780–1835*. New Haven: Yale University Press, 1977.

Courtney, Luther Weeks. *Hannah More's Interest in Education and Government*. The *Baylor Bulletin*, Baylor University, Waco, TX, 32, No. 4, Dec. 1929.

Crane, R. S. "The Humanities and Theses of Education in the Eighteenth Century." In his *The Idea of the Humanities and Other Essays Critical and Historical*. Chicago: University of Chicago Press, 1967, I, 89–121.

Crittendon, Walter Marion. "The Life and Writings of Mrs. Sarah Scott—Novelist (1723–1755)." Diss. University of Pennsylvania, (Philadelphia) 1932.

Derry, John W. *A Short History of Nineteenth-Century England*. London: Blandford Press, 1963.

Devlin, D. D. *Jane Austen and Education*. New York: Macmillan, 1975.

*Dictionary of National Biography*. Eds. Sir Leslie Stephen and Sidney Lee. 63 vols. New York: Macmillan, 1885–1900.

Doran, John. *A Lady of the Last Century*. [Elizabeth Montagu.] 7 Boston, Niccolls, n.d.

Durant, W. Clark, ed. *Memoirs of Mary Wollstonecraft by William Godwin*. New York: Greenberg, 1927.

Ellis, Grace Atkinson, ed. *Memoir, Letters, and a Selection from the Poems and Prose Writings of Anna Laetitia Barbauld*. 2 vols. Boston: Osgood, 1874.

Flexner, Eleanor. *Mary Wollstonecraft: A Biography*. Baltimore: Penguin, 1972.

Fontainerie, F. de la. *French Liberalism and Education in the Eighteenth Century: The Writings of la Chalotais, Turgot, Diderot, and Condorcet on National Education*. 1932; rpt. New York: Franklin, 1971.

Forry, John Harold. "A Study of the Novels of Mrs. Mary Robinson (1758–1800)." Diss. University of Pittsburgh, 1952.

Garber, Frederick, ed. and introd. *The Italian, or the Confessional of the Black Penitents. A Romance*. By Ann Radcliffe. New York: Oxford University Press, 1968.

Gardiner, Dorothy. *English Girlhood at School: A Study of Women's Education through Twelve Centuries.* London: Humphrey Milford, 1929.

Gay, Peter, ed. *John Locke on Education.* New York: Columbia University, 1964.

George, Margaret. *One Woman's "Situation": A Study of Mary Wollstonecraft.* Urbana: University of Illinois Press, 1970.

Gregory, Allene. *The French Revolution and the English Novel.* New York: Putnam's, 1915.

Hall, Walter Phelps. *British Radicalism 1791–1797.* New York: Longman, Green, 1912.

Halsband, Robert. "The Female Pen: Women and Literature in Eighteenth Century England." *History and Today*, 24, No. 10 (Oct. 1974), 702–09.

Hans, Nicholas. *New Trends in Education in the Eighteenth Century.* London: Routledge and Paul, 1951.

Harden, O. Elizabeth McWhorter. *Maria Edgeworth's Art of Prose Fiction.* The Hague: Mouton, 1971.

Hemlow, Joyce. *The History of Fanny Burney.* Oxford: Clarendon Press, 1958.

Hill, C. P. *Who's Who in History. Volume III. England 1603–1714.* Gen. ed. C. R. N. Routh. Oxford: Blackwell, 1965.

Holcombe, Lee. *Victorian Ladies at Work: Middle Class Working Women in England and Wales 1850–1914.* Hamden, Conn: Archon Books, 1973.

Horner, Joyce M. *The English Women Novelists and their Connection with the Feminist Movement (1688–1797). Smith College Studies in Modern Languages*, 11, Nos. 1–3. Northampton, MA: The Collegiate Press, Oct. 1929–Jan, April 1930.

Huchon, R. *Mrs. Montagu and her Friends. 1720–1800: A Sketch.* London: Murray, 1907.

Humphreys, A. R. "The 'Rights of Woman' in the Age of Reason." *Modern Language Review.* 41 (1946), 256–69.

Jaeger, Muriel. *Before Victoria.* London: Chatto and Windus, 1956.

Johnson, Richard Brimley, ed. *Bluestocking Letters.* London: Lane, 1926.

Hilbish, Florence May Anna. "Charlotte Smith, Poet and Novelist (1749–1806)." Diss. University of Pennsylvania (Philadelphia), 1941.

Jones, M[ary] G[wladys]. *Hannah More.* Cambridge: Cambridge University Press, 1952.

Kamm, Josephine. *Hope Deferred: Girls' Education in English History.* London: Methuen, 1965.

Kelly, Gary. *The English Jacobin Novel 1780–1805.* Oxford: Clarendon Press, 1976.

Lacour, Léopold. *Trois femmes de la révolution* [Olympe de Gouges, Théroigne de Mericourt, Rose Lacombe]. Paris: Plon-Nourrit, 1900.

Leavis, Queenie Dorothy. *Fiction and the Reading Public.* London: Chatto and Windus, 1965.

Lefanu, Alicia. *Memoirs of the Life and Writings of Mrs. Frances Sheridan . . . also Criticisms and Selections from the Works of Mrs. Sheridan: and Biographical Anecdotes of her Family and Contemporaries.* London: Whittakers, 1824.

Leranbaum, Miriam. "'Mistresses of Orthodoxy': Education in the Lives and Writings of late Eighteenth-Century English Women Writers." *Proceedings of the American Philosophical Society*, 121, No. 4 (August 12, 1977), 281–310.

Lincoln, Anthony. *Some Political and Social Ideas of English Dissent.* Cambridge: University Press, 1938.

Littlewood, S. R. *Elizabeth Inchbald and her Circle: The Life Story of a Charming Woman (1753–1821).* London: O'Connor, 1921.

Luke, Hugh J., Jr. "Drams for the Vulgar: A Study of some Radical Publishers and Publications of Early Nineteenth-Century London." Diss. University of Texas (Austin), 1963.

Luria, Gina. "Mary Hays: A Critical Biography." Diss. New York University, 1972.

MacCarthy, Bridget G. *The Later Women Novelists 1744–1818.* New York: Salloch, 1948.

—. *Women Writers: Their Contribution to the English Novel 1621–1744.* New York: Salloch, 1948.

MacGregor, Margaret Eliot. *Amelia Alderson Opie: Worldling and Friend. Smith College Studies in Modern Languages*, 14. Northampton, MA: The Collegiate Press, Oct. 1932–July 1933.

McKee, William. *Elizabeth Inchbald, Novelist.* Washington, D.C.: The Catholic University of America, 1935.

McKillop, Allan Dugald. "Charlotte Smith's Letters." *The Huntington Library Quarterly.* 15, No. 3 (1951–52), 237–55.

MacLean, Kenneth. *John Locke and English Literature of the Eighteenth Century.* New Haven: Yale University Press, 1936.

May, Gita. *Madame Roland and the Age of Revolution.* New York: Columbia University Press, 1970.

Mews, Hazel. *Frail Vessels: Women's Role in Women's Novels from Fanny Burney to George Eliot.* London: Athlone Press, 1969.

Mitford, Mary Russell. *Recollections of a Literary Life; or, Books, Places, and People.* 1852; rpt. New York: AMS Press, 1975.

Moers, Ellen. *Literary Women.* New York: Doubleday, 1976.

—. "Vindicating Mary Wollstonecraft." *The New York Review.* 19 Feb. 1976, pp. 38–42.

Moler, Kenneth L. *Jane Austen's Art of Allusion.* Lincoln: University of Nebraska Press, 1968.

Monk, Samuel H. "Anna Seward and the Romantic Poets: A Study in Taste." *Wordsworth and Coleridge: Studies in Honor of George McLean Harper.* Ed. Earl Leslie Griggs. Princeton: Princeton University Press, 1939, pp. 118–34.

Monroe, Paul. *A Text-Book in the History of Education.* New York: Macmillan, 1923.

Moynihan, Robert D. "Clarissa and the Enlightened Woman as Literary Heroine." *Journal of the History of Ideas.* 36 (Jan–Mar 1975), 159–66.

Murray, E. B. *Ann Radcliffe.* New York: Twayne, 1972.

Myers, Mitzi. "Aspects of William Godwin's Reputation in the 1790's." Diss. Rice University (Houston, TX), 1969.

*The National Union Catalogue: Pre-1956 Imprints.* 629 vols. London: Mansell Information, 1968–79.

*The New Cambridge Bibliography of English Literature 1660–1800.* Ed. George Watson. Cambridge: Cambridge University Press, 1971. Vol. II.

*The New Encyclopaedia Britannica.* Chicago: Hemingway Benton, 1974. Vols. VI, VII.

Paston, George [pseudonym of Emily Morse Symonds]. *Lady Mary Wortley Montagu and her Times.* New York: Putnam's, 1907.

Paul, C. Kegan. *William Godwin: His Friends and Contemporaries.* 2 vols. London: King, 1876.

Perkins, David, ed. *English Romantic Writers.* New York: Harcourt, Brace & World, 1967.

*The Oxford Companion to English Literature.* Ed. Sir Paul Harvey. 4th ed., 1932; rpt. New York: Oxford University Press, 1969.

Phillips, Margaret, and W. S. Tomkinson. *English Women in Life and Letters.* Oxford: Oxford University Press, 1927.

Pinchbeck, Ivy. *Women Workers and the Industrial Revolution 1750–1850.* New York: Crofts, MCMXXX.

Pollin, Burton R. *Education and Enlightenment in the Works of William Godwin.* New York: Las Americas, 1962.

—. "Mary Hays on Women's Rights in the *Monthly Magazine.*" *Études Anglaises.* 24, No. 3 (1971), 271–82.

Pollock, Walter Herries. *Jane Austen: Her Contemporaries and Herself.* New York: Longman, Green, 1899.

Posgate, Helen B. *Madame de Staël.* New York: Twayne, 1968.

Ramelson, Marian. *The Petticoat Rebellion: A Century of Struggle for Women's Rights.* London: Lawrence and Wishart, 1967.

Reisner, Edward H. *Nationalism and Education since 1789: A Social and Political History of Modern Education.* New York: Macmillan, 1923.

Reynolds, Myra. *The Learned Lady in England 1650–1760.* Boston: Houghton Mifflin, 1920.

Riddehough, Geoffrey B. "Priscilla Wakefield." *Dalhousie Review,* 37, No. 4 (Winter 1958), 341–47.

Rodgers, Betsy. *Georgian Chronicle: Mrs. Barbauld and her Family.* London: Methuen, 1958.

Roper, Derek. "Mary Wollstonecraft's Reviews." *Notes and Queries.* 203 (Jan. 1958), 37–38.

Rosbottom, Ronald C., ed. *Studies in Eighteenth Century Culture.* Madison: University of Wisconsin Press, 1976. Vol. V.

Rowbotham, Sheila. *Hidden from History: 300 Years of Women's Oppression and the Fight Against It.* London: Pluto Press, 1973.

Sadleir, Michael. "'Minerva Press' Publicity: A Publisher's Advertisement of 1794." *The Library, A Quarterly Review of Bibliography.* Transactions of the Bibliographical Society of London. 4th series. New York: Oxford University Press, 1941. Vol. XXI, 207–15.

Schapiro, J. Salwyn. *Condorcet and the Rise of Liberalism.* New York: Harcourt, Brace, 1934.

Scott, Walter S. *The Bluestocking Ladies.* London: Green, 1947.

Seeley, L. B. *Fanny Burney and her Friends: Select Passages from her Diary and Other Writings.* New York: Scribner and Welford, 1890.

Showalter, Elaine. *A Literature of their Own: British Women Novelists from Bronte to Lessing.* Princeton: Princeton University Press, 1977.

Smith, Florence M. *Mary Astell.* New York: Columbia University Press, 1916.

Soulbury, Viscount. "Women of Influence, 1750–1800." *Quarterly Review.* 297 (Oct. 1959), 400–07.

Steeves, Edna L. "Pre-Feminism in some Eighteenth-Century Novels." *Texas Quarterly.* 16, No. 3 (Autumn 1973), 48–57.

Storr, Marthe Severn. *Mary Wollstonecraft et le movement dans la littérature anglaise.* Diss. Paris, 1931.

Thackeray, A. I. *A Book of Sibyls.* London: Smith, Elder, 1883.

Tomalin, Claire. *The Life and Death of Mary Wollstonecraft.* London: Weidenfeld and Nicolson, 1975.

Tompkins, J. M. S. *The Popular Novel in England. 1770–1800.* 1932; rpt. London: Methuen, 1969.

Treasure, Geoffrey. *Who's Who in History. Volume IV: England 1714–1789.* Gen. ed. C. R. N. Routh. Oxford: Blackwell, 1969.

—. *Who's Who in History. Volume V: England, 1789–1837.* Gen. ed. C. R. N. Routh. Oxford: Blackwell, 1974.

Tytler, Sarah [pseudonym of Henrietta Keddie], and J. L. Watson. *The Songstresses of Scotland.* 2 vols. London: Strahan, 1871.

Utter, Robert Palfrey, and Gwendolyn Bridges Needham. *Pamela's Daughters.* New York: Macmillan, 1936.

Varma, Devendra, ed. *The Orphan of the Rhine.* By Eleanor Sleath. 4 vols. 1798; rpt. London: Folio Press, 1968.

—, ed. *Castle of Wolfenbach.* By Eliza Parsons. 2 vols. Minerva Press, 1793; rpt.

Vicinus, Martha, ed. *Suffer and Be Still: Women in the Victorian Age.* Bloomington: Indiana University Press, 1972.

Wallas, Ada. *Before the Bluestockings.* London: Allen and Unwin, 1929.

Wardle, Ralph M. "Mary Wollstonecraft. *Analytical Reviewer.*" *PMLA,* 62 (1947), 1000–009.

Warner, James H. "*Émile* in Eighteenth Century England," *PMLA,* 59, Part 1, No. 2 (1944), 773–91.

Wheeler, Ethel Rolt. *Famous Bluestockings.* London: Methuen, 1910.

White, Cynthia. *Women's Magazines 1693–1968.* London: Joseph, 1971.

Whitford, Robert C. "Madame de Staël's Literary Reputation in England." *Studies in Language and Literature.* 4, No. 1 (Feb. 1918), 7–56.

Whitmore, Clara H. *Woman's Work in English Fiction: From the Restoration to the Mid-Victorian Period.* New York: Putnam's, 1910.

Williams, David. "Condorcet, Feminism, and the Egalitarian Principle." In *Studies in Eighteenth Century Culture.* Ed. Ronald C. Rosbottom. Madison: University of Wisconsin Press, 1976. V, 151–63.

—. "The Politics of Feminism in the French Enlightenment." In *The Varied Pattern: Studies in the Eighteenth Century.* Eds. Peter Hughes and David Williams. Toronto: Hakkert, 1971, pp. 333–51.

Williams, Jane. *The Literary Women of England.* London: Saunders, Otley, 1861.

Woolf, Virginia. *A Room of One's Own.* 1929; rpt. New York: Harcourt, Brace, and World, 1957.

—. *The Second Common Reader.* New York: Harcourt, Brace, 1932.

# Index

Addison, Joseph (1672–1719) 241
  *Spectator*, # 92 (11ᵗʰ ed, 1711–12) 60, 71,
    83, 86, 87, 207, 241
*Agatha: Or a Narrative of Recent Events* (1796)
  180
Aldis, Charles (1775?–1863) 203
  *Defence of the Character and Conduct of the
    Late Mary Wollstonecraft Godwin* (1803)
    203
Amelia Alderson (see Amelia Opie) 11, 103,
  110, 201, 202, 230, 252, 262
Alexander, William (1726–82) 62
  *History of Women* (1782) 1, 2, 3, 5, 24, 62,
    237, 241
*Analytical Review* 102, 116, 140, 169, 177, 241
*Anti-Jacobin Review and Magazine* 105, 164,
  169, 241
Astell, Mary (1666–1731) 1, 3, 4, 11, 23, 58,
  59, 102, 263
  *Letters Concerning the Love of God* (1697) 60
  *A Serious Proposal to the Ladies* (1694, 1697)
    59, 241
  *Some Reflections upon Marriage* (1700) 90,
    241
Austen, Jane (1775–1817) 1, 4, 18, 197, 206,
  233, 242, 259, 260, 262, 263
  *Emma* (1815) 106, 117, 119, 134, 136,
    137, 213, 214, 217, 235, 241, 248
  *Northanger Abbey* (1818) 5, 18, 206, 207,
    228, 242
  *Pride and Prejudice* (1813) 39, 227, 229,
    242

Bage, Robert (1728–1801) 66, 67, 111, 154,
  159
  *The Fair Syrian* (1787) 91, 242
  *Hermsprong* (1796) 111, 159, 242
Baillie, Joanna (1762–1851) 167, 170, 196,
  202
  *The Country Inn* (1804) 231
  *Plays of the Passions* (1798) 167, 196
Barbauld, Anna Laetitia Aikin (1743–1825)
  10, 23, 242, 243
  "On Female Studies" in *Memoir, Letters*
    (1874) 184, 187, 193
  "What Is Education?" in *Monthly Magazine*,
    5 (1798) 172
Barbauld, Anna Laetitia, and John Aiken 10,
  23, 242, 243
  *Evenings at Home* (1792–96) 166, 190, 242
Behn, Aphra (1640–89) 3, 12, 52, 63, 64
Bennett, John, Rev. (na) 151, 162, 167, 177
  *Letters to a Young Lady* (1789) 167, 177,
    200, 203, 204, 243, 256
Berry, Mary (1763–1852) 155, 165
  *Social Life in England and France* (1831)
    155, 243
*Bildungsroman* 110
Bluestockings 10, 11, 12, 15, 29, 30, 52, 59,
  65, 161, 208, 251, 264
Boscawen, Frances (1719–1805) 10
Bronte, Charlotte (1816–55) 218
  *Jane Eyre* (1847) 218, 223, 235, 243
Brunton, Mary Balfour (1778–1818) 243
Burke, Edmund (1729–97) 10, 139, 162

*Reflections on the Revolution in France* (1790) 129, 162, 243

Burney, Charles (1726–1814) 24
   *Recollections of Dr. Johnson* 24, 243
   [nd, on Anna Barbauld) 243

Burney, Fanny [d'Arblay] (1752–1840) 10, 11, 18, 38, 130, 161, 167, 169, 197, 243, 261, 262, 263
   *Camilla* (1796) 167, 168, 172, 173, 174, 179, 180, 186, 188, 189, 190, 195, 196, 217, 243
   *Cecilia* (4th ed, 1782) 17, 32, 39, 43, 51, 52, 137, 168, 196, 231, 235, 243
   *Evelina* (1778) 17, 19, 21, 28, 38, 39, 52, 115, 243

Cadell and Davies [publishers] 69, 148, 154, 210, 219, 242, 244, 247, 251, 253, 254, 255

Cappe, Catherine Harrison (1744–1821) 243
   *An Account of Two Charity Schools for the Education of Girls* (1800) 71
   *Reflections upon the Education of Children in Charity Schools* (1792) 125, 256

Carlisle, Isabella Byron Howard, Countess (–d. 1795) 244

Carter, Elizabeth (1717–1806) 11

Cavendish, Margaret (1623–73) 14

Centlivre, Susannah (1669–1723) 64

Chapone, Hester Mulso (1727–1801) 32
   *Letters on the Improvement of the Mind* (1772) 16

Chesterfield, Philip Dormer Stanhope, Earl of (1694–1773) 16 244
   *Letters to His Son* (1774) 16, 244

Chirol, J. L. (na) 210
   *An Enquiry into the Best System of Female Education* (1809) 244

Cleland, John (1707–89) 21
   *Memoirs of a Woman of Pleasure* (aka *Fanny Hill*, 1748–79) 21, 38, 244

Condillac, Étienne Bonnot de (1714–80) 244
   *Essay on . . .Human Knowledge* (1756, trans. *Essai . . . connaissances humaines)* 17

Condorcet, Marie Jean Antoine Nicolas de Caritat, Marquis de (1743–94) 245

Darwin, Erasmus (1731–1802) 103, 226
   *Plan for the Conduct of Female Education in Boarding Schools* (1797) 116, 245

Day, Thomas (1748–89) 17, 21, 37, 85

Decker, Thomas (c. 1572–c. 1632) 53

Defoe, Daniel (1660–1731) 75, 245
   *An Essay upon Projects* (1697) 73, 245
   *Moll Flanders* (1722) 21

Delaney, Mary (1700–88) 10, 36

Dickens, Charles (1812–70) 245
   *Tale of Two Cities* (1859) 55, 245

Drake, Judith (fl. 1696) 58, 59, 61, 62, 123, 157
   *An Essay in Defence of the Female Sex* (1696) 59

Duncombe, John (1729–86) 64
   *Feminead* (1754) 64, 86, 169, 245

*Eccentric Biography, or Memoirs of Remarkable Characters, Antient and Modern* (1804) 203

Edgeworth, Maria (1767–1849) 107, 110, 129, 130, 131, 151, 152, 169, 197, 201, 202, 205, 208, 221, 224, 259, 261
   *Castle Rackrent* (1800) 151, 205, 246
   *Helen* (1834) 103, 104, 201, 225, 256, 257, 259, 263
   *Letters for Literary Ladies (1795)* 128, 129, 130, 151, 246
   *The Parent's Assistant* (1796) 110, 246

Edgeworth, Maria, and Richard Lovell Edgeworth (1744–1817) 103, 169, 246
   *Practical Education* (1798) 110, 113, 119, 127, 128, 131, 205, 226, 235, 246

*Elfrida or Paternal Ambition* (anon.,1786) 32, 83, 246

*The Female Aegis, or, the Duties of Women* (1798) 187, 189, 191, 246

*Female Restoration, by a Moral and Physical Restoration of Female, Talents* (anon., 1780) 61, 246

Fénelon, Archbishop François de Salignac de la Mothe (1651–1715) 246
   *The Education of Girls* (1891 trans. of . . . *l'éducation des filles*, 1687) 16, 246

Fenwick, Eliza (1766–1840) 108, 119, 129, 201
    *Secresy* [*sic*] (1794) 119, 246
Fielding, Henry (1707–54) 246
    *Tom Jones* (1749) 20, 42, 70, 246
Fielding, Sarah (1710–68) 18, 48, 59, 66, 86, 95, 151, 179, 229
    *David Simple* (1744, perhaps first novel by a gentlewoman) 18, 48, 95, 246
Fordyce, James, Rev. (1720–98) 15, 16
    *Character and Conduct of the Female Sex* (1775) 16, 246
    *Sermons to Young Women* (1765) 16, 247
Genlis, Stéphanie Félicité Ducrest de Saint Aubin, Comtesse de (1746–1830) 247
    *Tales of the Castle* (1785, trans. of *Les Veillées du château*) 63, 65, 67, 71, 81, 247
Gibbon, Edward (1737–94) 69
    *History of the Decline and Fall of the Roman Empire* (1776–88) 69, 247
Girondins 105
Gisborne, Thomas, Rev. (1758–1846) 159, 162, 167
    *An Enquiry into the Duties of the Female Sex* (11th ed, 1797) 160, 247
Godwin, William (1756–1836) 39, 103, 104, 105, 201, 257, 260, 262, 263
    *An Enquiry Concerning Political Justice* (1793) 117, 247
    *Memoirs of the Author of a Vindication of the Rights of Woman* (1798) 110, 247
    *St. Leon* (1799) 151, 181, 247
Goethe, Johann Wolfgang (1749–1832) 17, 247
    *Werther* (1774) 17, 38, 39, 41, 108, 247
Goldsmith, Oliver (1728–74) 17, 50
    *Vicar of Wakefield* (1766) 17, 50, 118, 247
Gouges, Olympe de (1748–93) 101, 114, 138, 247, 261
    *Déclaration des droits de la femme et de la citoyenne* (1791) 105
Gregory, John (1724–73) 15, 16
    *A Father's Legacy to his Daughters* (new ed., 1774) 16, 244, 247, 255

Halifax, George Savile, Marquess (1633–95) 247
Hamilton, Elizabeth (1758–1816)) 103, 201
    *Letters on the Elementary Principles of Education* (3rd ed. 1801–02) 204, 209, 211, 248
    *Letters of a Hindoo Rajah* (2nd ed., 1776) 142, 152, 248
Hays, Mary (1759/60–1843) 68, 101, 104, 108, 110, 113, 201, 248, 249, 262, 263
    *An Appeal to the Men of Great Britain* (1798) 248
    *Female Biography* (1803) 123, 201, 207, 248
    (?) *Julietta* (1802) 206, 216, 217, 218, 225, 228, 229, 233, 248, 249
    *Letters and Essays* (1793) 107, 128, 143, 248
    *Memoirs of Emma Courtney* (1796) 106, 248
    *Memoirs of Queens* (1821) 221
    *The Victim of Prejudice* (1799) 102, 114, 115, 117, 138, 248
D'Holbach, Paul Henri Thiry, Baron (1723–89) 248
Holcroft, Thomas (1745–1809) 63, 104, 201, 247
    *Anna St. Ives* (1792) 114, 135, 194, 249
Imlay, Gilbert (b. 1754) 136, 138, 151
Inchbald, Elizabeth Simpson (1753–1821) 249
    *Lover's Vows* (new ed., 1798) 114
    *Nature and Art* (1796) 110, 117, 118, 249
    *A Simple Story* (1791) 116, 117, 134, 135, 249
Jackson, Mary Elizabeth (na). 110, 249
Jacobins 105
Johnson, Joseph [publisher of *Analytical Review*] 93, 98, 102, 111, 154, 161, 201, 205
Johnson, Samuel (1709–84) 10, 12, 14, 61, 70, 89
Kames, Lord Henry Home (1696–1782) 16, 249
Keir, Susanna Harvey (1747–1802) 249
    *Interesting Memoirs* (2nd ed., 1785) 26, 34, 37, 54, 55, 249
Kemble, Fanny (1809–93) 234
Kenrick, William (1725–79) 16

Knox, Vicesimus (1752–1821) 66
   *Essays Moral and Literary* (6th ed., 1778–79)
     78, 80, 249
*Lady's Monthly Museum* (started 1798) 108,
     120, 153, 164, 165, 181, 183, 186, 195,
     207, 250
Lambert, Anne Thérèse de Marguenat de Cour-
     celles, Marquise de (1647–1733) 250
   *Advice of a Mother to her Daughter* (1790,
     trans. *Avis d'une mère . . .* [1728]) 28,
     250
Lane, William [publisher] 111, 154
Lee, Sophia (1750–1824) 137, 206
   *Life of a Lover* (1804) 206, 212, 231, 250
Lennox, Charlotte (1720–1804) 19, 61, 72,
     179
   *Euphemia* (1790) 180, 182, 185, 250
   *The Female Quixote* (1752) 19, 72, 250
   *Henrietta* (1758) 21, 50, 72, 250, 264
Locke, John (1632–1704) 4, 21, 211, 250,
     261, 262
   *Essay Concerning Human Understanding*
     (1690) 31, 55, 66, 77, 250
   *Thoughts Concerning Education* (1685) 85,
     250
Mackenzie, Henry (1754–1831) 17, 23, 250
   *Mirror* (1779–80) 23, 46, 48, 51, 250
Makin, Bathsua (1600–75) 57, 122
   *An Essay to Revive the Antient* [sic] *Education
     of Gentlewomen* (1673) 57, 250
Mathias, Thomas (1754–1835) 162
Méricourt, Théroigne de (1762–1817) 138,
     261
Mill, John Stuart (1806–73) 239
Millar, John (1735–1801) 89
Molière, Jean Baptiste, Poquelin (1622–73)
     250
   *Les Femmes savantes* (1672) 17, 42, 250
   *Les Précieuses ridicules* (1659) 17, 251
Montague, Elizabeth Robinson (1720–1800)
     251
   *Letters* (1809) 13, 16, 17, 24, 25, 30, 32,
     41, 60, 63, 71, 77, 79, 102, 107, 108,
     109, 117, 127, 128, 129, 130, 140, 143,
     146, 151, 156, 167, 168, 171, 177, 180,
     184, 200, 201, 203, 204, 209, 211, 212,
     219, 220, 224, 226, 227, 230, 233, 235,
     236, 241, 242, 243, 244, 246, 247, 248,
     250, 251, 252, 253, 254, 256, 257, 259,
     260, 261, 262, 263
Montagu, Lady Mary Pierrepont Wortley
     (1689–1762) 251
   *Letters from the Levant* (1763) 63, 251
   *The Works* (6th ed., 1803) 4, 12, 13, 15, 39,
     57, 64, 66, 100, 104, 132, 202, 217
Montesquieu, Charles Louis de Secondat, 251
   Baron de la Brede et de la (1689–1755)
     251
*The Monthly Magazine* 118
*The Monthly Museum* 108, 120, 153, 164, 165,
     181, 183, 186, 195, 207, 250
Moore, Edward (1712–57) 13, 17
   *Fables for the Female Sex* (1744) 13, 251
More, Hannah (1745–1833) 4, 11, 13, 17, 52,
     76, 132, 159, 160, 164, 165, 167, 169,
     175, 177, 184, 191, 193, 197, 200, 202,
     215, 251, 252, 260, 261
   *The Bas Bleu* (1786) 29, 251
   *Cheap Repository Tracts* (1795–98) 161
   *Coelebs in Search of a Wife* (3rd ed., 1808)
     202, 219, 251
   *The Search after Happiness* (1773) 13
   *Strictures on the Modern System of Female
     Education* (1799) 160, 167, 252
   *Village Politics* (1792) 175
Murray, Judith Sargent 57
   "On the Equality of the Sexes" (1790) 57
Murry, Ann (1750–c.1818) 79, 111
   *Mentoria, or the Young Ladies Instructor*
     (1778) 79
Opie, Amelia Alderson 11, 103, 110, 201, 202,
     230, 252, 262
   *Adeline* Mowbray (1804) 203, 206, 211,
     216, 229, 230, 231, 234, 252
   *Dangers of Coquetry* (1790) 117
   *Father and Daughter* (1801) 231, 234, 252
Paine, Thomas (1737–1809) 93, 102
Parson, Eliza Phelp (d. 1811) 252
   *Errors of Education* (1791) 111
Pennington, Lady Sarah (d. 1783) 16, 252

Pigott, Charles (d. 1794) 159
  *The Female Jockey Club* (1794) 159
Pilkington, Laetitia (1712–50) 64
Piozzi, Hester Lynch Salusbury 252
  [see Hester Thrale] (1741–1831) 252
Polwhele, Richard (1760–1838) 162, 167
  *The Unsex'd Females* (1798) 164, 169, 253
Pope, Alexander (1668–1744) 1, 7, 17, 253
  *Essay on Man* (1733–34) 1, 7, 253
  *Rape of the Lock* (1712) 13, 253
Poulain de la Barre, François (1648–1723) 57,
    58, 67, 69, 70, 82, 87, 99, 131, 155
  *Woman as Good as the Man* (1677, 58
    [trans. of *Des l'égalité . . .*)
Priestley, Joseph (1733–1804) 104
Price, Richard (1723–91) 104
Radcliffe, Ann Ward (1764–1823) 18, 107,
    134, 136, 137, 148
  *The Italian* (1797) 148, 154, 253, 260
Radcliffe, Mary Ann (1746–1818) 107, 110,
    130, 142, 149, 150, 152, 156, 196, 208,
    230, 233, 235, 253
  *The Female Advocate* (1799) 107
  *Memoirs* (1810) 17, 21, 26, 34, 37, 38, 45,
    51, 54, 55, 59, 62, 106, 107, 110, 116,
    149, 164, 169, 179, 181, 203, 205, 208,
    221, 227, 232, 233, 239, 241, 242, 243,
    244, 245, 247, 248, 249, 252, 253, 254,
    255, 260, 261
Raikes, Robert (1735–1811) 23
Reeve, Clara (1729–1807) 19, 45, 75, 100,
    103, 104, 214
  *Plans of Education* (1792) 75, 104, 115,
    122, 150, 247
  *School for Widows* (1791) 104, 150, 151,
    253
Richardson, Samuel (1689–1761) 14, 18, 37,
    58, 59, 66, 253
  *Clarissa* (1747–48) 32, 35, 36, 39, 40, 54,
    91, 93, 94, 138, 194, 231, 253, 262
  *Pamela* (1740) 17, 21, 35, 36, 39, 85, 89,
    93, 94, 97, 114, 142, 171, 216, 253,
    264
  *Sir Charles Grandison* (1753–54) 35, 72, 73,
    74, 79, 253

Robinson, Mary Darby (1758–1800) 253
  *Thoughts on the Condition of Women* (1799)
    102, 108, 110, 124, 138, 152, 254
Robinsons, J. J. & G. [publishers] 111, 112,
    142, 154, 211, 212, 226, 247, 248, 249,
    250, 254, 256, 257
Rogers, Samuel (1763–1855) 170
Rousseau, Jean-Jacques (1712–78) 254
  *Eloisa* (3rd ed 1764, trans. of . . . *La Nouvelle
    Héloise*) 17, 39, 254
  *Emilius, or an Essay on Education* (1763,
    trans. of *Émile* [1762]) 18
  *The Social Contract* (1762, trans. of *Du
    contrat social*) 101, 254
Rowe, Elizabeth (1674–1737) 64
Scott, Sarah (1720–95) 55, 59, 66, 72, 88, 99,
    260
  *A Journey Through Every Stage of Life* (1754)
    99
Scott, Sir Walter (1771–1832) 202, 233, 255
De Scudéry, Madeleine (1607–1701) 63
Shelley, Percy Bysshe (1792–1822) 101, 111,
    260
  "The Revolt of Islam" (1818) 101
Sheridan, Frances Chamberlaine (1724–66)
    254
  *Memoirs of Miss Sydney Biddulph* (1761–67)
    17
Sheridan, Richard Brinsley (1751–1816) 17,
    41
  *The Rivals* (3rd ed., 1775) 17, 19, 42, 254
Slave Trade 41, 252
Smith, Adam (1723–90) 148
Smith, Charlotte Turner (1749–1806) 254
  "To Dependence" in *Elegiac* 147
  *Sonnets* (1784) 65, 148, 187, 253, 254
  *Emmeline* (1788) 118, 138, 254
  *Montalbert* (1795) 136, 141, 151, 255
  *Marchmont* (1796) 117, 254
  *The Old Manor House* (1793) 114
  *The Young Philosopher* (1798) 118, 255
Smith, Sydney (1771–1845) 199, 206, 207,
    211, 215, 218, 222, 223, 232, 233,
    234, 236
  *Essays Social and Political* (1882) 199, 207

Smollett, Tobias (1721–71) 18
*Humphry Clinker* (1771) 19, 22, 35, 42, 55, 255
Staël-Holstein, Germaine Necker, Baronne de (1766–1807) 255
*Corinne* (189- trans. of *Corinne, ou Italie* [1807]) 202, 203, 206, 220, 221, 223, 224, 234, 255
*De la Littérature* (1800) 210, 232, 255
Steele, Richard (1672–1729) 75, 241
*Spectator,* # 66 60, 71, 83, 86, 87, 207, 241
Sterne, Lawrence (1713–68) 18
*Tristram Shandy* (1760–67) 43, 255
Swift, Jonathan (1667–1745) 15, 16, 75, 255
*The Tatler,* # 63 75, 85
Talbot, Catherine (1721–77) 12, 45, 244
*Tendenz* novel 17, 110
Thrale, Hester [Hester Piozzi] (1741–1821) 10, 38, 161, 202
Trimmer, Sarah (1741–1810) 23, 103, 132, 201, 207
*The Oeconomy of Charity* (rev. ed., 1787) 256
*Twin Sisters, or the Effects of Education* (1788–89) 111, 256
Vesey, Elizabeth (1715–91) 10
Voltaire, François Marie Arouet de (1694–1788) 256
Wakefield, Priscilla Bell (1751–1832) 103, 108, 201, 263
*Leisure Hours* (3rd ed., 1798) 108
*Reflections on the Present Condition of the Female Sex* (1798) 110, 115, 124, 256
Walker, Mary (nd) 17
*Letters of the Duchess of Crui and Others* (1776) 17, 30, 256
Walpole, Horace (1717–97) 163

West, Jane (1758–1852) 111, 162, 163, 167, 200, 202
*Advantages of Education, or the History of Maria Williams* (1793) 111
*Gossip's Story* (1796) 168, 179, 180, 188, 256
*Infidel Father* (1802) 205
*Letters to a Young Lady* (1806) 167, 177, 200, 203, 204, 243, 256
*Tale of the Times* (1799) 179, 188, 194, 256
Williams, Helen Maria (1762–1827) 103, 104, 201, 259
*Julia* (1790) 38, 55, 118, 137, 151, 217, 230, 250, 256
Wollstonecraft, Mary (1759–97) iii, 4, 39, 48, 58, 62, 84, 101, 102, 114, 134, 159, 163, 183, 203, 216, 241, 257, 259, 260, 261, 262, 263, 264
*The Female Reader* (1879) 116, 256
*Letters Written . . . in Sweden, Norway, and Denmark* (1796) 117, 257
*Mary, a Fiction* (1788) 102, 134, 136, 257
*Original Stories from Real Life* (1788) 110, 133, 257
*Thoughts on the Education of Daughters* (1787) 64, 66, 86, 91, 116, 136, 183, 257
*A Vindication of the Rights of Woman* (1792) iii, 91, 159
*The Wrongs of Woman* (1798) 101, 135, 136, 137, 138, 182, 257
Woolf, Virginia (1882–1941) 65, 106
*A Room of One's Own* (1929) 65, 106, 107, 264
Woty, William (1731–91) 64
Yearsley, Anna (1756–1806) 104

www.ingramcontent.com/pod-product-compliance
Lightning Source LLC
Chambersburg PA
CBHW080344030726
47598CB00009B/2627